—

THE ONE AND THE MANY

—

THE ONE AND THE MANY

Contemporary Collaborative Art in a Global Context

Grant H. Kester

DUKE UNIVERSITY PRESS   DURHAM AND LONDON   2011

Designed by Heather Hensley

Typeset in Warnock Pro by Tseng Information Systems, Inc.

Library of Congress Cataloging-in-Publication Data appear on
the last printed page of this book.

Duke University Press gratefully acknowledges the support
provided through the Arts and Humanities Innovation
Fund and the Office of the Dean of Arts and Humanities
at the University of California, San Diego, and the Creative
Capital | Andy Warhol Foundation Arts Writers Grant
Program, which provided funds toward the production of
this book.

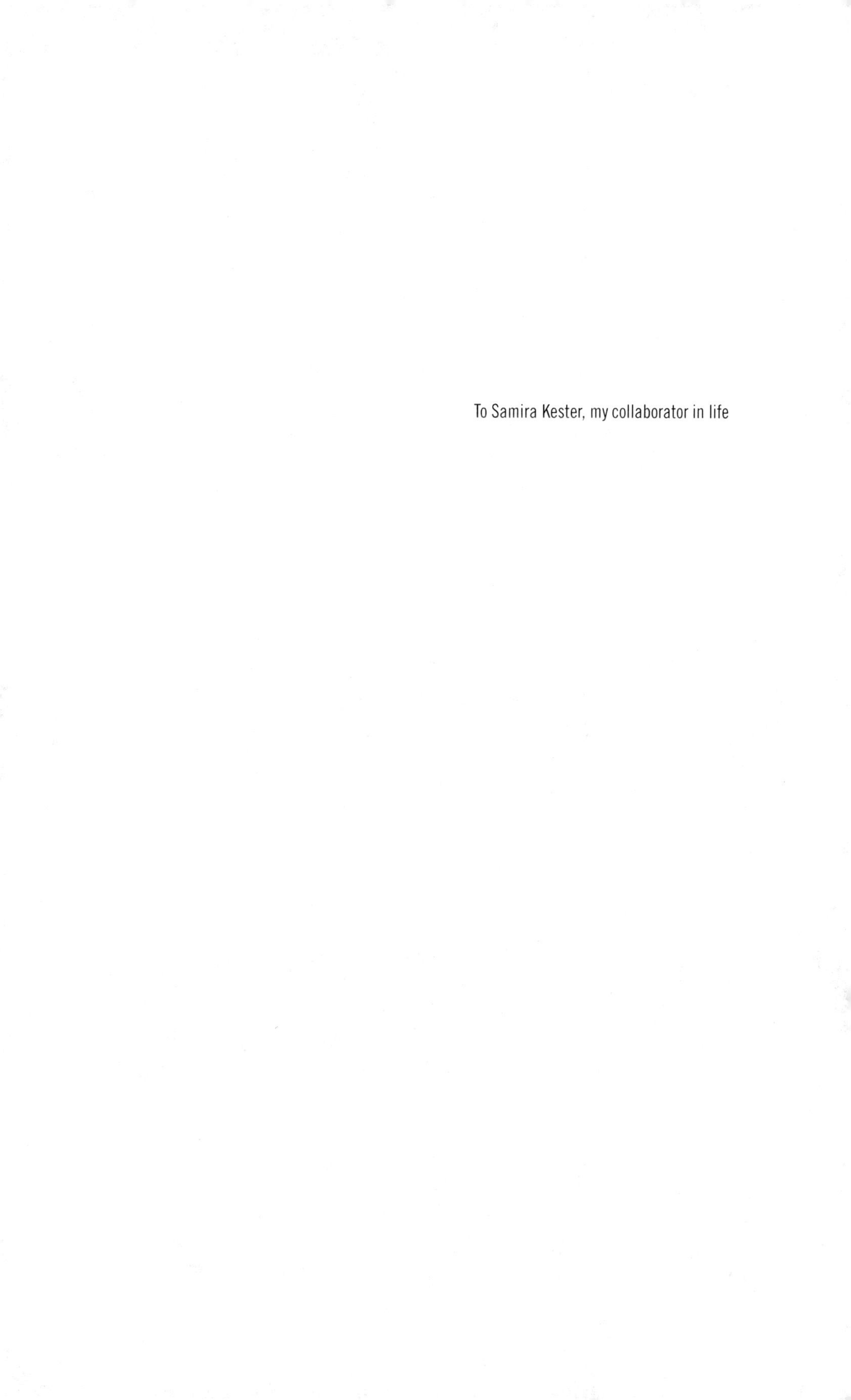

To Samira Kester, my collaborator in life

CONTENTS

ACKNOWLEDGMENTS

It is a commonplace that any book is the product of collaboration rather than singular authorship, but in this case it has the virtue of being true. *The One and the Many* was only made possible by the generosity of a great number of colleagues and friends. I'd like to give special thanks to Navjot Altaf, Shantibai, Gessuram, and Rajkumar of Dialogue; Silvina Babich, Alejandro Metin, and Rafael Santos of Ala Plastica (Rafael has since left the group); Christoph Schäfer and Margit Czenki of Park Fiction; Rick Lowe of Project Row Houses; Amadou Kane-Si and Muhsana Ali of Huit Facettes Interaction; and Jay Koh and Chu Yuan of NICA. Thanks also to Annie Mendoza, Navjot Altaf, and Rajkumar for help with translations in San Diego and Bastar, and to Patrick Deegan and Noel Hefele for conducting interviews in conjunction with the *Groundworks* exhibition in Pittsburgh. The travel necessary to research this book would not have been possible without the generous support of the Creative Capital/Warhol Foundation Arts Writers Grant Program, one of the only programs of its kind available to art historians and critics writing on contemporary art. Research for this book was also supported by the Getty Research Institute (during a 2004 fellowship), and the Division of the Arts and Humanities and the Center for the Humanities at the University of California, San Diego. I would also like to thank Anne Douglas and Carole Gray at Gray's

School of Art at Robert Gordon University in Scotland (who invited me to participate in the "Working in Public" seminars in 2007), and Tim Collins and Reiko Goto, formerly of the Studio for Creative Inquiry at Carnegie Mellon University (who invited me to organize the *Groundworks* exhibition in 2005). Thanks are also due to Lea and Pekka Kantonen and Jan Kaila in Helsinki; Mick Wilson, Martin McCabe, Ed Carroll, and Ailbhe Murphy in Dublin; Doug Ashford and Walid Raad at Cooper Union in New York; and Raul Cárdenas Osuna of Torolab in Tijuana; along with Nancy Adajania, Teddy Cruz, Steve Fagin, Tom Finkelpearl, Geeta Kapur, Bill Kelley, Suzanne Lacy, Malcolm Miles, Carmen Mörsch, Per Nilsson, Javier Rodrigo, Shubhalakshmi Shukla, and Jennifer Flores Sternad for conversations that helped in the development of this work. Thanks also to Ala Plastica, Chu Yuan, Dialogue, Galleri Nicolai Wallner, Lisson Gallery, the Museum of the City of New York, Park Fiction, the Paul Strand Archive at Aperture Foundation, Project Row Houses, and David Zwirner Gallery for photos and permissions.

INTRODUCTION

If oneness in art works inevitably implies the use of force against the many—
phrases like "mastery over materials" in aesthetical criticism betray this state
of affairs—then it follows that the many must also fear oneness.
T. W. ADORNO, *AESTHETIC THEORY*

This book began with a question. Why have so many artists over the past decade and a half been drawn to collaborative or collective modes of production? This is a global phenomenon, extending from the fashionable biennales of Europe to the villages of central India, from the Hamburg waterfront to the arctic circle of Finland, and from generously subsidized new media centers to struggling community art programs. While each practitioner comes to collaborative work with a unique perspective, these individual creative choices, taken in the aggregate, reveal much about both the current political moment and the broader history of modern art. We must begin, of course, by coming to terms with collaboration itself. Its primary meaning is straightforward enough: "to work together" or "in conjunction with" another, to engage in a "united labor." It is shadowed, however, by a second meaning: collaboration as betrayal, to "cooperate treasonably, as with an enemy occupation force."[1] This ambivalence, the semantic slippage between positive and negative connotations, is, I think, fitting. There are other terms that one might employ to describe this work: "cooperative," "collective," and so on. Where collaboration is redolent of Vichy France, collectivity evokes associations of forced labor camps, even as cooperation leads us through a chain of associations to "cooperative" witnesses and a complicitous submission to authority.

It is telling that within the continuum of terms we use for working together, each carries with it a counter-meaning: a warning, so to speak, of its ethical undecidability. I'm reminded of a lecture I once gave on collaborative art to an audience of distinguished academics. Over the course of an otherwise unremarkable presentation, I noticed one audience member becoming increasingly agitated. Eventually, he could contain himself no longer and burst out with an impassioned jeremiad about the dangers that inevitably follow when trying to work creatively in groups. We are well acquainted with the conformist demands that collective social formations make on individual participants, but the threat, as Adorno reminds us, runs in both directions.[2] The many have equally to fear the power of the one, for whom the world in all its concrete particularity is a mere resource to be joyfully manipulated and transformed. Is the identity of the many based on coercive consensus or radical plurality? Is the one defined by narcissistic projection or an opening out to alterity? These are some of the most pressing political and ethical questions of our day, and they are also central to the collaborative art projects I'll be exploring here.

There are, of course, no unequivocal signifiers, just as there is no art practice that avoids all forms of co-option, compromise, or complicity. It seems wiser to openly acknowledge this impurity than to assume that it can somehow be defeated at the level of terminology. We can identify many modes of collaborative practice, many ways of being together, in contemporary art. Perhaps most visible are what we might term "artist-to-artist" collaborations of the kind Charles Green describes in *The Third Hand: Collaboration in Art from Conceptualism to Postmodernism*. Green discusses such collaborative "teams" as Marina and Ulay Abromovic, Christo and Jeanne Claude, and Gilbert and George, focusing primarily on the dynamics of collaborators who are also linked through personal relationships ("publicly-bonded couples," as Green has it).[3] His key theoretical innovation, the concept of the "third artist," marks a form of creative praxis that emerges at the intersection of these complex, overlapping relations. If art is understood as an expression of autonomy and unity (the unity of authorial intention and of the work itself as a semantic construct), then any concession to contingency and multiplicity will be perceived as a transgression. At the same time, most of the examples outlined in Green's book simply expand a capacity for conventional artistic expression and production to multiple participants (e.g., two "performance artists" working collaboratively rather than one in isolation). In many of the projects I'll be examining here, the artistic personality itself (defined by its commitment to mastery and self-projection) is understood as a locus of creative transformation. Further, they often challenge the traditional perception of the work of art as an event or object authored beforehand and subsequently presented to an audience.

Modernism is identified with the emergence of the solitary genius out of the lumpen collectivity of the medieval guild or lodge—a transition symbolized by the apocryphal tale of Charles V kneeling to retrieve Titian's brush during a visit to the master's studio. The modern artist would soon make his triumphant debut on the stage of European culture, blinking in the glare of his newfound fame like Plato's slave freed from the dark cavern of communal illusion. The future of (European) art from this point on was preordained as the titanic struggle of progressive individualism against the stultifying conformity and consensus imposed, variously, by the salon, bourgeois consumerism, political propaganda, and, eventually, the history of modernism itself. More recent art historical research has done much to discredit this simplistic account (works produced in guilds and lodges were often neither collectively authored nor anonymous).[4] However, the figure of the singular, auratic artist, reinforced by notions of artistic genius first formalized by Kant, remains the bulwark of the long history of modernism, and the epistemological template for much contemporary criticism and curatorial practice. We can also identify intellectual and creative tendencies that challenge, or at least complicate, conventional notions of authorship during the modern period. In fact, one of the primary trajectories of modernist art involves the gradual erosion of the authoring conscious via techniques such as automatic drawing, frottage, montage, the splatter and dripping of paint, and so on.

The history of modernism can be viewed from this perspective as enacting a relentless disavowal of agency (and the rational, calculating mind it was seen to represent): a surrendering of authorial power to the unconscious, chance, or desire. There is, as well, a more formal tradition of distributed or collective authorship that looks back, to the artisanal guilds of an idealized Middle Ages (William Morris and the Arts and Crafts movement, Jugendstil, Der Blaue Reiter), or forward, to a utopian fraternity of artists and technicians (Constructivism, David Alfaro Siquiero's "polygraphic team"). Emerging at differing historical moments and in varying geopolitical contexts, these new collective formations also performed a defensive function, serving as a protective enclave against an indifferent mass culture and an openly hostile art establishment. The collaborative and collective traditions of the interwar years (dadaism, surrealism, etc.) were revitalized during the 1960s and '70s by Situationist, activist, and feminist groups, ranging from Womanhouse in the United States and Tucuman Arde in Argentina, to Welfare State in England and Hi Red Center in Japan.[5]

During the 1980s and '90s a new generation of collectives emerged (Border Arts Workshop, Group Material, REPO History, Guerilla Girls, Gran Fury, Platform, Wochenklausur, and Grupo Etcetera, among many others) that experimented with multiple authorship and novel reconfigurations of the artist's relationship to audience, with a particular focus on public space and activist intervention. Typical projects include Gran Fury's *Silence = Death* campaign in the late '80s; Group Material's *Democracy* project at the Dia Art Foundation in New York, which featured an extended series of dialogues and exhibitions on participatory democracy; and Platform's *Delta* installation, which used a micro-hydro turbine to mark the tidal movements of one of London's hidden rivers. Feminist collaborative practices by figures such as Judy Baca, Mierle Laderman Ukeles, Leslie Labowitz, Suzanne Lacy (whose concept of "New Genre" public art played a key role in debates during the 1990s), and Jo Spence, Loraine Leeson, and the Hackney Flashers group in London, provided a particularly important point of contact at that time between the traditions of conceptual art, public art, and activism.[6] As curator Okwui Enwezor has argued, those moments at which the constitution of the artistic personality is most radically in question often coincide with periods of more general political and social crisis. "Such crises," Enwezor writes, "force reappraisals of conditions of production, reevaluation of the nature of artistic work, and reconfiguration of the position of the artist in relation to economic, social and political institutions."[7] We might consider here the link between William Morris's involvement in syndicalist politics in nineteenth-century England and the founding of the Arts and Crafts movement, the obvious influence of the Russian and Mexican Revolutions on early twentieth-century avant-gardes, and the dramatic expansion of experimental tendencies in the arts during the political upheavals of the 1960s and '70s.

The current moment is defined by a complex and contradictory mixture of cultural and geopolitical forces. The last two decades have witnessed the rise of a powerful neoliberal economic order dedicated to eliminating all forms of collective or public resistance (institutional, ideological, and organizational) to the primacy of capital. Within this movement, the state and civil society have taken on a central role as zones of contestation and targets of conquest by corporate power. Thus, during the economic crisis that followed the demise of the subprime mortgage system in the United States, the primary response involved a return to market-complementing Keynesian economic policies rather than a more substantial challenge to the imperatives of capitalism. And even these relatively modest gestures were greeted with vehement opposition and warnings that the United States was in danger of devolving into "socialism." Of course, the neoliberal juggernaut is asynchronous. Some European countries still manage to retain remnants of the postwar social compact, subsidizing higher education, the arts, healthcare, and so on, while other countries (Venezuela, e.g.) have managed to resuscitate the otherwise vilified discourse of state socialism as a tool for the (ambivalent) promotion of economic and social justice. But their ability to maintain the standard of living of their middle classes is tenuous at best. Even now, the nations of the European Union find themselves increasingly reliant on the cheap labor of foreign immigrants, leading to the demoralizing spectacle of anti-immigrant racism in historically tolerant cultures like those of Holland, Denmark, and Ireland.

Predictions of a newly decentralized "Empire" notwithstanding, the reality is that the command and control of global capital has never been more centralized. Class divisions and the monopolization of major industries (energy, finance, pharmaceuticals, media) are reaching levels not seen in the United States since the late nineteenth century. At the same time, we have witnessed the recent emergence in India and China of powerful capitalist managerial blocs with significant nationalist ambitions of their own. Combined with mounting U.S. dependence on China's central banks, the most likely future scenario is a series of low-intensity skirmishes among competing nation-states over tariffs, energy resources, immigration, debt, and labor markets. As the U.S. loses its economic dominance, especially in domains where it can no longer rely on sheer military aggression to impose its will, the risk of destabilizing nationalist conflict is likely to increase. This hyper-rationalized economic order is accompanied, and complicated, by the rise of right wing, theocratic fundamentalism in the United States, the Middle East, and regions of Southeast Asia, along with the dramatic penetration of Protestant evangelical Christianity into the faith "markets" of South America and Asia. Thus, we have a convergence across the developed and developing world of patriarchal, absolutist, faith-based cadres, operating in many cases at the highest level of political power, and exercising considerable influence over large segments of the public.[8]

Despite this bleak picture, there is also a growing sense of political renewal around the world. From the worker-run factories of Argentina to Tahrir Square, and from university-based protest movements in Europe and the United States to campaigns for tribal rights in India, we encounter new forms of social organization, resistance, and identity. This is a time of both peril and opportunity, as the dominant political narratives used to explain and justify social and economic inequality, the distribution of resources and opportunities within society, and the relative responsibility of the state to the public at large, are being contested and destabilized. As these narratives lose their legitimacy, space is opened for new stories and new visions for the future. In the past history of the United States, to use one example, these moments of transition produced rapid transformations in the political self-understanding of the country, as decades of incremental struggle were, in a matter of a few years, realized in quite dramatic changes. This was evident during those moments of systemic crisis and incipient disorder (the Progressive era, the Great Depression, the Sixties) when previously unimaginable rearticulations of the political (the right to collective bargaining, public education, state regulation of corporate conduct, the expansion of voting rights, etc.) were given enduring form through legislation, legal enfranchisement, changes in public discourse, and so on. Of course, these periods are brief, and the pressure toward reversal and renormalization almost immediate, but they led to substantial improvements in the quality of daily life for millions of Americans. No doubt, similar examples could be provided for other countries and political cultures.[9]

So what can we predict for the future? The continuing revival of religious theocracy marching in lockstep with corporate capital, or the triumph of immaterial labor as computer programmers and artists harness the "swarm intelligence" of the multitudes? Incipient fascism, as the United States reenacts the interpenetration of state and capital of Weimar-era Germany, or the spread of Bolivarian socialism through the southern hemisphere? Any and all scenarios seem equally possible and equally improbable. It is a sign of the uncertainty of the moment—the unresolved play of cultural, economic, and political forces currently unfolding before us. It is this sense of possibility, and imminent threat, that animates the remarkable profusion of contemporary art practices concerned with collective action and civic engagement. The cycle of contestation and reconsolidation in the political sphere is paralleled in the history of modernism itself, as formerly transgressive modes of artistic practice achieve canonical status, only to be unsettled in their turn by a subsequent transgression for which they function as the necessarily reified counterpoint. As a result, the "work" of modern art can be understood less in terms of formal or stylistic change per se, than as an ongoing struggle to identify, and then displace, normative conventions (whether these are discovered in the surrounding sociocultural environment or within the history of art practice itself). It is this procedure of distanciation and critique that constitutes the essential content of the contemporary aesthetic (or at least one of its most characteristic functions). Thus, we might view the recent proliferation of collaborative practices as part of a cyclical paradigm shift *within* the field of art, even as the nature of this shift involves an increasing permeability *between* "art" and other zones of symbolic production (urbanism, environmental activism, social work, etc.). As the history of modernism has repeatedly demonstrated, the greatest potential for transforming and reenergizing artistic practice is often realized precisely at those points where its established identity is most seriously at risk.

As I will suggest subsequently, there are really two decisive shifts at work. First, there is growing interest in collaborative or collective approaches in contemporary art. And second, as I've already noted, there is a movement toward participatory, process-based experience and away from a "textual" mode of production in which the artist fashions an object or event that is subsequently presented to the viewer. This shift is evident across a wide range of practices, from neoconceptual, biennial-based works by figures like Rirkrit Tiravanija and Thomas Hirschhorn, to more recognizably activist projects by groups like Park Fiction and Ala Plastica. The breadth of this shift is somewhat unusual. During the 1980s, the last time that collaborative work was on the radar screen of the mainstream art world, there were obvious methodological differences between the projects of groups like ACT UP, Colab, the Social and Public Art Resources Center, and Group Material, and the recognized avant-garde represented by Neo-Expressionist painting and postmodern appropriation, which both remained mono-authorial and fairly traditional in terms of media. Today the boundaries between socially engaged art practice and the avant-garde are harder to determine, with mainstream artists like Hirschhorn, Francis Alÿs, and Liam Gillick working in public space, engaging social networks, and so on. The interrelationship among and between these various modes of collaborative practice will be an important subtheme of this book.

2 — ART PRACTICE AND THE INTELLECTUAL BAROQUE

The One and the Many builds on research that I began in *Conversation Pieces: Community and Communication in Modern Art* (2004). Where that book concentrated on what I described as "dialogical" art practices (projects organized around conversational exchange and interaction), *The One and the Many* casts a wider net, examining the broader methodological field constituted by recent collaborative and participatory art. I will, however, continue to elaborate on the concept of dialogical production in the current study, especially as it relates to questions of creative labor. Since the publication of *Conversation Pieces*, interest in "relational" aesthetics and art practices concerned with social networks has increased dramatically within the art world. This is due in part to the growing importance of biennial exhibitions as both gatekeepers and commissioning agents for contemporary art projects that must, by their nature, be ephemeral or temporary. This institutional framework is paralleled by the emergence of entrepreneurial curators, like Nicholas Bourriaud, Catherine David, Okwui Enwezor, Uta Meta Bauer, and Hans-Ulbrich Obrist, who have done much to encourage art world interest in such work. Further, the range of collaborative art has continued to expand over the past decade, extending into work in new media (online collectives, concepts of distributed creativity, etc.) and protest-based practices catalyzed by the anti-war and anti-globalization movements in the United States and Europe, as well as an active tradition of demonstration-based collective work in South America (Grupo Etcetera and Taller Popular Serigrafia in Argentina, e.g.). There is, in addition, a long history of collaborative work in activist theater (much of it inspired by the writings of Augusto Boal) and community-based art.[10]

A substantive account of this entire field would require several volumes. It has been my preference to provide a more sustained analysis of a smaller number of projects rather than a synoptic overview. As noted above, I'll focus here on site-specific collaborative projects that unfold through extended interaction and shared labor, and in which the process of participatory interaction itself is treated as a form of creative praxis. In many cases these projects have been developed outside of traditional art venues such as biennials, galleries, and museums, and were produced instead in conjunction with local communities, neighborhoods, or sites of political resistance (Park Fiction's work challenging gentrification in Hamburg, e.g., or Dialogue's creation of water pump enclosures in central India). At the same time, as I've already noted, collaborative work has gained increasing legitimacy in the mainstream art world, as evidenced by the visibility of figures such as Alÿs, Gillick, Hirschhorn, and Tiravanija, who employ methodologies (video collectives, workshops, public meetings, etc.) that would have been identified, and possibly dismissed, as "community art" only a generation ago.[11] I'm interested in the differential articulation of participation and collaboration across a range of practices and sites, and what it can reveal about the more general condition of contemporary art. Thus, this book will also feature extended readings of projects by more recognized figures and groups (Alÿs, Superflex, and Santiago Sierra in particular).[12]

The proliferation of collaborative and participatory work suggests certain transformations in the nature of contemporary art practice that have broader implications for art historiography and theory. There are three areas in which these transformations have been particularly significant. First, contemporary collaborative art practices complicate conventional notions of aesthetic autonomy. These practices mark a (cyclical) renegotiation of aesthetic autonomy via the permeability that exists between art production and other, adjacent, forms of cultural production and activism. This raises an important set of ontological questions. What constitutes "art" at this historical moment, and what are its constituent or defining conditions? A second set of questions concern the epistemological status of this work. What forms of knowledge do collaborative, participatory, and socially engaged practices generate? These questions have come to the fore in recent debates over the differentiation of "aesthetic" and "ethical" criteria in the evaluation of artistic production. The issue of evaluative criteria is further complicated by the contrasting modes of transgression at work in the aesthetic and political fields, which I outlined above. How do we determine which transgressions *matter* in the arts? In the political sphere the act of transgression is typically framed through an appeal to some ethical criteria (respect for difference, the cultivation of the full range of human capacities, equal opportunity for participation in decision making, etc.). There is some reluctance, however, to explicitly acknowledge the kinds of ethical claims that art practices advance. Instead, the procedures of distanciation and destabilization are presented in much current criticism as intrinsically valuable. Finally, collaborative practices have important hermeneutic implications. While many projects that I examine include a physical component, the artists involved also identify various dialogical *processes* as integral to the content of the work. This suggests a model of reception, and a set of research methodologies, that are potentially quite different from those employed to analyze object-based art practices. The extemporaneous and participatory nature of these projects requires the historian or critic to employ techniques (field research, participant-observation, interviews, etc.) more typically associated with the social sciences.[13]

Taken in the aggregate, collaborative practices suggest a paradigm shift in contemporary art production. As I've already suggested, they deviate in certain key ways from textual forms of production in which the work of art is presented to an audience or viewer fully-formed. In using this designation I'm not suggesting that collaborative or participatory practices are somehow more rooted in the political or social "real." The concept of textual production refers here to the status of authorship and reception in the work, rather than proximity to conventional notions of the political. Moreover, as I'll outline in subsequent case studies, these are not hard and fast distinctions. Rather, "collaborative" and "textual" approaches can more accurately be described as predispositions within contemporary art practice that vary from artist to artist and project to project, depending on the artist's relationship to the materiality of a given work and to the viewer. Thus, collaborative practices don't supersede this textual approach. They simply offer a different articulation of a capacity that I take to be central to the constitution of modern art more generally: the ability of aesthetic experience to transform our perceptions of difference and to open space for forms of knowledge that challenge cognitive, social, or political conventions. This is, of course, a fairly vague definition, but I hope to make its meaning clearer through the case studies and project descriptions that follow.

An analysis of this paradigm shift requires, in turn, a reevaluation of existing art theory and the ways in which art theory and criticism are used to legitimate specific forms of art production. Therefore, my investigation of collaborative practice will also entail an extended engagement with the normative conventions of art theory itself. I'll be using the concept of an avant-garde "discourse," or "tradition" to describe a set of features common to a range of otherwise diverse contemporary practices. While the notion of an avant-garde tradition may seem oxymoronic, it is my contention that certain historically specific modes of artistic production have achieved a canonical status in contemporary theory and criticism. The constituent elements of this avant-garde tradition include a particular model of reception (based on shock or disruption), the a priori assumption of the viewer's perceptual or cognitive naïveté, and a belief in the intrinsically transgressive or liberatory power of desire or a-rational somatic experience. This mode of production remains quite vital and pervasive in contemporary art. My description of it as a "tradition" is not meant as a judgment of its efficacy or value, but is simply intended to denaturalize it as a particular system of art production rather than the necessary condition of all advanced art.

This model of artistic production emerged in conjunction with the assimilation of Continental (and primarily French) philosophy in the United States and European art worlds during the 1990s. Of course, various forms of theory began to play an increasingly central role in artistic production and criticism during the 1970s and early '80s. One could produce a revealing portrait of the art world based solely on changing intellectual fashions over the past four decades—from *Zen in the Art of Archery* to *The Poetics of Space*; from von Bertalanffy and systems theory to Wittgenstein and the *Tractatus*; from Lacan and psychoanalytic theory to Saussure and semiotics; from the cultural studies of Raymond Williams to the cultural anthropology of Clifford Geertz; from the feminism of *Screen* to the queer theory of *GLQ*; and from the Western Marxism of Gramsci, Lefebvre, and Benjamin to postcolonial theory via Fanon, Bhabha, and Spivak. By the early 1990s, this relatively inchoate mélange had been gradually winnowed down to the familiar patrimony of Deleuze, Derrida, and Foucault, and more recently, the quartet of Agamben, Badiou, Nancy, and Rancière.[14] While other sources and theoretical paradigms continued to be referenced, the poststructuralist tradition gained a quasi-hegemonic prominence in art critical discourse and was widely reproduced through the expansion and professionalization of graduate education in art history, studio art, and curatorial practice. The academic regularization of "theory" inevitably led to pressures to produce a uniform and consistent narrative based around a relatively limited number of canonical authors. As a result, theoretical paradigms that emerged out of the distinctive political conditions of Fifth Republic France were, in many cases, unproblematically imported into dramatically different contexts and settings. The result has been a complex and often contradictory dialogue between the art world and the academy. François Cusset describes this exchange in *French Theory: How Foucault, Derrida, Deleuze and Company Transformed the Intellectual Life of the United States*:

> When revolution is reinterpreted as stylized rebellion, when social forces are turned into identity politics, when writing is replaced by reading, when texts published by Gallimard or Éditions de Minuit wind up translated by specialized university presses, when mottos coined during Left Bank marches are being re-used in New York art galleries, then indeed one can speak of a "structural misunderstanding," not in the sense of a misreading, an error, a betrayal of some original, but in the sense of a highly productive transfer of words and concepts from one specific market of symbolic goods to another.[15]

While Cusset is concerned to deny any connotation of "betrayal" in the broader assimilation of French theory, the transition he describes (from revolution to "stylized" rebellion, from Gallimard to "specialized university presses," from Left Bank marches to "New York art galleries") inevitably implies a process of deracination or compromise; a movement from populist political engagement to more marginal forms of cultural production. I will return to this contrast in greater detail subsequently. For now, I simply want to note the growing interdependence between art practice and the academy, and the institutionalization of "theory" itself. Within this system the artist or the intellectual is simultaneously dependent on the dominant social order (through its subsidy of academic or cultural production) and external to it (through his or her capacity to achieve a critical distance from normative conventions), both alibi and critic. This development was anticipated almost twenty years ago by Pierre Bourdieu, who writes of the "reproduction of the corps" necessary to sustain institutional power in the academic system (an analysis that could be applied, in modified form, to the art world itself) and of the central role played by the "consecrated heretic" and "ritual sacrilege" within this system.[16]

Of course many of the insights on which this study depends (intersubjective models of identity, the aesthetics of collective or collaborative production, the micro-politics of various cultural practices) are themselves informed by the traditions of post-structuralism. It is, nonetheless, necessary to subject these same theoretical models to critical scrutiny, precisely because they have increasingly taken on the form of received wisdom within the art world. There are also certain assumptions about the nature of political resistance and cultural production specific to critical theory produced in the wake of May 1968 that require reconsideration. While this tradition is hardly monolithic, it nonetheless exhibits certain generic characteristics, especially around the question of the individual's relationship to the collective and the relative efficacy of organized forms of political action. As I will discuss in chapter 1, the concept of a textual politics (centered on a process of critical reading, or decoding) is symptomatic of an underlying tension within post-structuralist thought in which the act of critique must be insulated from the exigencies of practice or direct action. We find a telling example of this tension in an incident recounted by the philosopher Alain Renaut in François Dosse's *History of Structuralism*:

> I remember [Jacques] Derrida, at the ENS [Ecole Normale Supérieure] on the rue d'Ulm, after having been stopped in Czechoslovakia. During his seminar, he said that he had been quite distressed because after

having spent his life as a philosopher deconstructing humanism and saying that the idea of the author and of responsibility did not exist, he had one day been stripped naked in Czechoslovakia at a police station. He had to admit that this was a serious infringement of human rights. On that day, Derrida demonstrated his great lucidity by saying that he was in a very bizarre intellectual situation. So he proposed a category of the intellectual baroque, because, according to him, the two levels did not intersect. But we cannot remain eternally in the baroque.[17]

We might view the intellectual baroque as an essentially aesthetic category in which a given critical or creative protocol takes on a life of its own, operating independently of the mechanisms of social and political change necessary to realize the ideals on which it is founded. The artists discussed in this book have each, in their own way, struggled with the dilemma of Derrida's "bizarre" situation. How does one reconcile the utopian or transformative insight disclosed by creative practice with the actuality of lived experience? Is it possible for these two levels to "intersect"? The nature of this intersection, between theory and practice, withdrawal and engagement, text and materiality, will be a central theme in the following study.

The book is divided into three chapters. The first, "Autonomy, Antagonism, and the Aesthetic," will include summary descriptions of three collaborative projects that will be examined more fully in subsequent sections (Park Fiction in Germany, Ala Plastica in Argentina, and Dialogue in India). The chapter's main focus involves an extended meditation on the significance of autonomy in the development of modern art and art theory. As I've suggested, one of the most decisive features of recent collaborative art practice is a rearticulation of aesthetic autonomy as art practices parallel, overlap with, and challenge the organizational and ideological protocols of urban planning, political activism, and other fields of cultural production. It is necessary then to determine more precisely how the concept of autonomy originated, what function it has played through the evolution of modern art, and what is at stake in its maintenance or transformation today. This investigation will begin with an analysis of aesthetic autonomy as it emerged during the early modern period in reaction to growing anxieties about the vulgar taste of an incipient middle class. I'll relate this defensive notion of autonomy to recent discussions of relational aesthetics by the curator Nicholas Bourriaud and the critic Claire Bishop, one of his primary interlocutors. These writers can help us more clearly identify an underlying set of assumptions regarding the autonomy of the work of art and the sovereignty of the artistic personality, which have exerted a strong normative influence on contemporary art production and criticism, with particular implications for the analysis of collaborative art. Finally, I will trace the rapprochement that occurs between this discourse and the traditions of post-structuralist theory during the 1980s and '90s, focusing in particular on the impact of the events of May '68.

The second chapter, "The Genius of the Place," builds on the theoretical framework established in chapter 1, providing a more detailed analysis of the specific material conditions and epistemological effects of collaborative experience. What forms of knowledge are catalyzed in collaborative interaction? How do they differ from the insights generated through the specular experience provided by object-based practices? The chapter begins with an extended reading of Francis Alÿs's *When Faith Moves Mountains* (2002), a large-scale performance staged near a shantytown outside Lima, Peru. Alÿs's work allows for a discussion of the status of labor in contemporary art. I identify a series of elisions in recent critical theory that led to a privileging of the un-worked and simultaneous over the labored and durational, and which have blocked a more substantive engagement with collaborative experience and interaction. I outline a new framework for the analysis of collaborative art practice, rooted in a reinterpretation of labor. It's first necessary to free the concept of labor from the productivist paradigm that has governed both historical and contemporary accounts. This analysis opens out into a broader examination of the history of artistic identity, pointing to certain fault lines in the constitution of modern subjectivity around notions of property and possessive individualism.

The chapter then turns to an investigation of the rhetoric of "development" in contemporary social policy and political theory. The relationship between developed and developing nations is paralleled at the regional level by a discourse that constructs the "rural" as the degraded antipode of the "urban." In each case, we encounter a set of oppositions that define the rural, or developing, culture as the parochial counterpart of an implicitly superior metropolitan culture. Insight and emulation can flow in only one direction: from the enlightened core to the blighted periphery. I'll investigate a series of projects that challenge or destabilize the rural/ urban dichotomy, and which produce strategic inversions in the field of developmental rhetoric sketched above, focusing in particular on the work of Dialogue, an art collective working in central India. I also address the complex and often contradictory interrelationship between collaborative art practices in the developing world and the operations of nongovernmental organizations, using the work of the Danish group Superflex as an example. The chapter concludes with a discussion of two extended collaborative projects, in Argentina's Rio de la Plata basin and in Myanmar.

If "development" provides a primary frame of reference for the projects discussed in chapter 2, "regeneration" is a central theme in chapter 3 ("Eminent Domain"), which examines collaborative groups working in urban settings. The discourse of development implies a primal, or pastoral, culture awaiting the civilizing effects of modernization. Regeneration, on the other hand, suggests a formerly healthy or advanced organism that has undergone a process of atavistic decline. In the history of the modern city this decline has often expressed a moral dimension: not simply the deterioration of a city's physical infrastructure, but the demoralization or spiritual degeneration of its (typically working-class) inhabitants. The signs of this demoralization include labor unrest, rising crime rates, the growth of poverty, the spread of disease, and so on. From Manchester in the 1860s to Detroit in the 1960s to modern-day Bangalore, the image of the city as a "natural" organism entails a strategic disavowal of its function as a system for the efficient spatial organization of industrial (or post-industrial) production. The pathological city, diseased and chaotic, effectively recodes the systemic effects of the capitalist economy (brought about by the division of labor, downward pressure on wages, cyclical crises of overproduction, and corporate disregard for public welfare) as the consequence of the moral depravity of the urban poor and working classes. As a result, contemporary urban regeneration schemes remain a site of significant political conflict.

In chapter 3, I'll discuss a range of projects that employ modes of collaborative and collective interaction to address the regeneration process and the imaginary construction of urban space. These projects explore the ways in which the image of the city is deployed to justify the authority of dominant economic and political interests, as well as struggles over the narratives used to advance or challenge specific public policies and projects. I begin chapter 3 with an extended analysis of work produced by Santiago Sierra in conjunction with beggars and the homeless. I discuss

Sierra's attempt to mobilize images of urban poverty in relationship to the visual culture of urban reform in the late nineteenth century (specifically, the work of the Danish-American journalist Jacob Riis), examining the ways in which both Riis and Sierra deploy images of the suffering body. Following this analysis I survey the cultural history of urban renewal (or urban regeneration as it is often known in Europe), focusing primarily on the relationship between urban renewal, public art, and gentrification in the United States during the 1960s and '70s, but with some reference to debates over regeneration in London during the 1980s as well. The second half of the chapter will concentrate on collaborative projects that involve the reclamation of urban space against the grain of gentrification and displacement, or that seek to activate urban space as a site of public, political discourse. The projects include Park Fiction's work in Hamburg's Hafenstraße neighborhood and Rick Lowe's Project Row Houses in Houston, Texas. Each of these projects asserts a claim of spatial sovereignty, while at the same time seeking to preserve a reflective relationship to the modes of collective solidarity necessary to sustain this claim, returning us to the questions of agency, identity, and labor introduced in chapter 2.

1

AUTONOMY, ANTAGONISM, AND THE AESTHETIC

Augustine writes in the *Confessions*, "What is time? If no one asks me, I know what it is: if someone asks me, I no longer know."[1] Here Augustine suggests that the moment that passes between posing a question and receiving a reply is marked by both risk and possibility: the risk of doubt and uncertainty, and the possibility of an opening out to the other. Paul Ricoeur, in *From Text to Action*, uses Augustine's quote to illustrate a familiar poststructuralist parable, as our "confused, formless . . . [and] mute temporal experience" inevitably succumbs to the instrumentalizing grasp of narrative discourse.[2] However, this passage carries another, equally subversive, message. Knowledge is reliable, safe, and certain as long as it is held in mono-logical isolation and synchronic arrest. As soon as it becomes mobilized and communicable, this certainty slips away and truth is negotiated in the gap between self and other, through an unfolding, dialogical exchange.

The Russian Constructivist El Lissitzky reiterated Augustine's famous query in the early twentieth century: "When someone would ask me what 'Art' is, then in that moment I do not know what it is. But when I'm not being asked, then I know what it is."[3] Lissitzky's paraphrase neatly conflates two of the central tenets of the modern avant-garde. First, avant-garde art constitutes a form of critical insight; its task is to transgress existing categories of thought, action, and creativity (beginning with the definition of art itself), to constantly challenge fixed boundaries and identities. And second, the formation of an artistic subjectivity capable of such insight requires a process of withdrawal and defensive interiorization. The uncertainty that the artist experiences in responding to an interlocutor is presented as a barrier and a constraint, while the certitude of his own, internal, definition of art is a necessary precondition for creative practice. It is precisely in *not* attempting to define or fix the meaning of art for the Other that the artist is freed to act with the greatest creativity, even as his own self-understanding provides an infallible compass. It's symptomatic that even in the midst of a Constructivist movement notoriously hostile to traditional notions of self-expression, we encounter this conflation of the task of modern art (the generation of counter-normative insight) and the experience of subjective individuation (the isolation of the artistic personality in a sequestered zone of autonomous self-reflection). For Lissitzky, the artist requires mono-logical clarity, needs to "know" what art is, precisely because he is challenging bourgeois tradition, popular opinion, or other forms of collective or cumulative knowledge, which are understood as intrinsically compromised. Armed with this wisdom, incubated within the far recesses of the self, the artist creates physical manifestations, works of art, designed to variously provoke, reveal, expose, and transgress.[4]

At the same moment, Lissitzky was acutely conscious of the new demands placed on artistic subjectivity by the Constructivist movement and the necessary contradiction between the imperative to subvert conventional knowledge, on the one hand, and the use of conventional forms of authorship to produce this subversion, on the other. "What is needed is a cooperative," he wrote in a letter to Jan Tschichold in 1925. "But there is still too much subjectivist leaven in us, since every attempt fails." Writing seven years later, Lissitzky reflected on the impact of the avant-garde assault on conventional artistic production: "We fought against 'art,' we spat on its 'altar'—and we got what we wanted. Now, of course, we need no new art monasteries and sacred groves, but, even flying through a storm as we are, we would like to be able to achieve a little more concentration and to carry our offspring to term."[5] This ambivalent relationship between individual and collectivity identity, between the work of art as experiential process and final product, is symptomatic. It isn't a question of privileging one term over the other, the collective over authorial sovereignty, or self-expression over the constraints of popular culture, but rather of recognizing the interplay of these ostensibly divided terms as a key nexus of creative action.

The tension between artistic and normative models of subjectivity was central to the development of modernist art over the past century, and continues to inform contemporary art practice and criticism.[6] The persistence of this dynamic is understandable. It was set in place initially by the overt hostility that greeted modernism's earliest outriders (the Romantic painters, the Realists, the Barbizon school, Der Blaüe Reiter, etc.) as they did battle with the still resonant forces of the salon and the academy. Withdrawal into the fortified enclave of the group or movement, and doughty faith in the integrity of one's personal vision against the grain of an art establishment mired in neoclassical repetition, were necessary for survival. The risk of significant ostracism and hostility has long ago subsided, but the *Weltbild* remains, a residue of modernism's initial struggle for legitimacy, internalized now by young artists at the earliest stages of their careers.

There is, of course, much at stake in the effort to preserve a cultural space that allows for critical reflection. Despite its many positive contributions, the impact of modernity on human subjectivity has also been profoundly damaging: the violence of industrial production, the brutal means/end rationality of the market, divisive class structures, the displacement or outright destruction of indigenous cultures, and oppressive forms of political totalitarianism have all diminished our understanding of what it is to be human. The history of modern art can be viewed, in large measure, as an ongoing struggle to develop a compensatory cultural response to the destructive and dehumanizing effects of modernity, whether this is done through the agency of a well-crafted object, paintings of bucolic Polynesians, or the therapeutic disruption of the viewer's perception. The artistic personality itself is perhaps the most symptomatic expression of this struggle. It exists as an explicit rebuke to the complacency, compartmentalization, and depersonalization imposed by the contemporary social order. Modern art has come to function as a privileged site of reflection on the forces of modernism—a quasi-autonomous space of commentary and engagement, whose critical optic has been made possible precisely by art's gradual displacement from its previously integral cultural role within premodern society. Now occupying the margins of society (in terms of broader cultural relevance if not its status as a signifier of class hierarchy), it exists at a critical remove, allowing the artist the distance necessary to recognize the flaws and limitations of modern life and consciousness, and to reveal those constraints to the viewer.

The modern artist's attack on society and societal norms has most often been mobilized through a critique of representation (or, more recently, "signification"). It was the way in which society chose to image itself, the fawning idealization of wealth in Baroque painting, the sentimentalization of bourgeois privilege in the nineteenth-century salon, and later an entire mass cultural apparatus predicated on illusion and manipulation, that provided the axis of attack for the modern avant-garde. In response, artists deployed a range of counter-representational strategies (the disruption of academic conventions governing the use of color, facture, and composition; the turn toward abstraction; and eventually a full-scale attack on the very principle of mimesis in visual art), calling attention to the mythifying powers of the conventional image and holding open space for a more complex aesthetic experience, capable of catalyzing self-reflection rather than Pavlovian consumption. The result was a modernist discourse centered on the theatrical struggle between good and evil images, and defined by heroic acts of exposure and revelation against the nefarious forces of duplicity and reification. Artists would wage war on the instrumentalizing powers of representation on behalf of the chaotic integrity of lived experience. This remained, of course, a deeply and self-consciously ethical tendency: a battle for the heart and mind of the modern subject. It sought to produce viewers more sensitive to the singularity and difference of the world around them, and less reliant on simplistic or reductive systems of meaning in trying to comprehend that world.

These two characteristics—the inviolable autonomy of the individual practitioner and a mode of ethico-representational engagement—remain an article of faith in even the most ostensibly participatory or interactive works of contemporary art. Consider curator Lars Bang Larsen's account of Michael Elmgreen and Ingar Dragset's *Cruising Pavilion* (1998), a cube-shaped space designed to facilitate public sex in Denmark's Marselisborg Forest:

> In a way, queer space is being queered; the codes and routines that hold it together as a cultural arrangement are worn thin. This is in keeping with a process that implicitly questions what can be particularly "gay" about any representation, when gay culture has gained relative access to the mainstream. . . . To find yourself in Elmgreen and Dragset's displaced ambiences is to feel the pull of your identity, whether you are straight or gay. . . . Space is fucked up because function is fucked up. "What are you about?" the work seems to ask. "What does your desire hang on to?" On the one hand, there is the suggestion of a fading "we" that refers to the loneliness of violently separate identities: on the other hand, the sense of a failure to condense things into a representational logic that can speak for the coherence and relevance of group identity.[7]

Larsen's talk of "codes" and "representational logic" is symptomatic. Confronted with a site whose inhabitants are already engaged in the creative deconstruction of conventional systems of meaning (subverting the public park into a space for proscribed forms of "private" sexual interaction), the artist's only conceivable option is to engage in a *further* act of deconstruction such that (ostensibly "mainstream") queer desire itself is problematized, interrogated, and challenged. Visitors to Elmgreen and Dragset's "fucked up" space are in familiar avant-garde territory. Larsen's description echoes Ad Reinhardt's famous cartoon of the philistine viewer chiding the abstract painting ("What does this represent?") only to have the painting spring to life, jab its anthropomorphic finger in the viewer's face, and demand in turn: "What do *you* represent?" The artist is responsible for arranging and administering an experience of therapeutic dislocation directed specifically at the representational matrix of identity, but it's a dislocation that remains strangely abstract. It's unclear whether gay (or straight) Danes need lessons in queer representation or identity politics or help in finding spots for public sexual encounters, but this question is really beside the point. The function of this project, in Larsen's view, is less to engage the actual inhabitants of Marselisborg Forest than to constitute an ideal formal manifestation within which engagement could, hypothetically, take place. It is an architectural symbol of this dislocation, a conceptual provocation that gains its aesthetic resonance from the juxtaposition of sterile minimalist form and the physical actuality of queer sex (the structure is replete with glory holes) (see Plate 1).

The works that I'll be discussing here challenge this paradigm in a number of ways. Most importantly, the various social interactions that unfold around a given project, rather than being ancillary to, or collapsed into, the *a priori* formal structure or design of a physical object (Elmgreen and Dragset's *Pavilion*, for example), are openly and often independently thematized as a locus for aesthetic practice. I'll be tracing a shift from an aesthetic discourse centered primarily on questions of visual signification to one concerned with the generative experience of collective interaction.

2 — PARK FICTION, ALA PLASTICA, AND DIALOGUE

We believe that the interesting and relevant art projects at the moment are developing new ways of cooperation and always build platforms of communication and exchange with others as well. We would go so far as to say, that this is a change of paradigm and that these collaborative qualities signify a new kind of avant-garde.
CHRISTOPH SCHÄFER, PARK FICTION

This experimental engagement with new forms of collectivity and agency is evident in Park Fiction's work in Hamburg, Germany, where they reinvented the process of participatory urban planning as an imaginative game.[8] The speculative quality of this work is literally embodied in their name (the "fiction" of a park), and in the audacity necessary to imagine a public park in place of the high-rise apartment and office buildings that were being proposed by the city's development community. Rather than simply protest and critique the process of gentrification that was beginning to unfold around Hamburg's waterfront (an area with a diverse, working-class population), Park Fiction organized a "parallel planning process" that began with the creation of alternative platforms for exchange among the area's existing residents ("musicians, priests, a headmistress, a cook, café-owners, bar-men, a psychologist, squatters, artists and interventionist residents"[9]). The element of fantasy is apparent in the proposals already completed for the park, including the Teagarden Island, which features artificial palm trees and is surrounded by an elegant forty-meter-long bench from Barcelona, an Open Air Solarium, and a Flying Carpet (a wave-shaped lawn area surrounded by a mosaic inspired by the Alhambra). Park Fiction combines this whimsical spirit with a well-developed tactical sensibility and a sophisticated grasp of the realpolitik involved in challenging powerful economic interests. They were able to build on a tradition of organized political resistance in the area around Hamburg's harbor that extends back to the occupation of the Hafenstraße (Harbor Street) neighborhood during the 1980s, when local residents took control of several city blocks and effectively halted the city's efforts at eviction. The residents of the Hafenstraße employed street theater, pirate radio, mural painting, and other cultural practices during the occupation to challenge the police, gain media attention, and encourage a sense of solidarity and cohesion within the embattled neighborhood. Park Fiction member Christoph Schäfer describes the leverage this history provided in the process of bringing the park into existence:

> The location for the park is directly at the river. It's a very expensive, highly symbolic place, where power likes to represent itself. . . . To claim this space as a public park designed by the residents really meant to challenge power—it's not an alternative corner or a social sandbox the parents can afford to give away. The resistance could only be overcome by a very broad and clever network in the community, by a new set of tactics, trickery, seduction and stubbornness and an unspoken threat lingering in the background of all this: that a militant situation might again develop that would be costly, and bad for the city's image, and deter investment in the whole neighborhood.[10]

It was necessary for Park Fiction to develop a close rapport with activist groups and organizations in the neighborhood. As Schäfer describes it, they only collaborated with institutions that had local "credibility." These included a community center, which was known for providing free and anonymous legal services, as well as a school that had supported the Hafenstraße squatters during the 1980s.

While operating in a very different cultural context, the work of the Argentinian collective Ala Plastica parallels that of Park Fiction in many ways. Their *AA Project*, located in the Rio de la Plata basin near Buenos Aires, mobilized new modes of collective action and creativity in order to challenge the political and economic interests behind large-scale development in the region. The construction of a massive transportation system (the Zárate-Brazo Largo rail complex) over the last two decades has exacerbated flooding and damaged the fishing and tourist economies in the delta, leading to high levels of unemployment and deteriorating social services. Ala Plastica initiated the *AA Project* with a process of spatial and cognitive mapping, developed in collaboration with the area's residents, along with a bioregional study of the Rio de la Plata and Parana delta. This mapping procedure was combined with various exercises designed to recover and collect local knowledge about the region. Ala Plastica sought to actualize the insights of the area's residents into the social and environmental costs of the rail complex and the proposed Punta Lara Colonia bridge. In order to challenge the institutional authority and "techno-political" mindset of the corporate and governmental agencies responsible for these projects, Ala Plastica worked with the area's residents to articulate their own visions for the region through the creation of communications platforms and networks for mutual cooperation. They helped design emergency housing modules for use during periods of flooding and provided communications training and infrastructure, with a particular focus on women. Building on a tradition of willow cultivation that dates back to the mid-nineteenth century, the *AA Project* identified new uses for willows and encouraged the emergence of local economies based on willow production. Throughout the *AA Project*, Ala Plastica worked closely with local activist groups and NGOs, including the Producers Cooperative of the Coast of Berisso and the Health and Plants Network of Argentina.

The *AA Project* was inspired by an earlier work, *Emergent Species* (1995), which involved research into the capacity of reeds and other aquatic plants to absorb pollution. In the process, Ala Plastica's members came to identify a significant correspondence between the structure of reed-bed propagation and a creative practice that links diverse particularities via a non-hierarchical network:

> We planned a project represented by the metaphor of rhizomatic expansion and emergence, alluding to the behavior of these plants and to the emergent character of ideas and creative practices. The connection of remnants within one another generated a practically indescribable warp of intercommunication deriving into innumerable actions that developed and increased through *reciprocity*: dealing with social and environmental problems; exploring both non-institutional and inter-

cultural models while working with the community and on the social sphere; interacting, exchanging experiences and knowledge with producers of culture and crops, of art and craftwork, of ideas and objects.[11]

We find a similar commitment to collaborative modes of creativity in the hand pump sites and children's temples produced by the Dialogue collective in conjunction with Adivasi tribal and peasant communities in central India over the past eight years (the Adivasi are India's indigenous population and have long suffered from economic and social discrimination). Access to clean water is a complex, and politically contentious, issue in rural India. As corporations penetrate farther into the countryside in pursuit of cheap labor, they put increasing pressure on natural resources to support their production facilities: in many cases either contaminating or privatizing local water supplies.[12] As a result, the Adivasi communities in the Bastar region where Dialogue has been working are engaged in struggles over land and water access, while also grappling with the impact of economic and cultural modernization. As Dialogue member Navjot Altaf writes, "What interested me most was the hybridism of the cultures [in Bastar]; contradictions and identity crises which are multiple and interrelated."[13] This macropolitical dimension is paralleled by a set of cultural traditions around water collection that place the greatest burden on young women and girls. Altaf and Dialogue began working in the villages around Kondagaon in Bastar with the simple goal of creating more efficient pump sites, using ergonomic designs that would ease the physical burden of collecting and transporting water. They developed the sites through a series of collaborative workshops that brought together Adivasi craftspeople, village residents, teachers, college students, hawkers, and other volunteers in the creation of quasi-sculptural constructions that surround the pumps. The constructions are practical (they include niches that allow water carriers to rest their vessels as they lift them to their shoulders), while also incorporating symbols and forms associated with local cultural and spiritual traditions. In the process of developing the pump sites, Dialogue's members came to realize their importance as gathering points for women and children—one of the few spaces in which they could meet and interact socially. This led in turn to the development of Children's Temples (Pilla Gudi) that could function as centers for activity and exchange among young people in the village.

Altaf views the collaborative interactions among artists and village residents, and between Adivasi and non-Adivasi, that occur in these projects as decisive. As she writes, "For us, organizing the workshops required to design and construct the pumps and Pilla Gudi is as important as creating the sites themselves. It encourages a communication network among artists from different cultures and disciplines, both within the area and outside, and with and among the young." These cross-cultural exchanges, Altaf notes, "lead the young to think about different ways of knowing and modes of working, enabling them to draw nourishment and sustenance from difference and similarities." The process of designing and constructing the pump sites and temples, the interactions of artisans, young people, and visitors, has encouraged a critical renegotiation of Adivasi identity. This renegotiation is particularly crucial in contemporary India, due to the rise of a right-wing fundamentalist movement over the past decade that has actively repressed non-Hindu cultures (like that of the Adivasi). At the same time, the mainstream educational system in India attempts to "neutralize" cultural difference, according to Altaf, through a policy of "Unity in Diversity" that minimizes the specific histories of the Adivasi and the Dalit (or "untouchables").[14]

I'll examine the projects of Park Fiction, Ala Plastica, Dialogue, and other groups more closely in the following two chapters of this book. In each case, the artists take on a strategic relationship to political collectivities currently in formation. Their projects begin with an opening out to their collaborators, which I have written about elsewhere in terms of a dialogical aesthetic.[15] The effect of collaborative art practice is to frame this exchange (spatially, institutionally, procedurally), setting it sufficiently apart from quotidian social interaction to encourage a degree of self-reflection, and calling attention to the exchange itself as creative praxis. A particular experience of openness is encouraged as participants are implicated in an exchange that is not wholly subsumable to conventional, pragmatic demands, but is consciously marked as a form of artistic practice. In fact, it is in part the lack of categorical fixity around art that makes this openness possible. The distancing from the protocols and assumptions of normative social exchange created by aesthetic framing reduces our dependence on default behaviors, expectations, and modes of being, encouraging a more performative and experimental attitude toward the work of identity. Despite their differences the projects of Park Fiction, Ala

Plastica, and Dialogue reflect a calling out to these experiences: a desire to work through them in a tentative, experimental, but nonetheless rigorous, manner.

The artwork is . . . no longer presented to be consumed within a "monumental" time frame and open for a universal public; rather it elapses within a factual time, for an audience *summoned* by the artist.
NICHOLAS BOURRIAUD, *RELATIONAL AESTHETICS*

How do we account for the recent proliferation of art practices concerned with the creation or facilitation of new social networks and new modalities of social interaction? Nicholas Bourriaud, co-director of the Palais de Tokyo in Paris, has argued that we are witnessing the transition to a "relational" aesthetic in contemporary art, defined by "meetings, encounters, events [and] various types of collaboration between people." And critic Claire Bishop, writing in *Artforum*, goes so far as to claim that "politically-engaged" collaborative art practice constitutes today's "avant-garde."[16] Bourriaud's analysis, or at least his nomenclature, has gained the most traction in the art world. By now the general contours of his argument (first floated in his eponymous 1998 book) are well established. We live in a "society of the spectacle," in which even social relations are reified ("The social bond has turned into a standardized artifact").[17] In response, a cadre of artists, beginning in the 1990s, developed a new approach to art involving the staging of "micro utopias," or "micro communities" of human interaction. These "convivial, user-friendly artistic projects," including "meetings, encounters, events, [and] various types of collaboration between people," provided a "rich loam for social interaction."[18] The "tangible models of sociability" enacted in these relational projects promise to overcome the reification of social relationships. In the process, these artists also sought to reorient artistic practice away from technical expertise or object-production and toward processes of intersubjective exchange.

On the one hand, Bourriaud offers a fairly straightforward rearticulation of conventional avant-garde discourse, in which the instrumentalizing attitude formerly understood as a potential result of exposure to mass culture has now colonized the most intimate modes and pathways of human interaction. No longer able to destabilize these effects through a kind of formal/representational "reverse engineering" (i.e., by creating objects and images that challenge, deform, or complicate the reductive visual codes of mass culture), artists must now engage them on the terrain of social interaction itself. It is not entirely clear why the "social bond" should be any more reified now than it was twenty, fifty, or even a hundred years ago. Rather, this claim seems to reproduce the epochal consciousness that is typical of the modernist project, in which art's ameliorative function is in some way demanded or called into existence by the exigencies of a singular historical moment defined by an experience of loss or lack. Thus, images used to be less manipulative or superficial, social interactions used to be more holistic, or society as a whole used to be less driven by greed and self-interest, and it is the artist's job to evoke or reclaim this lost, utopic experience. Bourriaud also describes relational practice as an epiphenomenal expression of the shift from industrial forms of labor to a service economy. If the artist under industrial production had the "job" of creating complex or well-crafted objects as an antidote to mass-produced dreck, then the "postindustrial" artist must now create alternative models of sociality to challenge the instrumentalizing of human social interaction characteristic of a postindustrial economic system. Although this explanation possesses a certain symmetrical elegance, it seems problematic to transpose economic transformations (which have, after all, been developing for fifty years or more) so neatly onto shifts in contemporary art practice. Further, this postulate relies on the highly questionable assertion (much beloved by advocates of the "immaterial labor" thesis) that the most symptomatic transformations in the contemporary economy are all centered in the realm of service-based labor or intellectual production.[19] While Bourriaud's writing is compelling, it is also highly schematic. Further, he provides few substantive readings of specific projects. As a result, it is difficult to determine what, precisely, constitutes the aesthetic content of a given relational work. At the same time, he has captured something that is undeniably central to a recent generation of artists: a concern with social and collective interaction. As he writes, "Today, after two centuries of struggle for singularity and against group impulses . . . we must [reintroduce] the idea of plurality [and invent] new ways of being together, forms of interaction that go beyond the inevitability of the families, ghettos of technological user-friendliness, and collective institutions."[20]

Drawing on the work of Félix Guattari and Gilles Deleuze, Bourriaud contends that relational art practices challenge the "territorialization" of conventional identity with a "plural, polyphonic" understanding of the subject. "Subjectivity can only be defined," Bourriaud writes, "by the presence of a second subjectivity. It does not form a 'territory' except on the basis of the other territories it comes across; . . . it is modeled . . . on the principle of otherness."[21] This profession of faith in the verities of the "plural" and decentered subject is by now routine, if not *de rigueur*, in art criticism. It exists in some tension, however, with Bourriaud's rather strenuous efforts to establish clear boundaries between the "new ways of being together" that he has privileged in his own curatorial work (by artists such as Pierre Huyghe, Liam Gillick, Rirkrit Tiravanija, and Christine Hill) and an abject Other, embodied in traditions of performance art and socially engaged collaborative practice that extend back to the 1960s. From the work of Conrad Atkinson, Grupo de Artistas Argentinos de Vanguardia, David Harding, and Helen and Newton Harrison, through Suzanne Lacy, Peter Dunn and Loraine Leeson, Carole Condé and Karl Beveridge, Group Material, and Welfare State, and up to groups such as Ala Plastica, Huit Facettes Interaction, Grupo Etcetera, Platform, Littoral, Park Fiction, Ultra Red, and many others, we find a diverse range of artists and collectives working in collaboration with environmentalists, AIDS activists, trade unions, anti-globalization protestors, and many others. This tradition is not only absent from Bourriaud's account, it is openly disparaged as naive and even reactionary. "Any stance that is 'directly' critical of society," as Bourriaud writes, "is futile." Bourriaud offers an ominous description of socially engaged art practice marching in lock-step conformity with a vaguely Stalinist political program ("It is clear that the age of the New Man, future-oriented manifestos, and calls for a better world all ready to be walked into and lived in is well and truly over").[22]

Bourriaud's caricature, which collapses all activist art into the condition of 1930s socialist realism, fails to convey the complexity and diversity of socially engaged art practice over the last several decades. Even Bourriaud's critics share this almost visceral distaste for socially engaged art. Writing in *Artforum*, Bishop imposes a similarly rigid boundary between "aesthetic" projects ("provocative," "uncomfortable," and "multilayered") and activist works ("predictable," "benevolent," and "ineffectual"). In a critique of Bourriaud published in *October*, Bishop feels compelled to reassure her readers: "I'm not suggesting that relational art works need to develop a greater social conscious—by making pin-board works about international terrorism, for example, or giving free curries to refugees."[23] For Bishop, art can become legitimately "political" only indirectly, by exposing the limits and contradictions of political discourse itself (the exclusions implicit in democratic consensus, e.g.) from the quasi-detached perspective of the artist. This is also the basis for Thomas Hirschhorn's anxious assertion that he is *not* a "political artist," but rather an artist who "makes art politically."[24] In this view, artists who choose to work in alliance with specific collectives, social movements, or political struggles, will, inevitably, be consigned to decorating floats for the annual May Day parade. Without the detachment and autonomy of conventional art to insulate them, they are doomed to "represent," in the most naive and facile manner possible, a given political issue or constituency.

This detachment is necessary because art is constantly in danger of being subsumed to the condition of consumer culture, propaganda, or "entertainment" (cultural forms predicated on immersion rather than a recondite critical distance). Instead of seducing the viewer, the artist's task is to hold him at arm's length, inculcating a skeptical distance (defined in terms of opacity, estrangement, confusion, or ironic distanciation) that parallels the insight provided by critical theory into the contingency of social and political meaning. The maintenance of this distance (literally embodied in projects such as Santiago Sierra's *Wall Enclosing a Space*, for the Spanish Pavilion of the 2003 Venice Biennale, in which only those carrying Spanish passports were allowed to enter the gallery) requires that the artist retain complete control over the form and structure of the work. Relational practice is thus characterized by a tension between two movements. One runs along a continuum from the specular to the haptic (the desire to literalize social interaction in nonvirtual space), and the other runs along a continuum from the work as a preconceived entity to the work as improvisational and situationally responsive. In order to preserve the legitimacy of relational practice as a hereditary expression of avant-garde art, it is necessary for critics like Bourriaud and Bishop to privilege the first movement over the second. It is for this reason, I would suggest, that a number of Bourriaud's relational projects retain an essentially textual status, in which social exchange is choreographed as an a priori event for the consumption of an audience "summoned" by the artist.[25] In addition to naturalizing deconstructive interpretation as the only appropriate metric for aesthetic experience, this approach places the artist in a position of adjudicatory oversight, unveiling or revealing the contingency of systems of meaning that the viewer would otherwise submit to without thinking. The viewer, in short, can't be trusted.[26] Hence the deep suspicion which both Bourriaud and Bishop hold for art practices which surrender some autonomy to collaborators and which involve the artist directly in the (implicitly compromised) machinations of political resistance.

On one level, this persistent discomfort with activist art is typical of post–Cold War intellectuals embarrassed by work that evokes leftist ideals. Precisely what makes relational artists such as Rirkrit Tiravanija, Thomas Hirschhorn, Pierre Huyghe, and Jens Hanning "new," in this view, is their attempt to redefine collectivity and intersubjective exchange outside of existing, and implicitly retrograde, political referents (the extent to which their projects actually accomplish a significant remodeling of collectivity is open to question). The modest gestures employed by Bourriaud's artists (offering to do someone's washing up, paying a fortune teller, hiring models, etc.) run no risk of being appropriated to dangerous *grand recits* that will, inevitably, be revealed as reactionary and compromised.[27] It would seem to be relatively uncontroversial to locate the relational projects embraced by Bourriaud (or Bishop) on a continuum with socially engaged projects that employ processes of collaborative interaction. However, for both of these writers activist work triggers a kind of sacrificial response—as if to even acknowledge this work as "art" somehow threatens the legitimacy of the practices that they do support.[28] In her *Artforum* essay Bishop dismisses activist art *en masse* as "politically correct," "Platonic," and even "Christian." A reductive version of engaged or activist art ("free curries for refugees") thus functions as a necessary foil, representing the abject, unsophisticated Other to the complex "aesthetic" works of which she approves.[29]

We can gain a more balanced perspective on recent collaborative art practices (and their critical interlocutors) if we locate them in a broader historical context relative to the traditions of the modern avant-garde. As I suggested above, the core function of art changes dramatically in the modern period. By the early nineteenth century art began to abandon its traditional function of transmitting and idealizing dominant forms of social or political power (as in medieval concepts of theophany, sacral or courtly art, or the flattering depictions of aristocratic leisure in the canvases of Boucher or Watteau), and instead took on the role of disrupting or destabilizing them. We can already detect this shift in Goya's famous portrait of *Charles IV with his Family* (1798) ("the corner baker and his wife after they have won the lottery," as Theophile Gautier described it). This thinly veiled criticism of monarchical power would have been almost unimaginable a generation before. It tells us much about the very different nature of bourgeois power, which was, at its earliest stage, defined by a capacity for self-reflection, often displaced into the institution of art. During the nineteenth century, provocation and critique would rapidly move from being an occasional or incidental aspect of art to its primary orientation, with the emergence of a series of avant-garde movements that sought, each in its own way, to challenge or destabilize normative bourgeois values. It is important to recall the remarkable consistency of avant-garde rhetoric across a broad range of otherwise disparate movements and tendencies. Of particular importance here was the notion of the artist as a provocateur, challenging modernity from a position of cultural exteriority that was typically leveraged via identification with an "other" identified either spatially (via a geographic displacement, to rural France, North Africa, the Middle East, Japan, etc.) or temporally (through the evocation of a past moment of cultural harmony or authenticity, as in the preRaphaelite's fetishization of the Italian primitives).

This agonistic posture changes art's self-understanding, its ontology, if you will, as well as the kinds of knowledge that it produces. First, modern art begins to define itself in opposition to, or as the negation of, certain characteristics identified with the dominant culture. Initially, genuine or authentic art was defined as the antithesis of the academic painting of the salon (which embodied dominant values through its allegiance to fixed representational protocols derived from classical models). Where academic art was labored and formulaic, authentic art would be spontaneous and improvisational. The decline of the academy and the growing influence of consumer culture during the early- to mid-twentieth century opened up a new axis of differentiation, as avant-garde art was defined against the grain of a rising wave of mass culture and propaganda that threatened to overwhelm it. By the post–Second World War period contemporary art was sufficiently institutionalized and capitalized that its survival was no longer at stake. The previously externalized threat represented by kitsch was internalized in anxieties about the proliferation of rogue tendencies within contemporary art itself.[30] In this process, particular modes of art practice (installation, performance, activist work) which failed to foreground their own media specificity with sufficient rigor became supplemental replacements for the faded mass cultural Other. The result is an aesthetic discourse based on notions of purity and contamination in which it is necessary to maintain a rigid segregation between corrupt and authentic practices. This approach lends itself to a hygienic attitude on the part of the critic, who must defend art from contamination: a fear that art will lose its specific identity if it becomes too permeable to other, impure, areas of culture.

As I've described it, modern art's self-definition unfolds via a modulating series of foils. The specific identity of the individual terms is less important than the kind of attitude art takes up relative to them as a whole. In each case there is an instrumentalizing relationship to the material, against which art is defined. This material, be it salon painting, kitsch, propaganda, or performance art, is reduced to a (reified) vehicle for the achievement of authentic art's own self-reflection (all mass culture is vulgar kitsch; all political discourse is propaganda; all performance art is merely theatrical). "Progress" in art is defined by this ongoing movement, as art's meaning becomes fixed, then finds itself called into question, only to eventually reassert its identity as art. As I've already suggested, the very capacity of art to attend reflexively to its own enabling conditions becomes its content, and it can only exercise this capacity by periodically identifying, and purging itself of, the "non-art" material it has accumulated in the process of reenergizing itself through contact with other cultural forms.

The second feature of this agonistic model involves the way in which the work of art produces meaning for an audience. Here, negation is produced in the artwork's relationship to the viewer via what I've described as an "orthopedic" aesthetic (in which the viewer's implicitly flawed modes of cognition or perception will be adjusted or improved via exposure to the work of art). The appropriate response to the work of art is no longer veneration or obeisance, but discomfort, rupture, or an uncanny derangement of the senses. These provocations can also perform an affirmative function, reinforcing a particular sense of identity among art world viewers (as liberal-minded risktakers). Or they are consumed rhetorically, as the viewer identifies, in a self-congratulatory manner, with the subject position of the artist rather than the hapless implied viewer. In fact, one comes to the space of art prepared for precisely this sort of provocation; disruption is, in a way, expected and even savored. This coincides with a textual model of art production, based in part on the rapprochement between neoconceptual art strategies and post-structuralist theory in the 1990s. Here the work of art functions as a hermeneutic device intended to destabilize fixed oppositions via some form of embodied conceptual provocation. Importantly, the work, whether it's a painting, installation, or event, is conceived by the artist beforehand and subsequently set in place before the viewer.

This approach is based on a principle of repetition; the work of art essentially replicates a vision or an idea generated by the artist and then presented to the viewer. While there is certainly an interactive dimension to even the most opaque or static art work, the "interaction" involved in textual production is understood primarily in terms of either contemplative decoding or somatic disruption. Artistic production in this mode is both teleological (resolved in the creation of a final, formally-delimited object, text, or event) and mimetic (the work of art functions as the physical manifestation of an idea first developed in the artist's imagination). The textual paradigm is defined by a spatial concept of agency, in which compositional and receptive roles are fixed. It thus forecloses the possibility that creative insight might be generated through less proprietary forms of compositional agency. That is, rather than viewing agency as the unique property of specific individuals, seeing it instead as fluid and transpositional over the course of a given creative action.

4 — THE RISK OF DIVERSITY

Nature in her physical creation points the way we have to take in the moral. Not until
the strife of elemental forces in the lower organisms has been assuaged does she turn to
the nobler creation of physical man. In the same way, the strife of elements in moral man,
the conflict of blind impulses, has first to be appeased, and crude antagonisms first
have ceased within him, before we can take the risk of promoting diversity.
FRIEDRICH SCHILLER, *ON THE AESTHETIC EDUCATION OF MAN*

We are witnessing today a certain disenchantment with the existing parameters of avant-garde art and an attempt to rearticulate the specificity of the aesthetic in relationship to both the viewer and to other cultural and political practices. Collectives such as Dialogue, Park Fiction, Ala Plastica, Huit Facettes Interaction in Senegal, and NICA (Networking and Initiatives for Culture and the Arts) in Myanmar, among many others, are engaged in a more or less conscious effort to renegotiate the condition of art's autonomy, and to shape a new paradigm. In place of an either/or mentality, which defines art through antithetical negation (art is not-activism, not-ethnography, not-popular culture), we encounter a relation of reciprocal elucidation relative to other fields of political and cultural action. And in place of a textual paradigm we discover practices centered on immersive interaction and a referential orientation to specific sites of social production. I would argue that some of the most challenging new collaborative art projects are located on a continuum with forms of cultural activism, rather than being defined in hard-and-fast opposition to them. Far from viewing this sort of categorical slippage as something to be feared, I believe it is both productive and inevitable given the period of transition through which we are living. It is, in fact, a persistent characteristic of modern art created during moments of historical crisis and change (Dadaism and Constructivism in the wake of the First World War and the Russian Revolution, the profusion of new movements and practices that emerged out of the political turmoil of the 1960s and '70s, etc.). Is Tatlin's *Monument to the Third International* an example of architecture, sculpture, or public art *avant la lettre*? What about John Heartfield's montages for *AIZ*? Are they art, graphic design, or experimental photojournalism?

The principle of aesthetic autonomy constitutes a central point of tension in this work. Within the modern tradition, it has, of course, never been a question of an absolute distance or separation "between" the aesthetic and the social or political. The political always operates through an aesthetic modality, and even the most strident claim of *art pour la art* poetic freedom is political at its core. Rather, it is the tension between these sites, their points of overlap, corroboration, and resistance, which have been most productive. Art may perceive itself as existing at some remove or distance from the social, but it also, always, imagines that it retains a causal or reflective relationship *with* the social world (whether as a reservoir for forms of affect and identity that are under assault in the modern life-world, as a therapeutic reprieve, or a symbolic embodiment of what-could-be). What remains of art, in the wake of a century and a half of avant-garde experimentation, if not the very concept of an autonomy or distance that enables a (critical) perspective on, and relation to, the existing social order? But for this distance, this autonomy, to retain its value, it must be recalibrated, it must respond to a specific social context and the particular ways in which art is mobilized during a given historical moment. Fluctuations within the field of aesthetic legitimacy are a necessary part of this process. The elasticity of the category "art" in response to changing historical conditions, the opening out and the closing down, the varying centripetal and centrifugal movements as art periodically encompasses and then expels other political and cultural modes is part of its very function within modernity.

On the one hand this autonomy is necessary in order to achieve an adjudicatory distance from dominant cultural, social, and political values (already here we are collapsing any distinction between "dominant" values that are imposed on a given social system and those values that evolve consensually). At the same time, autonomy implies a relationship of segregation or exclusion. It is this second connotation that fuels hygienic criticism: the defensive fear of affiliations or interconnections with contaminated or impure realms (and the corollary assumption that all forms of cultural production within modernity, aside from the arts, are complicit with, or symptomatic of, a repressive social order). The persistence of this fear among critics, curators, and artists is understandable. An antagonistic relationship to the viewer and a defensive relationship to other domains of cultural practice are written into the very DNA of modernist art.

We can gain a deeper understanding of the complex function of aesthetic autonomy in contemporary art if we examine its initial historical articulation. As Martha Woodmansee suggests in her revealing study of German aesthetic philosophy, the development of a concept of aesthetic autonomy is closely identified with the emergence of the modern literary market. Woodmansee analyzes the impact of rising literacy rates in Germany during the mid-1700s. The new "reading craze" (*Lesewut*) that swept Germany at that time led to a dramatic increase in the number of authors, publishers, bookstores, and libraries. As a result the comfortable intimacy that the first generation of *Aufklärer* writers enjoyed with their aristocratic patrons was rudely disturbed. Rather than flocking to the edifying works of Lessing, Hölderlin, and von Kleist, the new reading public displayed a seemingly inexhaustible appetite for ghost stories and romances. Friedrich

Schiller lamented the flood of "mindless, tasteless, and pernicious novels, dramatized stories, so-called journals for the ladies and the like" that were destroying the taste of the German reading public.[31] As a result of the fragmenting impact of modernity, the public is now bifurcated between those few who possess sufficient humanity to comprehend and take pleasure in complex art, and the untutored masses, which remain insensitive to it.[32] Further, any attempt to reach these mass readers in a familiar or colloquial language is doomed to failure, as their own perceptions, their own cultural responses to modernity, can only ever be failed and compromised.[33]

Confronted with a new mode of literary production devoted to entertainment rather than improvement, and alarmed by the declining prestige of serious literature, authors such as Schiller and Karl Philipp Moritz promulgated a radical new definition of art; a "remapping" as Woodmansee describes it, in which art, unique among all forms of human culture, is understood to have a wholly immanent value.[34] "The first, essential condition for the perfection of a poem," Schiller observes, "is that it possess an absolute intrinsic value that is entirely independent of the powers of comprehension of its readers."[35] If their poems, plays, and novels failed to capture the interest of newly literate Germans, then the problem rested with the readers themselves, who were too dependent on the simple pleasures of sensation and spectacle to meet the challenge posed by advanced literature. "The rabble seek only diversion," Moritz complains, and beautiful works of art are "passed by with indifference."[36] In fact, the public's lack of interest in, or outright resistance to, one's work became a badge of honor, a guarantee of its aesthetic integrity ("War," as Schiller claims, "is the only possible relationship to the public").[37]

But revulsion at the cultural enfranchisement brought about by literacy and the literary market is only one of the forces driving the initial articulation of an autonomous aesthetic. Woodmansee reveals a surprising, and heretofore unrecognized, affiliation with the discourse of German Pietism. The connection is explicit in the writing of Moritz, whose 1785 essay, "An Attempt to Unite All the Fine Arts and Sciences under the Concept of That Which is Complete in Itself," published five years before Kant's third *Critique*, describes the ideal work of art as a "self-sufficient totality" produced for its own sake.[38] Moreover, for the work to remain pure and authentic, it must be produced from an entirely disinterested perspective; the artist must disavow any benefit or fame that might accrue as a result of its creation. As Moritz writes, "If the thought of approval is your main consideration, and if your work is of value to you only insofar as it brings you fame, then you are working in a self-interested manner: the focal point of the work will fall outside the work: you are not creating it for its own sake. . . . You are only seeking to 'dazzle the rabble.'"[39]

As Woodmansee notes, this insistence on art's necessary detachment from the praxis of life departs dramatically from the long history of Western aesthetics, in which art was understood to have a functional role within society (to educate, or indoctrinate, the viewer, to reproduce or disclose the natural world, and so on). While there is no significant precedent for this view in the European philosophical tradition, it replicates almost exactly the discourse of German Pietist theology, which exerted a powerful influence on Moritz's generation. As Moritz himself described it, Pietist doctrine "posited . . . absolute self-sufficiency, or freedom from dependence upon anything external to [god] Himself, as a necessary condition of the pure perfection of the Deity." Pietist teachings, according to Moritz, demanded "total abandonment of the self and entry upon a blissful state of nothingness, with that complete extermination of all so-called self-ness or self-love, and a totally disinterested love of God, in which not the merest spark of self-love may mingle, if it is to be pure." We are, in short, "enjoined to love God disinterestedly," not as a "source of private gain."[40] This same attitude is "transported, almost verbatim," according to Woodmansee, into Moritz's concept of art. The "aesthetic attitude" provides a "pleasant forgetfulness of ourselves. . . . We seem to lose ourselves in the beautiful object, and precisely this loss, this forgetfulness of ourselves, is the highest degree of pure and disinterested pleasure which beauty grants us."[41]

The discourse of aesthetic autonomy operates through a form of "displaced theology," preserving a residual metaphysical element in the fantasy of an entirely pure self-transcendence and the work of art as a substitute for god's absolute self-sufficiency and freedom from external determination. It's not simply the theological principle of disinterest that is retained, but also a set of assumptions about the viewer or reader. Woodmansee's research helps us recognize the essentially religious character of the division between the artist and the "vulgar masses" evident in early aesthetic philosophy (as well as the subsequent evolution of modernist art theory). In the writings of Schiller, Moritz, and others, we encounter an adjudicatory apparatus that positions the philistine viewer (the "rabble" who are incapable of properly appreciating advanced art) as impious or immoral (slaves to the easy seductions of romance novels), and art as the instrument of their salvation. The artist, possessing a god-like ability to transcend the debilitating influence of banal popular literature and an increasingly materialist society, is able to ameliorate the blinkered ignorance of the multitudes through the process of "aesthetic education."

This underlying pessimism about the capacity of the viewer or reader is an article of faith in the tradition of modernist aesthetics, evident in Schiller's seminal *Letters on the Aesthetic Education of Man* (1794). Written in the aftermath of the French Revolution, Schiller's book is in large measure a meditation on the impossibility of progressive political change. As demonstrated by the recent "events" in France, man has not yet developed the moral character necessary to overcome his animal nature. As a result, the moment that the iron hand of political domination is lifted, he descends into lawlessness and violence. Of course it isn't man *qua* man Schiller is evoking here, but rather the "lower and more numerous classes," who are possessed by "crude, lawless instincts."[42] "We must continue to regard every attempt at political reform as untimely," Schiller writes, "and every hope based upon it as chimerical, as long as the split within man is not healed."[43] The split is between the "cultivated classes," possessed by a cold, calculating rationality, and the violent, impulsive lower orders, lacking in self-discipline and reason. The state can't impose a reconciliation of these two opposed forces via external compulsion. Rather, it requires a subtler reprogramming, a form of experience that reaches us through our senses and feelings, providing a point of mediation between the rational and the sensual. It requires, in short, an aesthetic education that will simultaneously bring compassion to the cultivated classes and self-discipline to the lower orders.[44]

The *Letters* exhibit all the conventional features of modern aesthetic autonomy. They are less discrete terms than serial moments in an unfolding, syllogistic chain, each leading inexorably to the next. First, we have the postulation of a singular moment of historical decline or degradation (the new "reign of material needs").[45] Second, we encounter a profound skepticism regarding the ability of the people (with the exception, of course, of the poet or artist) to transcend these constraints, and the presumption that any form of conventional social or political action will founder on the shoals of an undeveloped human nature. And, finally, we have the contention that the solution to this impasse involves a fundamental reconfiguration of the human spirit, which can only be provided by aesthetic experience. It requires, more specifically, an encounter with a work of art that is radically autonomous. In order to produce this transformation, the work of art must refer to nothing but itself and make no concession to the knowledge, experience, or interest of the reader or viewer. Sufficiently insulated from the exigencies of daily life, the work of art will provide a quasi-religious experience of undetermined freedom (in the virtual realm of aesthetic play), training us to act more responsibly in the "real" world of daily life. "The psyche of the listener or spectator must remain completely free and inviolate," Schiller insists. "It must go forth from the magic circle of the artist pure and perfect as it came from the hands of the Creator."[46] The lack of determination or predication by external forces is essential to the operation of an autonomous aesthetic, producing in the viewer or reader a kind of therapeutic regression. Man must "momentarily be free of all determination," Schiller writes, returning "to that negative state of complete absence of determination in which he found himself before anything at all had made an impression upon his senses."[47]

The work of art trains us for social interactions that we aren't yet prepared for in real life. Actual social or political change is deferred to an indefinite and idealized future, when the aesthetic will have finally completed its civilizing mission. It's not simply the belief that artistic experience is in some essential ways distinct from political experience, but the more extreme proposition that any form of political action is premature until humanity allows itself to be guided by aesthetic principles.[48] The political becomes the second negational axis along which art defines and differentiates itself (paralleling the institutions of the market system). The realm of political action is always characterized by compromise and failed ideals. Schiller thus instantiates one of the central logical contradictions of modern aesthetics: art has no purpose and possesses an entirely "intrinsic" value, yet art is also the sole experiential mode capable of reversing the deleterious effects of modernity.[49]

In contemplating a beautiful object . . . I roll the purpose back into the object itself:
I regard it as something that finds completion not in me but in itself and thus
constitutes a whole in itself and gives me pleasure for its own sake.

FRIEDRICH SCHILLER, *ON THE AESTHETIC EDUCATION OF MAN*

In poetry we are no longer referred back to the world, neither to the world as shelter nor
to the world as goal. . . . This means primarily that words, having the initiative, are not
obliged to serve to designate anything or give voice to anyone, but that they have their
ends in themselves.

MAURICE BLANCHOT, *THE SPACE OF LITERATURE*

The *Aesthetic Education* provided a template that has been followed by subsequent critics and theorists with remarkable devotion, as each element is retained and rearticulated. We might consider the parallel with Clement Greenberg's notion of formal "movement" in the development of avant-garde art in the post–Second World War period (as the sublimated expression of a currently unrealizable political movement). For Greenberg, and many American artists during the early years of the Cold War, substantive political change was blocked by the impasse between a tarnished communism and a reviled capitalist consumer culture.[50] As a result, the only option available was retreat into the protected enclave of the canvas, where the artist could preserve the freedom necessary for unconstrained aesthetic play. Schiller's aesthetic finds a more contemporary expression in the dilemma of French intellectuals and artists in the late 1960s. Here the impossibility of positive political change (embodied in the perceived failure of May '68) legitimated a withdrawal into a zone of subversive textual play and *écriture*. Each of these cultural moments proceeds via a conservational displacement or deferral of political critique into a more abstract critique of epistemology *per se*, evident in Greenberg's attack on representational art and Roland Barthes's attack on conventional forms of signification.

Peter Starr, in his illuminating intellectual history of May '68, identifies a "logic of failed revolt" that informed the thinking of the generation of French theorists who rose to international prominence during the 1970s. Starr traces this logic through the writings of Louis Althusser, Roland Barthes, Hélène Cixous, Gilles Deleuze, Jacques Derrida, Michel

Foucault, Julia Kristeva, Jacques Lacan, Claude Lefort, and others.[51] Their work is situated on the cusp between a more formally coherent structuralist movement (associated with the anthropological research of Claude Lévi-Strauss and the influence of Saussure's linguistics), and the diverse range of post-structuralist approaches and methodologies that grew out of this movement. In the writings of Deleuze, Guattari, Foucault, and others, the events of May '68 were accorded an epochal significance, signaling a fundamental rupture in the nature of political life in France, with implications for industrialized societies around the world. For Alain Badiou, May '68 was a "truth event" that shattered the existing parameters of the political. For Michel de Certeau "the revolutionary speech of May '68 . . . puts language on trial and calls for a global revision of our cultural system," and for Félix Guattari the "earthquake" of May '68 "presented problems that affected society as a whole."[52] The cultural and political staging of May '68, as Starr notes, centered on the perceived alignment between the forces of order and the counterposed forces of change or revolution (embodied in the main labor union—the Confédération Générale du Travail, or CGT, and in the French Communist Party, or PCF). In the political narratives of the post-structuralist generation the PCF and CGT, rather than constituting a real or substantive locus of resistance, were "pseudo-rivals" whose function was to maintain the illusion of an oppositional movement in French politics. Their conflicts with the French state or private sector were little more than stage-managed spectacle.[53]

The underlying lesson of May '68 was based on the twin principles of "specular doubling" and "structural repetition," in which all attempts to challenge entrenched power end up inadvertently reproducing it. In Starr's account, each principle "begins with the uncovering of a pseudo-opposition between the principles or structures of the established social order and an oppositional force whose action is found to be deeply complicitous with those principles or structures (repeating them and/or being recuperated by them)." The "back to back dismissal" of these terms provides the "pretext for articulating a 'Third Way'" that is "neither the Gaullist establishment nor its communist pseudo rivals in the PCF and CGT, but May's 'authentic' revolutionism."[54] The third way constitutes a new form of oppositional intelligence that would abjure the mechanisms of the state, the party, or the union, assuming an entirely new counterinstitutional form. As Claude Lefort writes:

It is against this system that the *enragés* strike a decisive blow. Not only do they know that nothing is to be expected from Power, nor from those parties and unions that feign to combat it, but who, were they compelled to take power, would do so only to make it serve new interests. . . . There is no need to look elsewhere for the grounds of their success. . . . They are cut loose from the old constraints . . . They create a new space. Or better, they hollow out a non-place where the possible is reborn.[55]

The third way was embodied by the student protestors who refused to "take" power and instead engaged in a series of exemplary gestures in the streets of Paris, seeking to spread the spirit of the revolution through sheer contagion rather than conventional forms of political organization and action. Here we rediscover the autonomy of the aesthetic: of a political expression that remains gloriously free, and insulated, from the contaminating influence of existing power structures, and of an "education" that communicates itself to us through a consensual enthusiasm beyond words or doctrine. But the very refusal to organize, to coordinate, and to negotiate created a further impasse. In order to actually initiate change, it was necessary to accept some level of engagement with extant institutions and policies and to translate across conflicting discursive modes, but this required, in turn, abandoning the liberating purity of the poetic gesture. "If one undertakes direct political action," Starr writes, "then the logics of specular doubling and structural repetition apply, but if one refuses such action, as the student revolutionaries had tended to do, then one's revolt will at best be hopelessly marginal, at worst, a reinforcement of institutional power."[56] The result was a compulsive effort to continually remain "outside" the circle of compromised legitimacy, leading to a *mise en abyme* trumping of exteriority and an almost paranoid fear of assimilation and co-option. "We push our refusal to the point of refusing to be assimilated into the political groups that claim to refuse what we refuse," as the Student-Writers Action Committee wrote in a statement on May 20th.[57]

It was necessary, then, to identify yet another "third way," another mode of action that could preserve the requisite revolutionary spirit without risking the inevitable compromise that would result from direct involvement with the mechanisms of social or political change. The solution was a tactical withdrawal into the protected field of the text. The novel, the poem, the film, the work of art, and theory itself would become the site for a process of "subtle" or "discrete" subversion.[58] The revolutionary would decamp to the institutional margins of political life—the university, the gallery, and the publishing house—to create a heterotopic space of experimentation.[59] As Starr describes it, the revolutionary impasse, or "double bind" (compromised engagement or surrender), had the effect of "displacing the political field toward the cultural in general and toward specifically transgressive forms of writing in particular."[60] Political change here and now is impossible because existing society is saturated by repressive forms of knowledge at the most basic level of human consciousness. Language itself polices and regulates our desires. As Roland Barthes famously claimed in his Inaugural Lecture at the Collège de France, "Language is neither reactionary nor progressive; it is quite simply fascist, for fascism does not prevent speech, it compels speech. . . . Once uttered, even in the subject's deepest privacy, speech enters the service of power."[61]

Here we find echoes of Schiller's skepticism and one of the key linkages between the post-structuralist theoretical tradition and early modern aesthetic philosophy: political action or change here-and-now is *intrinsically* futile. Existing systems of power and resistance to power are so corrupt, so inhumane, so irredeemably compromised, that one must reject any accommodation with, or proximity to, them. The only possible way to move forward and to retain the purity and integrity of the revolutionary message, is to work indirectly, via the insulating protection of ancillary, quasi-autonomous, institutions (the arts, higher education), to develop covert, subversive "interventions" in the cultural sphere, which will reproduce the contagion logic of the street action at the level of the individual reader, viewer, or student.

May '68 failed because existing modes of human consciousness and political agency were simply incapable of sustaining an authentic revolutionary impulse. Until we disrupt the fascism of language, until we purge the human psyche itself, all attempts at political change in the "real" world will remain ineffectual, and even destructive. "If the world could not be changed," as François Dosse observed of the intellectual aftermath of May '68, "the self could be."[62] Just as Schiller and Moritz insisted that a proper aesthetic education could only come about through exposure to a work of art that remained radically autonomous, resisting all forms of external determination, Barthes will call for forms of writing that refuse the utilitarian demands of conventional signification: "To write can no longer designate an operation of recording, of observing, of representing, of 'painting'." The very playfulness of the signifier, "unimpoverished by any constraint of representation," will model for the reader a new, non-instrumentalizing consciousness.[63] "We" can't yet be trusted with the freedom that would result from a total revolution. Instead we must practice this freedom in the virtual space of the text or artwork, supervised by the poet or artist. Like Schiller's ideal aesthetic subject, "momentarily free of all determination," Barthes's reader is "a man without history, without biography, without psychology; he is only that someone who holds gathered into a single field all the paths of which the text is constituted."[64]

As Barthes describes it in his influential essay "The Death of the Author," writing as a creative, politically transformative act can only occur through the absolute freeing of the text from any external determination or referential function. Even the attribution of meaning to the author constitutes an intolerable violation of the text's aesthetic freedom: "Once an action is recounted, for intransitive ends, and no longer in order to act directly upon reality—that is, finally external to any function but the very exercise of the symbol—this disjunction occurs, the voice loses its origin, the author enters his own death, writing begins."[65] Barthes's "Inaugural Lecture" signals the crucial shift that followed May '68:

> For those of us, who are neither knights of faith nor supermen, the only remaining alternative is . . . to cheat with language, to cheat language. This salutary trickery, this evasion, this grand imposture, which allows us to understand language outside the bounds of power, in the splendor of a permanent revolution of language, I for one call literature.[66]

Barthes attaches an almost mystical significance to the gesture of dissolving or disrupting the signifying process ("Writing ceaselessly posits meaning but always in order to evaporate it"). Thus, literature "liberates an activity which we might call counter-theological, properly revolutionary, for to refuse to arrest meaning is finally to refuse God and his hypostases, reason, science, the law."[67] Barthes's counter-theological attitude retains a displaced theological element, as Woodmansee might describe it, in the notion of a rigorously purified zone of autonomous aesthetic experimentation. The writer's hand "detached from any voice, borne by a pure gesture of inscription, traces a field without origin—or which, at least, has no other origin than language itself, that is, the very thing which ceaselessly questions any origin." The experience of aesthetic "bliss," according to Barthes, is decisively "asocial . . . it is the abrupt loss of sociality, and yet there follows no recurrence to the subject (subjectivity), the person, solitude, *everything* is lost, integrally."[68] The process of creation allows the artist or intellectual to do *something*, to take some action, however nominal or symbolic, while remaining protected from the compromises entailed by more direct political engagement.[69]

The collapsing together of the entirety of religion, law, science, and reason into a single, monolithic expression of man's inherently instrumentalizing nature is symptomatic. The shibboleth of reason can only be defeated by a full-scale assault on any and all forms of coherent meaning—narrative writing, historical continuity, collective identity, and conscious agency— waged through the daunting weapons of experimental literature and New Wave cinema. Fascism will, finally, be undone by Robbe-Grillet novels and Godard films. Barthes's concept of textual *jouissance* carries with it the characteristic contradiction of modern aesthetic autonomy, evoking a monadic art practice that occupies a position of radical exteriority ("outside the bounds of power"), while able to act back on the world with the most uncompromising ethical authority. This contradiction is anticipated by Schiller's contradictory concept of a *Spieltreib*: precisely a play *drive* that is simultaneously free and yet driven or oriented toward an ethical telos. The tension between an open-ended aesthetic experience and the conative energy of a play drive is reiterated at a second level in the concept of an aesthetic encounter that claims to liberate or empower the reader precisely by subjecting him or her to a shattering ontic dislocation. The frustrated militance of the street protest is displaced and transposed to a symbolic aggression enacted against the viewer or reader, who stands simultaneously for the forces of rationalist reaction and their benumbed victims, in need of both a punishing attack and a cathartic awakening. Thus, Maurice Blanchot, a central figure for the post-structuralist tradition, celebrates the violent "combat" that occurs between the writer and the reader.[70] For Lyotard, language and linguistic communication can only ever be a field of battle, populated by "opponents" engaged in a series of strategic "moves" and "countermoves" intended to advance their position relative to the "balance of power." For Lyotard's interlocutors, utterance is mere "ammunition" in the endless game of "agonistic" conflict.[71] As Alain Badiou writes, "All art, and all thought, is ruined when we accept this permission to consume, to communicate and to enjoy. We should become the pitiless censors of ourselves."[72] While for Ernesto Laclau and Chantal Mouffe, a "radical" democratic politics can only ever emerge through an "antagonistic" rupture that "escapes . . . language, since language only exists as an attempt to fix that which antagonism subverts."[73]

Signification was only the first in a series of systems implicated in the purging and purification of cultural discourse and human consciousness. The basic linguistic operation of signification, the linking of a given sign with a given, referential, object, was simply the *ur-form* of a much broader and more insidious system of consensual meaning that ran like a fault line through Western modes of thought and being. Just as the relationship between signifier and signified implies a sort of linguistic agreement (the shared assumption that this word or image "stands for" a given idea), any social formation that depends on the interdependence, reliance, or predication of one subject on another became suspect, whether in the guise of a family, a community, a union, a party, civil society, or the state. The concept of friendship itself was shown by Derrida to be irredeemably compromised by its dependence on an Othered "enemy" whose difference provides the necessary ground for the recognition of a convivial amity.[74] The revolution will begin, then, not with collective experience, but with a single "dissident" subject—the monadic individual whose consciousness must first be wiped clean of the contaminating influence of conventional modes of signification and identity ("*Everything* is lost," as Barthes writes). "What has emerged in our postwar culture," Julia Kristeva wrote, "are singular forms of speech and *jouissance*." The poet and the intellectual will "give voice to the singularity of unconsciousness, desires, needs. Call into play the identities and/or languages of the individual and the group. Become the analyst of the impossibility of social cohesion."[75] The "impossibility" of social cohesion will become a *leitmotif* of post-structuralist thought. It is precisely when we come together (in collective forms of action and identity) that we are most at risk of succumbing to our instrumentalizing nature.

The ethical/epistemological couplet of the singularity and the collective is paralleled by a second, temporal, discourse that presents "revolution" (rather than more gradual change or reform) as the only acceptable paradigm for political transformation. Duration is irreconcilably tinged by its associations with narrative and teleology. Therefore, meaningful change can only occur through an absolute rupture of historical continuity: a single moment that breaks radically with its syntagmatic precedent.[76] The "event" of revolutionary change, like the aesthetic object itself, must be pure, autonomous, and non-referential, owing nothing to the existing distribution of social and political forces. Only this sort of revolution can hope to outpace our tendency to revert to reifying patterns of thought and action when working collectively. It does so by tapping into a reservoir of pre-symbolic, and intrinsically non-instrumentalizing, desire. The apparent contradiction of an open-ended aesthetic encounter that is simultaneously capable of orienting us toward an ethically correct form of self-reflection is resolved by the fortuitous discovery of an immanent and non-instrumentalizing force or *Pulsion*.[77] Since conventional subjectivity itself is inherently debased, this tendency must be "discovered" at an almost biological, or bodily, level. Rather than being forced into the proper mode of being through external coercion or determination, it's simply a matter of freeing a liberatory impulse already buried *within* us, at our ontic core, beneath the accumulated detritus of *cogito*, language, and Western metaphysics. The gradual accretion of these personal epiphanies, little May '68s of the mind, will prepare us for the revolution yet to come.

The ethical normalization of desire as an intrinsically non-instrumentalizing somatic force is an article of faith in the post-structuralist tradition, evident in the utopian language of bodily "sensations" and libidinal "intensities" in Lyotard and Deleuze, as well as the signal value assigned to the play of difference and the signifier, or the quasi-erotic *jouissance* of the "writerly" text by Derrida and Barthes. Desire constitutes a natural state of non-aggression and primal sociality that preexists our very identity as discrete subjects. Like the utopian sociality of the traditional aesthetic *sensus communis*, desire reassures us that we are, at the most basic level of our existence, predisposed toward heterogeneity and pleasurable co-existence. We need only free ourselves of the baleful influence of language, culture, and history to re-actualize the Edenic experience of being-as-becoming. The possibility that our immanent desire might, in fact, be grasping, violent, or self-interested is overcome by the simple expedient of insisting that the only proper desire occurs prior to individuation, before there is even a "self" to be interested. Yet the moment that a coherent self does evolve out of this inchoate but benign field of energy, what is to prevent the consequent emergence of a violent and defensive subjectivity? If a possessive relationship to the world, and to other subjects, is part of the very constitution of a volitional self, how are we to proceed? Precisely by subjecting that "self" to a process of compulsory decentering and dislocation. The cognitive subject, as both the symptom and the cause of the Western metaphysical sickness, must be pulverized, demolished, and rendered pure. The various modes of sensory provocation, semantic ambiguity, and cognitive disruption enshrined in the avant-garde tradition will return us, momentarily, therapeutically, to a pre-symbolic state of null subjectivity; reconnecting us with the utopic energies of desire and pre-differentiated existence.

The concept of rupture outlined above entails a kind of ontic scorched-earth policy; the self as it currently exists (specifically, the centered, self-identical Cartesian version that one typically encounters in post-structuralist literature) is beyond redemption. This requires, in turn, a strategic disavowal of the specific situational practices and experiential realities of individual human agents. This disavowal is rooted in the Structuralist tradition, which postulated an overarching system that limits, constrains, and determines individual agency. The systems of language (Saussure), myth (Lévi-Strauss), the unconscious (Lacan), ideology (Althusser), and discourse (Foucault) are entirely autonomous: impervious to the reciprocal actions of conscious subjects. In each case, we see an effort to distill out the underlying structure of a given system of meaning as an object of knowledge, precisely by discarding the practical experience of its participating subjects (individual utterance/speech acts, volitional action, the experience of historical continuity, referential forms of meaning, etc.) as naive, complicit, or unsuitable for proper theoretical reflection (cf. Schiller's reader, benumbed by romance novels). "Man" is no more than an "effect" of language or discourse, a "rift" in the Order of Things, a "desiring machine," with no conscious agency.[78]

Individual utterance, action, or ideation can only ever be treated as a symptom of some deeper structuring logic. "Reality" as it is experienced and lived is constantly set aside, bracketed, and critiqued in order to disclose the deeper truth created by a previously hidden structure that organizes our actions and our very consciousness behind our backs. As Pierre Nora, Foucault's editor at Gallimard, wrote: "When men speak they say things they are not necessarily responsible for, and end up doing things they did not necessarily want to do . . . forces they are not conscious of course through them and dominate them."[79] The result is a kind of inverted image of aesthetic autonomy, in which the individual is wholly and completely determined, even as the structure itself appears entirely closed and self-referential. As I've noted above, post-structuralist thought will wrestle with this contradiction by restoring some nominal agency to the subject through a de-individuated notion of desire or bodily conatus (a key term which I will return to in chapter 2).[80] The result, evident in contemporary art theory, is a neo-romantic discourse that attributes various intrinsically utopian or liberatory powers to the body, desire, sensation, and so on. However, the problem of agency and collective experience isn't resolved in this manner, merely deferred. In each case, the problem begins with the reliance on a reductive model of the volitional self and agency and its predicable antithesis: an equally reductive, de-centered, a-rational self. The hapless modern subject is either controlled by a *Matrix*-like system of external domination, with no hope of independent action, or exposed to a relentless program of destabilization, violent confrontation, and therapeutic de-centering.

The only exception to this unremittingly mechanistic picture of human behavior is the theorist, writer, or artist; the single agent who retains some power beyond inchoate desire or bodily sensation, some autonomy relative to structures of meaning, and some capacity to act back on the world in a coherent and expressive manner.[81] The central intellectual task assigned to this felicitous agent is the search for hidden structures and their subsequent revelation. Eve Kosofsky Sedgwick offers a useful interpretation of the rhetoric of exposure and revelation in her analysis of the "paranoid consensus" that has come to dominate contemporary critical theory informed by structuralism, psychoanalysis, and Marxism. Based in part on the historical identification of critical theory with the act of revealing the (structural) determinants that pattern our perception of reality, the paranoid approach obsessively repeats the gesture of "unveiling hidden violence" to a benumbed or disbelieving world.[82] As enabling and necessary as it is to probe beneath the surface of appearance and to identify unacknowledged forms of power, the paranoid approach, in Sedgwick's view, attributes an almost mystical agency to the act of revelation in and of itself. As she writes:

> The paranoid trust in exposure seemingly depends . . . on an infinite reservoir of naiveté in those who make up the audience for these unveil-

ings. What is the basis for assuming that it will surprise or disturb, never mind motivate, anyone to learn that a given social manifestation is artificial, self-contradictory, imitative, phantasmatic or even violent?[83]

As Sedgwick notes, the normalization of paranoid knowing as a model for creative and intellectual practice among writers, theorists, and, I might add, artists, has entailed "a certain disarticulation, disavowal, and misrecognition of other ways of knowing, ways less oriented around suspicion."[84] Sedgwick juxtaposes paranoid knowing (in which "exposure in and of itself is assigned a crucial operative power") with reparative knowing, which is driven by the desire to ameliorate or give pleasure. As she argues, this reparative attitude is intolerable to the paranoid, who views any attempt to work productively within a given system of meaning as unforgivably naive and complicit, a belief authorized by the paranoid's "contemptuous assumption that the one thing lacking for global revolution, explosion of gender roles, or whatever, is people's (that is, other people's) having the painful effects of their oppression, poverty or deludedness sufficiently exacerbated to make the pain conscious (as if otherwise it wouldn't have been) and intolerable."[85] Traditional theology discovers signs of divinity in the world, like the image of the Virgin Mary miraculously preserved in a grilled cheese sandwich, precisely because they are already present in the cognitive apparatus of the faithful. The counter-theology of the post-structuralist tradition seeks to root out signs of complicity and fatal coherence with the same zealous predisposition.[86]

ART THEORY AND THE POST-STRUCTURALIST CANON — 6

This ultimate, Utopic, generation is *by far* the most revolutionary one the system has ever produced.

ANGELO QUATTROCCHI AND TOM NAIRN, *THE BEGINNING OF THE END*

While there are obvious differences among the key figures associated with post-structuralist theory, the broader assimilation of their work within the humanities and social sciences has led, perhaps inevitably, to a certain homogenization. Four decades after Derrida's influential 1966 appearance at the Johns Hopkins Humanities Center, we can identify a recognizable "post-structuralist" discourse that has attained a canonical status in the academic systems of Europe, the United States, and Latin America.[87] Over the preceding pages I've attempted to sketch out the broad contours of this discourse. The assumptive world of post-structuralist thought is defined by several key characteristics. Chief among these are a series of tactical inversions directed at the traditions of Western metaphysics and subjectivity. These include the privileging of dissensus over consensus, rupture and immediacy over continuity and duration, and distance over proximity, intimacy, or integration. Other significant features include an extreme skepticism about organized political action and a hyper-vigilance regarding the dangers of co-option and compromise entailed by such action, the ethical normalization of desire and somatic or sensual experience, and the recoding of political transformation into a form of ontic disruption directed at any coherent system of belief, agency, or identity. It is the task of the artist or intellectual, in particular, to supervise this process through the composition of axiomatic texts (writing, poetry, film, objects, events, etc.) that seek to destabilize the viewer or reader through an essentially individual hermeneutic engagement. The artist's relationship to the viewer or reader is necessarily distanced and custodial. And the viewer or reader, in turn, can only ever be acted *upon* by the artist or work of art.

While this tradition has been profoundly generative, it also carries with it certain limitations and lacunae that are all the more debilitating because of its canonical authority. As I noted in the introduction, what would have been identified twenty years ago as a distinct "post-structuralist" strand within the larger field of critical theory has been so successfully assimilated that it's now largely synonymous with critical theory *per se*. The generation of thinkers who stormed the Sorbonne is now taught with near catechistic devotion at the most privileged institutions of higher learning in the United States, Latin America, and Europe.[88] Foucault, Derrida, Lyotard, Deleuze, and, more recently, Agamben, Nancy, Levinas, Rancière, and Badiou, are ubiquitous not only in the academy but also, perhaps especially, in the art world, their names regularly invoked in catalog essays, artist's statements, reviews, course reading lists, and dissertations. Today post-structuralism constitutes a kind of globalized theoretical *lingua franca* in the arts and humanities.

While critics such as Jack Burnham and others began referencing sources in structuralism and semiotics (Lévi-Strauss, Saussure, Greimas, etc.) in the late 1960s and early 1970s, the initial rapprochement between contemporary art and post-structuralist theory occurred during the late '70s and early 1980s, when the works of Derrida, Baudrillard, Lacan, and Barthes were first widely available in English.[89] The key term here, imported from semiotics, was "signification," which was mobilized in debates around photography and film. The photographic image (which stood at the time as the *ur-form* of realist ideology) was relentlessly deconstructed, its contingency revealed, its framing conventions exposed, in numerous works by Sarah Charlesworth, Silvia Kolbowski, Barbara Kruger, Sherrie Levine, Richard Prince, Cindy Sherman, and their various followers.

Semiotics allowed for the initial consolidation of a textual paradigm in art practice and criticism, as a body of theory designed to reveal the contingency of *linguistic* meaning was transposed into discussions of visual art. This was a decisive shift, leading to the concept of the work of art as a subversive text that would denaturalize photographic truth and thereby trigger a cascading series of insights into the contingency of all forms of coherent meaning (with a particular focus on the construction of gender and sexuality). Postmodern art criticism promulgated a hermeneutic system, based on the act of "reading" the image, which was largely drawn from the canon of structuralist and post-structuralist literary theory.[90] Postmodern techniques of image appropriation would simultaneously undermine the artist's status as the "author" of photographic meaning, and the referentiality of the photograph itself. Following the line of aesthetic autonomy established by Barthes, the role of the appropriated image isn't to "stand for" something in the world, but precisely to break free from the demands of representation and reveal the contingency of the signifying process itself. The artist retains his or her characteristic autonomy at the margins of the dominant culture as a Virgil-like figure laying bare the apparatus of photographic meaning to viewers wandering stupefied through the "forest of signs."

By the early 1990s the discourse of art theory began to expand from a concern with signification in the cinematic or photographic image to a concern with the more general signifying processes at work in the constitution of individual, collective, and even geopolitical identity. At the same time, the largely gallery-bound work of the 1980s (Cindy Sherman's Cibachrome prints, the photographs of Richard Prince and Sherrie Levine) gave way to a more ephemeral, public, performative approach associated with the international biennial and Kunsthalle circuit (e.g., the work of

Elmgreen and Dragset, Superflex, Tiravanija, Hirschhorn, Liam Gillick, Pierre Huyghe, Carsten Holler, Christine Hill, Jens Haaning, Ben Kinmont, Philippe Parreno, N-55, etc.). It is largely from this body of work that Bourriaud's "relational aesthetics" artists are drawn. Its practitioners are primarily, though not entirely, European, in part because many European nations still provide economic support (in the form of stipends, bursaries, or fellowships) for younger artists and art students. In addition, European cultural institutions devoted to contemporary art enjoy much more generous levels of state funding than comparable institutions in the United States and elsewhere. The result is a quasi-formal system of public patronage that frees younger artists from the demands of the art market and commodity production and has opened space for an ephemeral, performance-based mode of practice.[91]

The rhetoric of disclosure and revelation remained central in this work, and the artist emerged as a nomadic agent of deconstruction, wandering from site to site to expose the contingency of meaning (Francis Alÿs and Christian Philipp Müller are emblematic).[92] During the 1990s, art practice was reinvented as a kind of potted cultural studies in which one selects a particular social, cultural, or representational system in order to "expose" or "deconstruct" the various ideological errors and complicities committed by its members. One could pick examples almost at random from the pages of *Frieze, Flash Art, Artforum,* or *Parkeet.* In *Chantier Barbès-Rochechouart* (1994) Pierre Huyghe erected billboards featuring re-staged photographs of workers at Parisian construction sites, ostensibly "deconstructing . . . the false promises of the advertising industry."[93] Phil Collins's installation *They Shoot Horses* (2004), which features extended video footage of Palestinian teenagers dancing to Western pop songs, exposes the ignorance of the "typical western viewer" who would otherwise be "condemned" to viewing young Arabs as "victims or . . . fundamentalists."[94]

Not surprisingly, post-structuralist thought has been a significant source of inspiration for this generation of artists. References to Deleuze, Derrida, Levinas, Agamben, Nancy, and Rancière (among others) are *de rigueur* in the critical staging of biennial-based work. Bourriaud, as I noted above, is particularly enamored of Guattari's notion of plural subjectivities, while *Documenta* 12 (2007) based its curatorial mission in part on the adumbration of Giorgio Agamben's concept of "bare life" by contemporary artists. The Swiss artist Thomas Hirschhorn has been especially conspicuous in calling attention to the role that critical theory plays in his work, patterning entire installations and projects around the proper names of his favorite thinkers (these include *Deleuze Monument* in 2000, *Bataille Monument* in 2004, and *24 Hour Foucault Project* in 2006). Recent projects such as *Utopia, Utopia = One World, One War, One Army, One Dress* (2006) literalize a textual paradigm, as Hirschhorn actually includes fragments of theoretical texts contributed by his frequent collaborator Marcus Steinweg. Steinweg writes in a poetic, quasi-philosophical mode that involves the incantatory repetition of key post-structuralist tropes (the oppressive nature of collective identity, the privileging of rupture and transgression, etc.). Here is a typical passage from "WORDPLAY" (written for the *Utopia, Utopia* installation), in which Steinweg, elaborating on Nietzsche's concept of a "Hyperborean" subject, rehearses the standard post-structuralist opposition between a transgressive, uncanny singularity and the universal, logocentric "we community":

> We Hyperboreans also means: we, the community of those who are without community, without we-community. We solitary ones. We singularities. We who touch the limits of the Logos that represents the principle of the Western we-community. We who have fallen out of the we-cosmos. We who have separated from the universality of a transcendental community, from the habitable zone of transcendental we-subjectivity. We homeless ones. We arctic natures. We monsters who are in contact with the limits of what is familiar, habitual and habitable . . .[95]

Steinweg returns us, yet again, to Kristeva's subversive intellectual, diagnosing the "impossibility of social cohesion." Communal or collective interaction can only ever be compromised, totalizing, and dangerous. The very act of participation, according to architects Markus Miessen and Shumon Basar, is tantamount to "war."[96] "Any form of participation is already a form of conflict," they contend, echoing Lyotard's assertions about language as a field of battle. The lone architect must assume the role of an "uninvited irritant" "forcing" his or her way into "other fields of knowledge" and "deliberately instigating conflicts" rather than "doing good" (that most abject of goals). The architect becomes the fiercest critic of transcendence, even as he or she claims a position that is radically external to all institutional, disciplinary, and epistemological boundaries.

As these examples suggest, by the 1990s, art practice and critical theory existed in an increasingly interdependent and even circular relationship: artists read, recited, and invoked the same theoretical sources as their critics—sources which were called upon, in turn, by the critics analyzing their work. Post-structuralist theory was disseminated in large measure through the art world and through university art history, literature, and cultural studies programs, rather than philosophy departments (where the philosophical premises and interpretations on which this theory is based might have been subject to more informed scrutiny). Relatively few art world commentators had the scholarly background necessary to engage with this work at a substantive philosophical level (to challenge, e.g., Deleuze's interpretation of Spinoza, Derrida's reading of Kant, or Rancière's account of Schiller). This led to the programmatic version of post-structuralist theory we frequently encounter in artists' statements and art criticism and theory. Post-structuralism, for many in the art world, is less a tradition that is actively engaged *with* than a system of thought that one subscribes *to*. The result is an often liturgical relationship to theory, and a related tendency to simply invoke theoretical precepts as axioms and then apply them to practice in an illustrative manner.[97]

We encounter in contemporary art discourse a set of assumptions about the expressive autonomy of the artist, the hermeneutic function of the artwork, the cognitive capacities of the viewer, and the relationship of art practice to broader social and political movements that have been heavily influenced by post-structuralist critical theory and the longer history of modernist aesthetics I've outlined in this chapter. The resulting model of art practice is characterized by a reductive model of human agency (and a problematic displacement of agency to pre-subjective "desire"), a tendency toward simplistic ethico-epistemological oppositions (coherence vs. incoherence, rupture vs. continuity, singularity vs. collectivity, dissensus vs. consensus, etc.), and a corresponding inability to grasp the tactical specificity of given sites of practice and modes of collective identity, or to work productively in the space "between" these oppositional categories. There is, in addition, a tendency to endow the artist with a singular capacity for transcendence (Miessen's "uninvited irritant"), thereby eliding his or her material specificity or situational accountability.

Finally, there is the problematic projection of a violent or disruptive conatus onto the viewer, as the aggression necessary to sustain certain forms of political action (demonstrations, street protests, etc.) is displaced onto the hermeneutic relationship between the audience and the work of art (via the post–May '68 "textualization" of politics). This displacement is sanctioned in turn by the assumption that more direct forms of political engagement are either futile or premature. "Nothing is possible without a far-reaching ecological transformation of subjectivities, without an awareness of the various forms of founding interdependence of subjectivity," as Bourriaud writes.[98] As a result, antagonism is de-specified, with no sense of its tactical relevance (are there points within a given project, e.g., during which dissensus is counterproductive, or ironic detachment simply alienates the artist from his or her collaborators?). By maintaining such an absolute division between the sequestered realm of art practice (textualized, detached, authorially-regulated) and social or political engagement (which is always at risk of compromise), this tradition has foreclosed the possibility that social interaction or political engagement *itself* might transform subjectivity or produce its own forms of insight. Instead, we must endlessly prepare our subjectivities for political action through a deferred aesthetic reeducation. A relational antagonism (to the viewer, to all other discursive modes, disciplines, and systems of knowledge) becomes self-justifying and is folded into the very identity of the producing artist as a reminder of a broader political transformation that is currently unrealizable but may one day come to pass.

For all of these reasons, activist and socially engaged art practices pose a particular challenge for many contemporary critics. As I noted earlier in this chapter, Bourriaud relies on a dated caricature of activist art (as coextensive with the worst traditions of agitprop) to legitimize the work he endorses. Thus, relational artists such as Carsten Höller, Philippe Parreno, and Pierre Huyghe are not, according to Bourriaud, "naïve or cynical enough to 'go about things as if' the radical and universalist utopia were still on the agenda."[99] Bishop, one of the more thoughtful critics of relational and activist art, nonetheless reverts to a similar dynamic. Activist art sacrifices its aesthetic credibility on the "altar of social change," Bishop warns, while authentic art (Lars von Trier, Phil Collins, Santiago Sierra) "fulfills the promise" of Schiller's aesthetic.[100] As the reference to Schiller suggests, we have come full circle, back to the long tradition of aesthetic autonomy. Bishop borrows this reference in turn from Jacques Rancière (a former student of Althusser), whose influential book *The Politics of Aesthetics* takes Schiller as a central point of reference.[101]

Rancière reiterates Schiller's skepticism regarding the fate of political action unguided by aesthetic sensibility. The French Revolution failed, as Rancière describes it, "because the revolutionary power had played the traditional part of the Understanding—meaning the state—imposing its law to the matter of sensations—meaning the masses."

> By so doing it was still in line with the old partition of the sensible where the culture of the elite had to rule over the wilderness of the common people. The only true revolution would be a revolution over-throwing the power of "active" understanding over "passive" sensibility . . . a revolution of sensory existence itself instead of a revolution in the forms of government.[102]

In order to resuscitate Schiller, Rancière must elide his expressed commitment to cultural elitism, but the underlying point (a revolution of the senses must precede any political revolution) remains intact. Rancière re-articulates the function of traditional aesthetic autonomy as the preservation of "heterogeneous" sensory experience and the "self sufficiency" of the individual subject. The "heterogeneous sensible" manages to elude determination (like Moritz's Pietist grace or anti-Oedipal "desire").[103] At the same time, Rancière claims to introduce a significant inflection of the traditional aesthetic. Rather than insisting on either the absolute autonomy of the aesthetic or its dissolution, he locates the power of the aesthetic in the "play" *between* art and life: a kind of quasi-autonomy. Rancière's formulation effectively restages the "third way" dynamic, relying as it does on two ostensibly opposed views that are revealed as equally compromised (both the museum-burning zealot and the *art pour la art* devotee threaten to destroy the truly revolutionary power of aesthetic "undecideability"). The solution to this "impasse," or antinomy, is not difficult to predict. Rather than withdrawing entirely into passivity and quiescence, the artist will remain engaged by working to subvert the consciousness of individual viewers. As with the logic of structural repetition I've already discussed, Rancière's resolution can only be produced by positing exaggerated or reductive versions of two ostensibly opposed positions. Few if any modernist artists or movements ever advocated a complete withdrawal from the social, or a total dissolution of art's specificity. "Undecideability" or "ambiguity," relative to the realm of politics, are inescapable and self-evident features of modern and contemporary art practice. The intellectual challenge doesn't lie in yet another reiteration of this familiar claim, but in working through the various ways in which this ambiguity is produced situationally, what effects it has in a given project and at a given site of practice.

Rancière has emerged in recent years as an art world favorite, in part I suspect because his work provides theoretical validation for an already cherished set of beliefs about the "political" function of the artwork. Bishop draws on Rancière's *The Politics of Aesthetics* to legitimate her appeal to "disruption" and shock as necessary prerequisites for authentic art ("A political work of art . . . transmits meanings in the form of a rupture").[104] In two influential essays published in *October* and *Artforum*, Bishop offers one of the most substantive critical engagements with both activist and relational art practices. All the conventional post-structuralist themes are in evidence. We have the valorization of a "tough, disruptive approach" and agonistic conflict (properly advanced art is patterned around "excruciating situations" and the experience of "grueling duration"), and the corollary reliance on a reductive opposition between a (good) de-centered and a (bad) unified subjectivity.[105] While activist or community-based projects traffic in proscribed forms of "unified" subjectivity and "transcendent human empathy" and are designed to "smooth over awkward situations," the work of artists such as Santiago Sierra and Thomas Hirschhorn inculcate a necessary "awkwardness and discomfort." Rather than promoting a reviled "social harmony," their works encourage a "relational antagonism" concerned with "exposing that which is repressed."[106]

In Bishop's account, the disruption and "antagonism" produced by Sierra and Hirschhorn involve various attempts to force privileged art world types to encounter the poor and working class as they slog through the galleries of their favorite biennial. Thus, Hirschhorn chose to locate his *Bataille Monument* "in the middle of a community whose ethnic and economic status did not mark it as a target audience for Documenta" (Bishop's circumlocution for an immigrant, working-class neighborhood in Kassel). By making Documenta's stalwarts take cabs (operated by Turkish drivers) to the *Monument*, Hirschhorn "contrived a curious rapprochement between the influx of tourists and the area's residents," making the "visitors feel like hapless intruders" (a gesture that echoes Sierra's use of retributive exclusion in *Wall Enclosing a Space*). Hirschhorn's work was thus "disruptively thought provoking," according to Bishop, as it "destabilized . . . any notion of community identity" (except, apparently, the "community" around the *Bataille Monument* itself, whose disconcerting race and class difference provided the *frisson* necessary to "provoke" Documenta's tourists).[107] Bishop describes her experience of a Santiago Sierra project for the 2001 Venice Biennial—in which he provided space in the Arsenal for street vendors to sell their wares—in similar terms. Her discovery of merchants selling knockoff Fendi handbags in a sanctioned art space ("Did they creep in here for a joke?") triggered a cathartic "moment of mutual non-identification," radically disrupting her "sense of identity."[108]

The corrective exposure to race and class Others engineered by Hirschhorn or Sierra generalizes both the viewer (all Documenta visitors are "tourists" whose relationship to a working-class Turkish community is necessarily inauthentic and voyeuristic) and the individuals whose "participation" is choreographed for their benefit (the street vendors function through a logic of simple juxtaposition, providing a spectacle of generic difference against the ground of a privileged art venue). The entire *mise-en-scène* is designed, in Bishop's description, to reiterate the chastising logic of post-structuralist poetics ("destabilizing," "disruptive," etc.). This approach, which might otherwise appear objectifying or ethically suspect, is legitimated by the textual paradigm and by the reflexive privilege accorded to the critique of signification elaborated around the photographic image during the 1980s. Having abandoned the naive assumption that signifiers and referents in the "real" world are necessarily linked, artists can now "appropriate" the human body itself. Liberated from its referential function, the body can be employed with the same tactical precision as any other semantic element toward the deconstruction of particular cultural or social discourses, thus neatly eliding the distinction between an image and a living being. In this view Sierra's work allows for only two possible responses. Either a genuine destabilization, in which viewers are made viscerally aware of their own complicity in an oppressive specular economy, or a critique of the ethical questions raised by the public display of the unemployed or homeless in an art gallery. The latter response can easily enough be dismissed as a defensive reaction formation to the unbearable "provocation" presented by Sierra's work, and thus a further demonstration of its efficacy. In each case, the ethical is collapsed into the a priori epistemological value assigned to disruption and provocation per se.

While socially engaged or community-based projects reaffirm their participant's most problematic assumptions about identity and difference, according to Bishop, authentic art practices (Sierra, Hirschhorn, etc.) "activate" the viewer. However, the decisive point in the reception of this work is not the distinction between an active and a passive viewer, but rather the broader set of assumptions *about* the viewer that are encoded in this activation: the particular form of agency it claims to give the viewer, and the essentially scripted nature of the viewer's presumed response. This is evident in Sierra's *Wall Enclosing a Space* for the Spanish Pavilion at the 2003 Venice Biennale (referenced earlier). If I don't have Spanish passport I'm not allowed in, so large numbers of art world *cognoscenti* from Europe and the United States were denied entry. "The wall polarizes the Biennial spectators on either side of a hypothetical stage," according to curator Rosa Martínez, "and formalizes physical and political tensions evocative of that strange territory of sealed cities and countries defined by contemporary exclusions."[109] The physical experience of having my free passage into the exhibit blocked isn't simply annoying or inconvenient. Rather, it has a pedagogical effect. My desire to see, to know, to consume "Sierra" has been interrupted, and I've learned, by extension, to empathetically identify with those global others who don't possess the geopolitical privilege and freedom of movement that I do. The artist has produced this lesson by momentarily inverting the conventional subject-position of the viewer. As Sierra describes it: "On one side, Spaniards; but not on the other side. . . . This fact is now emphasized and displayed, to prompt one to think of one's belonging."[110]

As with Elmgreen and Dragset's *Pavilion*, the assumptions about the viewer encoded in this work are clearly hypothetical (e.g., that Biennial visitors are blithely ignorant of their own privilege, and that having had their entry to the Sierra exhibit blocked they would necessarily respond with the proper insight and mend their ways, or have their "mindset . . . laid bare," in Sierra's words).[111] Given the vast number of biennial-based works over the past twenty years that have been devoted to discomfiting the viewer, it seems likely that their experience of these provocations is considerably more complex and contradictory, and that they may include elements of pleasure or even self-affirmation. In fact, the work of Sierra and others is as likely to consolidate a particular sense of identity among art world viewers (as tolerant, enlightened, willing to accept risk and challenge) as it is to effect any lasting ontic dislocation. Unfortunately, mainstream critics and curators continue to offer the same credulous accounts

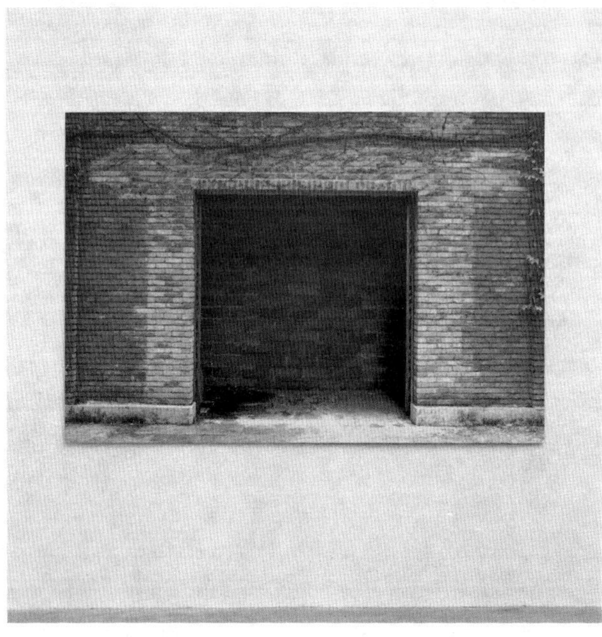

FIGURE 1 Santiago Sierra, *Wall Enclosing a Space, Spanish Pavilion, Venice Biennial, Venice Italy 2003* (2003). Courtesy of the artist and Lisson Gallery, London.

of Sierra "exposing" the operations of power, thus eliding any discussion of the more complex relay of exchanges, assumptions, and experiences his works might catalyze among actual audience members.

The almost reflexive application of a critical discourse based on authorial singularity and the artwork as a prefabricated and essentially specular event or object can prevent a fuller understanding even of those projects produced by artists working under its auspices. Thus, Hirschhorn's *Bataille Monument* project also involved an extended collaboration with Turkish-German youth from the neighborhood, who helped him construct a temporary library, snack bar, and television studio (which they used for the duration of the exhibit). This aspect of the project is unremarked in Bishop's account, perhaps because it so closely resembles the retrograde "community-art" tradition. In some cases, the artists themselves seem simultaneously drawn to, and embarrassed by, the collective, participatory dimension of their own work. In writing about his large-scale performance *When Faith Moves Mountains* (a project in which several hundred volunteers worked together to move a sand dune outside Lima, Peru, in 2002), Francis Alÿs avoids any extended discussion of the actual mechanics of the collaborative interaction and negotiation necessary to bring the work into existence, focusing instead on hermeneutic issues around the work's transmission in the art world, or on the symbolism of the performance as a "mythic" image. It was a *"beau geste,* at once futile and heroic, absurd and urgent," according to Alÿs. The Guggenheim describes it as a "powerful allegory, a metaphor for human will." The five hundred collaborators are thus reduced to an undifferentiated collective mass, laboring among clouds of sand as a literal illustration of Alÿs's poetic imagination.[112]

I've spent some time sketching out the broader intellectual history behind current critiques of activist and socially engaged art for two reasons. First, because these critiques raise some relevant and important questions about this work and can help in delineating a more rigorous analysis. And second, because the critiques themselves are symptomatic of certain limitations within current art critical discourse. It is a discourse, as I've argued above, that has achieved near canonical authority in the contemporary art world. While I've attempted to problematize it, my goal isn't to question its legitimacy, but simply to make it visible in the first place as *one* potential framework for the analysis of contemporary art. Several of the collaborative projects that I'll begin discussing in the following chapter challenge this discursive system. They are, by and large, concerned with the generation of insight through durational interaction rather than rupture; they seek to openly problematize the authorial status of the artist, and they often rely on more conciliatory (and less custodial) strategies and relationships (both with their participants and with affiliated movements, disciplines, etc). While they may be implicated in forms of collective action that take up an oppositional or antagonistic relationship to particular sites of power, they differentiate this antagonism from the modes of self-reflexive sociality necessary to create solidarity within a given organizational structure. In short, they challenge the conventional aesthetic autonomy of both the artist and art practice, relative to a given site, context, or constituency. It is this challenge, embodied in practice, which requires a new analytic approach. In the following chapter I'll outline such an approach, centered on a concept of collaborative labor.

THE GENIUS OF THE PLACE

Every now and then a chorus could be heard from the top of the dune:
"Water, water, water." But the camera kept rolling.
MEDINA ET AL., *FRANCIS ALŸS: WHEN FAITH MOVES MOUNTAINS*

I ended the last chapter with a brief discussion of Francis Alÿs's *When Faith Moves Mountains*, a performance created with a cast of several hundred volunteers in the sand dunes of Ventanilla, outside Lima, Peru. The event, commissioned for the 2002 Lima Biennial, generated a great deal of interest in the art world and helped to consolidate Alÿs's international reputation. Turner Publications in Madrid released a book documenting the performance in 2005, and it was prominently featured in a monograph on Alÿs published by Phaidon in 2007. In addition, an installation focused on the event was exhibited at museums in Mexico City, Lima, and Los Angeles. *When Faith Moves Mountains* elaborates on a concern with the symbolism of wasted or futile labor that was evident in Alÿs's earlier performances, but at a much grander scale. At the same time, the emphasis that Alÿs placed on the experience of collaborative interaction in this project marked a significant departure from his previous work. While he employed participants in performance-based pieces such as *Song for Lupita* (1998) or *Rehearsal 2* (2001–6), their primary role was to "act out" certain scripted gestures designed to convey a symbolic or metaphoric meaning. The volunteers in *Faith* were also assigned a fixed task by Alÿs (the shoveling of the dune), but he now contends that the execution of the task itself had the effect of transforming the consciousness of the participants ("It did, maybe just for a day, provoke this illusion that things could possibly change.").[1] The critic Jean Fisher, writing on *Faith* in the Phaidon monograph, contends that the process of moving the sand dune catalyzed a "spirit of conviviality" capable of "initiating and uniting community as a shared experience of a thought, from the group of mostly engineering students who participated in the event at the site, to the people of the pueblo jóven who took it upon themselves to protect the site while the work was in progress, to the art world, which receives the idea through the chain of documentation and commentary—a movement connecting the local to the global." Drawing on Heidegger and Agamben, Fisher suggests that the performance revealed a "new thought of the political, here understood . . . as 'conviviality,' or the founding moment of community."[2] This is a significant claim, with particular relevance for the themes developed in this book. What forms of knowledge were mobilized in the act of shoveling sand? And how do they relate to insights made available to viewers who experienced the performance as an image in subsequent screenings or gallery installations?

Fisher's quote collapses the distinction between the experience of the participants engaged in the collective act of moving the dune and the subsequent re-presentation of the event as a film or installation in the art world, describing instead a continuous line of transmission from the local to the global. As I'll discuss shortly, this is a symptomatic elision. *Faith* presents us with a useful test case of some of the operative tensions in contemporary art between the textual paradigm outlined in chapter 1 (the work of art as an event, object, or image fabricated by the artist for the viewer's consumption) and a growing interest in methods of collaborative production that mobilize very different forms of intersubjective affect, identification, and agency. The creation of this performance involved weeks of effort and the composition of a complex social and organizational network. The museum presentation, however, focused primarily on the spectacle of the volunteers shoveling in the sand. The installation that I saw at the Hammer Museum in Los Angeles (September 2007–February 2008) centered on the projection of a fifteen-minute film documenting Alÿs's initial scouting of the location, the arrival of the volunteers, and the actual labor of the shoveling.[3] In addition, photographs of the performance, along with several short texts and e-mail exchanges between Alÿs and his collaborators, Cuauhtémoc Medina and Rafael Ortega, were displayed under Plexiglass on a set of low worktables. The images include a signed photograph of Alÿs, Medina, and Ortega standing together at the site of the performance with bullhorns and cameras as they prepare to direct and document the labor of the five hundred volunteers, mostly young college students from Lima wearing matching shirts emblazoned with the project logo.

Although the video includes comments by several (unidentified) student volunteers, Alÿs's installation does little to convey the nature of their participation, or their particular investment in the Sisyphean task that he has assigned them. They have been summoned by Alÿs not as collaborators (that status is reserved for Medina and Ortega), but as bodies to illustrate a "social allegory" about the inevitable failure of Latin America to successfully modernize.[4] Thus, in Medina's words, *When Faith Moves Mountains* represents the "application of the Latin-American principle of non-development: an extension of the logic of failure, of the programmatic dilapidation, the utopic resistance, the entropic economy and the social erosion of the region. But moreover, the action was conceived as a parable of short productivity: a huge endeavor whose major achievement was *no achievement at all.*"[5] Images of failure and futility run throughout Alÿs's work, from the aging Volkswagen trying unsuccessfully to climb a Tijuana hill in *Rehearsal 1* (1999–2003) to the Mexico City sweepers in *Barrenderos* (2004), paid to push garbage through the streets of the city until its accumulated mass is impossible to move. Progress in Latin America is always failed, compromised, or postponed.[6] No matter how hard Alÿs's street sweepers or student volunteers work, they will never be able to gain access to the benefits of modernity precisely because modernity, as a process led by the North, depends on the strategic underdevelopment of the economies of the South.

The fact that Alÿs uses human labor as the vehicle for his allegory is symptomatic, linking two main vectors of his practice. The first, as noted above, is based on the correlation between labor and productivity. The very "failure" of Latin America to successfully modernize is registered as a kind of melancholic protest against the imperatives of efficiency. Latin America chooses to stay in a "sphere of indeterminate action," as Alÿs writes, in order to "define itself against the imposition of Western modernity."[7] Hence, the struggling Volkswagen, the idled *barrenderos*, and the shoveling volunteers are all engaged in a conspicuous expenditure of wasted labor ("maximum effort, minimal result," as Alÿs writes of *Faith*).[8] For his part, Medina justifies his involvement in the project by contrasting it with his own history of failed militancy at the University of Mexico in the 1980s: "What made me go back and do this at the age of thirty-six was that we were making a metaphorical political comment instead of just undertaking another futile political action."[9] This notion of futility and waste brings us back to the ambivalent lesson of May '68 outlined above. Political or social progress is destined to be frustrated and deferred, due to the inevitable co-option of the forces of organized resistance.[10] The improvements in social justice and economic equality that have been achieved in the Latin America polity through a century or more of contestation against the logic of modernity and the forces of neocolonial exploitation fall away in this narrative, which reduces critique to a simple logic of inversion: modernity's demand for efficiency and productivity will be subverted by a deliberate embrace of inefficiency and futility.[11] Alÿs's metaphoric construction of modernity thus entails a hollowing out of Latin American history, as well as a detached, delectory relationship to that history as a subject of poetic contemplation.

The symbiotic relationship between efficiency and inefficiency in Alÿs's work is paralleled by a second set of oppositional terms associated with its critical and theoretical framing in the art world. This opposition is neatly captured by Jean Fisher in the essay cited above. Activist art, according to Fisher, operates on the basis of a naive faith that "words and images are directly communicable." Alÿs, for his part, refuses the semantic labor of meaning and engages instead in a Heideggerian "suspension of signification," producing a "heretofore un-thought configuration of reality."[12] We encounter a similar argument in Russell Ferguson's catalog essay on Alÿs for the Hammer Museum exhibition. Alÿs's work "refuses closure" and "rejects conclusions," according to Ferguson, and embraces instead an ambivalent "politics of rehearsal."[13] Alÿs reiterates this claim in his own account of the project. Confronted with an impossible situation (an invitation to produce a project for the Lima Biennial in the midst of the social turmoil surrounding Alberto Fujimori's failing dictatorship), he sought to create "a sensation of 'meaninglessness' that shows the absurdity of the situation."[14] Alÿs elaborates on this point in an interview with Ferguson, arguing that the "poetic act" entails the deliberate "suspension of meaning, a brief sensation of senselessness that . . . makes you step back or step out and revise your prior assumptions about this reality."[15]

The central role played by physical labor in Alÿs's work, at the symbolic level, is thus reiterated by a concern with semantic labor in the work's reception as an allegorical image. Productive labor, whether the linking of signifier and signified or the removal of trash from the streets of Mexico City, is always complicit with the totalizing forces of modernity. Alÿs thus projects a form of textual politics that operates through the valorization of semantic failure (the refusal of narrative closure, the suspension of signification, the negation of meaning) onto the geopolitical situation of Latin America. In doing so, he effectively reiterates the "third way" logic of May '68. Given the relentless instrumentality of modernization, and the ostensible failure, or complicity, of leftist political resistance to this process, the artist has no choice but to operate through a form of poetic withdrawal and allegorical distanciation. In his writing for the *Faith* installation Alÿs seems cognizant of the problematic nature of this transposition and his tendency to poeticize Latin America's ostensibly futile resistance to modernization, leaving it to "future minds" to decide if "this attitude is more cynical than siding with the evils of development."[16]

The arduous process of moving the sand dune clearly functioned as an imagistic resource for Alÿs. This is evident in the careful attention given to the visual staging of the event; the deliberate arrangement of the workers' bodies in a single line across the face of the dune, the matching shirts with logos, the detailed storyboards outlining the shot-by-shot composition of the film, and perhaps most significantly, in the particular location Alÿs selected as the site for the performance. The dune is directly in front of a large shantytown with a population of over seventy thousand immigrants, displaced farmers, and political refugees.[17] Few if any of the shantytown residents were involved in the project as volunteers (although some, apparently, witnessed the performance itself). Instead, the town and its population function as a kind of backdrop, an image of the political "real" (the impoverished, marginal space left to the victims of development and modernization) against which the metaphoric gesture of fruitless labor could take on added resonance. Alÿs appears to have made a deliberate choice to not directly engage the residents of the shantytown in his performance, fearing perhaps that any possible interaction would literalize his critique of modernization and collapse the distance from the site of the political necessary to produce a properly metaphoric meaning, even as it risked the accusation that he was engaging in a further, symbolic, exploitation of the landless workers who lived there. The gap between figure and ground, performance and shantytown, thus acts as a spatial expression of the poetic autonomy that Alÿs views as central to the integrity of his work. It preserves the crucial distinction between art and mere activism even as it protects the political Other from instrumentalization at the hands of the artist. It also reveals the double movement of this gesture: on the one hand, a necessary skepticism regarding the pitfalls of political engagement, and on the other, a reduction of the political to the realm of the impure, the compromised, and the co-opted.

Alÿs has described *Faith* as "land art for the landless," because it "deromanticizes" the insular land art traditions of Richard Long and Robert Smithson.[18] It's not clear, however, in what way *Faith* serves the interests of the shantytown's inhabitants or is made "for" them. Perhaps a more accurate description would be land art "on behalf of" or "in the name of" the landless, but surely this construction, this relationship, is no less problematic than the attempt to represent the landless as the subject of his work. On the one hand, as noted above, Alÿs associates art with a poetic "suspension of meaning" (and, in particular, a disruption of conventional signifying practices). On the other, his desire to address the impact of modernization in Latin America obliges him to retain a conventional system of signification in which modernization is represented by various allegorical substitutes. To the extent that his goal is to suspend signification, this strategy fails (we know precisely what the Volkswagen or the *barrenderos* are "supposed" to mean because Alÿs and his commentators have told us). Meaning is less negated in this gesture than it is temporally displaced through a semantic relay. The ambiguity required of a poetic text is then collapsed into the content of the work, through the metaphorical staging of Latin America's ambivalent relationship to modernization and development.

In *Faith*, the referent of modernization is spatially proximate, in the dilapidated, overcrowded houses of the shantytown that form the backdrop of the performance. The pressures exerted by this context expose certain fault lines in Alÿs's creative practice. Despite the proximity of the shantytown, Alÿs can't represent or reference the landless workers directly without sacrificing the nominally poetic distance produced by allegorical substitution. Instead, the college students were bused in from Lima as surrogates for the absent landless workers. Their deployment as a metaphoric vehicle is, presumably, less problematic, due to their relatively privileged status. But precisely in refusing to engage the residents of the shantytown, by excluding them from the labor of the performance, they are all the more easily reduced to a generic abstraction (the "landless worker"), whose mute presence lends the work its aura of political authenticity. It seems difficult, in fact, for Alÿs to imagine a form of creative interaction with the shantytown's residents outside the ethical constraints imposed by a textual paradigm (to either enact or suspend a representational relationship). He is clearly more comfortable with *Faith* as a poetic image or narrative that has been "freed" from its referential dependence on the event itself.[19]

In a letter to the theorist Susan Buck-Morss (who contributed an essay to the *Faith* catalog published in Madrid), Alÿs modestly cedes authorship of the original event, and the complex social interactions that led to its realization, claiming responsibility only for its subsequent re-presentation in the art world in the form of a film. "That second part of the work [the film] belongs to me clearly," according to Alÿs. "Whether the first part, the day itself, belongs to me, to the volunteers . . . to Cuauh or Rafa . . . or to the dune itself, I would personally find difficult to tell."[20] Alÿs's generous renunciation of singular authorial possession (even the sand dune is allowed some creative autonomy) is complicated by two factors. First, the action performed by the participants was predetermined and choreographed by Alÿs himself. Their agency in the project was reduced to the simple act of either bestowing or withholding their physical presence and cooperation. This reproduces the binary structure evident in his relationship to the shantytown (either consent or refusal; the enactment or suspension of representation). Second, it is precisely in the circulation of the event-as-image before a "global audience," as Alÿs writes, that he is able to accrue the symbolic capital necessary to enhance his career as an artist. Thus, his willingness to surrender authorship over the event entails no particular sacrifice of his authorial autonomy or prestige. I'm less interested here in the ethical issues that this gesture might raise (Alÿs is certainly entitled to claim or disavow authorship over the event or the video without necessarily diminishing the significance of either one) than in its implications for our understanding of collaboration as a form of artistic production.

When Faith Moves Mountains suggests some of the challenges that artists accustomed to a textual mode of production face when they seek to embed their practice more fully in a given social context through a collaborative or reciprocal relationship to site. The complexities of these relationships, the contradictory forms of negotiation and solicitation, recognition and disavowal, projection and transference, produced through intersubjective exchange, are evident in the treatment of *Faith*'s student volunteers. While Alÿs is reluctant to identify the event qua event with his own artistic practice, he does acknowledge its creative or generative capacity, which he associates with the voluntary nature of the student's participation ("the volunteers that could pull out at any moment and virtually break the line").[21] By volunteering for the project their involvement was insulated from baser motives and inclinations. Neither compelled nor rewarded, it could maintain the purity necessary to function as a poetic symbol. Their labor thus possessed a dual nature, expressing both the failure of Latin American modernization and the presence of an underlying human capacity for joyful selflessness:

> The *sine qua non* condition of the action was voluntary collaboration, i.e., an exercise of generosity. One of the piece's intentions was to explore alternative methods of action to those of the capitalist system and its mass media. To pay people for their participation would have contradicted the concept of the piece by involving economic coercion instead of a conflux of individual wills. Faith cannot be bought.[22]

While faith can't be bought, it can, apparently, be strongly encouraged. In his account of the actual process involved in recruiting volunteers, Medina describes walking through the corridors of Lima's universities, megaphone in hand, "rallying" the students with the soft coercion typical of Latin American political demonstrations.[23] In an interview in the Madrid catalog, critic Gerardo Mosquera remarks on the significance that Alÿs, Medina, and Ortega attach to the experience of the participants ("Its worth noting how the three of you value the physical act of moving the dune, while to me as a spectator it doesn't seem as important."). "It could be due to guilt," Medina replies. "We had five hundred people stupidly working on the action. It wasn't about an act of generosity, about volunteers offering to cooperate in the making of a work of art. It was half a day of brutal, murderous work under a relentless sun. You bear the responsibility of having involved people in an unreasonable effort."[24]

Medina's response provides an instructive contrast to the image of *Faith* as a festival of ludic conviviality. For Alÿs, the "infinitesimal displacement" of the sand dune was "a tiny miracle."[25] "We were trying to suggest the possibility of change. And it did, maybe just for a day, provoke this illusion that things could possibly change."[26] The "illusory" nature of this experience, in Alÿs's account, is symptomatic. The only hope for a positive form of action, capable of resisting co-option and complicity, lies in the orchestration of a singular moment of joyful collectivity that is so brief, so ephemeral, so utterly disconnected from any broader or more sustainable narrative of resistance or emancipation, that it vanishes almost at the moment it is expressed. Thus, the only pure moment, the only poetic moment (and here aesthetics is very much a discourse of purity) must occur prior to the contaminating, predicative, constraints of practice, application, or engagement. Alÿs's work returns us to the ethical normalization of desire and the logic of an infinite regression. The goal of art is to reproduce that most preliminary and unadulterated expression of liberatory desire before it achieves coherence or articulation: to be decanted and preserved for some potential future use.

Faith reveals both the possibilities and the disjunctions of contemporary collaborative art practice. Its attempt to convey a kind of "degree zero" of community (Fisher's "founding moment") speaks to the necessity that many artists feel to start over, at the most basic level, in understanding the embodiment and constitution of collective interaction in the post–Cold War era.[27] Yet it also demonstrates the impoverished notion of praxis that is often encountered in textual projects. Alÿs's work, with its poetic celebration of the futile, the failed, and the incomplete, offers itself as a critique of modernization at the very moment when the success of modernization has never appeared more inevitable, and the presumed futility of resistance to it more habitual. It combines a necessary historical consciousness of the myriad ways in which political change has failed, or can fail, with a conspicuous blindness to those moments of success in the past and the present from which artists might learn or gain inspiration. The experience of the volunteers, which no doubt exists somewhere between the extremes of coercion and unfettered desire, is significant, even if it is difficult to gauge in the museum presentation of *Faith*. But the students were set to a task over which they had no real control. The experience of creative autonomy, the power to envision and carry forward an action, remains the singular province of the artist.

The fact that agency is not fully and equitably distributed in the *Faith* performance doesn't invalidate it as an art practice, any more than the fact that the installations of Santiago Sierra or Thomas Hirschhorn may reinforce, rather than disrupt, the self-perception of art world viewers. The more relevant question, and the question that can help us grasp the complex and necessary interdependence of the aesthetic and the ethical, is to what extent the work remains mindful of the violence of community and of representation itself. There are other possibilities, of course, other ways of working, in which the experience of collaborative labor is seen as generative, not simply symbolic, improvisationally responsive rather than scripted, and in which the distribution of agency is more reciprocal. The questions of labor, development, and modernization that are so complexly rendered in Alÿs's project will also be central themes in the following discussion. Is there a way to make labor productive differently? I'll explore this question with a series of case studies, beginning with the work of the Dialogue collective in central India.

2 — ENCLOSURE ACTS

How come we hadn't seen the [Adivasi] memorial pillars as artworks earlier but now we are seeing them that way? It's not only a difference in thinking and perception, but also a difference in how we were able to borrow something, some imagery, from other artworks. . . . We began going through the fields and grass and really looking carefully at these things. There is no tradition of reading an image as such, but here we were looking at every little figure.

GEESURAM, KONDAGAON ARTIST, 2007

My colleague said, "You're drifting from what you came here for. Now you want to work with kids." I said, "I'm not drifting, I've worked with children in the past. I'm just throwing myself open, and seeing how children deal with situations. How elders deal with situations. How artists deal with situations." I was trying to work past my preconceptions. I was leaving myself open . . .

The town of Kondagaon is located in Bastar district, Chhattisgarh, 225 kilometers south of Raipur, in central India. Bastar's economy is centered on farming and rice cultivation (the area has long been known as India's "rice bowl"). It is also home to a large Adivasi tribal population. The Adivasi are India's indigenous people (the name means "original inhabitants" in Sanskrit) and have lived here for thousands of years. In many ways, little has changed. Village life still centers on the seasonal cycles of rice cultivation and the monsoon, the weekly *hatt*, or market, and the rituals of the Sacred Grove.[28] Electricity and running water remain rare outside of the scattered towns. In the past decade, however, the Adivasi and peasant communities of Bastar have begun to suffer from some of the most corrosive effects of modernization, even as they receive few of its benefits. The expansion of multinational timber and mining corporations into central India (marking Bastar's transition from India's rice bowl to its "mining bowl," as activist Nath Ratneshwar has observed) has threatened not only the ecosystems on which tribal and peasant communities depend for survival, it has also destabilized long-established living and working patterns in the villages. "I pray the government finds some minerals under your hut or fields" has become a new Adivasi curse.[29] Unemployment, eviction from the land, and disruption of traditional farming patterns are all increasingly common features of Adivasi life.

Equally damaging are attempts to erode or displace Adivasi spiritual and cultural traditions by groups such as the Rashtriya Swayamsevak Sangh (RSS), a Hindu Nationalist organization linked with the BJP (Bahratiya Janata Party). The RSS and other right-wing Hindu fundamentalist organizations seek to "civilize" the Vanavasi ("forest dwellers," their preferred term for the Adivasi) by converting them to Hinduism.[30] This is occurring even as Adivasi craft practices, previously anchored in village rituals, are appropriated by Indian businessmen eager to adorn their Delhi and Mumbai boardrooms with tokens of the same "native" Indian-ness that their corporations are rapidly destroying. Adivasi villages are thus poised between the depredations of industrial capital and the fetishizing appetites of consumer culture. Scholar Dip Kapoor has analyzed the many ways in which NGOs, development agencies, political activists, and other groups have sought to make use of Adivasi culture and community life.[31] Kapoor, who spent nearly a decade working in Khond villages in Orissa, outlines the various permutations of this appropriative drive in his recent research. He examines the discourse of Ghandian environmentalists, who cast Adivasi village life as a romanticized, pastoral antidote to the instrumentalizing forces of modernity; Indian NGO and development workers, who view the Adivasi as childlike primitives in need of modernization and technical know-how; and Naxalite resistance fighters, for whom tribal communities are merely another cadre to be mobilized in their war against the Indian state.[32] In each case, the conflicted and hybrid nature of contemporary Adivasi life is neglected or overlooked. There are relatively few attempts to engage with the specific situation of Adivasi communities here and now, and the unique challenges that they face at the interstices of modernity and tradition.[33]

These questions of adaptation and survival, resistance and assimilation, bring us back to Kondagaon, and the outlying village of Kopaweda. Over the past decade Mumbai artist Navjot Altaf and Kondagaon artists Rajkumar, Shantibai, and Gessuram, have built a small, independent art center in Kopaweda. They created the center in order to develop projects with the Adivasi and peasant communities in the area.[34] After receiving some initial support from the India Foundation for the Arts (IFA) in Bangalore, the center has become entirely self-sustaining, relying on money generated by Altaf and her collaborators through the sale of their own work. The center is named Dialogue, which reflects a key component of their creative philosophy. While their projects often take physical form (typically as spaces related to collective activities, such as water collection or children's play), they are equally concerned with the processes of reciprocal learning generated in the planning and creation of these spaces, as well as the forms of social interaction catalyzed by their subsequent use.

Survival in Kopaweda depends on water; drinking, washing, bathing, cleaning, and cooking all require regular trips to one of several pump sites scattered throughout the village. The Nagar Palika (municipal government) spends very little money on infrastructure in Kondagaon, so wells typically consist of little more than a simple pump surrounded by a muddy pool. The pool in turn becomes a breeding ground for malaria and other

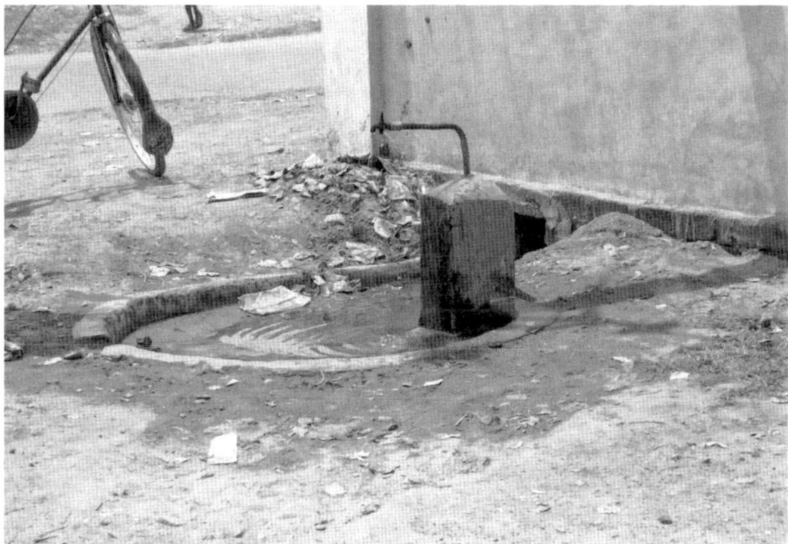

FIGURE 2 Water Pump, Kondagaon, Bastar District, Chhattisgarh, India (2007). Photograph by Grant Kester.

diseases, due to accumulated debris from washing and bathing and the presence of watering animals. The work of collecting water is performed almost entirely by the women and children of the village, who travel back and forth to the pump sites up to a dozen times a day. In addition to the backbreaking labor of transporting the water, the women suffer from musculoskeletal disorders as a result of the awkward torsion involved in lifting heavy vessels onto their shoulders and heads. This division of labor reflects one of the central features of village life: a patriarchal structure in which women are closely monitored by fathers, husbands, uncles, and brothers. Their movement through the village, their social interactions, and their daily work are subject to a pervasive scopic regime.

Over the course of several months, Altaf and her collaborators analyzed the spatial choreography of village life, the protocols governing the movement and aggregation of bodies, and the distribution of power, labor, and access among men, women, and children. The water pump quickly emerged as a central nexus of meaning in village life, essential to daily survival while remaining almost entirely inexpressive at the symbolic level, due in part to its association with women's labor. In 2000 they began to develop plans for restructuring the pump sites by organizing a series of extended meetings with Adivasis and non-Adivasis from the vicinity of

Kondagaon. The ensuing discussions were wide-ranging, addressing the role of art in the villages, the selection of specific sites, the politics of water supply and land access (Adivasi land is rapidly being bought up by wealthy Hindus), and caste issues associated with Hindu perceptions of the Adivasi as unclean. The final pump site designs were generated collaboratively by Altaf, Rajkumar, Shantibai, and Gessuram in response to the issues introduced at these meetings. After extensive negotiations with village elders and the Nagar Palika, they built the first water pump structure, or Nalpar, in 2001. As of 2007, they had constructed three Nalpar sites in Kopaweda and another four elsewhere in Kondagaon.

The format of each site is similar: a smooth concrete pad that is large enough to accommodate several women at once, a more efficient pump design, an enclosure incorporating Adivasi cultural symbols related to water (the zigzag or chevron) or formal references to pumps, faucets and clay pots made by village artisans, and a system of paved trenches to channel and collect runoff water into smaller reservoirs for irrigation, building, and the watering of animals. As noted in chapter 1, the construction and design of the Nalpar sites was undertaken collaboratively, with a particular focus on workshops that combined Adivasi and non-Adivasi artisans, so that the creation itself became both ritualized as a public event and socially transformative. The concrete pad allows for the efficient evaporation of water, while also providing a platform for social interaction among the women, encouraging a convivial interruption of work routines. The Nalpar acts as a stage for women's labor, setting off and framing the act of washing, cleaning, and water collection, and marking the pump site as a significant center of activity in the village. The sites also operate on a more practical, ergonomic level, incorporating niches and platforms that allow the women to rest their carrying vessels before raising them up to their heads (see plates 3 and 4).

The surrounding enclosure is perhaps the most distinctive formal element in the Nalpar. Some are shaped like large pots or Pop Art faucets, while others are more abstract. My concern here, however, is less with the enclosure's decorative or symbolic function than with its effect on the phenomenological condition of the Nalpar site. The scale and structure of the enclosure is significant. It must be high enough to provide some degree of privacy, and it must be partially closed off while still allowing ease of access for women burdened with heavy vessels or laundry. The Nalpar is both a physical object and a gesture, an enunciation, within the space of the village. To enclose is to claim or possess, but also to shelter: to segregate but also to protect. The Nalpar is simultaneously integral to village life (literally, it is the source of water which sustains life) while also set apart from it, both connected and uncoupled. The Nalpar produces two distinct but related effects. First, it claims this space (a space already largely assigned to women by virtue of the gendered division of labor) as a site of dialogue and recreation, as well as work, among women. This appropriative act is essential to its effect. While men aren't prevented from entering the Nalpar enclosure (and still drink at the sites), its very separateness as a space of women's work discourages their extended presence.

The physical barrier of the Nalpar wall excludes the men and effectively screens the women from their view. At the same time, the enclosure creates within itself a new space in which the women can share work and build a sense of solidarity apart from the normal cultural relations and spatial protocols of village life—a zone of cohesion, intimacy, and reconsolidation.[35] Through its very monumentality it declares that this space, this labor, and these relationships have a symbolic, as well as practical, value. Over a period of almost seven years the Nalpar sites have effected a subtle but significant remapping of the psycho-geography of village life in Kopaweda. They have provided, for perhaps the first time, a protected and recognized space of interaction and reflection for women, available in the course of their daily routines (see plates 5 and 6). There are few, if any, sites of this nature in the village. In the temple, the home, the festival, and the market, men and women tend to interact within traditional hierarchal structures.

In many ways the Nalpar sites are quite simple, operating at the most practical, physical, level to facilitate the postures and rhythms of human labor (water collection, washing, drinking). At the same time, the ways in which these sites function within the broader social ecology of the village raise significant questions about the complex calibration of collective and individual identity. They constitute, in the totality of their physical, aesthetic, and social operation, a form of embodied practice with implications that extend beyond the boundaries of Bastar. In particular, they complicate some of the more reductive assumptions found in recent art theory and criticism regarding the function of individual and collective identity. As I discussed in the first chapter, something very like a theoretical canon, in its influence and uniformity, has emerged in Euro-American art writing over the past decade and a half, influenced by the rapprochement between post-conceptual art practice and post-structuralist literary theory during the 1990s. This discourse typically operates through a juxtapositional logic, in which a "good" form of subjectivity, defined as fluid, open, shifting, and incapable of violence, is contrasted with an antithetical form of "bad" subjectivity, defined as fixed, closed, coherent, and violently instrumentalizing. It is linked, in turn, with debates in political theory (e.g., the work of Giorgio Agamben, Jean-Luc Nancy) over the relationship between collective or communal identity (assumed to be oppressive and universalizing) and a radical singularity that is seen as intrinsically liberatory.

Claire Bishop exemplifies this juxtapositional logic in the *October* essay I cited earlier, contrasting an abject community-based or "relational" art practice with the "tougher, more disruptive" approach of European biennial stalwarts Thomas Hirschhorn and Santiago Sierra. "The model of subjectivity that underpins their practice," as Bishop writes, "is not the fictitious whole subject of harmonious community, but a divided subject of partial identifications open to constant flux. If relational aesthetics requires a unified subject as a prerequisite for community-as-togetherness, then Hirschhorn and Sierra provide a mode of artistic practice more adequate to the divided and incomplete subject of today."[36] As Bishop's quote suggests, those forms of identity that appear incoherent, singular, fragmented, or partial are viewed as intrinsically superior (regardless of their situational orientation), necessarily preferable to those that are premised on a more coherent, stable, or collective sense of self. Here the problematic synchronic bias of post-structuralist theory reveals itself, leading to a tendency to reify states of being. Thus, identity is treated as either static or fluid, coherent or incoherent, stable or destabilized, porous or impermeable, singular or collective. In each case, ethical privilege is assigned to only one of two fixed positions (an entirely benign, ceaselessly changing, presubjective desire on the one hand, and a violent and objectifying drive on the other), and only disruption and fragmentation are seen as epistemologically productive.

The Nalpar sites offer another lesson. Identity is always carried forward through a double movement, a diachronic oscillation, between the assertion and the dissolution of self. A moment of enframing and conative assertion is necessary and generative (both epistemologically and ethically) in the reparative construction of identity. The space of the Nalpar is not heterotopic or fluid, but exclusive and concentric. Its efficacy resides precisely in the claiming of space and the power to limit access (via social norms) to women, in a context in which that power is systematically denied elsewhere. In fact, as the Nalpar suggest, the concept of a heterotopic space, in which the hierarchies of daily life are suspended in a fluid play of difference, is just as clearly ideological as its Habermasian counterpart, the ideal speech community, so long as neither acknowledges the a priori determinants and constraints of identity in a given circumstance. Object-based art practices lend themselves to what we might term an axiomatic form of criticism. The work, by its very physical stasis and receptive anonymity, instantiates certain propositions about the viewer's experience that necessarily remain hypothetical and untested (except through the surrogate consciousness of the critic). Collaborative or collective art practices, however, place a very different set of demands on the critic. They require a mode of thinking rooted in the situational operation of identity and driven by a reciprocal testing of the assumptions of both theory and practice.

One of the most significant questions raised by collaborative art practice concerns the pragmatic interrelationship between solidarity, violence, and resistance. The Nalpar sites certainly express the drive to enframe and annex space. They effectively erode the zone of observation that is projected onto and through the village by men (who gain a sense of self precisely through the exercise of this scopic and spatial control). To the extent that this action was perceived by the men of the village as curtailing their agency and freedom of observation it involved a form of violence; a diminishing of the sphere of the Other. But this violence is clearly of a different order than the violence involved in attempting to possess, objectify, or negate another subject. It is intended to limit another subject's power over oneself, sustaining the integrity of self relative to others, rather than establishing one's dominion over them. The solidarity or "togetherness" produced in the Nalpar doesn't claim transcendence or universality, but neither does it dissolve into "constant flux" or monadic isolation.

As Dialogue's work suggests, the "community" of Kopaweda is defined by a series of strategic exclusions oriented around gender and imposed through the framing of space and movement via habit and convention. There is no attempt here to romanticize village life, but rather a frank acknowledgment of its biases and limitations. At the same time, there is a willingness to see the emplotment of space and movement as fluid, rather than timeless, and to rewrite the script that governs the gathering and segregation of bodies in the village. While Dialogue seeks to intervene in these protocols, to generate an alternative schema, it does so through reciprocal engagement with the residents of the village (in particular the women, but also the male elders). In contrast to the programmatic imposition of a priori technologies and techniques typical of many development agencies, Dialogue's innovations were generated in and through the experience of the site itself.[37]

The Nalpar sites soon attracted groups of children as well as women collecting water (children in Kopaweda have few places to play). Adivasi culture has traditionally recognized the necessary autonomy of children from adult life through the institution of the Ghotul, a kind of dormitory/ clubhouse in which unmarried adolescents teach younger children songs, dances, poems, wood carving, and other art forms. The Ghotul also encourages the young men and women of the village to form romantic relationships, which are understood as temporary and provisional (it is assumed that they will change partners regularly), prior to formal marriage and monogamous commitment. The government, however, has repressed the Ghotul system, which many Hindus consider immoral because it allows boys and girls to interact, and even have sex, without adult supervision.

For their next series of works Dialogue chose to reinvent the tradition of the Ghotul, creating a space where the village children could congregate, play, and educate one another outside the formal schooling of the temple or classroom. They described this new space as a Pilla Gudi, or "children's temple." The first Pilla Gudi was designed by Rajkumar in 2001 for the nearby village of Kusma. Rajkumar's Pilla Gudi was based on a famous Adivasi "Mother Goddess" temple at Matnar, about 150 kilometers from Kondagaon. The interior ceiling of the Matnar temple features a series of carved deities who gaze down upon the worshippers below. For

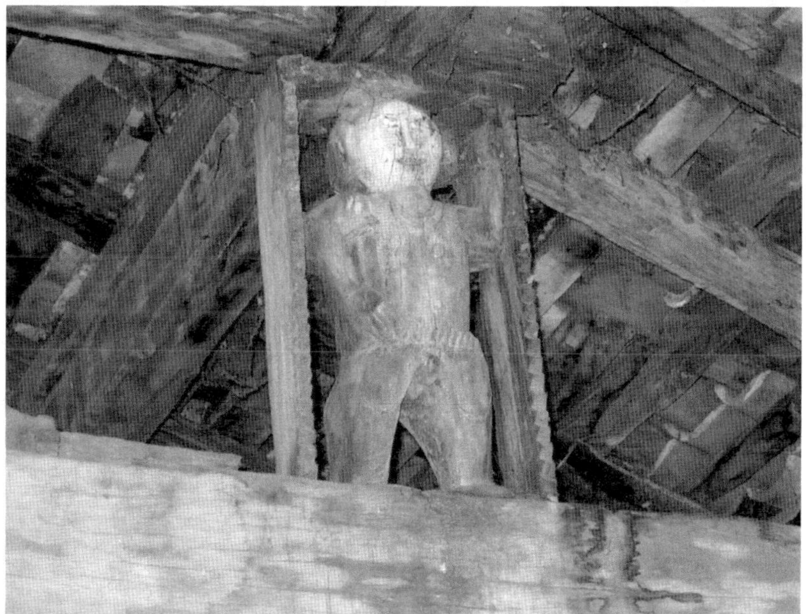

his Pilla Gudi, Rajkumar replaced the sculptures of deities with large mirrors laid flat against the ceiling's surface. When the children look up, they see their own images reflected back. The performative submission implied in the act of gazing upward to the temple ceiling is transformed: an external, metaphysical authority is replaced by a reflective self-imaging in which agency and divinity are attributed to the children themselves. This secularizing gesture takes on added significance given the growing pressure exerted by Hindu fundamentalism in rural India. The members of Dialogue also developed art workshops for the children in the Pilla Gudi, which employ the mirrored ceiling, its reflections and distortions, as a way to initiate discussions about image and self in the village community (see plates 7 and 8).

The second Pilla Gudi was created by Altaf at Shilpi Gram, a workshop established by the celebrated Adivasi artist Jaidev Baghel. It functions as an open-air meeting and performance space, with a circular, concrete seating structure oriented around a central, stagelike space. The central space consists of a large, concave dome buried in the earth and filled with sand. The dome shape, hidden beneath the sand, again inverts the form of a nearby temple. Altaf titled this Pilla Gudi *12 + 1 = 13 (Hence it is not a Circle),* because one section of the seating structure is broken apart and set slightly askew. Whoever sits in this section is expected to improvise the day's activities or introduce questions for discussion among the other children. This is an apt image for Dialogue's work as a whole: both inside and outside the circle of community, integrated with, but also distanced from, village life. The third Pilla Gudi was designed collaboratively by Altaf, Rajkumar, and Shantibai working with the children of Kopaweda. It is located near a small cluster of living spaces and workshops built by Dialogue at the edge of the village. The children wanted a space that could function simultaneously as a meeting place and a playground, so their early sketches describe a building with a low-pitched roof, connected to the ground by a series of smooth, flat buttresses. The completed structure follows this design quite closely, and allows the children to literally play on the roof of the building, again inverting traditional architectural syntax in which roof-as-shelter becomes roof-as-playground, or ceiling-as-heaven becomes ceiling-as-mirror. The children also asked that the Pilla Gudi be located at the periphery of the Dialogue compound, and that it face away from the other Dialogue buildings to create a space protected from adult scrutiny. As both the Nalpar sites and the Pilla Gudi suggest, visuality plays a crucial role in Dialogue's work; relationships of seeing and being seen, observation and reflection, are worked out in both the architectural form and the social operation of each of their projects. Like the Nalpar sites, the Pilla Gudi provides a space of enclosure and situational autonomy that encourages new modes of interaction and conviviality. The twelfth seat, the mirrored ceiling, and the roof-as-playground literalize the child's agency, their capacity to remake and reinvent the world, to act rather than being acted upon (see plate 9).

The production of art in Adivasi culture is traditionally governed by ritual protocols (totems, memorial pillars, etc.). Here the object's manufacture, the labor of its making, is swallowed up by its ceremonial or mnemonic function. The object is as natural and increate as the gods it signifies, or merely a vehicle for commemorative reflection. Dialogue's collaborative process had the effect of reframing the object and making visible the labor of its production in new ways. In particular, Dialogue's workshops and projects encouraged a recognition of the necessary contingency of the object, an attention to the object not as a vehicle for the transmission of some a priori meaning (the authority of a god, the memory of a loved one), but as something produced through certain formal techniques and stylistic norms. In making these conventions, and the agency of the artist who deploys them, visible, they also raised the possibility that these same conventions might be subject to change or transformation.[38] From the contingency of the created object they moved to the contingency of the rituals and institutions that structure village life. And it is this playful, transformative, spirit that led to the Pilla Gudi and the Nalpar.

If ritual constitutes one axis of object production in Kondagaon, the second is provided by the trade in Adivasi and tribal crafts among the agents and dealers who service metropolitan galleries, collectors, and art fairs. While some production for local ritual and worship still occurs, the bulk of the demand now comes from the urban and international art market. Jaidev Baghel's workshop trains dozens of young artists in bell metal sculpture and casting techniques to meet this demand. Baghel's sculptures incorporate traditional Adivasi themes and motifs (animal forms, gods and spirits, geometric patterns) that have existed for hundreds, if not thousands, of years. In fact, it is this very sense of integration, of Baghel's affiliation with an unbroken Adivasi tradition, which appeals to collectors. The work performs a kind of nostalgic reenactment of pre-modern India as a pastoral *Gemeinschaft*. If the artist's agency and the process of production are effaced in ritual, they are fetishized by the market. Baghel acts as the living embodiment of an ancient tradition in which the artist conveyed venerable truths in a common symbolic language.[39]

In this dynamic, Adivasi culture functions as the static, unchanging, antithesis to India's chaotic modernity. As I've already noted, Adivasi communities today are riven with distinctly modern forms of conflict and exploitation. But the discourse of tribal art discourages any direct reflection on, or representation of, this experience. We encounter here one of the central structuring oppositions of modern art, as it defines itself against the grain of the pre-modern. The pre-modern artist is, in this discourse, wholly integrated with his culture; there is no gap, no distance, in the signifying relationship between artist and society. But the artist pays a price for this intimacy and interdependence. He is entirely subordinate to that culture: incapable of independent or critical thought; de-individuated in the warm, but stifling, embrace of the collective. The modern artist, on the other hand, is an emblem of the pervasive alienation of modern life,

Temporal Register (Telos)

PRE-MODERN	MODERN
• Fixity	• Change
• Stasis of thought	• New insight or innovation
• Meaning is given	• Meaning is problematized

Spatial Register (Proximity)

PRE-MODERN	MODERN
• Integration	• Distance
• Individual artist is subordinate to the collective	• Individual artist is free and autonomous
• Art affirms dominant values	• Art critiques dominant (i.e., repressive) values

no longer able to identify with the values of his own society. The loss of his former sense of belonging is compensated for by a new, critical capacity that turns that distance to his advantage. His relationship to society becomes detached, critical, and ironic: the fearless individual holding out against the repression of *Das Man*.

The pre-modern artist functions here in a supplementary or subaltern capacity relative to the modern (implicitly Western) artist. Baghel's relationship to Adivasi culture, for example, can never be reflexive, distanced, or critical, only dependent and mimetic, while the modern artist must jealously guard his expressive autonomy against the imposition of shared or collective values. This relationship is structured by a set of oppositions that operate along both a spatial and a temporal axis. On the one hand is the shift from the artist submerged in the collective to the artist autonomous and distanced from the collective. And on the other is the shift from art that simply replicates or transmits dominant values to art that disrupts, critiques, or challenges those values. These resolve themselves into a set of ethical and aesthetic oppositions that privilege individuation, critical distance, and change over collectivity, integration, and stasis.

We encounter here a familiar art historical narrative that celebrates the triumph of the expressive individual over the collective, of innovation over tradition, and autonomy over interdependence. As I'll discuss shortly, the artist's ability to generate new insights and actively transform, rather than passively reflect, the surrounding social order bears the mark of an entrepreneurial model of subjectivity associated with the rise of bourgeois political culture. This narrative is, of course, reversible. In fact, a common trope within the modernist tradition of the nineteenth and early twentieth centuries involved the attempt to reconstruct or recover the lost ideal of an art that is integrated with, rather than alienated from, the social. By and large, however, the dominant model of avant-garde art during the modern period assumes that shared or collective values and systems of meaning are necessarily repressive and incapable of generating new insight or grounding creative praxis.

This assumption of the intrinsically repressive nature of collective experience and the redemptive power of individuation is a staple of contemporary art theory and criticism. I would argue that a closer analysis of collaborative and collective art practices can reveal a more complex model of social change and identity, one in which the binary oppositions of divided vs. coherent subjectivity, desiring singularity vs. totalizing collective, liberating distanciation vs. stultifying interdependence, are challenged and complicated. It is certainly necessary to maintain some critical distance from a given site of practice, and the complex constellation of forces, identities, and discourses that structure and subtend it. But this distance is not an absolute and constant characteristic of artistic subjectivity; it is not given by the artist's sheer existence and self-declaration as artist. Distance understood in this manner can lend itself to programmatic and insular forms of production in which the artist's a priori assumptions are never fully tested against the exigencies of site and situation, only imposed upon them. It entails a fundamentally passive notion of site as either a compliant receptacle for the artist's singular vision, or a set of compositional or scenic elements to be captured for subsequent use in film, video, or installation work. In these cases, aesthetic distanciation, far from generating new insight, can actually encourage the stasis or fixity of thought, and reproduce the prescriptive, administrative ethos of state-based institutions and agencies.

The practices under discussion here suggest a different model of practice. In Dialogue's work, for example, critical distance is produced out of the interactions that occur at a given site. This distance is always partial and contingent, coexisting with moments of relative integration or proximity in a diachronic unfolding. Insight is generated not via distance per se, but in the play that occurs between these moments. On the one hand, Dialogue's projects evolved out of a deep knowledge of Kondagaon accumulated through years of observation, interaction, and coexistence. They didn't approach the craft practices of the area from a position of exteriority, seeking to critique or dismantle them as symptoms of the regressive conservatism of village life. Nor did they romanticize them. They learned how to work productively within these traditions, even as they were able to maintain a productive distance from them. A recognition of the contingency of the crafted object opened out into a broader exploration of the plasticity of craft itself as a form of social architecture that could be mobilized to reshape village protocols. Their work is based neither on a claim of seamless integration with Adivasi culture, nor on an equally absolute distance from it. Rather, it affects a kind of toggling back and forth between inside and outside, engagement and observation, immersion and reflective distance, effectively producing a diagonal movement within the diagram above. Thus, forms of social integration can also produce new insight, while aesthetic distance can result in conceptual or cognitive stasis.

This cognitive movement is produced through the physical, discursive, and haptic experience of shared labor among Dialogue's members in the conceptual development and fabrication of the Nalpar and Pilla Gudi, and in their common habitation in the village. It is parallel to, and intertwined with, the pragmatic, applied labor necessary to design and construct the sites. The effect is a "co-laboring" of sorts, that is displaced from normal routines and reflectively conscious of the village as a social and spatial totality. It is a labor that is grounded in, and oriented toward, a practical end (the creation of a pump site), but at the same time not merely programmatic or mimetic (the physical enactment or reproduction of a pre-existing plan). Rather, the collaborators are conscious of the process of design and creation as provisional and generative. This labor is not realized or subsumed solely in the final product (the completed pump site), but in their own, transformed, consciousness of the village.

The workshop is a site at which village social protocols are both reinforced and, potentially, destabilized. While Jaidev's workshops at Shilpi Gram (in wood carving, bronze and bell metal sculpture, etc.) didn't exclude women, the normative conventions of art production in the village ensured that they continued to function primarily as assistants to men rather than working as artists in their own right. In many cases village women had to take jobs in farming, construction, and brick making in order to support their husband's art production. Any challenge to the male prerogative in art making was greeted by derision, hostility, and even violence. Shantibai's husband, a well-known wood carver named Raituram, was ridiculed by other men in the village when she began making her own sculptures with Navjot's support. He resented the attention that she received and they eventually divorced (although he finally reconciled with Altaf and supported her work in the village). The identity of "artist" was not given for Shantibai, but rather was something she had to consciously claim and reinvent. In this process she turned to the Adivasi tradition of the memorial pillar, which was typically used to commemorate a dead relative. Shantibai transformed the pillar, using it to mark and situate her own life story. She created a series of cylindrical columns combining memorable scenes and incidents (a drunken mason dangling from a scaffold, her first car ride, Rajkumar's motorbike) into an unfolding visual narrative. This re-authoring of self involved a claim of expressive agency, but it also had the effect of changing the nature of Adivasi art.[40] Inspired by Shantibai's example and Altaf's encouragement, several of the women who had been supporting or assisting male artists in Kopaweda began to produce their own work.

Dialogue's workshops are premised on the concept of craft not as a fixed tradition (the impoverished antithesis to the exemplary virtuosity of the modern avant-garde) but as a cultural practice that can be amended, transformed, and reconstituted. It is this recognition of the underlying plasticity of craft, and its reciprocal integration with a complex network of social and cultural conventions, which differentiates Dialogue's approach from the workshops at Shilpi Gram. At the same time, the replicability of craft practice is essential to the social operation of the workshop. Craft knowledge is discursive and transmissible. It is a skill that can be taught and passed on, and in doing so it provides a platform for shared labor that can be used to mobilize new relationships. A generative understanding of craft practices is well established in Indian culture. It was Gandhi, after all, who reclaimed the spinning wheel as a symbol of protest against English domination. In her book *When Was Modernism* the art historian and critic Geeta Kapur describes the complex cultural politics surrounding craft in

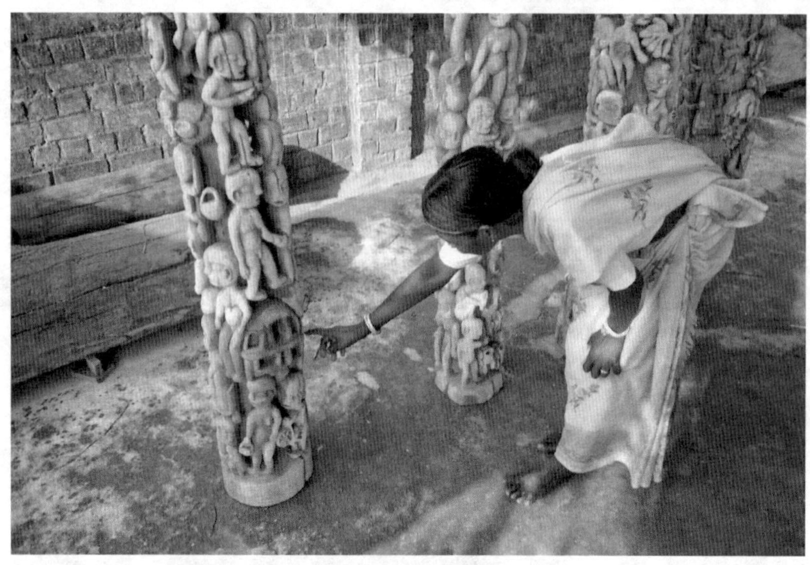

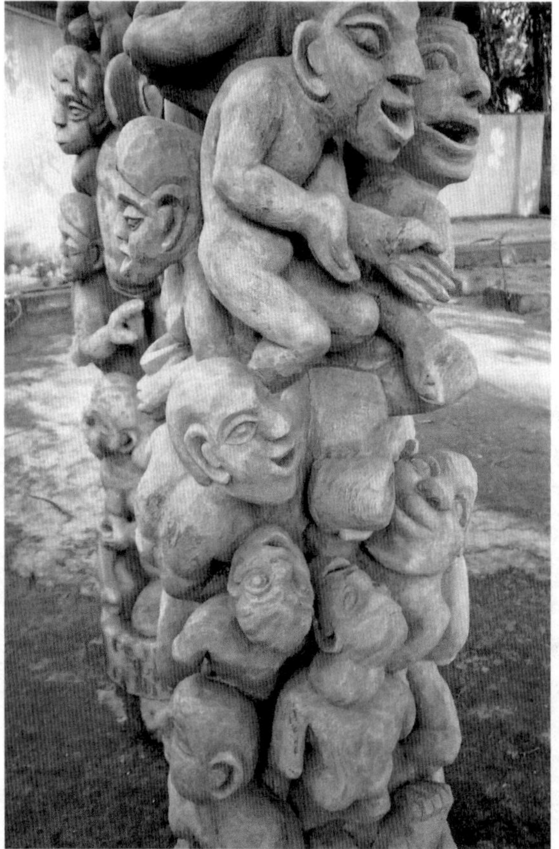

FIGURE 4 Shantibai with sculptures at the Dialogue center in Kopaweda, Kondagaon, Bastar District, Chhattisgarh, India (April 2007). Photograph by Grant Kester.

FIGURE 5 Shantibai with sculptures at the Dialogue center in Kopaweda, Kondagaon, Bastar District, Chhattisgarh, India (April 2007). Photograph by Grant Kester.

post-Independence India, beginning with K. G. Subramanyah's attempts to challenge the hegemony of European notions of fine art by valorizing India's artisanal practices as part of a "living tradition."[41] One trajectory of this valorization leads to the romanticized image of the tribal artisan that fuels the Indian craft market, and provides support for many of Kondagoan's artists. However, it is important to recall Gandhi's insistence that the spinning wheel was not merely a symbol of resistance but also an organizational tool, capable of altering the balance of economic power between India and Great Britain through the cultivation of domestic textile production.

The workshops initiated by Dialogue encouraged the emergence of new temporalities and new forms of social interaction. Their work requires the kind of deep understanding of site, and the social structures of village life, that comes only with long habitation and a recognition of the full complexity of craft and artisanal production. At the same time, it requires an understanding of craft, gender norms, or caste divisions as something available to be reshaped, redeployed, and experientially tested. Throughout this process, Altaf has consistently sought to problematize her own position as an urban, non-Adivasi artist. Altaf, Rajkumar, Shantibai, and Gessuram developed a set of performative protocols to guide the decision-making processes necessary to work together creatively and minimize implicit hierarchies (acknowledging differing forms of communication—written vs. verbal—differing notions of time and duration, models of decision making, kinesthetics, conventions, etc.). Any collectively generated written material (statements, grant applications, etc.) is produced by transcribing a series of conversations, circulating the transcripts, discussing them in subsequent conversations, and then engaging in further revisions of the final text. They've also worked together to collectively define a series of key words related to their practice ("interaction," "labor," "criticism," "dialogue," etc.) that expose some of the significant conceptual and cultural differences between Hindu and Adivasi culture.[42]

In her work at Kondagaon, Altaf has refused the role of the nomadic provocateur who appears briefly at a given site, stages an "intervention," and then departs. Nor would she claim to speak with any absolute authority on behalf of Adivasi or peasant experience in India. Both positions effectively bypass the question of ethics—the first by claiming a capacity for ironic detachment or critical distanciation that ostensibly renders such questions irrelevant, and the second by assuming a natural correspondence between the artist's interests and those of her collaborators. And both positions are equally naive. The point of attending to the specific epistemological and material effects of collaborative labor and dialogue is not to effect yet another reversal, privileging dialogue and physical interaction as somehow more authentic, or less instrumentalizing, than textual or specular modes of experience. It is, rather, to understand what is different about these modes of interaction as a form of creative practice. "To speak," as Luce Irigaray reminds us, is "never neutral."[43] Nor is bodily knowledge or interaction ever "outside" power. While Altaf, Raj Kumar, Shantibai, and Geesu have made a concerted effort to acknowledge differences of power and privilege, the fact remains that Altaf's class and caste status, as well as her position as a metropolitan artist, have provided her with educational opportunities, material comfort, and a level of access to national and international art circuits that is largely unavailable to her collaborators.

At the same time, this privilege is ambivalent. When Altaf first arrived in Kondagaon she was treated with a superficial deference due to her caste, but she was also viewed with considerable suspicion for the same reason. Jaidev Baghel and many of the male artists at Shilpi Gram were especially resistant to her extended presence, fearing that she was there simply to appropriate Adivasi forms and styles. In a thinly veiled criticism, he complained to Altaf that, "All the failures from the city come here, take advantage of this place, go back [to the city], get romanticized and become famous."[44] Notwithstanding the fact that Navjot chose to remain in Kondagaon, and that she had already achieved recognition as an artist before her arrival, Baghel's comment reflects a legitimate fear of the colonizing tendencies of urban artists in India (and elsewhere). Taken in conjunction with Altaf's willingness to question gender relationships in Kondagaon (encouraging the movement of women into art production and intervening when she would witness incidents of domestic violence or abuse in public), the result was a lengthy period of subtle and not-so-subtle hostility among several of the men in the village toward her work there. It was only after several years of sustained engagement and the demonstration of her commitment to Kondagaon as a site of practice and not simply a reservoir of stylish indigeneity, that Altaf was able to build a network of collaborators and establish sufficient trust within the village community to work in a sustained manner.

Differences of cultural capital, access, and mobility inevitably had an impact on Altaf's interactions within the village, as well as her reception in the global art world. They are unavoidable precisely because Altaf has chosen to work across boundaries of class and caste. The goal of Dialogue is not to magically dissolve these tensions, or to produce some ideal and unconstrained model of community, but rather to make the negotiation and the "working through" of difference an explicit part of their practice. Francis Alÿs, as I noted above, attempted to insulate himself from these tensions by working with architecture and engineering students from Lima rather than with the residents of Ventanilla, where his performance was actually staged. His use of the students as metaphoric stand-ins created a distance between the image he sought to create and the actual site of failed modernity that was both literal and figurative, even as it produced another set of instrumentalizing relationships around that very act of representation. He further emphasized this poetic segregation through his strategic disavowal of agency and accountability for the performance itself ("Whether the first part, the day itself, belongs to me, to the volunteers . . . or to the dune itself, I would personally find difficult to tell"). As with Altaf's work, these are both ethical and aesthetic decisions, or rather, they point to the inevitable imbrication of ethical and aesthetic concerns in collaborative practice.

THE ATELIER AS WORKSHOP — 4

The workshop has emerged as a significant nexus of creative production in a wide range of collaborative and collective projects. Thomas Hirschhorn's *Bataille Monument,* discussed above, featured workshops and media training for Turkish youth, and Park Fiction (whose work will be discussed in the following chapter) generated ideas for its Hamburg park through a series of informal planning workshops. Other groups that have developed the workshop as a method of production include Sarai Media Lab in Delhi (in their *Cybermohalla* project), Partners for Urban Knowledge, Action and Research (PUKAR) in Mumbai, Networking and Initiatives for Culture and the Arts (NICA) in Yangon, Myanmar, Oda Projesi in Istanbul, Tranvia Cero in Quito, and Torolab and Bulbo in Tijuana. U.S. examples include Ha Ha's influential *Flood* project in Chicago, Temporary Services Prisoners' Invention workshops, Temescal Amity Works in Oakland, and Rick Lowe's *Project Row Houses* in Houston (discussed in chapter 3). There are also numerous examples of projects grounded in direct action and participatory planning that parallel art-based forms of cultural activism, such as the media workshops developed as part of the Prestes Maia occupations in São Paulo between 2002 and 2007, Can Masdeu's environmental workshops in Barcelona, and Max Rameau's *Take Back the Land* project in Liberty City, Florida. Interest in the workshop as a social form has grown in conjunction with a critical remobilization of craft practices, evident in Littoral's engagement with textile production in England and Ala Plastica's interest in willow cultivation in the Rio de la Plata basin.

These concerns are also evident in the work of the Dakar-based group Huit Facettes Interaction. Huit Facettes was formed in 1995 when eight Sénégalese artists (Moustapha Dim, Abdoulaye Ndoye, Amadou Kane Sy, Fodé Camara, Cheikh Niass, Serigne Mbaye Camara, El Hadj Sy, and Jean Marie Bruce) traveled to Belgium at the invitation of a Flemish art center in Turnhout.[45] During their visit they met members of Vredeseilanden, a Belgian NGO that supports sustainable agricultural practices for family farmers, with a particular focus on the global South. The artists were surprised to learn that Vredeseilanden was organizing projects in Sénégal, and arranged to visit the area where the NGO was active when they returned home. It was this visit that led them to the village of Hamdallaye Samba Mbaye in the south of Sénégal, near the Gambian border. Working in collaboration with Vredeseilanden, they developed Les Ateliers d'Hamdallaye (The Workshops of Hamdallaye) in 1996, recovering the nineteenth-century tradition of the atelier as a site of learning, exchange, and shared labor, rather than cloistered isolation.

For Les Ateliers d'Hamdallaye they invited artists and filmmakers from Flanders, French-speaking Belgium, Rwanda, Dakar, and southern Sénégal to work with them for a period of two weeks in Hamdallaye, developing projects that responded to the culture and influences of the region. As Amadou Kane Sy wrote, the program was conceived "as a way of bringing together contemporary urban artists, a village community and a nongovernmental organization. The issues faced in the project could be traced

to relationships and ties within a precisely demarcated social territory—
a rural one—since the workshops fostered interaction between spheres
that are traditionally alien to one another."[46] While the resulting artworks
included paintings, drawings, sculptures, and animations, these interactions—European with African, Rwandan with Sénégalese, rural with
urban—were an equally important part of the project. The atelier became a
center for cultural, social, and artistic exchanges, not simply among the invited artists but also among and with the residents of Hamdallaye, through
a series of workshops devoted to fabric dying, glass painting, embroidery,
sculpture, soap making, and other crafts, organized by Huit Facettes member Fodé Camara.

The Atelier of Hamdallaye project both emulated and complimented a
Sénégalese practice of week-long cultural festivals in which a given village
community invites artists from surrounding villages to live with them and
share their work. The festivals began a few years earlier in the villages east
of Kéréwane. As Kane Sy observes, "During these periods of celebration
[*réjouissance*], all of the different villages that live in the zone were invited
inside one of the villages, which was responsible for organizing the event.
This offered everyone the chance to exchange their different cultural and
agricultural practices."[47] In fact, Huit Facettes was invited to Hamdallaye
specifically to participate in one of these festivals. The festivals provide
more than simply an opportunity to share craft skills or farming techniques. They have come to play an important role in maintaining the social
ecology of the region and are credited by many with the relative absence of
significant interethnic and intertribal conflict among village communities
in the area around Hamdallaye. The co-presence of artists from different
villages and different tribal and ethnic backgrounds, sharing knowledge,
culture, food, and shelter has had a transformative effect.

In fact, Sénégal has a long history of peaceful coexistence among diverse ethnic and tribal communities.[48] One of the Atelier of Hamdallaye
projects, an animated film developed by Rwandan and Sénégalese youth
working with a visiting filmmaker from Belgium, focused specifically on
this tradition. *Message to our Rwandan Brothers* used sculpted chairs (constructed of earth, straw, and other natural materials) to represent quarrel-
ing individuals who are finally reconciled around a table, as a background
chorus chants: "Friend from Rwanda, if I could get a ticket to go visit you
and comfort your troubles, I would come right away." The film draws on a

Wolof proverb that states: "There is no misunderstanding, there is only a lack of working together." It is this tradition that Huit Facettes sought to honor, expanding the scale of the interaction from the local to the global. They have a particular interest in the political implications of these exchanges, seeking to reverse the process by which cultural institutions in Europe and North America, by virtue of their economic resources, exert a centripetal influence as nodal points of production, exchange, and discourse in the global art world.

Their goal isn't to curtail international exchange, but to decenter it. Rather than Sénégalese artists meeting in Belgium, for example, they will organize events that bring artists together in the countries of the global South, challenging the geopolitical privilege of the North. By rooting these exchanges in the proximate conditions, spaces, and protocols of Dakar or Hamdallaye, for example, rather than London or New York, the character of the interactions will be transformed, responding to an African context rather than the (naturalized) Euro-American framework of the international art scene. This form of horizontal rather than vertical interaction is a key part of Huit Facette's practice. As Kane Sy has noted, "Until recently, it was easier for African artists coming from English, Portuguese, Spanish or French speaking countries to meet others in the North (Europe, US, etc.). Until now everything or nearly everything was conceived, determined, and run by the West (market forces, corporate spearheads [*fer de lance*] and advancement of the neoliberal economy is largely to blame). In my view, to create working relations in the sense of 'south-south' is to offer the opportunity to have access to things in a world whose history and geopolitics are differentiated from ours."[49]

Following the success of Les Ateliers d'Hamdallaye, Huit Facettes went on to produce a similar workshop-based event, *Ici et Maintenant* (or *Here and Now*) in Joal-Fadiouth, outside Dakar, in 1998. The process of geopolitical de-centering in these projects operates not only in the relationship between Europe and Africa, but also across the divisions between the rural and the urban, and rich and poor, in Sénégal itself. The Nigerian critic Okwui Enwezor has noted Huit Facette's concern with the "increasing social stratification that defined the relationship between the elite and the poor in the city, a stratification that also had impoverished the relationship of their individual work [as artists] to the society in which it was produced." "This stratification and alienation," as Enwezor notes, "is even more acute in the lines that separate rural and urban communities in Senegal."[50] Kane-Sy has described Huit Facette's work in rural Sénégal as "a procedure or process that . . . has given us [contemporary Sénégalese artists living in the city] a point of anchorage or reconciliation with the part of society that feeds us and from which we were cut off. One particular elite rejoins its roots in the same socio-cultural context."[51]

The significance of this shift of emphasis (from the urban to the rural) should not be underestimated in an art world that continues to privilege the city as the only relevant site of art practice and dissemination (evident in the tendency to identify major biennial exhibitions with particular cities, and in the ongoing relationship between new museum construction and the process of urban redevelopment). As Kane-Sy writes, "It is habitual to think that art may, and must, rhyme with urban existence alone."[52] The core/periphery logic of globalization thus reiterates a more general prejudice within the discourse of modernism that contrasts the city, as the site of an advanced, cosmopolitan culture, with the conservatism, stagnation, and "idiocy," in Marx's famous words, of rural life. The renewed interest in rural cultures and contexts evident in the work of Huit Facettes and Dialogue, as well as groups such as Ala Plastica, Littoral Arts, and the collaborative team of Tim Collins and Reiko Goto, has effectively challenged this simplistic opposition, drawing attention to the complex changes being registered in the countryside through the process of globalization, and exploring the necessary interdependence of the urban and the rural.[53]

Les Ateliers d'Hamdallaye shares several important features with the work of Dialogue. First, it unsettled the metropolitan bias of art practice in Sénégal and created a space in which rural and urban artists could experience a rapprochement. Seydou Wane, the head of Vredeseilanden at Kolda, described Les Ateliers d'Hamdallaye as "a sort of reconciliation between the city and the country . . . each wants to go toward the other. Now for the people of Hamdallaye the village is practically a monument. And in Dakar, all those artists want to return to Hamdallaye. One has to feel something very profound [happened] here."[54] It also involved the strategic mobilization of craft practices. This engagement with craft had two, related, effects. First, the exchange of craft skills facilitated some degree of economic independence and autonomy for women in the village, who were able to sell their work to neighboring villages and participate in what had previously been male-dominated circuits of craft production and sale.

And second, the shared labor of the cultural festival functioned to encourage intertribal and interethnic dialogue (the same process unfolded in Dialogue's work in Kondagaon across caste lines, and with Hindu and Adivasi participants).

5 — LABOR, PRAXIS, AND REPRESENTATION

The question of labor brings us back to *When Faith Moves Mountains* and Francis Alÿs's shoveling students. While Alÿs acknowledged the generative power of the performance itself for the participants, his primary concern was with the image of the event as a symbolic resource denoting the futility of Latin American modernization. This notion of failed or futile labor is not unique to Alÿs, of course, but has emerged in a number of recent art projects. Thus, we have Phil Collins's Palestinian teenagers dancing themselves into exhaustion in *They Shoot Horses* (2004); Artur Zmijewski's *The Singing Lesson I* (2001), in which deaf and mute students attempt to sing a mass in a Polish church; and Santiago Sierra's various "underclass" representatives, paid to perform meaningless or idiosyncratic tasks (e.g., *Workers Who Cannot Be Paid, Remunerated to Remain Inside Cardboard Boxes* in 2000, and *Worker's Arm Passing Through the Ceiling of an Art Space from a Dwelling* in 2004). Labor in contemporary art is typically figured as inefficient, irrational, or oppressive because of its perceived complicity with a generalized discourse of instrumentalizing productivity that ranges from the exploitation of the market system to the semantic processes of language. The alternately grueling or quixotic tasks assigned to Alÿs's students or Sierra's unemployed workers will, in this scenario, reveal the monstrous conceit behind any attempt to "produce" meaning, change, or collectivity.

The conventional, representational, relationship to labor conveyed by Sierra's work has a venerable history, extending back at least as far as Courbet, whose *Stonebreakers* presented the laboring body as a calculated affront. It is subtended, however, by two more-complex registers of meaning. The first concerns the symbolic value of the artist's own labor, which offers a model of authentic creativity defined in implicit opposition to the alienated labor of the market system. The artist's labor, in the act of creation, marks an autonomous and free exercise of will, as beauty (or transgressive meaning) is extracted from the dross of quotidian reality. The second register involves the hermeneutic labor required of the viewer when confronted with difficult or challenging works of art (discussed earlier in my analysis of Schiller). The modern viewer is obliged to "work"—cognitively, perceptually—against the semantic resistance posed by the complex art object. In the presence of such works, he or she will experience amazement, discomfort, shock, and outrage, while cultivating a more enlightened, self-reflective mode of subjectivity. As with the first register, this labor is defined in implicit opposition to the banal, programmatic forms of perception that are presumed to characterize our normal existence. In fact, we might say that modern avant-garde art is defined precisely by the (naturalized) tension between these two registers of labor (the exemplary labor of the artist's production and the corresponding mimetic labor of the viewer's reception). The viewer's consciousness, like the natural world, is a malleable resource set in place before the shaping will of the artistic personality.

The dialogical projects under discussion here present a mode of collaborative art practice in which the tension between semantic and symbolic labor is not collapsed per se but openly thematized and made an explicit object of inquiry and creative engagement, and in which the linkage between creativity and a certain form of singularized aggression and self assertion is de-naturalized. In the projects of Dialogue, Park Fiction, Ala Plastica, Huit Facettes, and other groups, we can identify a form of collaborative interaction that has the capacity to transform the consciousness of its participants and to disclose new modes of being-together (precisely the point that Jean Fisher wished to make about the *Faith* performance). As I've already noted with Altaf's work, this is a labor that occurs through the thickly textured haptic and discursive exchanges that unfold in these projects over a period of months and even years. It is linked in turn with a cognitive movement, a reflective shuttling or oscillation, between contingency and freedom, figure and ground, immersion and distanciation, which generates new insight. We can discover a number of precedents for this categorical movement in the genealogy of post-structuralism. Bataille, in *The Accursed Share*, advocates a liberating play between submission and transgression. Law as such is inevitable, according to Bataille, and any attempt to challenge it directly only leads to a new set of interdictions (as we see in post-Revolutionary France or Russia). Instead of seeking to overturn the law, we should use it for our own purposes, transforming the pain of punishment into the pleasure of a subversive *jouissance*. We might also consider Julia Kristeva's concept of the "thetic" subject shifting between unity and division, or her quasi-Schillerian notion of a poetry that addresses both the present reader and a reader "yet to come."[55]

More recently, Jacques Rancière has resuscitated this line of thought in his analysis of the aesthetic (discussed above), in which art is neither fully collapsed into the political nor entirely autonomous from it, but rather gains its power from its ambiguous or "undecideable" location between autonomy and subordination.[56] He offers a parallel formulation in his treatment of reception in "The Emancipated Spectator." Here Rancière attempts to transcend the false opposition between an immersive notion of theater (in which the viewer passively consumes the material presented on stage) and a theater that seeks to "activate" the spectator by collapsing the barrier between stage and audience (the correlation with recent debates in artistic practice is apparent). This latter strategy inevitably succumbs to the "demand that the theater achieve, as its essence, the gathering of an un-separate community" based on the "Platonic assignment of bodies to their proper—that is, to their 'communal'—place." The spectator is thereby "restored to the status of a member of a community . . . carried off in a flood of the collective energy."[57] Here, again, we encounter the Manichean juxtaposition of two equally untenable positions. Conventional "immersive" theater, which seeks only to manipulate viewers and render them docile, is contrasted with an experimental theater that claims to activate the viewer on behalf of some naively metaphysical notion of "community." Rancière's resolution to this impasse takes the form of a "third way" that "invalidates the opposition between activity and passivity . . . and the communitarian idea of the theater that . . . makes it an allegory of inequality." As he elaborates:

> The crossing of borders and the confusion of roles shouldn't lead to a kind of "hyper-theater," turning spectatorship into activity by turning representation into presence. On the contrary, the theater should question its privileging of living presence and bring the stage back to a level of equality with the telling of a story or the writing and the reading of a

book. . . . It calls for spectators who are active interpreters, who render their own translation, who appropriate the story for themselves, and who ultimately make their own story out of it. An emancipated community is in fact a community of storytellers and translators.[58]

Rancière returns us, not surprisingly, to Barthes's "writerly text" and the notion of the reader, or viewer, as an empowered "producer" of meaning ("The goal of literary work . . . is to make the reader no longer a consumer, but a producer of the text").[59] The author's death in this scenario is, of course, largely rhetorical: authors still exist and are more necessary than ever in order to provide newly empowered readers with sufficient material to catalyze their own agency. The terms of Rancière's contract are revealing. A "Platonic" theater of "community" based on the privileging of "presence," and indifferent to processes of representation, is utterly incapable of inculcating any critical distance or insight. For that, we still require the conventional spatial and institutional categories of the "learned" author and the receptive but somnolent reader. Thus, Rancière warns us against a too hasty inversion of the intellectual authority of the author or artist. "We don't need to turn spectators into actors," he writes. "We needn't turn the ignorant into the learned or, merely out of a desire to overturn things, make the student or the ignorant person the master of his masters."[60] Determinant agency continues to rest with the "master," while the reader is allowed a compensatory form of emancipation by "translating" the author's text in his or her own terms.

The text, the "mediating third" that both links and bifurcates author and reader, viewer and work, self and other, is necessary to guard against the objectification and instrumentalization that is the inevitable consequence of any attempt to achieve a more direct relationship to others. In the absence of this tutelage the reader will relapse into a naive faith in referential meaning and lose sight of the productive indeterminancy of all signifiers. Authority as such is not dissolved or questioned, but simply displaced. Rancière retains key elements of Schiller's "aesthetic education," as the bringing-to-consciousness of the un-enlightened by an advanced cadre of artists and poets. The deferral and displacement that is characteristic of the aesthetic is thus premised on a necessary gap between (transformed) consciousness and (subsequent) action. Enlightenment or emancipation must precede action in the world. While the specific form taken by this action can't be anticipated, its broader orientation is dependent on the a priori transformation of a guiding intelligence.

These are by now familiar, even conventional, formulations, both influencing and influenced by the "third way" logic of May '68 that I outlined earlier. While they are helpful in expanding our understanding of cognitive movement, they remain oddly dependent on an oppositional system of meaning in which certain static functions or states of being (the "centered" and "de-centered" subject, art that is wholly autonomous from the political and art that is entirely subordinate to it, "passive" and "active" viewers, etc.) are presumed to exist in order to justify a particular notion of transgression. There is a tendency among artists informed by this tradition to project generic theoretical postulates onto a given context, situation, or site: to treat site as an opportunity to "discover" these ostensibly hidden structures (centered identities, fixed meanings, etc.) as if they were ideological subtexts buried in a Victorian novel, only in order to reveal them to the astonished reader. As a result, art practice rehearses the same revelatory gesture, the same disclosure of contingency and structural determination, in an almost compulsive manner. Like Marx's hazy images of life following the revolution, we never investigate the productive movement that might occur after the obligatory admission of contingency is extracted from the viewer.

Over the past decade this approach has become ubiquitous in contemporary art. In less skillful hands it can have the effect of blinding the practitioner to the generative complexity and contradiction of a given site, reducing it instead to a kind of embodied illustration of theoretical axioms. Nor does this tradition offer a convincing account of how cognitive movement might actually be produced in and through practice, rather than simply compelled by the presentation of a particular image, scene, or event. It is this notion of practice as a sequential unfolding, extended through the cumulative experience of discrete moments of interaction and negotiation, conflict and reconciliation, which interests me in the work of Dialogue, Huit Facettes, Park Fiction, and other groups. This is also why I consider a revised concept of labor of particular importance in theorizing this work. Unfortunately, concepts of labor and duration are anathema in recent theory and criticism, which instead prize the instantaneous, the sublime, and the "un-worked."[61] Art must be precisely the inverse of labor (understood as coerced, externally imposed, and temporally extensive) to play its assigned cultural role.

Jean Luc-Nancy's writing on community is emblematic in this regard. Community, for Nancy, can only be ethically constituted if it arises in an instant, in a moment of "unworked" epiphany. As soon as the experience of community involves a durationally extended process of social and discursive exchange, it descends into mythic essentialism. Thus, Nancy's "inoperative" community is a "workless and inoperative activity. It is not a matter of making, producing or instituting a community," and "community is given to us—or we are given and abandoned to the community; a gift to be renewed and communicated, it is not a work to be done or produced."[62] In his understandable desire to foreclose the potential violence of direct, intersubjective exchange, Nancy reduces all human labor ("work," "making," "production,") to a simple expression of conative aggression, functioning only to master and negate difference. The result is a fetishization of simultaneity (cf., the sublime, shock, or disruption) and a failure to conceive of the knowledge produced through durational, collective interaction as anything other than compromised, totalizing, and politically abject. Labor can only ever be the domain of coercion and exploitation, irrevocably linked with the fixed ontological structure of bourgeois subjectivity (centered and violently instrumentalizing).

We encounter a similar tension around verbal and haptic experience in the post-structuralist tradition, beginning with Saussure's decision to concentrate exclusively on language (as a synchronic totality) at the expense of an investigation of the diachronic processes of human speech (he famously considered speech acts, or parole, an unsuitable object of "scientific" inquiry). Derrida extends this schism in his opposition between the "phonocentrism" of speech (the realm of authorial presence and Platonic truth) and the ludic domain of *écriture*. Only the written text is open to the liberatory play of meaning, while speaking and listening, and by implication, the haptic texture of human social exchange, is consigned to the realm of logocentric fixity.[63] While there is nothing that makes reading a book or watching a play any less active than any other form of mediated social interaction, neither is there anything that makes it *more* active or more likely to encourage reflective engagement. One need not subscribe to phonocentric notions of presence to believe that forms of social interactions outside those mediated by authored texts, crafted objects or scripted events are subject to their own unique conditions and capable of producing different experiential effects. These tendencies have discouraged a deeper engagement with diachronic experience and with the process of collective and collaborative interaction in contemporary critical theory. In order to move beyond this impasse it is necessary to investigate more closely the historical emergence of the much-reviled bourgeois subjectivity and its relationship to modern concepts of labor.

6 — THE DIVIDED AND INCOMPLETE SUBJECT OF YESTERDAY

Labor, in the early modern period, must be understood as a predicative term, emerging in conjunction with its counterpart: property. It was the mobility of property, the novel idea of possession as a right that could be earned, and lost, that set the modern period apart. The movement of landed property was, of course, always virtual, a transfer of rights, but it had a profound significance.[64] This "great transformation" was not simply economic; it dramatically changed the way in which political subjectivity was defined in the early modern era.[65] One's social status, for so long predestined by birth and blood, could now be radically altered by the creative externalization of self in the act of rendering nature productive. This new model of identity arises in the context of a changing political scene in Europe, associated with the emergence of a proto-capitalist class of merchants and gentry. Its earliest manifestations occur in England, in response to the pressure exerted by economically powerful, but un-titled, landowners during the 1600s and early 1700s. One of the principal targets of this nascent class was the concept of divine right. The king must be obeyed because, within the great chain of being, he sits in closest proximity to God. Further, man must accept his natural subordination within the hierarchy of religious and secular power.

We encounter the first significant challenge to this system in the natural law tradition of the early seventeenth century, which sought to construct new forms of political legitimation in the face of the gradual desacralization of authority in early modern Europe. The tattered canopies of God and King would be replaced by the self-legislating subject of liberal humanism; a subject whose identity is predicated on the possession of inherent powers or faculties as well as on the physical possession of property. The natural law tradition identified certain quasi-anthropological moments rooted in the distant past (if not in the constitution of the human personality itself), which could be used to ground and legitimate the new political claims of the third estate. For the Dutch jurist Hugo Grotius and the theorist Samuel Freiherr von Pufendorf, two leading exponents of the natural law tradition, the "state of nature" was a communal affair in which God gave the resources of the earth to all men in common. As Grotius wrote in *De jure belli ac pacis libri tres* (1625):

> Soon after the creation of the world, and a second time after the Flood, God conferred upon the human race, a general right over things of a lower nature.... In consequence, each man could at once take whatever he wished for his own needs, and could consume whatever was capable of being consumed.[66]

In this "original community of the land" (*communio fundi originari*) everyone is free to take what he or she needs from the common land in order to survive. Eventually, this condition of divinely mandated communism gave way to some form of private possession (earned by labor, not endowed by God). The transition from common access to private property was crucial for seventeenth- and eighteenth-century European political thought.

Property, and most importantly, the act of possession, emerge in the philosophy of the Enlightenment as one of the chief markers of legitimate subject status—not merely the possession of property, but more specifically, the faculty of possession, as it is exercised by the subject. This performative aspect is essential. One becomes a subject through the act of possessing things as property. This socially and historically contingent act is at the same time founded on an inherent capacity of the human subject; it brings this subject into harmony with universal moral laws. Labor and property are linked by the power attributed to labor in transforming both nature, and, crucially, the laboring subject. This is articulated through the natural law concept of the extension of personality. Grotius and Pufendorf predicate their account of property on the division between the "I," or what philosopher Karl Olivecrona terms the "spiritual ego," and the body. The I is the foundational site of identity; it possess the body and the actions of the body. Taken together, the body and its actions constitute the individual's suum, "that which belongs" to the individual. Thus, according to Grotius, "life, body, limbs, reputation, honor, and our own actions belong to ourselves."[67] Of particular importance is the fact that the suum can be extended to encompass things outside the subject's body. This "extension of personality" is such that one can acquire a moral warrant for these things (land, goods, and so on) and incorporate them into the suum. Once these things are assimilated into the personality, any attempt to remove or damage them constitutes an injury that is morally commensurate to physical harm to the body.[68] We should think of the suum not simply in terms of a spatial metaphor (as the "sphere" of the subject), but also as a faculty or power to assimilate and extend this sphere on the basis of a moral justification.[69]

The postulates of the natural law tradition gradually coalesce into more coherent form in early liberal political philosophy, which will contend that a social order based on the primacy of property and individual possession is intrinsically egalitarian and will naturally prevent the systematic inequality and arbitrary abuses of power characteristic of absolutist government. The discipline imposed by the vicissitudes of the market, and internalized by each individual at the behavioral level, will replace the external authority previously exercised by an omiscient God or monarch. This system is not, however, without its own internal contradictions. The only way you can achive subjectivity, and experience freedom, is at the expense of an "other" person or thing which serves as the vehicle through which you actualize, experience, and express that subjectivity. Within the larger economy (of identity-as-capital) there must always be something that you own or possess—a constant supply of material to be controlled, transformed or appropriated.[70] The actual form taken by the property is less important than the kind of relationship that it sets in place between you and the world around you. It is an active, acquisitive relationship in which the world exists as the vehicle for your own redemption and fulfillment as a subject.[71]

The possibility that one's subjectivity, one's status as a subject, can be expanded or enhanced, as well as eroded or diminished, creates a fundamental instability within bourgeois society. The bourgeois subject is not autonomous and internally coherent, but intrinsically permeable and dependent (on the labor of others and on a continuing supply of materials, frontiers, or "things of a lower nature") for its self-constitution.[72] Further, the relative privilege, the ontic spaciousness, of the bourgeois subject, far from being earned through a fair and equal competition, the outcome of which offers a meaningful indication of the relative fortitude of their conative drive, is, in fact, biased by preexisting distortions in the field of social and economic opportunity (in Locke's time, the fact that the common or unclaimed land on which a subject might actualize his will, and achieve political sovereignty, was being rapidly enclosed by the already wealthy landowners who controlled Parliament).

On the one hand, labor is proof of the superiority of the bourgeoisie to the parasitic and effete aristocracy, and on the other, a reminder of the contingency of its hard-won status. The myth of its absolute autonomy can only be sustained by an active suppression or denial of this underlying dependence on the labor of the Other. In the social sphere, this suppression is produced through an ethical discourse that identifies the non-propertied (the poor or working class) as failed subjects whose powers of appropriation are insufficiently developed (from which flows a long tradition of conservative political discourse that views the poor as lazy, morally depraved, etc.).[73] Thus, bourgeois identity, at its earliest stages, is divided and relational.[74] The decisive shift is from a static identity (dependent on fixed proximity to God or King) to an identity that is produced through labor (the externalization of will and the extraction of value via the transformative effect of labor), as a model of economic activity replaces a model of metaphysical hierarchy as the basis of identity claims.

This performative understanding of identity differentiates modern, bourgeois, subjectivity from the relatively fixed ontology of pre-modern identity. The essentially fluid, processual, status of bourgeois identity, and its dependence on a possessive relationship to the external world (and a competitive relationship to other subjects), introduces certain tensions around modes of collective or communal solidarity that might impinge on or restrict the expressive powers of the individual bourgeois subject. It also results in a moral economy based on an economic vitalism in which the possession of wealth is viewed as evidence of a superior productive capacity and, by extension, an enhanced social status. As I will discuss in chapter 3, it is precisely the concept of a fundamental "conative" drive to expand the self, drawn from Spinoza and the traditions of natural law, that Deleuze will employ in developing a notion of radical singularity in his own writing. The free exercise of this conative power, its enhancement and extension, becomes the precondition for an ethical form of being.

The arid proceduralism of natural law thus carries a radical implication. Bourgeois identity is marked by a colonizing expansion of self, yes, but also an opening out of self to Otherness. It has no intrinsic substance, only a potential or capacity, waiting to be actualized by the subject through their engagement with the material and social world. The common roots of both bourgeois subjectivity and modern artistic identity are apparent in this formulation.[75] What is decisive about bourgeois subjectivity is not its relational or contingent status per se, but rather, the way in which this relational identity is mobilized. One can easily enough acknowledge one's de-centered and dependent status and nonetheless continue to behave in an objectifying and instrumentalizing manner. This is evident in the tradition of evangelical Christianity that developed in Europe and the United States in the eighteenth and early nineteenth centuries (a variant of which continues to exercise a decisive influence on American culture and political life to the present day). Striving to attract an emerging middle and lower-middle-class audience, evangelicals such as John Wesley, William Wilberforce, and, later, Henry Ward Beecher and Henry Grandison Finney, jettisoned the limiting, Calvinist notion of predestination. Instead, entrepreneurial Christian subjects could perform their own salvation, bypassing church hierarchies and establishing a personal relationship to God. This shocking exercise of free will was legitimated by a deliberate display of self-abnegation before the supreme authority of Christ. In so doing, evangelicals could simultaneously embrace their own broken and divided condition while also enjoying a drastic expansion of self and conative power through identification with a God-like moral authority. "It is the description of real Christians," as Wilberforce writes, "that they are gradually changed into the image of their Divine Master."[76] There are, it is clear, many ways to be de-centered.

Despite this complex history, the notion of the naively self-identical bourgeois subject remains an idée fixe for many contemporary artists and art theorists. For both the modernist avant-garde and the discourse of bourgeois liberalism, the conative drive is understood as a quasi-anthropological feature of human subjectivity—its primary motive force. From Alfred Jarry to the most recent Venice Biennale, the avant-garde has often defined itself in opposition to what it perceives as a paradigmatic bourgeois identity: a Piñata-like caricature that embodies all the most reviled characteristics of the boorish middle class: its heedless narcissism, its reactionary fear of difference, and its destructive compulsion to extract profit from every possible source. By the 1980s, under the influence of Continental philosophy and its critique of the Enlightenment, this figure gained a new theoretical pedigree and was reborn as the Cartesian subject. A more sophisticated incarnation of the bourgeois subject, the soul-destroying power of the Cartesian subject was seen to reside not simply in its class origins, but in its very ontological condition: centered, autonomous, and self-identical. The necessary antidote to this mode of subjectivity was a shattering dislocation: exposing the false consciousness of bourgeois subjectivity via the quasi-religious revelation that its cherished selfhood is actually relational, de-centered, and contingent.

The relationship of the artist to the viewer implied by this tradition is essentially adjudicatory and conspiratorial. It transposes the generic attributes of a stereotypically bourgeois sensibility onto the viewer, who is assumed to possess a "natural" inclination toward reductive or instrumentalizing behavior that requires remediation and correction by the work of art. This skepticism also links the modern avant-garde to the proponents of natural law, and to the broader philosophical history of liberalism, for which self-interest is the founding condition of human subjectivity. For Grotius, there is no inherent human disposition toward conviviality. Rather, community and the sacrifice of self-interest are only forced upon us by the finitude of natural resources (or, for Hobbes, by the unbearable violence of man's warlike nature). In the absence of these external compulsions, humanity's inherent tendency would be toward dispersal, singularity, and division.

As I've suggested, the contingent and relational nature of bourgeois subjectivity is hardly a repressed secret, awaiting only the epistemological dynamite of the avant-garde artist or critical theorist to break it free and catalyze a new era of peace and harmony. The challenge posed by modern identity lies not with our illusory autonomy per se, but with our relationship to our own intrinsically dependent nature. The important point is not to simply acknowledge the (suppressed) "truth" of our divided selfhood in some singular epiphany, but rather, to develop the skills necessary to mitigate violence and objectification in our ongoing encounters with difference, even after we acknowledge our relational identity. The cultivation of this insight requires a temporally extensive form of social interaction in which modes of expression, enunciation, and reception are continuously modified and reciprocally responsive. It is also dependent on somatic, one might even say aesthetic, forms of knowledge: the exchange of gesture and expression, the complex relationship to habitus and habit, and the way in which conflict, reconciliation, and solidarity are registered in and through the body.

This is the experiential knowledge that is catalyzed in the workshops of Park Fiction, Dialogue, Ala Plastica, and Huit Facettes. The exchanges initiated in their projects constitute a form of labor that is distinct from the "work" of possessive individualism. Their goal is not the violent extraction of value or the suppression of difference, but a co-production (literally, a "co-labor") of identity at the interstices of existing cultural traditions, political forces, and individual subjectivities. Here the movement between contingency and freedom is seen as productive not simply because it exposes the contingency of the subject but because it enables constructive praxis. These projects require an analytic vocabulary that is capable of addressing the sustained experience of collective or collaborative interaction, the verbal and non-verbal encounters that occur not just among the members of specific groups, but between and among these artists and the broader network of participants catalyzed by a given project.

These issues return us to the rearticulation of aesthetic autonomy outlined in chapter 1. Modernity is marked by the "freeing" of the work of art (from its dependence on social or religious ritual and its spatial subordination to architecture) via the mobility of easel painting and the emerging market for the circulation and exchange of art works. In the same way, the expressive autonomy of the artistic personality implies a cognitive freedom. The artist is released from the oversight of direct patronage, and thereby able to take up a more critical relationship to dominant social and political institutions, leading to the generation of counter-normative insight. In the modern tradition this capacity for independent, potentially transgressive, thought was initially identified with the concept of "genius." Genius, for Herder as for Kant, involved the ability to create new modes of expression that challenged the constraints of existing genres and conventions (genius "gives the rule to art," as Kant famously wrote). Genius borrows two salient characteristics of bourgeois subjectivity. The first is the notion of artistic production as a form of ex nihilo creativity (a concept previously reserved only for divine creation). Like the bourgeois individual conjuring himself into existence through the sheer creative force of his labor, genius is transformative and indeterminate.[77] Rather than reproducing existing identities, models, or forms, it holds open a space for the generation of new meaning and new insight, beyond the brute facticity of what is.

This capacity carries a utopian potential. At the same time, it leaves aside a rather significant question. How do we determine which forms of new insight, and which efforts to destabilize existing systems of meaning, are liberating or empowering, and which are harmful or destructive? It is typical in contemporary cultural theory to attribute an a priori ethical valence to disruptive or destabilizing actions, based on the contention (discussed earlier) that all such efforts are driven by, or oriented toward, an inherently benign mode of pre-symbolic desire. I would suggest, however, that this determination can only be made a posteriori, through an evaluation of practice, and through the knowledge produced by practice itself. The projects of Dialogue, Park Fiction, Huit Facettes, and Ala Plastica, among other groups, constitute a form of research into the production of collective and individual identity. They suggest, in a pragmatic, experiential manner, that it's possible to uncouple the process by which identity is constituted within modernity (performative, relational, interdependent) from the conative drive of possessive individualism. They offer a potential resolution of the impasse between identity and agency through the formation of self in a manner that is both reflective and capable of coherent action. They challenge us to recognize new modes of aesthetic experience and new frameworks for thinking identity through the haptic and verbal exchanges that unfold in the process of collaborative interaction. They call upon us, in turn, to reconsider the formation of modern subjectivity. Thus, Dialogue's work in Bastar differentiates between the violent projection of self and its protective assertion in the claiming of spatial autonomy. The result is a mode of creative practice in which conventional notions of site and expressive autonomy are reconfigured.

The concept of genius also relies on a conative, possessive, model of subjectivity (hence the value accorded to singular authorship in the modernist tradition) in which the artist lays claim to particular formal or expressive innovations. Expression has commonly been viewed in this tradition as the re-presentation of an a priori content (the artwork as a material extension of the unique being of the individual artist). This semiotic model of expression persists, in modified form, in the neoconceptualism of artists such as Sierra, Alÿs, Hirschhorn, and Vanessa Beecroft, in which the artist visualizes an image, scene, or event (shoveling students, posing models, tattooed workers, etc.) that is subsequently brought into physical existence. While the image or idea may be generated in response to a particular context or situation, the artist's relationship to site is largely appropriative, and the locus of creativity resides primarily at the level of autonomous conceptual ideation. The world, in turn, becomes an extension of the artist's suum, a kind of reservoir from which he or she may draw at will in elaborating his or her particular vision.

The projects of Huit Facettes, Park Fiction, Dialogue, NICA, and Ala Plastica suggest that it is possible to produce new or counter-normative insight via a process of shared, rather than singularized, expression. Here the act of expression is generative and contingent. Rather than transmitting a preexisting content, expression takes place through an unfolding, extemporaneous process among an ensemble of collaborative agents. The locus of creative production is displaced from the level of independent ideation on the part of the artist to an indeterminate, collectively authored exchange among multiple interlocutors. The relative autonomy of each participant is alternately diminished and enhanced as the subjectivity of the viewer (distanced, critical, receptive) fluctuates with the subjectivity of the producer (immersive, haptic, participatory). In conventional expression the artist's vision is enacted for, or against, the viewer through a form of unilateral modeling (the artist's mode of perception stands as the telos toward which the viewer aspires, or by which they are guided). The viewer's feedback, as such, is seldom a significant factor, and even their presence before the work is understood only hypothetically.[78]

Dialogical practices involve the co-presence of bodies in real time. They encourage a heightened awareness of bodily schema—our capacity to orient ourselves in space relative to the world around us—and an increased sensitivity to the process by which our bodies feel, relate, and produce meaning. Further, they revolve around an experience of reciprocal modeling, as each subject shifts roles, anticipates, mirrors, and challenges the other. In the same manner, these groups conceive of site less as a reservoir of formal or representational material that is ready-to-hand, than as a space in which action is constituted and reconstituted on an ongoing basis.[79] Hans Joas, in *The Creativity of Action*, describes what he terms the "meaningful loss of intentionality" that occurs when we relinquish some degree of rational control due to the ambiguity or emotional quality of a given situation.[80] We might speak, then, of a meaningful loss of intentionality in dialogical practice as the artist opens out to the effect of site, context, and the collaborative Other. Here the mindful surrender of agency and intentionality is not marked as a failure or abandonment (of the prerogatives of authorship or the specificity of "art"), but as a process that is active, generative, and creative.

As I've noted above, this doesn't imply an absolute or permanent dissolution of artistic agency, only that the question of agency (its attribution, concession, and negotiation) is openly thematized in the work. Nor does this approach eliminate the possibility that a given project will entail some level of instrumentalization, misrecognition, or negation among its participants. It simply locates creative praxis within a different set of coordinates and, in so doing, raises a series of ethical questions that are neither more nor less compelling than those encountered in the work of figures such as Sierra, Tiravanija, and Beecroft. Having said that, dialogical practices do challenge some traditional assumptions about the status of the ethical in modernist art. The diagram I introduced above conveys the underlying teleological orientation of the modernist avant-garde, in which the historical transition from integration to aesthetic autonomy is valorized and necessarily linked with the emergence of art practices that are critical and transgressive in nature, rather than formulaic. We are presented here with an essentially synchronic system in which art is either integrated with existing social and discursive structures, and thereby incapable of producing new insight, or alienated from them, and therefore inherently dissident or liberatory.

It is this binary discourse that is being challenged today, across a broad range of collaborative art practices. In particular, we are witnessing a re-temporalization of the aesthetic as artists explore the capillary movement of agency and identity through cycles of coherence, dissolution, and reformation. As we've seen in the work of Park Fiction, Dialogue, and others, the relative integration of the artist within a given context, site, or milieu over time can result in projects that precipitate creative, counter-normative insight. At the same time, artists who habitually position themselves at a detached, *flaneur*-like remove from the site of practice can easily enough produce works that are banal, repetitive, or disconnected from the complexities and contradictions of lived experience. Moreover, techniques of disruption and destabilization, far from opening up new trajectories of thought, can actually reinforce an instrumentalizing, custodial relationship between the artist and the viewer when applied in a reflexive and unthinking manner. In the following discussion, I'll continue this inquiry, examining the renegotiation of aesthetic autonomy as it is unfolding in the dialogue between art and other, adjacent, practices associated with the discourse of development.

7 — MEMORIES OF DEVELOPMENT

In the previous discussion, I analyzed collaborative practice at the level of individual bodies and modes of subjective agency, with some reference as well to village-based social protocols. I want to return now to the broader political issues with which this chapter began: specifically, international development and modernization. Francis Alÿs and his collaborators described *When Faith Moves Mountains* as a "parable of under-productiveness" marking the "failed modernization" of "southern countries."[81] Further, the projects of Huit Facettes, Dialogue, and other groups discussed here raise questions that are relevant to current debates in rural development, activism, and participatory planning. These overlaps aren't surprising. As I noted in the introduction, one of the salient features of contemporary collaborative art practice is an increasing permeability between art production and other cultural practices and organizational forms. The work of activist groups, social movements, and NGOs provide a particularly important point of contiguity, as well as differentiation. It is necessary, then, to examine the larger discourse of modernization and development in relationship to, and against which, these practices define themselves.

Mechanisms of "international development" have played a central role in relations among the United States, the wealthy industrial nations of Europe, and the countries of the global South since the early 1950s. The formal institutions of international development (the U.N. Development Program, U.S. Agency for International Development, World Bank, and International Monetary Fund) emerged in response to a number of significant geopolitical changes brought about by the end of World War II, including a redistribution of economic and military power between Europe and the United States (symbolized by the Marshall Plan), and efforts by the U.S. to maintain an international sphere of influence in competition with the USSR.[82] The overt paternalism of early international development, which treated recipient nations as passive subjects in need of the civilizing influence of Western aid, was complicated in the 1960s and '70s by the emergence of anti-colonial liberation movements in Africa, Asia, and Latin America.[83] A further challenge to the hegemony of Western interests emerged in the work of the so-called "dependence" theorists (a group comprising North American neo-Marxists such as Paul Baran and Latin American academics such as Rodolfo Stavenhagen in Mexico, Fernando Cardosa in Brazil, and Raúl Prebisch in Chile).[84]

The *dependentistas* argued that development aid, far from empowering the poorer countries of the South (the "periphery"), actually functioned to enrich the economies of the North (the "core") at their expense. While the development process provided new markets for industrialized nations, it did little to increase the autonomy of the developing world, which instead becomes subordinate to Northern economies (the influence of this analysis on Medina and Alÿs is evident). The dependency school advocated instead the cultivation of "self reliance" among Southern economies, most famously represented by Julius Nyerere's Ujamaa movement in Tanzania. Throughout the 1970s the discourse of development continued to be negotiated between the normative forces of capitalism, Cold War realpolitik, and the quasi-revolutionary energies of the Third World and the "Non-aligned Movement" (cf. the 1955 Bandung Conference and the Belgrade Conference in 1961), which sought to challenge the top-down, market-driven approaches of the USAID, UNDP, and World Bank.

By the early 1980s a backlash from Western countries against the perceived radicalization of the development process combined with the relative success of some Southeast Asian economies to justify a turn toward neoliberal policies of "structural adjustment" or economic reform.[85] Structural adjustment approaches assumed that the client countries first had to fix, or "reform," themselves before development aid would have any positive effect. Here development implies a progressive movement out of, or beyond, a prior stage of stagnation or retardation. More specifically, it entails the anthropomorphic projection of certain values associated with bourgeois subjectivity onto entire cultures and countries. Thus, the "undeveloped" nation or culture, like the poor or working-class subject, has failed the test of modernity. Arrested in a primitive or infantile state, the undeveloped culture is typically viewed as incapable of the (economic) discipline necessary to compete in the global marketplace. Rather than greater autonomy and differentiation, what was required was a more faithful emulation of Euro-American market values. Thus, the ethical implications of the original dependency thesis were inverted by what we might term a neoliberal dependency thesis, which lamented the "dependence" of Third World nations on Western largesse. In order to receive support from the World Bank or IMF, countries were forced to surrender control over their internal affairs and conform to the dictates of neoliberal economic policies which required the privatization of publicly owned companies, the suspension of trade protections and price controls, the reduction or elimination of social welfare and public services, and the opening of their economies to foreign investment. This "shock therapy" would bring the recipient country in line with a harsh market-centered regime that would have been impossible to fully impose in the U.S. or Europe. The results, from Sudan to Tanzania and from Argentina to Mexico, were depressingly similar: increases in social inequality and disorder, exacerbation of social tensions and ethnic differences, increased unemployment, and rampant currency devaluation.

Despite its dismal record, structural adjustment policy had emerged by the 1990s as the new "common sense" of global development and one of the most visible manifestations of a nascent neoliberal ideology that was transforming domestic policy in the countries of the developed world as well (under the guise of "neoconservatism").[86] One of the primary goals of neoliberalism is to erode the autonomy of public institutions, which are seen to represent a space of collective articulation that is potentially resistant to the privatizing drive of the market system. In practice, this has entailed an assault on all forms of collectivity or solidarity that challenge the imperatives of capital, aside from ideologically compliant forms of organized religion. State-based institutions (legislative entities, regulatory agencies, public schools and universities, social service programs) have been a chief target. In the United States, where the drive toward privatization is perhaps the most advanced, an alliance of corporatist Republicans and fundamentalist Christians has worked steadily for some twenty years to weaken or destroy government regulation of the private sector,

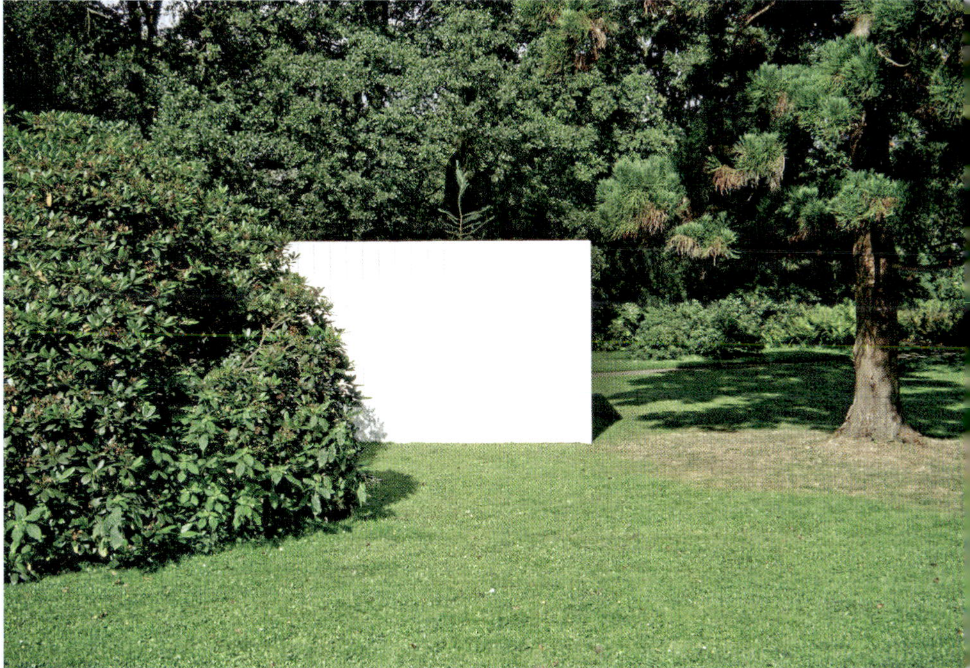

PLATE 1 Michael Elmgreen and Ingar Dragset, *Powerless Structures, Fig.55 (Pavilion)* (1998). Photograph by Bent Ryberg; courtesy of Galleri Nicolai Wallner, Copenhagen.

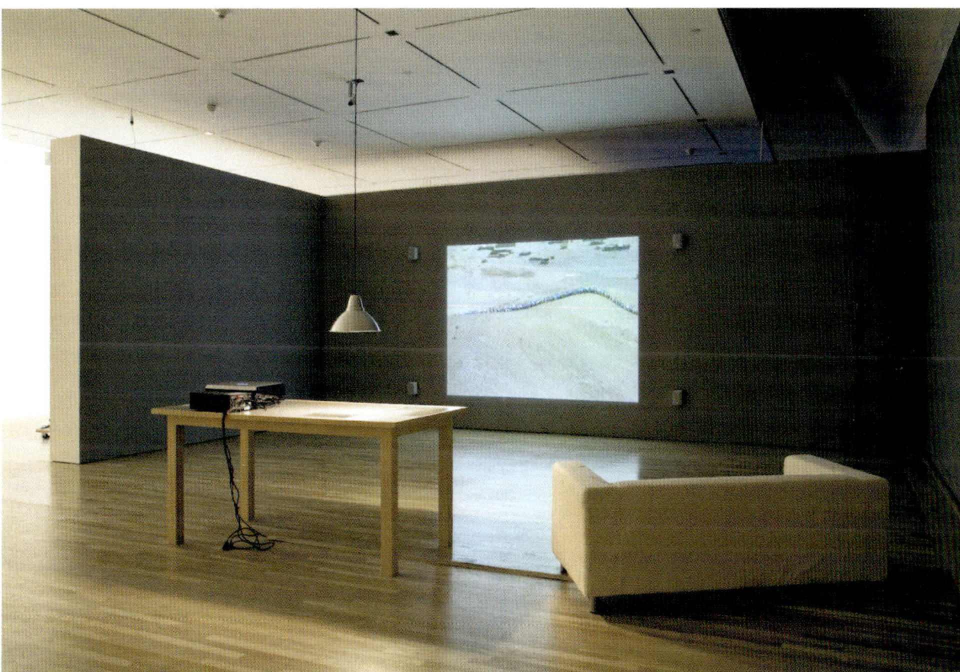

PLATE 2 Francis Alÿs, *When Faith Moves Mountains* (2002). In collaboration with Cuauhtémoc Medina and Rafael Ortega. 16mm film transferred to video. 36 minutes. Installation at the Hammer Museum, Los Angeles. Courtesy David Zwirner, New York. Photograph by Joshua White.

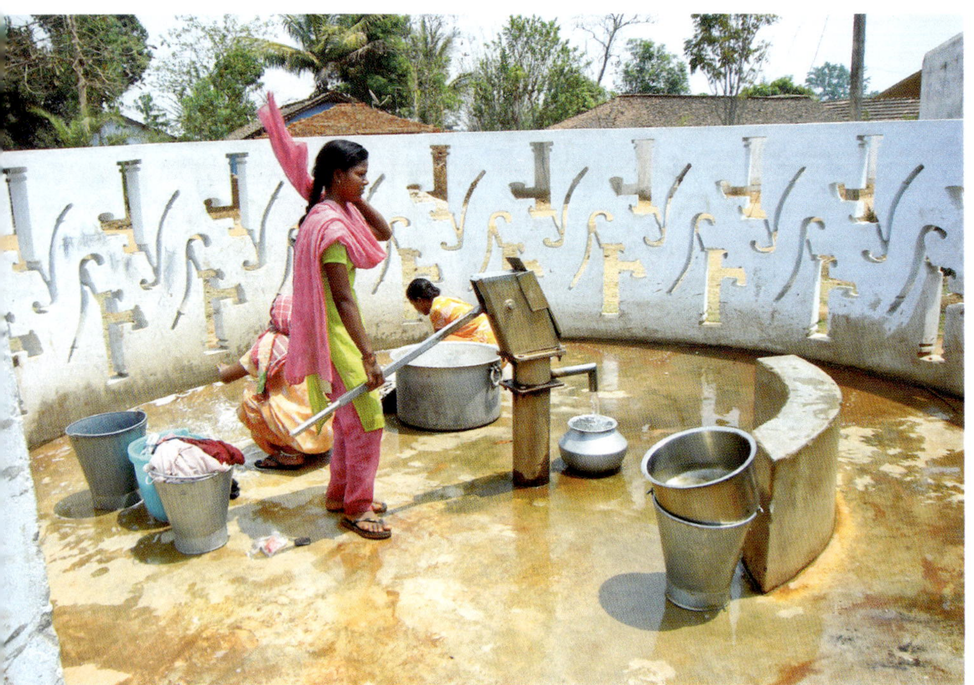

PLATE 3 Navjot Altaf, Rajkumar, Shantibai, and Gessuram, *Nalpar* (Water Pump Site), Kondagaon, Bastar District, Chhattisgarh, India (2004). Photograph by Grant Kester.

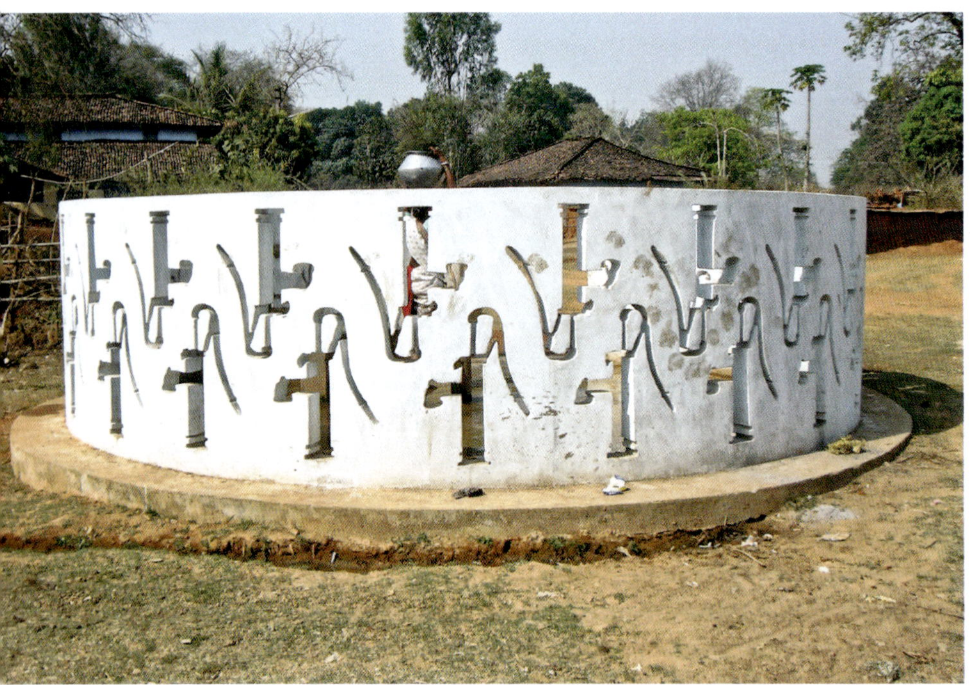

PLATE 4 Navjot Altaf, Rajkumar, Shantibai, and Gessuram, *Nalpar* (Water Pump Site), Kondagaon, Bastar District, Chhattisgarh, India (2004). Photograph by Grant Kester.

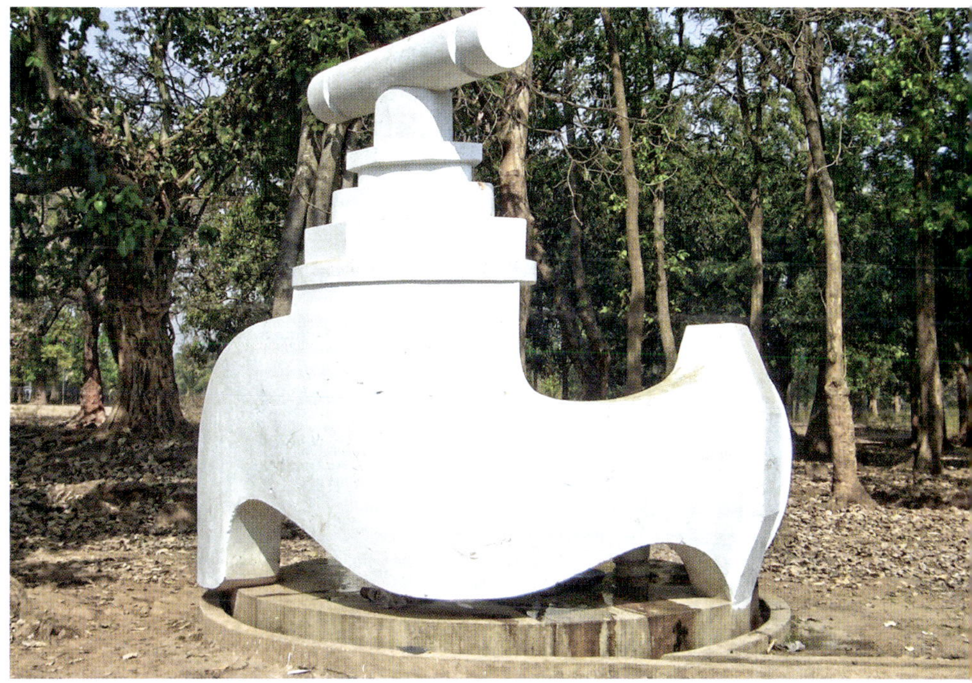

PLATE 5 Navjot Altaf, Rajkumar, Shantibai, and Gessuram, *Nalpar* (Water Pump Site), Kondagaon, Bastar District, Chhattisgarh, India (2003–4). Photograph by Grant Kester.

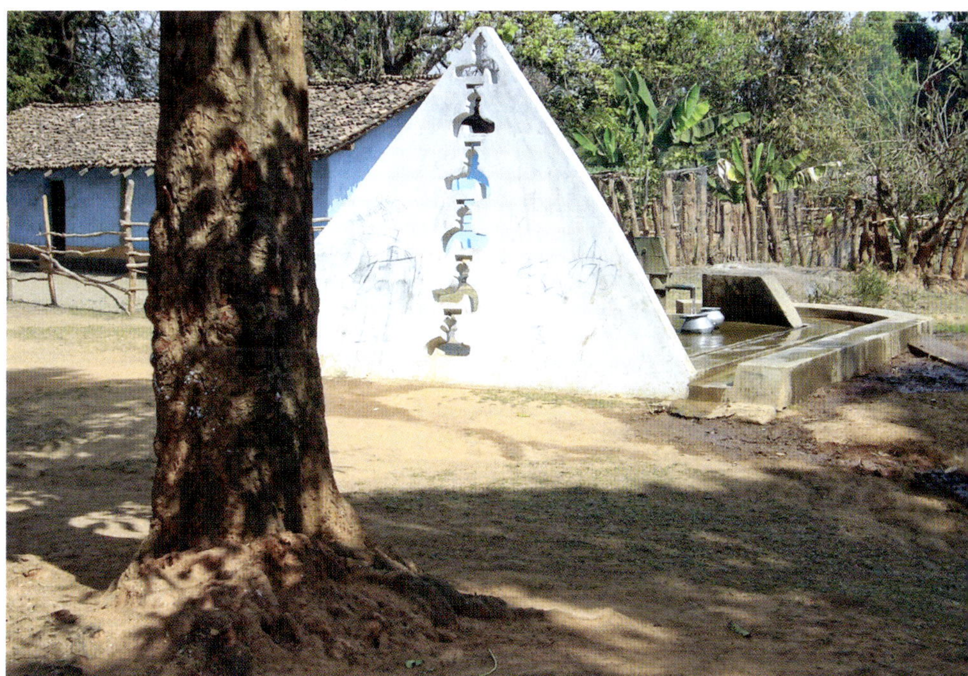

PLATE 6 Navjot Altaf, Rajkumar, Shantibai, and Gessuram, *Nalpar* (Water Pump Site), Kondagaon, Bastar District, Chhattisgarh, India (2003–4). Photograph by Grant Kester.

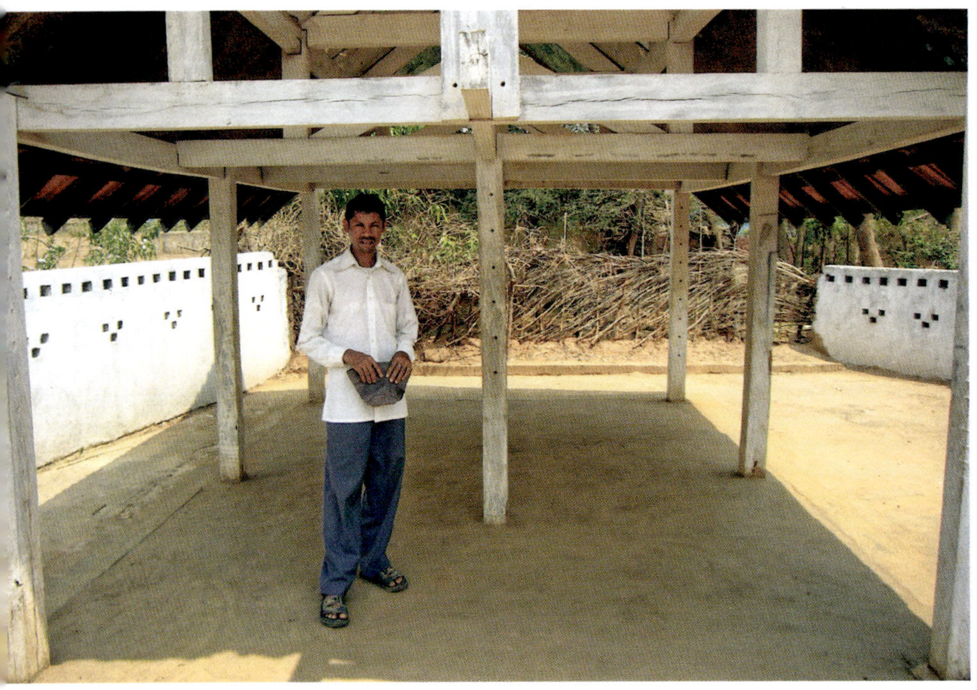

PLATE 7 Rajkumar, *Pilla Gudi* (Temple for Children) in Kusma (2001). Photograph by Grant Kester.

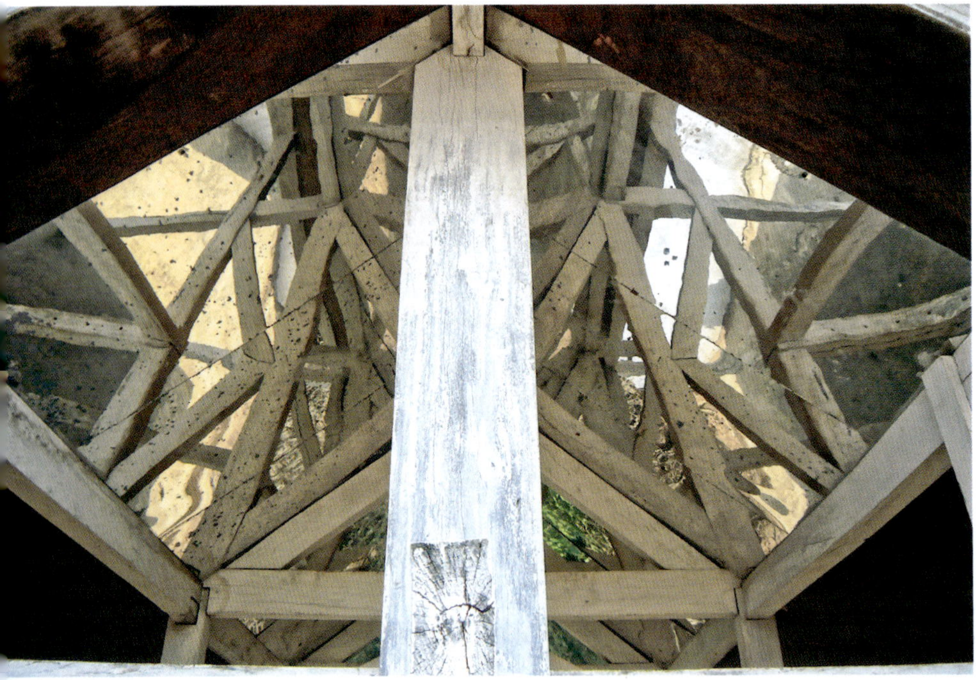

PLATE 8 Rajkumar, *Pilla Gudi* (Temple for Children) in Kusma (2001). Photograph by Grant Kester.

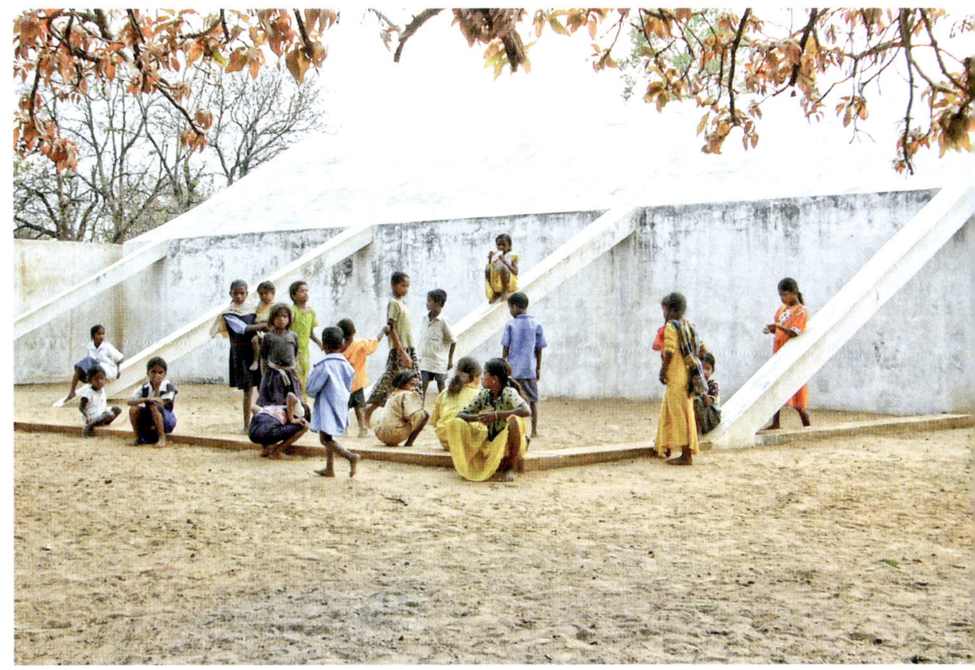

PLATE 9 Navjot Altaf, Rajkumar, Shantibai, Gessuram, and the children of Kopaweda, *Pilla Gudi* (Temple for Children), Kondagaon, Bastar District, Chhattisgarh, India (2006). Photograph by Grant Kester.

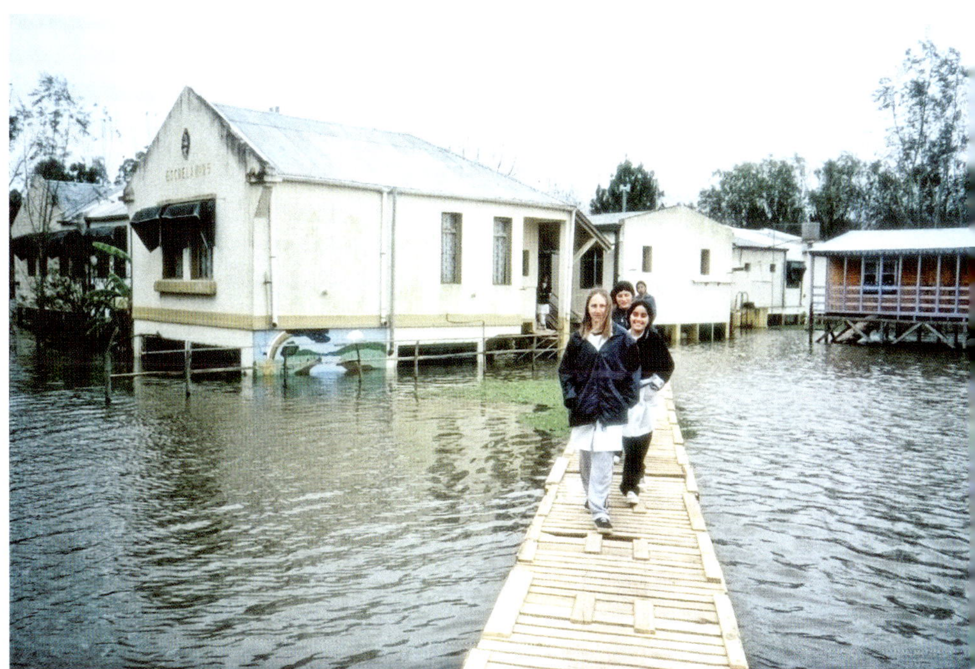

PLATE 10 Ala Plastica, *AA Project ("Isleños Unidos")* (2003). Photograph by Thomas Minich.

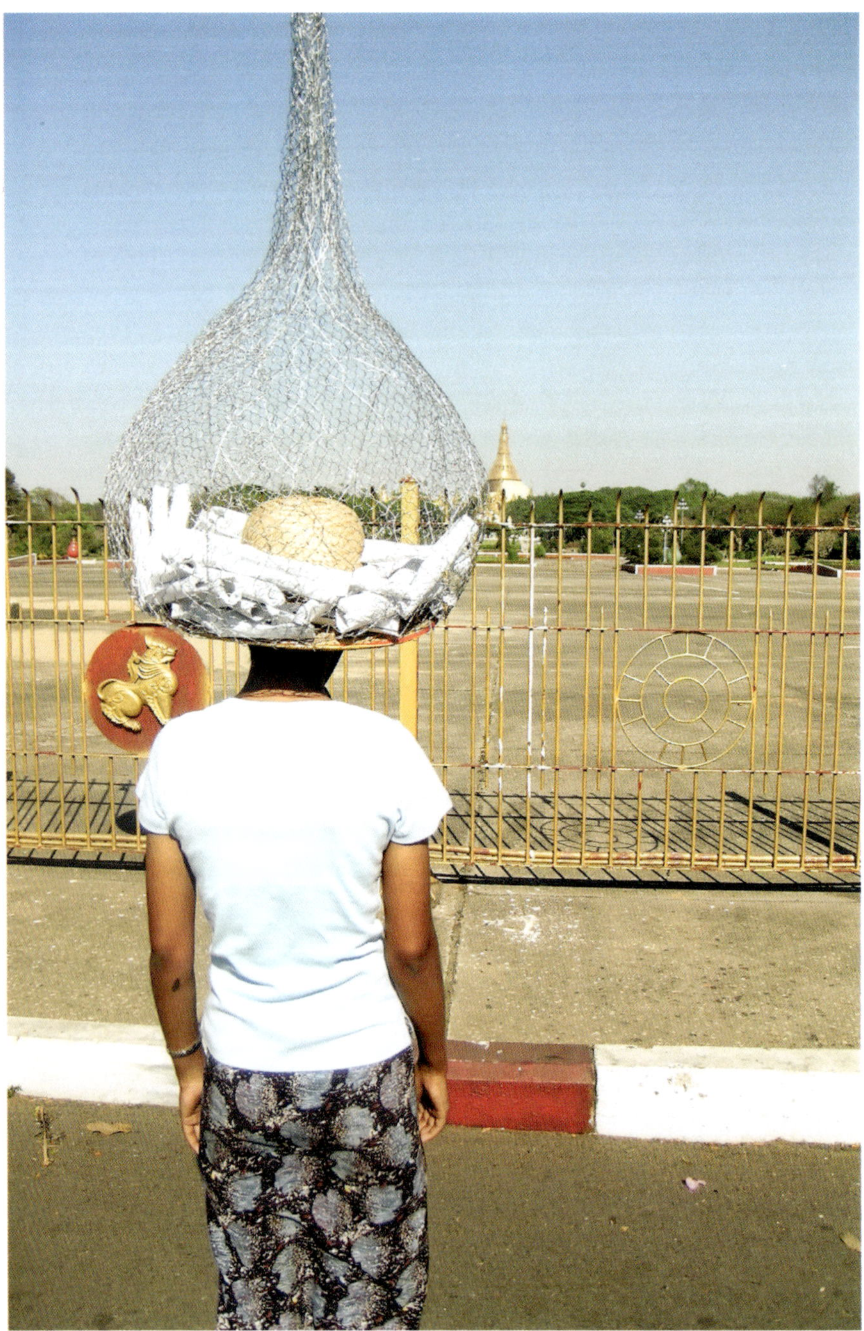

PLATE 11 Chu Yuan and Myanmar/Burmese collaborators, *Offering of Mind: Muslim Bamar-Indian Young Professional*, performed photography in front of Swedagon temple and park grounds, Yangon/Rangoon (2005). Photograph by Chu Yuan.

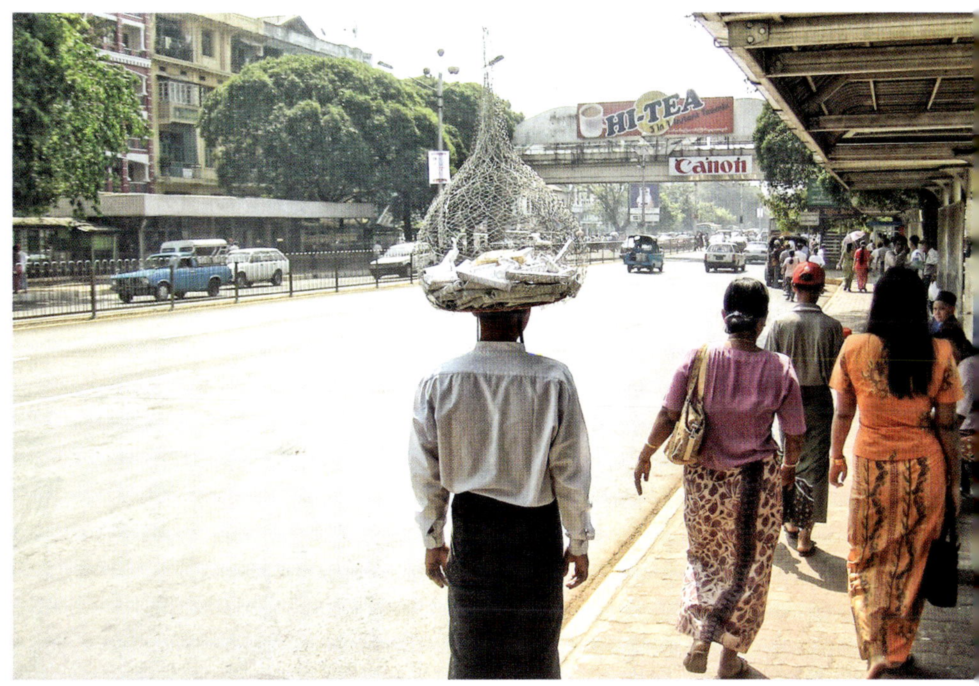

PLATE 12 Chu Yuan and Myanmar/Burmese collaborators, *Offering of Mind: Buddhist Bamar Aspiring Entrepreneur*, performed photography in downtown Yangon/Rangoon (2005). Photograph by Jay Koh.

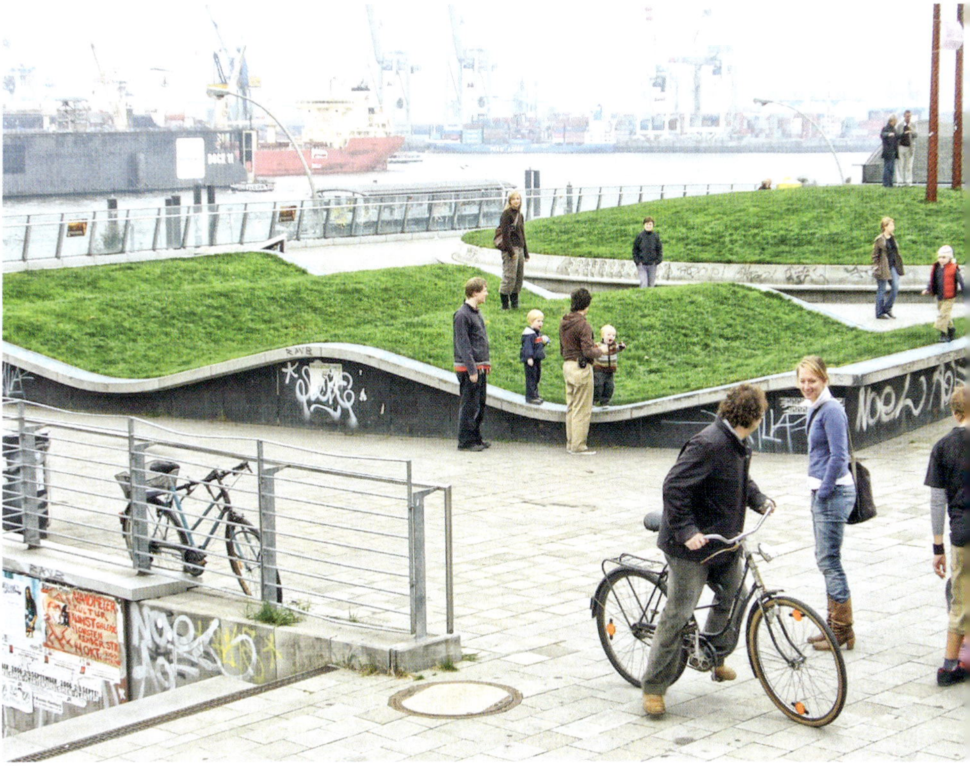

PLATE 13 Park Fiction, Public Park ("Flying Carpet Lawn"), Hamburg, Germany (2007). Photograph by Grant Kester.

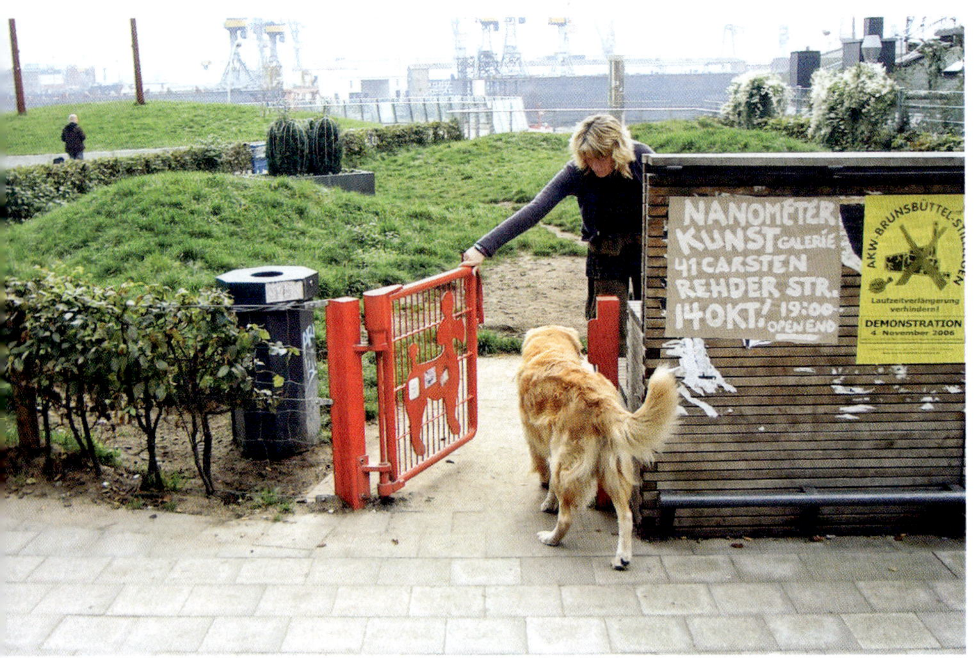

PLATE 14 Park Fiction, Public Park (area for dogs), Hamburg, Germany (2007). Photograph by Grant Kester.

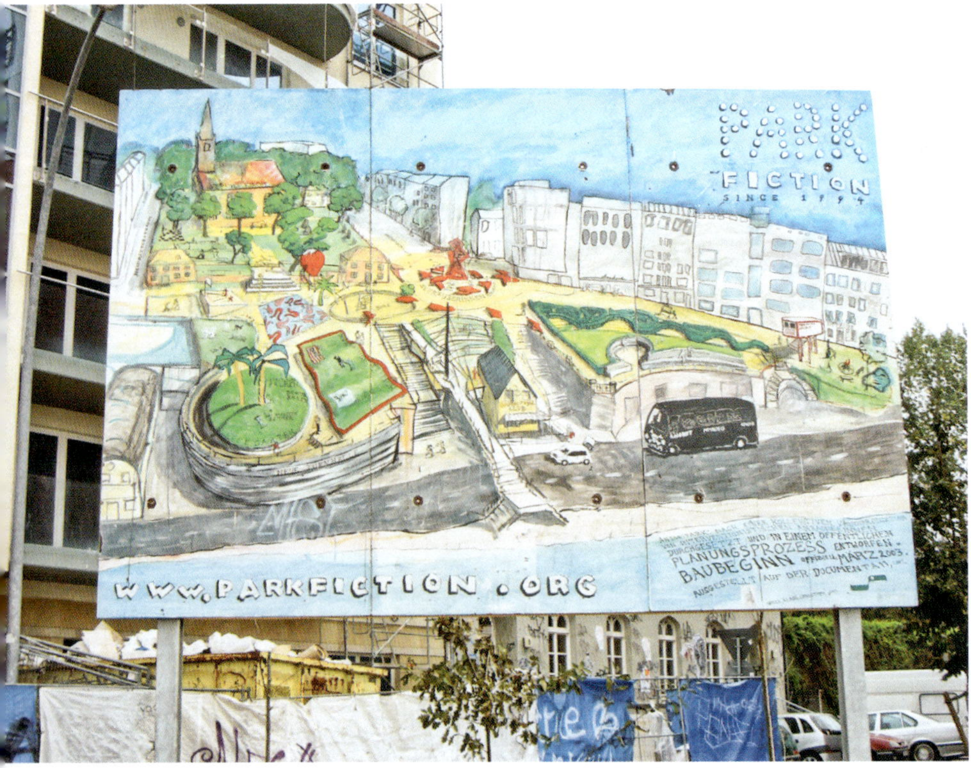

PLATE 15 Park Fiction, Billboard, Hamburg, Germany (2007). Photograph by Grant Kester.

dismantle forms of public education, and eliminate services for the poor and the working class. They seek, in particular, to undermine the state's capacity to provide a space in which systematic inequalities are acknowledged, legitimated, and acted upon via policy, regulation, and institutional reform.

British Prime Minister Margaret Thatcher, an early exponent of the neoliberal worldview, famously claimed, "There is no such thing as society."[87] That is, there is nothing, no form of social reciprocity or obligation, no space of collective action and exchange, outside the market and the family. As Thatcher's quote suggests, civil society as such has no relevance in the neoliberal worldview. It is against this ground that contemporary collaborative and collective practice needs to be understood. Artists around the world are increasingly conscious of the stakes involved in this emptying out of public space, discourse, and action. It is for this reason as well that various public and quasi-public organizational forms and practices (the operations of non-governmental agencies, activist groups, and social movements) have emerged as a key point of contact, influence, and exchange for contemporary artists.

Structural adjustment policies continue to provide the basis for most international development assistance. However, they have been paralleled over the past decade by a significant increase in various forms of "humanitarian" relief (typically in response to natural disasters such as drought, flooding, or famine, or for populations displaced by war or sectarian violence). As the Swiss development scholar Gilbert Rist has noted, this "adjustment with a human face" brought about a "strange alliance between the World Bank and the NGOs around the concept of basic needs." "Here," Rist argues, "was a new way of making people believe in the harmless—even positive—character of a procedure with catastrophic effects. By a semantic trick, two opposites were joined together so that the value accorded to one was reflected upon the other, much more questionable, term. A 'human face' was thus supposed to make adjustment acceptable."[88] Rist presents us with a typical example of hegemonic power attempting to blunt or deflect criticism of its actions through the use of a humanizing alibi. We encounter this same interpretation in the work of figures such as Giorgio Agamben, for whom humanitarian agencies "maintain a secret solidarity with the powers they ought to fight," or Michael Hardt and Toni Negri, who contend that groups such as Médecins sans Frontières or Oxfam are "completely immersed in the biopolitical context of . . . Empire" and constitute "the most powerful pacific weapon of the new world order."[89]

Despite the fact that humanitarian aid has saved thousands of lives, its very co-existence with the mechanisms of structural adjustment (perhaps even receiving funding from the same sources) is sufficient to render it suspect. This criticism raises an important but complex question: what is the relationship between local, situational action and a larger political context? For many theorists this question continues to center on the possibility of some systematic or revolutionary change that would radically and irrevocably transform the overarching values and drives of capitalism. This implies, in turn, a mode of autonomous political action capable of maintaining an absolute detachment from the contaminating mechanisms of the capitalist system. The "first basic task of the revolutionary communist movement," as Guattari and Negri contend in *Communists Like Us*, is to affirm the movement's "radical separation not only from the State which it directly confronts but also, more fundamentally, from the very model of the capitalist State and all its successors, replacements, derived forms and assorted functions in all the wheels of the socius, at all levels of subjectivity."[90] But how do we determine precisely which "forms and assorted functions" within a given social system are safe and which are contaminated by the capitalist State and its myriad offshoots? Guattari and Negri's account risks collapsing literally every form of sociality and subjectivity into the maw of an undifferentiated capitalist juggernaut. The revolutionary must effect a "radical separation" from virtually any social interaction, identity, or organization that is even tangentially connected to a monolithic "capitalist State." All partial, incremental, or gradual change is compromised and tainted, functioning only to prop up and legitimate existing power structures and defer the possibility of a permanent and fundamental transformation of the capitalist system.[91]

Negri develops this theme more fully in *Empire* (co-authored with Michael Hardt). Pointing to the negative consequences of post-colonial nation building in Cuba, Vietnam, and Algeria. Hardt and Negri reject "any political strategy that involves . . . trying to resurrect the nation-state to protect against global capital."[92] In their analysis the state's only function is negative: to contain desire and objectify difference on the basis of a monolithic collective identity (the nation, the people, etc.). This rejection of the state coincides with Hardt and Negri's insistence that political and economic power is no longer centralized in specific countries or institutions, but is instead dispersed through a rhizomatic network of corporations, NGOs, banks, and governments, no one of which is wholly determinant.[93] The only appropriate mode of resistance to the newly subtle and dispersed mode of capitalism is sporadic, uncoordinated, and singular. There is no need to challenge the institutions of political and economic power with collective forms of resistance or to build political alliances across national boundaries, because power has thoughtfully reconfigured itself to be decentralized. Thus, we must meet the rhizomatic forces of capital with the Deleuzean "flows" of migration and unplanned and local gestures.[94] The working class, understood as an agent of collective political struggle and transformation, has been replaced by an inchoate army of laborers scattered across the globe, whose most radical political option is "nomadic" immigration to the metropolitan centers of the developed world to serve as low-waged labor. Hardt and Negri would leave no civic or institutional insulation whatsoever between the mobile and predatory forces of global corporate capital and the poor and working classes, to whom even the solace of a "communicable solidarity" is denied. Their analysis operates through a kind of negative teleology in which all possible outcomes of the cultural and political logic of modernity are anticipated in the specific experience of the Euro-American nation-state. There is no point in trying to organize trade unions in China or work toward a more egalitarian government in Nicaragua because "we" (white Europeans and Americans) have already been down that road.

This impatience with, and even disdain for, the impure processes of negotiation and mediation involved in political change is a typical feature of recent critical theory. Gilles Deleuze famously recoiled at the very concept of "human rights":

> The reverence that people display toward human rights—it almost makes one want to defend horrible, terrible positions. It is so much a part of the softheaded thinking that marks the shabby period we were talking about. It's pure abstraction. Human rights, after all, what does that mean?[95]

The local or situational victories we can achieve in the way people are treated here and now (through the discourse of "human rights," e.g.) are irrelevant if the language used to achieve them is in any way implicated in a broader discursive and political system that operates elsewhere in a violent or instrumentalizing manner (a legacy of the textual politics I outlined in my discussion of May '68). This skepticism is understandable. Capitalism has long excelled at co-opting or absorbing resistance, but it's also the case that oppositional movements have historically extracted significant concessions from the capitalist system, in its various guises. Whether you choose to see these as representing meaningful progress or merely reformist delusion, many of the most important changes that have occurred in the global polity over the past century (the expansion of the franchise, public education, protection of civil rights, regulation of corporate conduct, the right to unionize, etc.) have been won precisely through negotiation and contestation with capital and the state in ways that were almost inevitably partial, impure, and compromised.

Deleuze's almost patrician distaste for the poisoned language of human rights provides an instructive contrast with Michel Foucault's more pragmatic approach. In fact, it was in part Foucault's willingness to accept some degree of compromise with existing political discourse that led to his falling out with Deleuze over the violence of the Red Army Faction in Germany.[96] While Foucault was certainly cognizant of the dangers of state power and the contradictions of liberal humanist ideals, he was also willing to align himself with groups that entered into negotiation with state agencies and which invoked decidedly humanist values in doing so. Thus, in his work with the International Committee Against Piracy (Comité International contre la piraterie) in 1981, Foucault chose to collaborate with French humanitarian groups such as Médecins du Monde and Terre des Hommes to protest attacks on Vietnamese boat people in the Gulf of Thailand. Foucault drafted a statement of support at the time, later published by *Liberation*, which began with a defense of fundamental human rights that would have no doubt dismayed Deleuze: "There exists an international citizenry, which has its rights, which has its duties, and which promises to raise itself up against every abuse of power, no matter who the author or the victims. After all, we are all governed and, to that extent, in solidarity."[97] Rather than waiting in millennialist anticipation for the emergence of a sufficiently pure political discourse, Foucault suggests that this discourse can be shaped, and reshaped, through concrete action. While existing modes of social change are inevitably informed by hegemonic power, they also have the capacity to transform subjectivity, generate insight, and catalyze new forms of solidarity.

As I've already noted, there is a significant level of interaction among and between activist groups, non-governmental organizations and associations, and artists in several of the projects under discussion here (and in contemporary collaborative art practice more generally). These interactions are characterized by moments of both correspondence and differentiation, both symmetry and resistance. They raise a number of relevant questions. How do practices grounded in a local context (the villages of Kondagaon, the dunes of Ventanilla, or the towns of the Rio de la Plata basin) relate to, corroborate, or challenge the larger protocols of globalization? To what extent does any artist become complicit with the logic of neoliberalism simply by working in conjunction with, or proximity to, NGOs or development agencies? And what is the broader political horizon for progressive social change today? Can we imagine a mode of resistance that operates outside the revolutionist paradigm advocated by Guattari and Negri, with its insistence on the "radical separation" of oppositional practice from virtually any form of social interaction or collective organization related to mechanisms of state power? This paradigm can lend itself to a reductive mode of thinking in which a properly chaste "revolutionary" desire (uncontaminated by any external determination) is juxtaposed to a compromised "reformist" practice that enters into negotiation with existing power structures, thereby softening social contradictions and legitimating the deferral of a "real" revolutionary transformation in exchange for merely local or provisional change.[98]

Where do we look today for evidence of a global revolutionary movement—socialist, communist, or otherwise—against which the relative legitimacy of any local political action could be measured? Hugo Chavez, the leading exponent of socialism in the southern hemisphere, has actually increased foreign direct investment in the Venezuelan economy.[99] While Chavez, Evo Morales of Bolivia, and Luiz Inácio Lula da Silva of Brazil, among other leaders, have done much to challenge neoliberalism in South America, they've often done so through engagement with, rather than separation from, the formal mechanisms of capital and the state (including the market systems of their own countries). Protests organized during periodic meetings of the International Monetary Fund, World Bank, World Trade Organization, and other organizations, have led to the emergence of a vibrant international community of anti-globalization activists, but it has remained relatively de-centralized and informal.[100] We find today not a (unified) global revolutionary movement but a mosaic of local and regional struggles, from attempts to organize workers in the *maquiladoras* of northern Mexico, to efforts by the Maori to retain control over land, resources, and their own cultural identity in New Zealand, from squatters in Hamburg and São Paulo to activist monks in Tibet and Myanmar, and from the *assentamentos* of Brazil to the worker-run factories of Argentina.[101]

These movements share many common values, including a commitment to participatory democracy, a resistance to the arbitrary imposition of state power and the exploitation of the market system, and a defense of local and indigenous cultures and communities. At the same time, each site, each repertoire of oppositional practices, has been invented out of a distinct set of forces, conditions, and institutional structures (involving activist groups, churches, NGOs, and private and governmental agencies that operate on the local, national, and even international level). An analysis of artistic practices developed in this context requires a more nuanced understanding of the interactions of these various individuals, groups, and institutions. While Doctors Without Borders may well be "the most powerful pacific weapon of the new world order," according to Hardt and Negri, it was also targeted by the U.S. National Security Agency as part of its illegal "terrorist" surveillance program.[102] This doesn't absolve Doctors Without Borders from criticism, but it does suggest that the actual political function of a given NGO or non-profit organization relative to the state is somewhat more complex and contradictory than Hardt and Negri's formulation would allow. It is also important to recognize just how diverse the "non-governmental" world is, ranging from the extreme conservatism of groups such as the World Family Policy Center and the Population Research Institute (which oppose birth control as a means of preventing the transmission of HIV/AIDS), to the Israeli Committee Against House Demolitions (which rebuilds Palestinian homes destroyed by the Israeli army) and the network of NGOs and associations that support the Sem Terra, or "landless movement," in Brazil.[103]

Rather than a simplistic opposition between "authentic" social movements and a monolithic system of NGOs entirely subordinate to the capitalist state, it seems more accurate to describe the emerging global civil society as a site of conflict and contestation, in which local and international activist groups, social justice movements, and union organizations both challenge and collaborate with an equally disparate network of non-profits, aid organizations, public agencies, and private foundations.[104] Given this diversity, it is necessary to establish the strategic relationship between a given project and the larger processes of globalization through a situational analysis of both the individual participants and the various institutional or organizational actors involved. As noted above, neoliberal development is characterized by the privileging of the market; an often paternalistic or judgmental relationship to local cultures, forms of knowledge, and social patterns; and a tendency to impose a priori technical or economic "solutions" in a programmatic and hierarchical manner, with little regard for the conditions pertaining at a given site. In the most successful collaborative projects we encounter instead a pragmatic openness to site and situation, a willingness to engage with specific cultures and communities in a creative and improvisational manner (e.g., Dialogue's work with craft production), a concern with non-hierarchical and participatory processes, and a critical and self-reflexive relationship to practice itself. Another important component is the desire to cultivate and enhance local forms of solidarity (among the women of Kopaweda, e.g.). These local identifications may, or may not, bear a relationship to larger political struggles or collective action. In some projects, as we'll see with the work of Ala Plastica, this relationship is explicit, while in others, local or provisional solidarities operate in a prefigurative manner.

THE LIMITS OF ETHICAL CAPITALISM — 8

In the following discussion I'll examine a series of collaborative projects in order to trace the complex interrelationship between non-governmental organizations, the mechanisms of international development, and contemporary art practice. The first set of projects, by the Danish group Superflex, center around the discourse of "ethical capitalism" in current development policy. In the *Supergas* project, Superflex worked with engineers and a sustainable agriculture organization in Tanzania to develop and market an affordable biogas generator to African farmers. The biogas unit turns human and animal waste into a gas fuel source. In *Guaraná*

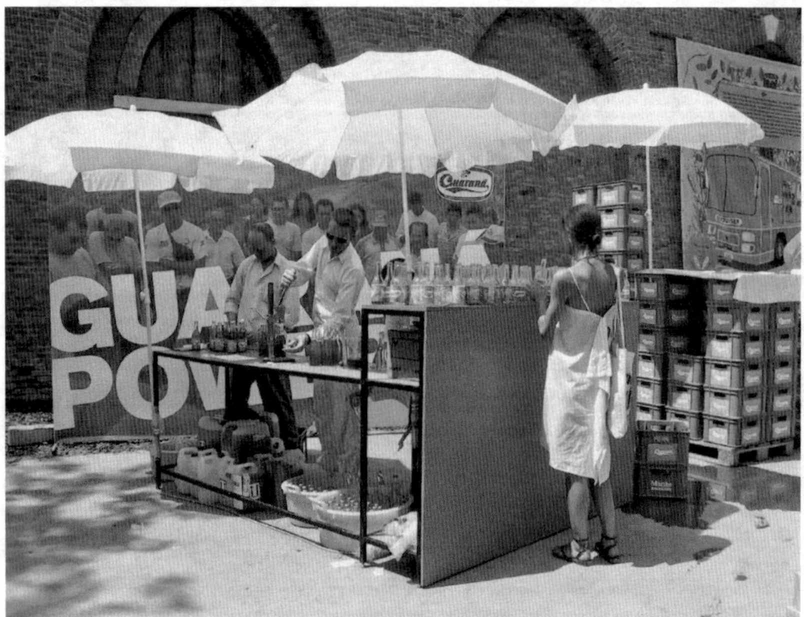

FIGURE 6 Superflex, *Guaraná Power Production/Bar*, Venice Biennial (2003). Photograph courtesy of Superflex.

Power, Superflex collaborated with a group of Guaraná berry farmers in Brazil to develop and market an energy drink to recapture some of the profits currently taken by the multinational beverage corporations that purchase their crops. Each functioned as a kind of pilot project, with the goal of achieving some wider replication: there have been (halting) attempts to market the biogas generator in other countries (Cambodia, Tanzania, and Thailand), and the Guaraná Power group has arranged for limited distribution of their drink. However, both projects have received their primary public exposure and legitimation thus far in art venues and before art audiences.[105]

The *Supergas* and *Guaraná Power* projects have clear affinities with the operation of NGOs: the members of Superflex worked with "disenfranchised" communities and sought to ameliorate their condition through locally situated interventions. They operated with the implicit understanding that they had something to offer these communities—new machinery, intellectual technology, or modes of social organization or subjectivity—which could help the disempowered improve their situation. In fact, images of Superflex's members assisting Tanzanians with the construction of a digester resemble nothing so much as earnest young Peace Corps volunteers spreading Western technological "know-how" through the developing world in the 1960s and '70s. Despite their somewhat labored efforts at tongue-in-check staging, which seem intended primarily for art world consumption, the members of Superflex appear to be sincere in their mission as emissaries of the developed world.[106]

The encouragement of grower's cooperatives or the circulation of new technologies among poor farmers is being carried forward in a nearly identical manner by literally hundreds of NGOs and aid agencies, as well as corporations, around the world. Danida, the Danish International Development Agency, has funded numerous projects organized along similar lines throughout Africa. Despite the obvious corollaries, Superflex's members have made a conspicuous effort to differentiate their work from the operations of nonprofit aid organizations in interviews. This ostensible difference is an article of faith in most sympathetic reviews as well:

> In order not to become involved in existing (power) structures in Danish government controlled development aid, Superflex is working to have their biogas project funded by companies and private and public foundations and funds. Superflex is thus accelerating a situation dramatically and effectively being a complex combination of art activism, "ethical" capitalism, and new development of ecological technology.[107]

> We don't want to help the way an aid organization does. Instead we offer a functional product that they are able to use on their own terms. . . . The goal of the "donors" in the classical aid-giving scenario is to raise the quality of life among the "recipients" by providing a road, a school, or some other amenity. Quality of life is, however, measured by Western or European values and norms and does not always work in a new context. . . . Many Africans talk about wanting to kick out all aid organizations, saying that they make their society passively dependent on the "helper's" contributions. They undermine creativity and initiative and thereby create victimized people.[108]

This confrontation demonstrates a clear difference between the objectives of the Superflex project and development aid: a functional product is offered for which an actual need has been identified and available resources (dung) are used. The argument here is not a social one, but rather an issue of economics. . . . Superflex thus distances itself from the traditional donor/recipient relation in which the latter becomes passively dependent on contributions, stifling creativity and initiative.[109]

As I've described it already, the negative ontology of traditional avant-garde art is based on difference from an implicitly inferior dominant cultural form (kitsch, craft, mass culture, etc.). This gesture entails, of course, a certain violence: the disparaged Other against which advanced art defines itself is necessarily reified, a caricature whose unalloyed simplicity or instrumentality justifies the complexity and ludic freedom of art as somehow unique and necessary. I suspect Superflex's almost instinctual effort to distance itself from the clearly analogous operations of aid organizations is motivated in part by this same tradition. Their ability to take up an adjudicatory, critically reflexive relationship to the operations of NGOs is precisely what defines their practice as "art." In order to produce this distance, Superflex, in what they apparently believe is a refreshingly non-conformist rejection of received wisdom, embrace the concept of "ethical capitalism."[110] Where NGOs make recipients "dependent," stifle "creativity and initiative," and inculcate a passive "victim" mentality, the market system makes them independent and entrepreneurial. Where NGOs force recipients to conform to Western values rather than meeting their real needs, the market gives people "functional products" that they can use "on their own terms."[111]

Unfortunately, this uncompromising criticality does not extend to Superflex's understanding of the market itself as a parallel organizational model. Instead, "market standards" remain a naturalized given which they accept more or less at face value. "We have always been oriented toward the market," explains Rasmus Nielsen. "We want our projects to be able to function according to market standards. It is not because we think corporations are particularly sympathetic, but rather out of an attempt to avoid the giver-receiver relationship established by NGOs."[112] Superflex attaches a particular importance to the act of *selling* the biogas digester to Tanzanians, thereby implicating them in a market-based transaction which will ignite their entreprenurial spirit. The ameliorative effects of the cash nexus are evident in a cartoon created to publicize the Supergas project. The cartoon features a proud villager bragging to a friend about the virtues of his biogas digester. "Where did you get that technology?" the friend asks. "I got it from Superflex's 'Wazungu' [white men]," he replies. "But this 'Wazungu,' they must be very rich and clever. How come they know our problems and work hard to help us solve them?" his friend inquires. "Oh! You boy," the friend responds, "'Wazungu' are not helping us, but we are helping each other. . . . I paid for this technology you see."[113]

NGOS practice a patronizing cultural superiority, but the "giver-receiver" relationship established by the market is refreshingly free of humanist cant and pretension. The market is an ideologically neutral device which artists can easily appropriate and turn to their own ends. Hence we have the unintentionally ironic situation of a group of Danish artists whose education and art practice have been subsidized by one of the most generous welfare states in Europe, working to encourage "entrepreneurial" independence among poor Africans, generously giving them the tools to "empower" themselves and overcome their "victimization" by Western aid agencies. The cause of African poverty in this view isn't the damaging economic reforms imposed by the World Bank and IMF, disproportionate debt, lack of resources, or kleptocratic government, but rather, an absence of "creativity" and "initiative" among the African people rendered passive and dependent by a surfeit of health clinics and primary schools. But farmers in Tanzania are hardly strangers to the vicissitudes of the market. And surely there is no reason to believe that the single purchase of a *Supergas* digester will be sufficient to overcome the decades of (accumulated) inertia and dependence encourged by conventional aid organizations. Superflex's embrace of market-based "solutions" and the cultivation of an "entrepreneurial" spirit among their Tanzanian collaborators is rendered all the more problematic because Tanzania was one of the first African nations to be subjected to forced structural adjustment policies by the IMF and World Bank, as early as 1979, leading to growing social tension over the resulting economic and class divisions.[114]

The critique of "dependency" among aid recipients is, of course, a key feature of neoliberal discourse, reiterating neoconservative attacks on state welfare provision in the United States during the 1980s by figures such as William Bennett. International aid, for all its limitations, encourages a form of reciprocal obligation between state entities and the poor that violates the moral economy of the the private market. With their appeals to "ethical" capitalism and the glories of "entrepreneurial" subjectivity, Superflex only manages to differentiate themselves from Danida by aligning themselves with Starbucks, whose support of "fair trade" initiatives is widely publicized. Superflex attempts to triangulate a critical perspective on NGOs and development dependency through the vehicle of market-based forms of social organization which are themselves deeply problematic. In an interview with Åsa Nacking they associate their approach with Muhammad Yunus's "Grameen Bank" system of microcredit in India, describing the Grameen system as a "virus" circulating among the poor that "provides the tools to enable a poor person to change his condition." "All humans are potential entreprenuers," they enthuse, speculating on the positive effects that would follow if the poor were given access to the same financial "tools" as the developing world.[115]

Despite its reputation, the Grameen Bank system has resulted in incidents of aggression and even violence in rural villages over loan repayment. Alex Counts, president of the Grameen Foundation USA, acknowledges that the microcredit model has "a dark side. . . . It brought a lot of solidarity but also brought an enormous amount of tension. If someone fell behind, people got very tense and even got hostile with each other."[116] By displacing conventional direct aid, the Grameen system increased debt entrapment among poor rural women, who are forced to repay loans at interest rates of up to 36 percent. "The poor are exploiting the poor," as Dr. Shudhirendar Sharma of the Dehli Ecological Foundation writes.[117] Notably, the microcredit "market" has now attracted the attention of Citibank and other global financial conglomerates. This isn't to discount the positive impact of the Grammen Bank system, but simply to acknowledge its necessary ambivalence and its explicit alignment with the discourse of neoliberalism, and to question Superflex's simplistic contrast between the intrinsically compromised operations of the nonprofit sector and the ostensibly untroubled procedures of ethical capitalism.

Ethical capitalism implies the assimilation of a resistance to the mandates of capital within capitalism itself through a kind of self-policing. It functions in two registers. First, through a quasi-socialization of risk via subsidized or simulacral versions of market tools (the Grameen Bank system relies, in fact, on NGO funding to remain solvent); and second, through a reduction of ethical claims to largely procedural forms of "transparency" and self-disclosure. Here ethics becomes a form of cultural capital. The necessary cost of doing business in a globalizing world is to appear ethical so as to not disturb the fragile sensibilities of your customers in privileged countries. The first register assumes that the poor need to be gradually weaned from their collectivist traditions and inoculated with the entreprenurial virus. The second is merely cover for business as usual. Neither are without problems, and neither is any less ethically compromised, or less prone to the projection of Western desires, than the work of the typical aid agency.

The *Guarana Power* project helps to complicate this analysis further. In the *Guarana Power* project Superflex worked with a collective of Brazilian Guarana berry farmers who were being pressured by beverage corporations such as Pepsi and AmBev to lower their prices. The result of their collaboration was a new energy drink (*Guarana Power*) that has so far received limited distribution (primarily at the opening of art exhibitions by Superflex). The bottle features the *Guarana Power* logo superimposed over the label of AmBev's competing Antarctica brand. While discussions of this project in the art world have focused primarily on issues of intellectual property and trademark infringement, it also suggests some of the constraints posed by Superflex's embrace of ethical capitalism. Neither Superflex nor the berry farmers have access to the capital, production facilities, or distribution networks necessary for their drink business to become self-sustaining in market terms. In fact, they are already in direct competition with a number of other locally produced, "fair trade," Guarana-based drinks (Mondo Guarana and Steaz: The First Fair Trade Energy Drink) being produced with equally altruistic motives but a somewhat stronger grasp of market fundamentals. In fact, the idea for the drink itself (and of consumption as a kind of surrogate form of political engagement or "empowerment) was taken from Mecca Cola, which is marketed by a French company that devotes a percentage of its profits to Palestinian charities (their slogan is: "Don't drink stupid, drink with commitment"). While Superflex's attempt to compete with multinational beverage corporations may constitute a symbolic gesture of resistance to globalization, it seems unlikely to improve the bargaining position of the Guarana farmers relative to Pepsi and AmBev.[118] One also suspects that the farmers themselves were less interested in exposing art world audiences to the evils of monopoly capitalism than in achieving some concrete improvement in their own living conditions.

As I've already suggested, the projects of Superflex reveal some of the symptomatic tensions in contemporary art practices that operate within, against, and adjacent to development agencies, NGOs, and other quasi-public institutions. What attitude does the artist take up relative to these institutions? Ironic distanciation? Adjudicatory critique? Sympathetic co-operation? The ambivalent character of Superflex's work is emblematic of these tensions. Are they reinforcing neoliberal orthodoxy, or exposing the contradictions of the "soft cops" of developmental aid? Are they building bold new models of social interaction, or merely recruiting incipient capitalists, in a kind of globalized version of Junior Achievement?[119] The very terms here suggest some of the challenges raised by these projects, as they consistently define Superflex's collaborators in behavioralist terms. For myself, the most productive aspect of the *Supergas* project isn't its earnest critique of NGO "dependency" (a critique which was articulated and debated within the aid community long before Superflex discovered it), but the particular effects of collaborative interaction itself: the habitus of shared labor and its relationship to new models of collectivity. This dimension of the work is generally treated as incidental or merely procedural in most accounts of the work.

It may well be that access to the biogas digester has made a significant practical difference in the lives of some Tanzanian (or Cambodian) farmers, but this is difficult to adduce, as there is little documentation of or reference to the experiences of the farmers themselves in the project's various art world instantiations. However, the broader goal of the project is not merely the provision of a new technology, but the fact that the sale (rather than the donation) of this equipment exposed the farmers to the redemptive pedagogy of the marketplace. The *Supergas* project thus endorses one of the central tenets of structural adjustment policy: that aid recipients must first be "reformed" (made more like "us"—properly self-actualizing bourgeois subjects) and that their poverty is the result of an insufficiently entreprenuerial spirit. It is on this level that the project can be said to reiterate, rather than challenge, the discourse of neoliberalism. The modularity of the *Supergas* digester, its status as a technology that can be transplanted from one site to another, is thus matched by the (ostensibly) benign universality of social relations governed by commodity exchange. It implies as well a relative indifference to the specific conditions of site, and a programmatic framing of the problem of site itself (the "solution," whether in Cambodia, Thailand, or Tanzania remains the same).

As I've already noted, Superflex's analysis of the politics of development aid exhibits a similar lack of situational nuance. Thus, aid agencies and NGOs can only ever function as agents of neocolonial domination. But NGOs, by definition, occupy a social or civil space that is at least partially independent from both the state and the private sector. As such, they exhibit no intrinsic political orientation, and have the potential to either reinforce or challenge the behaviors and values of each, depending on their integration with, or relationship to, specific institutional structures, ideologies, modes of resistance, or moments of crisis. For Deleuze, Negri, and others, the state, along with its network of ancillary NGOs, is wholly subsumed within the logic of capitalist globalization. For Superflex, this critique is inverted: the "problem" of the (Danish) state is precisely its *resistance* to the entrepreneurial spirit of the market and its tendency to inculcate a smothering, quasi-socialist passivity among aid recipients. In each case, the political and epistemological space occupied by public institutions and NGOs is assumed to be entirely corrupt and strategically irrelevant.

Superflex's idiosyncratic analysis of development aid achieves the rather remarkable feat of reconciling two entirely opposed intellectual traditions. On the one hand they evoke a decontextualized version of the leftist critique of the welfare state that emerged in the work of theorists such as James O'Connor, Claus Offe, Frances Fox Piven, and Richard Cloward during the 1970s and early '80s, in which welfare is seen as co-opting or defusing political energies among the poor and working class that might otherwise be channeled toward revolutionary struggle.[120] And on the other, they redefine revolution as the liberation of an individual, entrepreneurial spirit against the reactionary forces of international aid, essentially replicating neoconservative critiques first developed during the 1980s, which accused the welfare state of inculcating immorality and lassitude among the poor and working class.

Given the increasing subordination of state institutions across the globe to the key tenets of neoliberalism (privatization of public resources, reduction or elimination of social services, attacks on organized labor, corporate deregulation, etc.), Superflex's enthusiasm for capitalism can seem either perverse or simply naive. The proximate cause, however, is less ideological than geographic. Superflex's members have come to maturity as artists in Denmark, one of the few countries that still offer its citizens free health care and higher education and generous support for the poor and unemployed. Nearly 60 percent of Denmark's adult population either receives entitlement payments from the government or is directly employed in the public sector.[121] We can gain some insight into the ways in which this system has patterned notions of critique and resistance in this comment by the Danish artist Michael Elmgreen:

> I was on social welfare for several years in order to pull myself together as an artist. Because I never entered a heavily subsidized and very expensive art academy, my education was very cheap for the state of Denmark. What I'm trying to say is that there are people who refuse to work and use their time in a productive way.[122]

Elmgreen effectively recodes the "refusal" of work (a gesture which is typically associated with a rejection of the dehumanizing effects of wage labor) into a refusal to imbibe more fully from the generous menu of benefits provided by quasi-socialist state institutions. One suspects that Superflex's desire to "free" Tanzania's farmers from the paternalistic oppression of Western NGOs stems, in part, from their own experience of the Danish welfare state. Their worldview has been formed in a kind of political time capsule, based on a version of the Euro-American state as it existed before Reagan and Thatcher, GAAT and NAFTA, and the overarching dominance of neoliberalism, where the greatest danger to be feared is the stultifying control exercised by an overly generous welfare system. But the political function of the state today is far more diverse, ranging from the quasi-totalitarian state capitalism of China to the theocracies of the Middle East. In the United States the state apparatus has been largely subordinated to the market (at least until the current economic crisis), while in parts of Europe, as we've seen, elements of the post–Second World War social compact remain largely intact (although this, too, is beginning to change: Denmark's center-right Venstre Party currently governs the country in coalition with the Conservative People's Party). It is essential that any critical analysis of the state-form account for this complex geopolitical differentiation.

The subsidization of art education in countries like Denmark, Sweden, Germany, Austria, Belgium, and elsewhere, along with a relatively generous level of state support for exhibition spaces, biennial exhibitions, and other venues dedicated to contemporary art, has liberated a generation of younger European artists from the immediate demand to produce salable goods imposed by the art market (at least in the early stages of their careers). Taken in conjunction with an increasingly standardized model of neoconceptual art practice, the result has been a loosely defined genre that we might term "EU art": open-ended experiments in the public realm that range from site-specific installations and performances to longer-term collaborative projects. Freed by an international network of grants, awards, stipends, bursaries, and museum and biennial commissions, these "itinerant" artists are able to wander the globe producing projects in varying sites and geopolitical contexts.[123]

This is the system of patronage and institutional alignment that, in large measure, supports the production and dissemination of the "relational" art practices championed by figures such as Nicholas Bourriaud. It constitutes perhaps the most visible manifestation of a much larger and more diverse body of new collaborative and collective art practice that has resulted from the renegotiation of aesthetic autonomy outlined earlier in this book. It implies, in turn, a new approach to art (or more accurately, an elaboration and rearticulation of modes of practice dating from the 1960s and '70s) based on the creation of adaptive and improvisationally responsive "projects" rather than fixed or static objects-for-display. The global expansion of this approach, and the cosmopolitan diversity of the works produced under its auspices, marks a salutary shift from the heliocentrism of the recent past in which contemporary art production was by and large rooted in a handful of metropolitan centers. At the same time, the abbreviated, nomadic, nature of many of these projects (the result in part of the commissioning process and the pressures of art world career development) can lead to a certain provincialism. The artist is never able to enter fully into the complexities of a given situation, and relies instead on a generic set of creative solutions and a priori assumptions that are imposed indiscriminately onto each site of practice. The result is an operative tension between the consciousness, intentionality, and creative autonomy of the artist, and the resistance provided by the ground of practice (the conditions, events, histories, and predispositions of site that challenge, contradict, or subvert this consciousness). It is also this tension that differentiates the museum or gallery space as an essentially accommodating receptacle for the artist's vision from the vicissitudes of the Tanzanian countryside.

The *Supergas* project provides an instructive contrast with the work of Dialogue and Huit Facettes. Each of these groups begin not with an a priori technical solution, but with a receptive opening out to the site of practice and a heightened sensitivity to the cultural and social protocols, temporal and spatial patterns, and modes of physical movement that define each context. Participants are not singularized and abstracted, but engaged through their immersion in, and distance from, collective systems of meaning and intentionality. The problematic of the site isn't predetermined. Nor is there a presumptive understanding that the subjectivity of individual collaborators is a "problem" in need to repair or remediation. In the case of Huit Facettes' work in Hamdallaye, for example, their goal was to learn from, elaborate, and disseminate an existing set of cultural practices that, in their words, could help "reopen spaces of inventiveness and creativity blocked by the 'fundamentalism of the market.'"[124] And rather than offering a corrective exposure to the experience of bourgeois individualism, the members of Dialogue sought to enhance solidarity among the women of Kopaweda. While the *Supergas* project advocated a form of social interaction governed by the reductive logic of the marketplace, the projects of Dialogue and Huit Facettes involved an extended renegotiation of subjectivity through consecutive stages of vulnerability and sovereignty, generosity and self-assertion.

Conventional NGOs and development agencies rely on a teleological orientation to site, entering into a given context with a predetermined set of technical or administrative solutions. The knowledge that they gain about a site is useful only to the extent that it can facilitate the successful deployment of these existing techniques. As a result, the site itself can never be generative, nor can it act back on or transform the consciousness of the development agent or the underlying logic of the remedial program dictated by the formal development process. The experience of creative agency remains the singular province of the representatives of this process, while local communities are seldom in a position to renegotiate the parameters of the development paradigm being imposed upon them. It should be noted that there have been many efforts over the past decade or more to promote a "participatory" model of development (e.g., "Participatory Rural Appraisal," or PRA), in which local communities are encouraged to "present, share, analyze, and augment their knowledge" as part of the development process.[125] Participatory planning, however, has not been without its critics, who point to the significant discrepancy between its promise to return decision-making power and agency to the local level and its application in the field.[126] All too often, "participation" functions in a primarily symbolic capacity, to legitimate decisions and plans that have already been made at a higher level of institutional authority. And the process of consultation itself often ignores the extent to which local differentials in power can work to suppress dissent, disagreement, and critique, creating the illusion of consensus and reinforcing rather than challenging existing power relations.

As I've already noted, teleological action entails a certain flattening out of the conceptual and affective topography of a given site. Hans Joas contrasts teleological action with a non-teleological approach in which the site of practice is reciprocally productive. "It is not sufficient to consider human action as being *contingent* on the situation," as Joas writes. "It should also be recognized that the situation is *constitutive* of action" (my emphasis). Drawing on the work of Dietrich Böhler, he outlines a "quasi-dialogical" understanding of action. "Situations," he writes, "are not merely a neutral field of activity for intentions which were conceived outside that situation, but appear to call forth, to provoke, certain actions already in our perception." As Joas describes it, quasi-dialogical action doesn't imply the abandonment of agency or intentionality, nor does it cast site as the source of an originary plenitude of meaning that constrains or predetermines all subsequent action. He merely suggests that teleological and quasi-dialogical orientations operate as "reciprocal preconditions of each other."[127] The particular constellation of forces in place at a given site, brought into conjunction with the consciousness and predisposition of participants, are generative in ways that exceed both the conditions of site and the subjectivity of individual actors. Alejandro Meitin of Ala Plastica clarifies this difference:

> We don't define our activities under the term "projects." Proyectar (which has the connotation of a "plan" in Spanish) presupposes having a knowledge beforehand of how things will finish. This implies as well a level of premeditation in terms of our relations and the results of our relations with the social groups with which we interact. We prefer to speak of "initiatives," and within those, various "exercises," that are

multiplied and involve various persons and groups with which we construct a dialogue. We develop actions on the basis of this receiprocity.[128]

This is an important distinction with significant implications for the analysis of dialogical art practices, while also suggesting some of the productive connections that exist between these practices and relevant aspects of the pragmatist tradition (cf. John Dewey, George Herbert Mead). It can help, in particular, to bring some greater precision to debates around the question of agency in contemporary collaborative and site-specific art practice. It is typical in these debates for critics who are skeptical of collaborative or collective approaches to base their critique on a reductive opposition between an authentic avant-garde art practice, in which the artist retains complete creative mastery, and a reviled "community-based" practice, which insists on the debilitating surrender of "all claims to authority and authorship" on behalf of some naive ideal of social unity.[129] Creative agency, in this analysis, only retains its generative power when it is consolidated in a singular individual; once it is shared, distributed, exchanged, or negotiated within a larger social body, its critical acuity is dissipated. This persistent anxiety about the erosion of individual expressive autonomy stems in part from the belief that only a single monadic consciousness (epitomized by the figure of the radical artist or theorist) can originate a form of revolutionary insight capable of challenging habitual forms of thought and power. There is a tendency here as well to equate critique solely with conventional avant-garde notions of situational transcendence and distanciation, and to valorize a conative model of artistic identity in which an intrinsically passive viewer, public, or site is subjected to the artist's transformative intelligence.

As I've tried to suggest with the preceding examples, it's possible for creative agency to be de-individuated without diminishing its critical or transformative power. In fact, I would contend that this capacity can actually be enhanced if the experience of creative agency itself is treated in a more reflective manner. The projects of Dialogue involve neither a proprietary relationship to agency nor its absolute disavowal. Instead, we encounter a process by which agency is left deliberately unguarded—both claimed and relinquished—while retaining its ability to reframe a given reality. It is necessary here to recognize the productive materiality of the collaborative process itself. While some dialogical projects involve the dematerialization of the conventional art object (as painting, sculpture, etc.), this doesn't mean that materiality as such is suspended in the aesthetic configuration of the work. Dialogical projects involve not the denial of materiality but its rearticulation. The material conditions of a given space, the physical orientation of the Nalpar sites in Kopaweda, the proximity of bodies in Hamdallaye, play an absolutely central role in the capacity of site to articulate and inflect the dialogical process. Even in those projects that leave little or no physical trace (Wochenklausur's *Boat Talks*, Alÿs's *When Faith Moves Mountains*), the habitus of interaction is an essential constituent of creative action (here we return to Alÿs's attribution of agency to the dunes of Ventanilla).

What we encounter in many of the projects under discussion here is not a disembodiment of artistic practice, but a process of social interaction mediated by a physical and cognitive co-laboring (the construction and occupation of the Nalpar sites; the sharing of artisanal practices in Hamdallaye; the participatory "desire production" of Park Fiction). Site is understood here as a generative locus of individual and collective identities, actions, and histories, and the unfolding of artistic subjectivity awaits the specific insights generated by this singular coming-together. As I've already noted, this entails a movement between immersion in site and distanciation from it. Dialogical practice thus remains open to the transformative effects of site while resisting the tendency to romanticize "local knowledge as an almost mystical, uniform, good."[130] As Dialogue's work suggests, it's possible to acknowledge the problematics of a given context or community (in this case the gender hierarchies of Kopaweda) without sacrificing the ability to work productively within that community. Conventional NGOs and development agencies often view local culture as the static expression of some quaint or anachronistic folkway, peripheral to the "real" goals of economic or technical modernization, or even as an outright hindrance to the development process. Groups such as Dialogue, Ala Plastica, Huit Facettes, and Park Fiction, on the other hand, understand cultural production as multivalent and generative; as something that can transform, rather than merely transmit, meaning and value. Moreover, this transformative process is intended to catalyze provisional forms of solidarity and collective action rather than cultivate possessive individualism. In this respect, they challenge the imperatives of the development process, which seeks to "reform" the ostensibly damaged sensibilties of its client subjects through the gospel of entrepreneurial capitalism.

9 — THE ART OF THE LOCALITY

In the archaeology of communication, the local has long been considered the enemy.
MICHEL DE CERTEAU, *THE CAPTURE OF SPEECH*

We see a similar concern with the tactical production of solidarity in the projects of the Argentinian collective Ala Plastica.[131] Ala Plastica has worked in the communities of the Rio de la Plata basin, south of Buenos Aires, for almost two decades.[132] The Rio de la Plata is an estuary formed by the confluence of the Uruguay and Paraná Rivers. In the past the economy of this largely rural area depended on tourism and small-scale agricultural production. In recent years, however, the communities of the delta have been disrupted by a series of major construction projects led by the Initiative for the Integration of Regional Infrastructure in South America (IIRSA), a consortium of development agencies, banks, and government agencies from twelve South American nations.[133] The IIRSA functions primarily as an instrument of neoliberal economic policy, seeking to "organize the South American space into transnational corridors" capable of generating "intraregional and global business opportunities . . . [and] trade flows." In practice this spatial "reorganization" has involved the creation of an industrial and transportation infrastructure that has diminished the autonomy of local communities, eroded geopolitical boundaries and cultural topographies that are resistant to the logic of globalization, and displaced decision making to an intra-national network of development banks and quasi-private agencies. In Argentina, the IIRSA spearheaded the construction of the Zárate-Brazo Largo complex, a four-meter-high rail and highway line that cuts through the heart of the estuary; the fifty-kilometer-long Punta Lara Colonia bridge; and a massive dam project that displaced sixty thousand residents. These projects have dramatically increased the risk of flooding in the region, devastated local economies (in both agriculture and tourism), and worked to fragment and disenfranchise the rural population of the Rio de la Plata basin. Like the Adivasi villagers of Bastar, the communities of the Rio de la Plata have experienced many of the social and economic costs of modern development but reaped few of its benefits.

Ala Plastica has worked on two, related, fronts. First, they have developed projects that explore the relationship between the metropolis of Buenos Aires and the poor, rural populations to the south. One of Ala Plastica's earliest works, *Emergent Species* (1995), addressed the problem of pollution carried by the La Plata River, which has become a dumping ground for Buenos Aires's sixteen million inhabitants. Working in conjunction with a group of environmental scientists, NGOs, and local communities, they created a series of aquatic plant beds near Punta Lara on the southwest edge of the La Plata River. "Emergent species" is the term given by plant biologists to semi-aquatic species that live both beneath and above the water. The reed, or *junco*, in particular, due to its unique root structure, has the capacity to encourage sedimentation, creating an environment supportive of other species and leaching contaminants from the water.[134] With the *Emergent Species* project Ala Plastica began to draw organizational metaphors from natural or ecological processes. In addition to the aquatic plantations, the project also involved the creation of a communications network connecting local communities, sympathetic government officials, scientists, and environmental NGOs. Ala Plastica thus linked the "emergent" characteristics of aquatic plants producing the conditions necessary to sustain a diversity of life forms to the "emergent character of creative ideas and practices" and a "corresponding rhizomatic expansion of community" (see plate 10).[135]

As their knowledge of, and engagement with, the Rio de la Plata region deepened, Ala Plastica's members became increasingly conscious of the complex social and environmental interconnections that linked the river not just to metropolitan Buenos Aires, but to the larger ecosystem of the Paraná and Uruguay Rivers as they flow into Argentina from the north. This is a vast watershed, covering one-fifth of the South American land mass. The result of this insight was a scalar shift in their field of action to what they describe as a "bioregional" level. They began developing the *AA Project* in 2000, working through Delta School No. 25 on the Irigoyen Canal.[136] Due to the lack of infrastructure in the region, schools play a key role as centers of community action, flood relief, and political organizing, as well as education. The school provided a natural base of operations, and allowed Ala Plastica to strengthen its connection with families in the area. The residents of the Rio de la Plata faced an uphill battle in their efforts to challenge or contest the IIRSA's plans for the region. In addition to its daunting institutional and economic authority, the IIRSA also possessed an important epistemological power through its command of a set of planning technologies that could enframe the Rio de la Plata as an instrumentalized totality. The IIRSA was able to construct the Rio de la Plata as an object of planning intelligence within a conceptual schema governed by the imperative to integrate Argentina more fully into the circuits of global capital. As a result, the IIRSA's plans effectively reduced the agency and autonomy of the estuary's inhabitants, whose presence was seen as incidental to the larger logic of economic modernization.

In order to challenge the authority of the IIRSA it was necessary to begin by reconceptualizing the mapping process itself: to undertake the "assembly of what had been fragmented," as Ala Plastica writes. The *AA Project* began, then, with a process of participative cognitive mapping designed to recover local knowledge of the region's topography, habitats, and cultural and agricultural traditions: to take the measure of what might be lost to the "imperial knowledge" deployed by the IIRSA.[137] This process is typified by the *Camino de la Sal* (Salt Trail) performance in 2005. Here Ala Plastica and El Albardon (a group that works to identify and preserve traditional uses of native plants) collaborated with several Kolla aboriginal community groups and NGOs in northwest Argentina to retrace the three-hundred-kilometer path taken by previous generations of Kolla, from Hornaditas in Humahuaca to the Tres Pozos Sanctuary at Salinas Grandes. As Ala Plastica describes it, "Kolla grandparents used to walk eight or nine days . . . with their donkeys loaded with corn, potatoes, fruit, medicine plants and other products to trade for salt and hoes, and to practice their oral narratives." The walk, led by seven Kolla elders, involved discussions, storytelling, and the exchange of information on plants and habitat, and helped to consolidate resistance among the scattered Kolla communities to the predatory actions of mining and pharmaceutical companies that have come to the Rio de la Plata.[138]

Taken as a whole, the oral histories, memory maps, narratives, family photographs, plant lore, and other materials assembled by Ala Plastica provided a multivalent picture of the delta region over time: the complex changes registered in the use of the land and cycles of flooding; the growing impact of pollution and industrial contamination on riparian cultures; and the steady erosion of small farms and cottage industries. They represent a form of knowledge "imbedded in local experience," akin to the

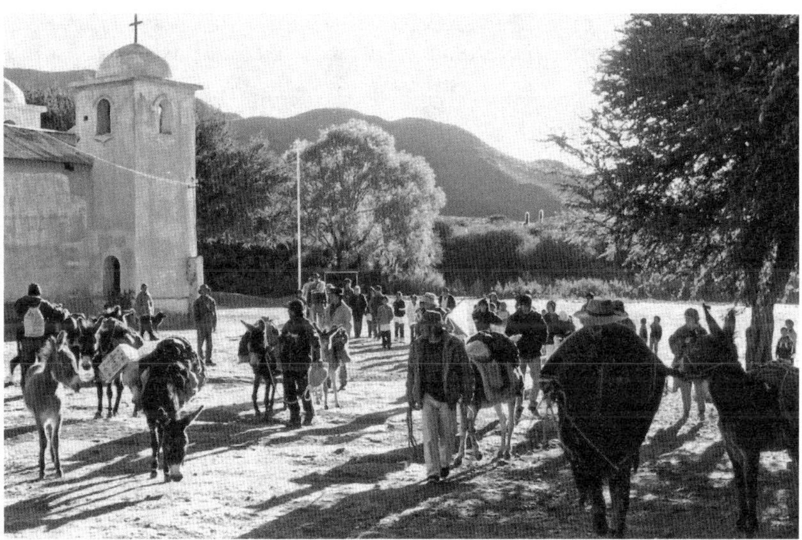

capacity that anthropologist James C. Scott has identified using the Greek concept of métis. Métis (taken from the goddess and mother of Athena) is differentiated from episteme—knowledge that is generic, repeatable, and codifiable—and techne, or technical know-how.[139] It has the implication, instead, of a form of knowing rooted in the specific conditions of a given site and the aggregated wisdom of the inhabitants of that site over time. Compared to the generalizing and abstract knowledge of Western science, imposed unilaterally on site, métis makes no claims for universality; it is "place specific," inflected by particular conditions and histories. It has parallels in turn with the early modern concept of the "genius" of place, the unique constellation of forces that permeate and give voice to a specific natural environment. This commitment to the empirical specificity of site and situation, against the instrumental abstraction of state planning, is essential to Ala Plastica's work. They speak of a "vocación del lugar" (a local calling) based on the process of "drawing closer" in their relationship to the Rio de la Plata.[140]

The material collected by Ala Plastica to "make visible local knowledge" was subsequently combined with data gleaned from conventional maps, land surveys, satellite imagery, and other sources to produce a spatial information bank that could help the residents conceptualize the region as a spatial, ecological, and geopolitical gestalt. The information bank facilitated a cognitive and conceptual movement between the registers of haptic immersion and visual and analytic abstraction, and has played a key role in helping Ala Plastica and other community groups and NGOs challenge "the one-sided techno-political conceptions" put forward by the IIRSA. It has been necessary in this process for the people of the Rio de la Plata to articulate their own, consensual, vision for the future of the region, and to insist on their consultative involvement in decisions regarding its future. The second stage of the *AA Project* involved a series of pragmatic interventions, inspired by the insights generated through the mapping and data collection process. These included the construction of embankments (to prevent flood damage) and emergency living spaces, and the development of training programs in carpentry, weaving, beekeeping, organic farming, and willow recovery, as well as the creation of a communications platform consisting of facilities for media production, Internet access, and training in the use of communications technologies. Women played a key role in this component of the project, as the men are often away from home for long periods hunting and fishing. The communications platform is intended to help community members exchange information on environmental threats and to generate alternatives to the proposals of the IIRSA. These include the "Integral Strategic Plan for the Conservation and Sustainable Use of the Paraná Delta" (PIECAS-DP), which was developed by Ala Plastica and their collaborators in conjunction with a broader coalition of activist groups and NGOs.

Ala Plastica doesn't seek to occupy the "wrong place," to use historian Miwon Kwon's description of artists who claim the role of interloper or provocateur, inserting themselves into a site in order to expose the contingency of the conventional forms of knowledge or identity operative there.[141] Here the capacity to produce a cognitive or perceptual disruption in a given social field is seen to reside wholly in the renegade intelligence of the artist. The artist crosses a proscribed threshold, entering a space where they don't belong. And precisely in that lack of belonging, in that transgression and estrangement, they are able to reveal the hidden logic of the site itself. Ala Plastica has worked in the Rio de la Plata for many years, and its members are viewed by their various collaborators as colleagues rather than foreign agents. For them, site is not simply a space of error, confusion, or blindness to be diagnosed and corrected. Rather, they locate the resources necessary to effect some transformation of political norms in the condition of site itself. The agency necessary to produce this disruption is distributed and negotiated rather than wielded. In the process, they seek to redefine the nature of place itself, drawing out its complexities and contradictions. Their work combines an epistemological critique (what forms of knowledge are appropriate or necessary to a given site?) with an investigation of governmentality (who is entitled to speak, or act, on behalf of this site, and who is subject to this authority?).

Ala Plastica operates as an NGO as well as an artistic group, working in conjunction with government agencies, community activists, and scientists. While they share certain commonalities with other NGOs, there are also clear points of differentiation. Perhaps the most important is their generative notion of site. As I've already noted, conventional NGOs typically arrive in a community with an a priori plan (a piece of equipment or technology, a proposal for restructuring local government, a set of prescriptive remedies, etc.). Consultation is limited to the effort to enlist local communities in the implementation of this modular plan. It is worth recalling that Saint Simon's original concept of an "avant garde" included industrialists and scientists as well as artists. All three figures were united by a distinctly modern notion of knowledge production in which a professional cadre would deploy its unique expertise in order to improve, guide, or rescue a passive mass audience. For its part, Ala Plastica doesn't claim to provide specific solutions to the social, economic, and environmental dilemmas facing the Rio de la Plata basin. As Ala Plastica member Alejandro Meitin has observed:

> Many expect art to contemplate ecological or social problems with a moral agenda . . . that will contribute to spreading around, in easily understood terms, contents produced by specialists. Absolutely not—what is sought rather is to give a chance to the specific potential that art has as a kind of knowledge: a way of perceiving, investigating and changing the world as a way of counterbalancing a world that is dominated by reason. . . . That is why we believe that it is not right for us to propose solving a problem; but rather, what is interesting is our being there at all, and our feeling-in-there that we become part of a new culture.[142]

This generative, improvisational relationship to site is also evident in a series of projects created by Jay Koh and Chu Yuan in Myanmar. Koh is a Southeast Asian artist who has developed performances, collaborative events, and exhibitions in Germany, Dublin, Finland, Mongolia, Malaysia, Cambodia, Vietnam, and Thailand over the past fifteen years. He's been active in Myanmar since 1997, building a rapport with local artists through informal conversations, the sharing of information and resources, and his own solo performances. As a result of these exchanges, a group of Burmese artists asked Koh to help them establish an independent art center in Yangon. Koh, along with his collaborator Chu Yuan, a Malaysian artist who was based in Singapore at the time, initiated the planning process by organizing an international symposium in 2002 ("Collaboration, Networking, and Resource-Sharing: Myanmar"). The symposium, one of the first of its kind in Myanmar, brought together a range of artists, writers, and educators from Asia and Europe to meet with their Burmese counterparts. It's important to bear in mind just how difficult even the simplest organizational process is in Myanmar. Under the ubiquitous gaze of the State Peace and Development Council (SPDC, formerly the State Law and Order Restoration Council) and a network of police spies, virtually any hint of political resistance or opposition is greeted with immediate arrest, imprisonment, and even torture. As Koh describes it, during the organization of the conference, "information had to be discretely channeled to military intelligence, to make it clear that the event was about sharing educational strategies and would definitely *not* be political."[143]

The task of creating a permanent physical space for the presentation of contemporary art was especially challenging because of Koh and Chu Yuan's status as foreigners. The Myanmar government is particularly fearful of foreign "infiltration" via cultural initiatives, which are seen as the "leading wedge of political opposition" and foreign domination.[144] This warning, from a current Burmese textbook, is typical:

As we are a civilized nation and gentle people we must preserve and protect our people's national pride. We have to be careful against foreign culture and tradition which will penetrate and influence our young people. . . . With the changes made along with globalization some big nations have made efforts to penetrate and influence developing countries with their culture, customs and traditions, which we need to prevent carefully. These big nations used to persuade young people from the developing nations by the way of cultural invasion such as music and arts. They started to bring in firstly music, culture and performing arts and then later thoughts, ideas and lifestyles of their choice.[145]

It is precisely the ability of cultural production to engage the imagination and transform consciousness (foreign "art" leads inevitably to foreign "ideas") that seems most threatening to the regime. As a result of this pervasive distrust, it's been nearly impossible for any foreign NGO or government to establish an independent art center in Myanmar since General Ne Win expelled the Goethe Institute in the mid-1960s.[146]

Cultural production in the country remains highly traditional. The art scene is driven by the demands of the tourist market and dominated by a master/apprentice model in which younger artists are subservient to, and dependent on, a small number of older, established artists. As a result of this hierarchical system of training and production, younger artists are reluctant to organize independently and unaccustomed to working collaboratively. In addition, the widespread presence of informants means that the members of most cultural organizations (writers unions, artist guilds, etc.) are habituated to a form of self-censorship. It has also resulted in a climate of suspicion, and even enmity, among different groups. In an interview with the author, Chu Yuan noted that Burmese artists "work in a 'family-minded' way, which basically means working only with those people whom they know and have established relationships with (either direct family connections or shared backgrounds)," in order to protect themselves from state surveillance. The "larger political situation in Burma," she continues, has been "internalized and reproduced in people's minds . . . they seem to thrive on conflict and on creating clear divisions between 'us' and 'them'; it's the only way they know how to operate."

Koh and Chu Yuan began by forming an ad hoc coalition of Burmese artists interested in working toward the establishment of an art center. They initially sought to function as facilitators, sharing their knowledge and expertise as curators and organizers. The coalition soon fell apart, due to internal divisions among the various member groups, and several of the artists asked Koh and Chu Yuan to play a more active role in moving the center forward. The Myanmar government told Koh and Chu Yuan that the process of approving and licensing the space would take five years, due to their status as foreigners and the unprecedented nature of their proposal. Working with a Burmese artist, they were able to obtain a local gallery permit instead, and opened the space within five months. NICA (Networking and Initiatives in Culture and the Arts) was launched in Yangon in early 2003.[147] It sponsored lectures, exhibitions, and workshops in writing, criticism, visual art, and information technology, along with a translation program designed to make English-language texts, such as John Berger's *Ways of Seeing*, available to Burmese readers, and to further disseminate the work of Burmese poets, artists, and writers. It also hosted a residency program that brought foreign artists and critics to Myanmar for exchanges and interactions with Burmese artists.[148] The IT component was particularly important, given the pervasive government control over media and information.

Despite the extreme vigilance of the Myanmar government regarding foreign cultural "penetration," Koh and Chu Yuan were able to mobilize the forces necessary to bring an independent art space into existence. Moreover, the NICA space engaged in activities (residencies, film screenings, translation programs, exhibitions) that had the precise effect of facilitating access to foreign cultural ideas and influences. They were able to do so in an environment in which foreign governments and NGOs had little success trying to operate. In fact, in 2006, while NICA was running some of its most effective programs, the Myanmar government forced the International Committee of the Red Cross to close its field offices in the country.[149] Koh and Chu Yuan's work with NICA was based on a detailed knowledge of Myanmar as a site of practice, and the complex protocols of authority, surveillance, accommodation, and resistance that were in operation there. The result, accumulated over seven years of sustained engagement, was a complex tactical understanding of the operation of both political and cultural power in Myanmar.

Koh and Chu Yuan came to recognize the essentially performative nature of public and private identity in Myanmar. This performative identity operates in two registers. The first register is intended for the panoptic gaze of the state, and centers on the public performance of docility and submission. As Chu Yuan has noted, "The Burmese people are natural performers because they have to perform every day of their lives; they have learned to speak and act differently with different people, depending on their perceived threat or trustworthiness. It's nearly impossible to get someone to tell you directly what they think, and we soon learned that the

Burmese believe that direct or open speech is an act of great foolishness." The second register involves a subtle subversion of this public or official persona via the uncoupling of speech from intention. It entails a certain tactical duplicity and an ability to communicate via unguarded channels of bodily movement and expressive nuance. In order to operate within this system, Koh and Chu Yuan had to develop a highly refined awareness of the manifold ways in which their own actions, gestures, and words were being received, translated, and understood. As Chu Yuan describes it, "I was told that whatever I said would be interpreted in at least ten different ways." She continued:

> We were constantly watched by different groups, from the dissidents to the authorities, who were all speculating about what we stood for and what we were trying to do in Burma. We found ourselves "performing" all the time; you're constantly aware that people are observing you and evaluating your actions, that everything you do carries some form of meaning to them. We carried out our performances in all the local art circles, modern and traditional, official and unofficial, to let everyone know that we were open and inclusive. This made NICA a "safe" space for locals to visit. We made contact with the dissidents, mostly indirectly, but we were able to send certain discrete signals to people.

It is this notion of feedback, or what we might describe as a process of biopolitical "tuning" between artist and site, that I find of particular importance. Koh and Chu Yuan grasped the complex choreography of communicative interaction: the ways in which the cognitive and the haptic, action and movement, pose and gesture, both produced and deferred meaning.[150] They also recognized the equally complex, and shifting, range of subject positions (dissident, informer, sympathizer, and skeptic) that were produced and reproduced within this semantic network. NGOs are, by necessity, driven by a more programmatic mandate (to implement particular systems of monitoring, relief, or technical assistance). As we've already seen in the work of Ala Plastica, artistic practices are able to operate in a more improvisational and unplanned manner. This reactive capacity is also evident in NICA's work. Koh and Chu Yuan were continually revising and reconsidering their plans in response to the changing forces of accommodation and resistance they encountered in Yangon. The idea of building an independent art space was generated by the local artists only after developing a level of trust in Koh and Chu Yuan through close observation and interaction. As Chu Yuan has noted, "It was clearly *not* a situation in which we could think ahead, plan a course of action and execute a pre-planned process."[151]

In addition to residencies, workshops, screenings, and exhibitions, NICA organized a number of collaborative, performance-based works. Chu Yuan's *Offering of Mind*, developed in 2005, involved a critical reconsideration of the concept of individual virtue or merit, which plays a central role in Burmese Buddhism. The SPDC has actively promoted those aspects of Buddhism (primarily the Theravada tradition) that encourage obedience and fatalistic resignation. Chu Yuan initiated the project as part of a performance art festival held at NICA in 2005. *Offering of Mind* drew on a practice in which worshippers donate gold to embellish *stupas* containing relics of the Buddha. The offerings are meant to help secure the donor's spiritual advancement in their next life. The Myanmar government has encouraged this belief, using it, as Chu Yuan notes, "to teach submission and non-resistance to one's fate in this lifetime." Thus, if the members of the ruling military junta are wealthy and powerful, it must be due to the virtue they exhibited in their past lives. Conversely, the poor have "earned" their poverty by failing to act nobly in their own past lives, and can only improve their condition in the future by sacrificing now.

Chu Yuan worked with several collaborators: an artist, an aspiring entrepreneur, a student, a young professional woman, a housewife/writer, a retired police officer who worked as a taxi driver, and a noodle vendor. Each collaborator was asked to write their "strongest wishes, hopes or thoughts" on pieces of paper and place them inside a *stupa*-shaped headpiece made out of wire. They then wore these headpieces as part of site-specific performances in locations that were related in some way to their own histories or aspirations, ranging from the venerable Swedagon Temple to the University of Rangoon to the streets of downtown Yangon. In *Offering of Mind* the condition of passive resignation is replaced by the open manifestation of desire, and the deferral of change is replaced by at least a symbolic form of action here and now. Simply calling attention to the rhetorical or declarative status of one's body in public space involves a considerable degree of risk (in the photographs documenting the performance the collaborators' faces must be turned away from the camera). The *Offering of Mind* per-

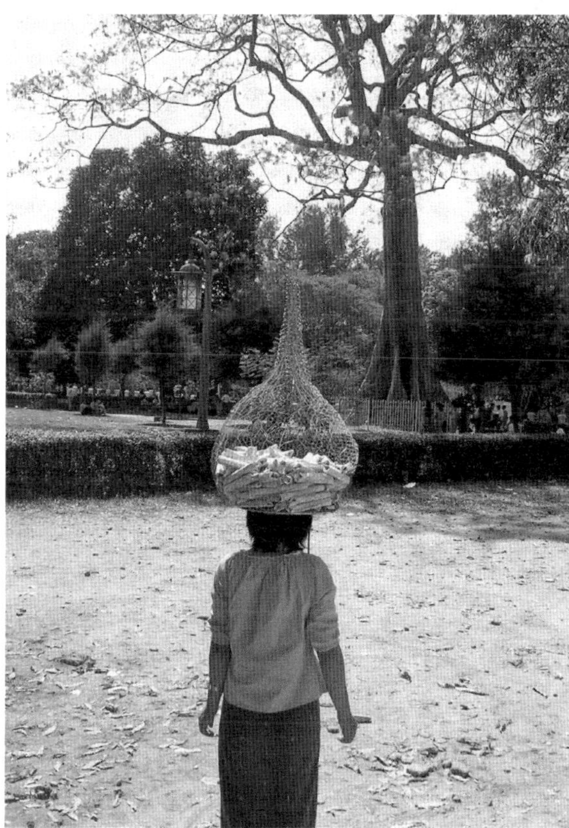

FIGURE 8 Chu Yuan and Myanmar/Burmese collaborators, *Offering of Mind: Christian Kachin Undergraduate*, performed photography on the campus of University of Rangoon (2005). Photograph by Chu Yuan.

formance thus exists on a continuum with other, more overt, gestures of resistance marked by the occupation of public space. It collapses, if only briefly, the division between the quiescent self-presentation demanded by the state and the normally privatized realm of expressive autonomy. As Chu Yuan writes, "This project functions as a visual representation of NICA's work in Myanmar: to encourage and cultivate the development, propagation and application of knowledge and ideas in the present. This becomes an offering of mind, in contrast to the offering of gold: to be applied in the present, in contrast to the ideology of gaining merit for one's next life" (see plates 11 and 12).[152]

Koh and Chu Yuan closed NICA's physical space in Yangon in 2007 after nearly five years in operation. However, they've continued to develop new projects in rural communities in Myanmar while also providing ongoing support for independent artist initiatives under the umbrella of what they call an "Open Academy."[153] As with Dialogue's work in Kondagaon, a seemingly modest cultural intervention nonetheless had a significant effect. In 2005, Studio Square, the first independent art space run entirely by younger Myanmar artists, opened in Yangon. And in 2007, another space, New Zero, opened as well. Although both maintained the "family-minded" model of closed membership, their emergence still signals a remarkable shift. In 2008, a young artist who had trained at NICA established Beyond Pressure, an independent group with an open, participatory operational structure. As the brutal suppression of protests by Buddhist monks in 2007 suggests, significant change in Myanmar may well be deferred by the intransigence of the military junta. But it's also important to recognize the capillary, cumulative, nature of political transformation, which is grounded in the gradual, often undetectable, accretion of events, relationships, and changes in individual consciousness. In this sense, we might say that NICA's work performed a prefigurative function in Myanmar: fostering experimentation with new modes of self-organization and collective action, and helping to overcome the endemic suspicion and mistrust encouraged by the state. Their work cultivates not an "agonistic" notion of democracy, but rather the conditions of mutual trust and civility necessary to sustain agonism and disagreement in the first place.[154]

The work of each of the groups I've discussed is characterized by a particular order of attention to the nuances of space and visuality, of integration and isolation, which structure a given site. In each case it involves a kind of noticing, distinct from normal perception, which emerges in the act of opening oneself to a specific context or situation. It is this capacity, this condition, which links the work of Dialogue, Huit Facettes, NICA, and Ala Plastica to the creative practice of a novelist, painter, or photographer who experiences a heightened sensitivity to the natural world or human social interaction—who notices things or events that carry meaning in hidden or unexpected ways. The mode of perception evident in these works is not instrumental (site is not a resource for the enactment of an a priori vision or a goal already-in-mind), but rather, anticipatory and open. At the same time, it is intensely focused and attuned, prepared but not projective. It is this unique form of perception, aggregated over countless discrete moments of insight that led Dialogue to recognize the potential of neglected water pump sites as a fulcrum for reconfiguring social interactions in Kopaweda, or NICA to master the delicate choreography of gesture and pose, inflection and enunciation, necessary to operate effectively under the gaze of an ever vigilant police state.

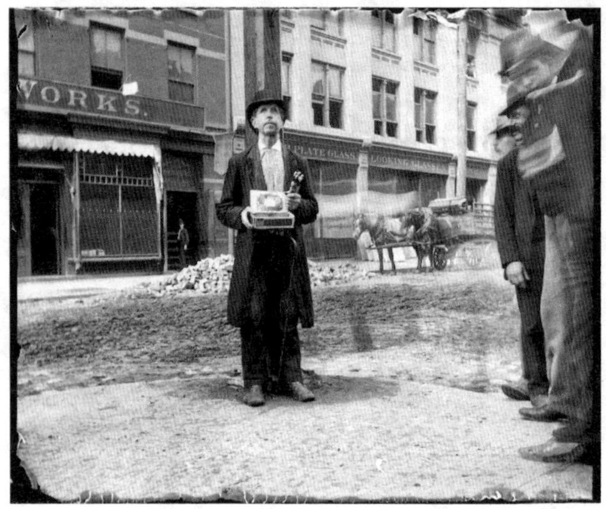

FIGURE 9 Jacob Riis, *Blind man (beggar) Father of the notorious Blanche Douglass* (c. 1890). Museum of the City of New York, The Jacob A. Riis Collection.

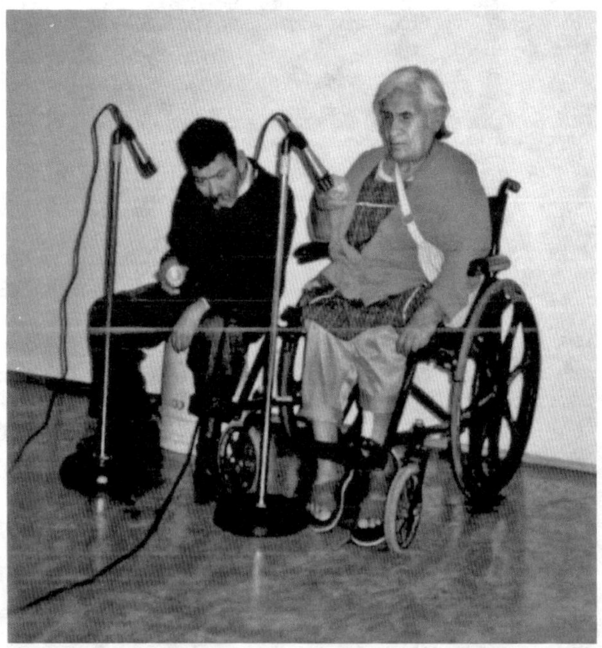

FIGURE 10 Santiago Sierra, *Two Maraca Players*, six speakers, amplifiers, microphones, and stool (2002). Courtesy of the artist and Lisson Gallery, London.

3

EMINENT DOMAIN: ART AND URBAN SPACE

I don't know the meaning of the word "representation." As hard as I try I can't find
any meaning to the word.
SANTIAGO SIERRA. INTERVIEW WITH ROSA MARTINEZ, "ENTREVISTA A SANTIAGO SIERRA, 207

The history of the long error is the history of representation.
GILLES DELEUZE, *DIFFERENCE AND REPETITION*, IX

We are faced with two photographs. In the first image a beggar
stands before us in a bowler and dirty frock coat.[1] He's positioned
at the edge of a city sidewalk, the façades of the buildings across
the street clearly visible behind him. A pile of bricks lies on the
opposite curb, possibly evidence of a nearby construction project.
The exposure time was relatively long, a half second or more, resulting in the blurred image of a pedestrian to his right. We also
see a horse-drawn cart standing motionless behind him. Several
men hover at the far right edge of the frame, trying to stay out
of the photograph as they stare at the beggar. One of them appears to be smiling, amused perhaps by the oddity of a photographer showing interest in such a lowly subject. We know that

he is a beggar because of the photograph's caption and because of his demeanor, which is open and receptive. We know that he is poor because of his shabby and unfashionable coat and soiled shirt, worn without a tie. We are drawn to his eyes, which are hollow and gaze upward at nothing. He is blind: even if the caption didn't tell us, we would know. He stands with the self-consciousness of someone who can't be entirely sure of his orientation to the world around him. The stiff formality of his posture signals both trust and patient subordination, like a servant waiting at a table. He, and his blindness and poverty, are clearly on display. He holds an open box, offering it to the photographer, and by implication, to passersby, for contributions. In his left hand he clutches the pencils that he is selling in exchange for this contribution. The beggar presents himself to the viewer as a dignified supplicant, molding his public image to reassure potential benefactors that he is making a good faith effort to support himself rather than seeking undeserved charity. He is not a shiftless pauper but chooses to labor despite his affliction. The act of selling pencils for a donation is evidence that he has not disavowed the moral economy of the market, that even disabled by blindness he chooses to remain a productive participant in the logic of exchange (cf. Superflex's decision to sell, rather than donate their biogas generators).

This photograph was made around 1890 by the Danish American journalist Jacob Riis. Riis is best known as a tireless advocate for tenement reform in New York City during the late nineteenth century. He was successful in mobilizing economic and political support for changes in city regulations governing the tenement buildings in which the vast majority of New York's poor immigrant population lived. He did so through a series of influential books and public lectures in which he presented evidence (photographs as well as written descriptions) of the demoralizing effect of life in the overcrowded neighborhoods of New York's Lower East Side. Like so many intrepid urban "explorers" before him (Gustave Doré, Henry Mayhew, Charles Booth, Charles Loring Brace), Riis brings a reassuring order to the dark underworld of the modern city through a process of classification and differentiation, attributing specific cultural and moral characteristics to each immigrant population (Germans are stolid and "order loving," Italians are hot-blooded, Chinese are inscrutable pagans, etc.). He devotes a lengthy discussion to beggars and paupers in *How the Other Half Lives* (1890), his most famous book describing life among the urban poor. "Pauperism," Riis writes, "grows in the tenements as naturally as weeds in a garden lot. A moral distemper, like crime, it finds there its most fertile soil":

> The thief is infinitely easier to deal with than the pauper, because the very fact of his being a thief presupposes some bottom to the man. Granted that it is bad, there is still something, a possible handle by which to catch him. To the pauper there is none. He is as hopeless as his own poverty. I speak of the pauper, not of the honestly poor. There is a sharp line between the two.[2]

Riis's distinction between the pauper and the "honest poor" returns us to the complex discourse of labor and identity first introduced in our discussion of property in chapter 2. Here one becomes a legitimate subject by extracting value from the natural world, thus demonstrating a capacity for productive work. The long-standing Euro-American anxiety about "indiscriminate almsgiving" is based on the fear that undeserved charity would simply escalate the moral deterioration of the poor and encourage their resistance to the discipline of the labor market. Figures such as the beggar or the mendicant pose a particular challenge to this moral order and feature prominently in the literature of the urban social reform movements that paralleled the rise of the modern industrial city.

Riis's image was preceded by several decades by Richard Beard's daguerreotype of a "Blind Bootlace Seller," reproduced as a woodcut in Henry Mayhew's four-volume *London Labour and the London Poor*, published in 1861.[3] Here we see the same public presentation of poverty and disability. *London Labour and the London Poor* again demonstrates the characteristic drive toward taxonomic classification elicited by the threatening class and ethnic diversity of the modern city. In his landmark study Mayhew exemplifies the Victorian ambivalence about the poor and working class, situating them along a moral continuum that has remained consistent up to the present day. The book's subtitle is "A Cyclopaedia of the Condition and Earnings of Those that *Will* Work, Those that *Cannot* Work, and Those that *Will Not* Work." Mayhew thus identifies three subject positions within the moral economy of labor: the able-bodied working class, the disabled, and the criminal. The third category constitutes a pariah class, outside the bounds of bourgeois morality and undeserving of assistance. The second category, those who are ostensibly "unable" to work, is more complicated. The blind beggar is emblematic.[4] Being blind diminishes the

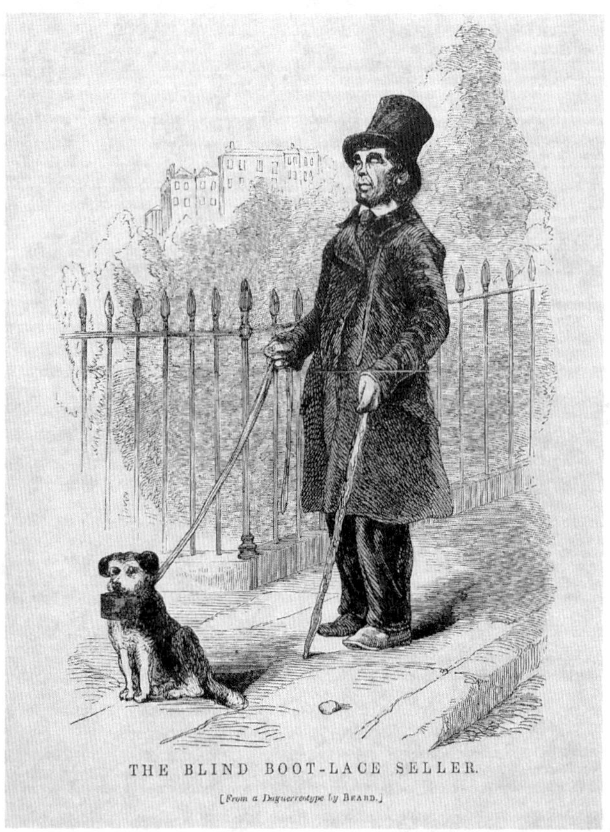

FIGURE 11 "The Blind Boot-Lace Seller," from a daguerreotype by Richard Beard, in Henry Mayhew, *London Labour and the London Poor* (1861).

stigma of poverty and begging. As Mayhew writes, "There must be some mitigating plea, if not a full justification, in the conduct of those [blind individuals] who beg directly or indirectly, because they cannot and perhaps never could labor for their daily bread."[5] Their "mitigating" physical condition notwithstanding, the blind or disabled must still make at least a symbolic effort to justify the provision of charity, and to preserve their own dignity. Pity is thus mixed with the recognition that the poor are "like" us, and occupy the same moral universe as the donor.

This exchange is rendered all the more complicated by the fact that the blind beggar represents a mode of penury that is located uncomfortably between the two categories of deserving and undeserving poor. As a result, the figure of the "fake" blind beggar poses a particular problem (Riis discusses it in conjunction with other "feints," such as the use of sick babies, to solicit charity). As Riis writes, "Professional mendicancy does not hesitate to make use of the greatest of human afflictions as a pretence for enlisting the sympathy upon which it thrives. Many New Yorkers will remember the French schoolmaster who was 'blinded by a shell at the siege of Paris,' but miraculously recovered his sight when arrested and deprived of his children by the officers of Mr. Gerry's society."[6] Our capacity for "sympathy" can thus be misused, or exhausted, by the duplicity of the poor. Mayhew describes a similar dynamic:

> It appears to me, then, that the blind have a right to ask charity of those whom God has spared so terrible an affliction, and who in the terms best understood by the destitute themselves, are "well to do"; those whom—in the canting language of a former generation of blind and other beggars—"Providence has blessed with affluence." This right to solicit aid from those to whom such aid does not even approach to the sacrifice of any idle indulgence—to say nothing of any necessary want—is based on their helplessness, but lapses if it becomes a mere business.[7]

The beggar is caught in a double bind. On one hand, he is obliged to present proof of his investiture in the logic of the market (the selling of nominal commodities such as pencils or boot laces). On the other, by treating begging as a "business," and the production of guilt, shame, or obligation in the passerby as a technical undertaking, he loses his legitimacy. It is precisely the pathos of his failed but earnest attempt at work, his striving, despite his affliction, to be a good worker, that earns him his reward. If he is too good, or too adept at mastering the psychology of begging, he becomes a criminal. His "helplessness" must thus be carefully preserved for it's his very lack of agency that allows the donor to savor the piety of selfless giving.

The strategic calibration of affect is a central concern of the broader social documentary and urban reform tradition as well. Just as the beggar must be adept at gauging emotional tolerances and choreographing his self-presentation, so too the reformer must navigate between compassion fatigue, voyeurism, and sheer apathy in rousing his complacent middle-class audience. Riis relied on a narrative discourse centered on melodramatic stories of the colorful characters inhabiting New York's impoverished underworld. He would present these stories in public lectures, illustrated with lanternslide projections and often accompanied by an organ player for further dramatic effect.[8] For many in his audience lower Manhattan was *terra incognita*, so Riis would pose as a kind of tour guide or surrogate, taking them on a vicarious journey to the hidden depths of the Lower East Side. The rhetoric of seeing and being seen, of blindness and revelation, that is both literally and symbolically represented by the figure of the blind beggar was central to Riis's work. Within this discourse, poverty exists because of the ignorance and indifference of the privileged classes. If they knew of its existence, they would hasten to ameliorate it. Thus, the proper role of the reformer is to expose the privileged to the suffering and abjection of the immigrant poor, to reveal that which had been hidden, unseen, or denied, and to thereby shock them out of their insulated complacency. Inevitably, the exchange was never quite so simple or straightforward. Riis's appeal to his audience's compassion was combined with a keen understanding of the less-elevated incentives provided by fear and self-interest. One of his most evocative stories describes a vengeful, unemployed father who journeys to the expensive stores on Fifth Avenue. With visions of his starving children filling his head, he attacks the throng of wealthy shoppers with a knife.[9] "The sea of a mighty population," Riis writes, "held in galling fetters, heaves uneasily in the tenements. Once already our city . . . has felt the swell of its resistless flood [a reference to the Draft Riots of 1863]. If it rise once more, no human power may avail to check it."[10]

The cultural history of urban reform is, of course, identified with an ostensibly objective investigative process supported by the facticity of the documentary photograph. Despite their undeniable veracity, it is clear that photographs of poverty and suffering carry no intrinsic or self-evident meaning. They can easily enough function as a site for the projection of any number of emotional responses—from voyeuristic fascination to empathetic recognition—depending on the viewer and the context of reception. This semantic mobility is evident in what is perhaps the best-known image of a beggar in the oeuvre of modernist photography, Paul Strand's *Blind Woman, New York* from 1916. The theme of the blind beggar has a venerable past in the history of art, extending back to Jacques-Louis David's *Belisarius Begging for Alms* and scenes of Bartimaeus, the blind beggar in the Gospel of Mark. Strand deployed this image as he was breaking with the soft, implicitly feminine, gum bichromate landscapes and society portraits that characterized early Pictorialist photography. In response, artists

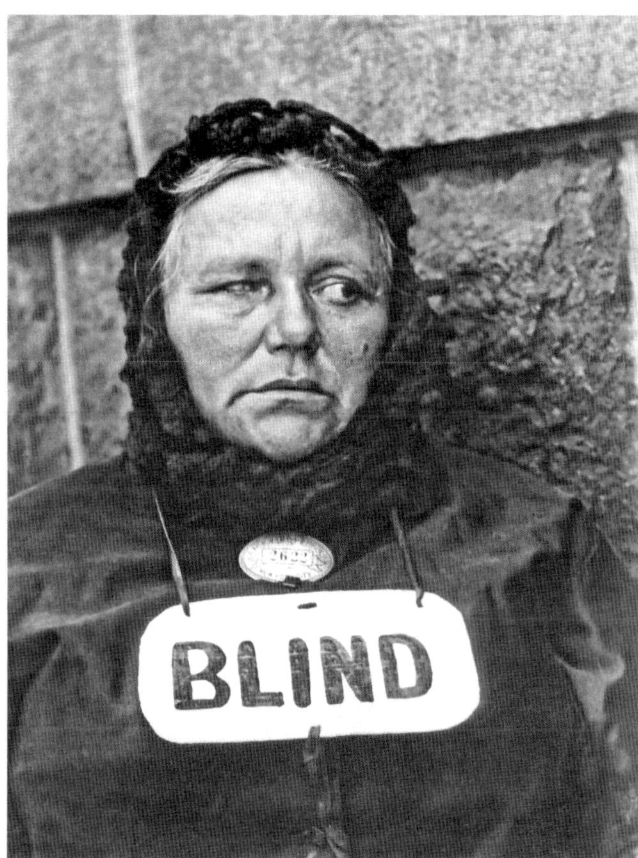

FIGURE 12 Paul Strand, *Blind Woman*, New York (1916). Copyright Aperture Foundation, Inc., Paul Strand Archive.

such as Strand and Alfred Stieglitz advocated a sharply focused, masculinist style of "straight" photography characterized by graphic contrasts and rectilinear compositions. In place of the genteel pastoralism of Pictorialist imagery, they produced gritty scenes of New York City street life. Strand, in particular, was fascinated with peddlers, alcoholics, beggars, and the homeless. As he described it, "I felt they were all people whom life had battered into some sort of extraordinary interest and, in a way, nobility."[11] Despite his subsequent commitment to political engagement in his work with the Photo League, Strand's image of the blind beggar is uncoupled from then-current debates over public policy or the particular situation of the urban poor in New York City. She becomes, instead, a generic and universalized emblem of the "nobility" of the human spirit under duress.[12]

The semiotic instability of the suffering body brings us to our second photograph. Here we see two figures, an older man and woman, seated side by side. The woman is in a wheelchair, while the man sits on a ten-gallon plastic paint bucket. The man slumps forward (there is no chair back for him to rest against), his left hand hanging limply on his knee. In his right hand he holds a maraca, possibly improvised from a tin can. The woman in the wheelchair sits up more fully and also holds a maraca in her right hand. The man wears a dark sweater and pants and the woman wears pants, a patterned blouse, and a cardigan. She has a small white bag around her shoulder. Two microphone stands have been placed directly in front of them, with each microphone angled sharply downward to capture the percussive sound of the maracas. They are seated indoors, against a blank white wall, as if performing for an unseen audience. The floor may be polished concrete or laminate; the murkiness of the photograph makes it difficult to discern precise details. This image is far more recent than the Riis photograph. It documents a January 2002 project in which the Spanish artist Santiago Sierra paid two blind *maraqueros* (beggars who play the maracas) to perform in the Galería Enrique Guerrero in Mexico City. While the image was taken only a few years ago, it resembles the grainy, underexposed photographs made to document early performance and conceptual art practices. This association is quite deliberate, as Sierra actually reprocesses original color photographs of his performances in black-and-white in order to evoke the aura of the experimental art scene of the 1970s.

Although they are separated by over a century, Riis's blind beggar and Sierra's *maraqueros* occupy a similar position within the moral economy of bourgeois society. For each of them the public space of the city serves as the locus of a complex exchange across class boundaries, centered on notions of obligation and guilt, shame and productivity. Riis's photograph of the blind beggar is meant in part to replicate his plaintive appeal before a more focused, and potentially more motivated, constituency (the audience or readership for Riis's own lectures and publications). For Sierra, the re-presentation of the *maraqueros* in a gallery space is intended to concentrate and intensify the forms of affect generated by their presence on the street. What the image can't show us is the sound of their playing, which has been heavily amplified through a set of large speakers in a "grating" manner. As a result, according to critic Jim Drobnick, "viewers were sonically confronted with the economic and class disparity structuring their 'pure' aesthetic experience."[13] Contained in the gallery space, the viewer can no longer ignore or walk past the *maraqueros* with eyes averted, but must acknowledge their presence directly. In each case, we are presented with a set of truth claims: Sierra brings us the actual bodies of the *maraqueros*, while Riis provides irrefutable evidence of a previously hidden urban poverty through the indexicality of the photographic image. This act of physical or visual dislocation bears a complex relationship to the beggars' own self-presentation on the street, both doubling and contradicting it. The beggars are sponsored, so to speak, called to appear before the viewer by an agent (the artist, the reformer) who seeks to deploy their bodies, and image, for his own purposes. The beggars' presence—in the gallery, in the lecture hall—constitutes an enunciation by the artist or reformer within which they function as the semiotic material ("signifiers" of various forms of social abjection or suffering). They no longer present themselves, but are, instead, re-presented by another, who speaks through, and on behalf of, their experience of suffering and privation.

For Sierra, as for Riis, the beggar has been summoned in order to teach us a lesson. Sierra, too, believes that he can shock (implicitly bourgeois) viewers out of their complacency and into the correct critical consciousness of both the Other's suffering and their own privilege. This claim is quite explicit in critical accounts of the work. Thus, for Cuauhtémoc Medina, "Sierra's work is designed to produce constant shock" as he "blows the whistle on the fraud that prevails in the history of emancipation." And for curator Rosa Martinez, Sierra's work "lays bare with jarring clarity the repetitive mechanics of labor exploitation and human submission for economic ends, thereby flouting the would-be purity of art."[14] Riis sought to convince his audience to support improvements in the living conditions of New York's immigrant poor. Sierra's goal is both less concrete and more ambitious. On the one hand, he seeks to rob the bourgeois viewer of the solace of art as a space of spiritual recreation insulated from the contradictions of daily social life. His use of beggars, migrants, prostitutes, and the homeless in his performances is intended to destroy the false ideology of aesthetic autonomy by "de-contextualizing and relocating socially distant signifiers" (the beggars, e.g., taken from the street to the gallery floor).[15] Sierra's willingness to employ the actual bodies of the poor and working class provides an instructive contrast with Francis Alÿs's use of surrogates in *When Faith Moves Mountains*. Alÿs rejected the ethical dilemma that

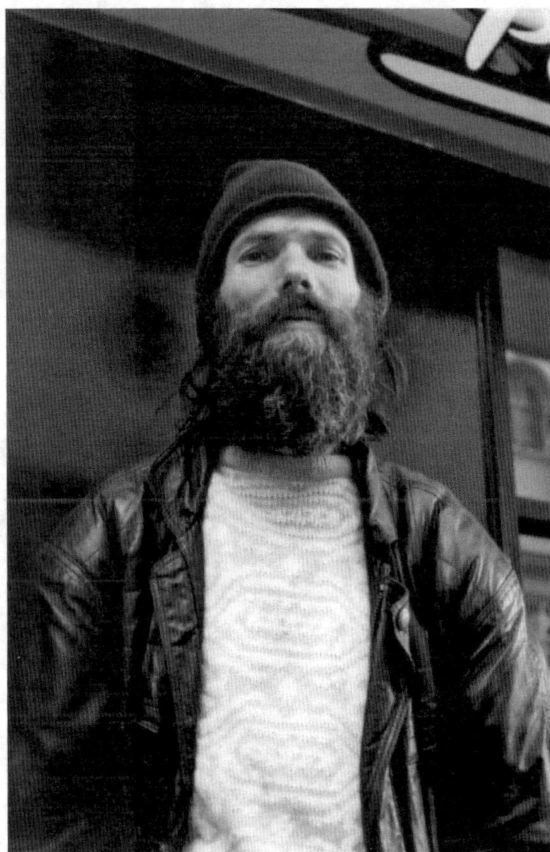

would have been raised by asking the inhabitants of Ventanilla's shanty-town to spend a day laboring in the sun by importing students from Lima. Sierra chooses instead to foreground and exaggerate this dilemma.

In *Person Saying a Phrase*, a project developed the same year as his *maraqueros* piece, Sierra paid a beggar on the streets of Birmingham, England to recite the phrase, "My participation in this project could generate $72,000 in profit. I am paid £5," in front of a camera. The resulting video, according to Martinez, "reveal[ed] the progression of surplus value in the system of artwork valuation, calling into question the aura of art as a moral institution by stressing its mercantile value."[16] Paul Strand used a beggar to make art by encouraging viewers to detach themselves from her specific condition as a victim of poverty and disability, and view her instead as a universal emblem of noble suffering or a poignant expression of the rough beauty of the street. Sierra inverts this logic and uses the beggar to "un-make" art, revealing the bankrupt ideology of aesthetic autonomy. As Drobnick argues, Sierra's "annoying, loud, out-of-place or otherwise noisome intrusions perturb both the quietude central to disinterested notions of aesthetic perception and the mythology that the artistic economy operates benignly or separately from the economy as a whole." Art, for Sierra, functions as a kind of alibi for bourgeois complacency, allowing viewers to experience unearned moments of aesthetic transcendence. In encountering his work viewers will be viscerally struck by the incongruity between their outrage at the ostensible exploitation exhibited in the gallery and their own manifest indifference to the larger system of capitalist oppression of which this is merely a singular, and comparatively mild, example.

Sierra's intervention assumes, of course, that there are still gallery-goers in the contemporary art world who retain some faith in the verities of a "disinterested" aesthetic, and that the violation of this faith is likely to transform their perceptions of poverty or their own class status. This assumption, however, strains credulity. If the past thirty years of artistic practice can be said to exhibit any coherent theme it would be the nearly single-minded drive to challenge, subvert, or transgress any fixed or rigid notion of aesthetic autonomy. At this point in the history of art, anyone who can enter a gallery, biennial, or museum and expect to receive an entirely pure or disinterested aesthetic experience possesses a capacity for denial that is unlikely to be disturbed by the presence of the odd beggar or prostitute. The "shock" produced by Sierra's work (such as it is) doesn't come from the largely ceremonial violation of the conventions of aesthetic autonomy, but rather, from his willingness to literally replicate the physical and economic coercion of the poor and working class.

There is, of course, a certain logic to this gesture if one remains invested in the traditional avant-garde notion of a pedagogical or therapeutic shock. If contemporary gallery-goers are so blasé that they can no longer be easily provoked, then the artist's only recourse is to raise the ante on provocation. By parading blind beggars, illegal workers, and drug-addicted prostitutes through the ostensibly sanctified spaces of the international art world, Sierra seems to say, "OK, try to take up an aesthetic distance from *this*." But, one might ask, if we are able to walk by the homeless and poor on the street in our daily lives, why should their presence in an art gallery make us any less prone to denial, indifference, or objectification than the typical Oxfam advertisement? It is precisely the assumption that the ethically correct form of revelation (of poverty and privilege) will occur simply because the exposure to class difference has been staged against the ground of an art space that seems most improbable in Sierra's work.

Sierra conflates a critique of aesthetic autonomy with a critique of bourgeois complacency. Each assumes a singularly provincial viewer whose naive "mindset" will be "laid bare" by his work.[17] This conflation is further complicated by his tendency to project his own guilt as a "white, Caucasian, male" on to the implied viewer or audience of his work. As he states in an interview with Martinez: "We First-Worlders and, above all, the world of culture, have no idea how grim and deep this issue [global poverty] is. We usually think it has been settled or mitigated."[18] "From Barcelona or Helsinki," Sierra continues, "we might conclude that mankind has evolved favorably from its infirmity. But all you need to do is take a flight to Manila or Medellín to see the collateral damage of our optimism. When you migrate the other way around, the feeling of being a dominator—as you put it—never leaves your mind."[19] Sierra's revelatory discovery of global poverty, and his own, apparently anguished, recognition of himself as "dominator" is turned on the viewer, who must undergo the same geopolitical catharsis presumably experienced by Sierra himself on his travels in the developing world. The viewer, as a result, is reduced to an abstraction: the oblivious and unknowing denizen of the "world of culture" who seeks only escapism and hedonistic denial and is wholly ignorant of the ongoing suffering of the "lumpen beyond their borders."[20] But perhaps the dismay generated by Sierra's work has less to do with the fact that art world viewers are recognizing the violence of poverty or homelessness for the first time, than with the sense that Sierra is reiterating, not challenging, this exploitation on the basis of an ill-conceived notion of both audience and critique itself.

The typological reduction of the viewer is matched in Sierra's work by an equivalent reduction of his participants to categories of abjection or social marginality. Like Strand's blind beggar, they aren't singular individuals, but representative types (the "junkie," the "illegal street vendor," the "prostitute," the "homeless") whose suffering represents the necessary consequence of the generic viewer's privilege. Sierra is drawn, in particular, to display the docile, constrained, overtaxed, and instrumentalized bodies of his "marginalized" subjects. They are deprived of agency and set to a task, the very monotony or absurdity of which will expose the violent illogic of the neoliberal economy. The fact that they do so through a formalized system derived from Minimal and Conceptual art, in which certain serialized and precisely scripted actions (sitting in a box for a set period of time, holding up a wall at a fixed angle, being tattooed with a line of a specific length) are enacted on and through their bodies is, presumably, meant to further underscore the tension between norms of aesthetic autonomy and the quotidian violence of global capitalism.

Sierra exhibits a remarkable faith in the self-evidence of this gesture, as if the sheer physical presence of these bodies will inevitably compel the correct response: a therapeutic "dislocation" in which the viewer is brought to recognize their own contingency and implication in the suffering of the Other.[21] But, as I've already suggested, images of suffering and poverty, duress and exploitation, carry no necessary or a priori meaning. Rather, the suffering body can be turned toward many different ends. While some might see a homeless beggar as the victim of a cruel and unjust economic system, others will view his bleak existence as the deserved result of personal failure and moral depravity. There is no ethically pure or unproblematic relationship to suffering, but rather, a continuum of orientations and attitudes that involve varying degrees of agency, self-reflection, defensiveness, and vulnerability. In *Fruits of Sorrow* Elizabeth Spelman identifies four modalities in the way our attention is brought to suffering. The first takes suffering as entertainment or spectacle, inviting a voyeuristic fascination in which the viewer experiences an outright pleasure with no sense of reciprocal identification. One thinks of the perverse genre of photographs made to commemorate lynchings in the southern United States during the Jim Crow era (in which the desecrated body is surrounded by a smiling and enthusiastic crowd). The second mode of reception involves the experience of pity. Here suffering provides a different form of pleasure: the quasi-distanced contemplation of one's own sentimental response. "In pity," as Lawrence Blum writes, "one holds oneself apart from the afflicted person and from their suffering, thinking of it as something that defines the person as fundamentally different from oneself." The solicitation of pity reinforces the position of the sufferer as *dependent* (on the good will induced in the viewer by the spectacle of their pain), and the viewer as the empowered agent within whose transformed consciousness their fate will be decided. Spelman is concerned here with what she describes as the "appropriation of suffering" and the way in which we make use of another's pain to fulfill our own need for spiritual transcendence or self-affirmation.[22]

The third mode of reception, which Spelman identifies with the writings of Hannah Arendt, conceives of suffering as a wordless given, the very existence of which compels our unequivocal ameliorative action. The witness, as Spelman writes, "is so stricken with the suffering of an other that one suffers as the other does. . . . Such sharing precludes or obviates the need for deliberation or discussion that are definitive of public life."[23] Any "public" discussion of suffering, according to Arendt, assumes that its evil is open to debate or "competing perspectives," and provides an opportunity for the non-sufferer to talk rather than act, to feel good about themselves (via pity or self-righteous indignation) and enjoy the experience of speaking on behalf of the other's pain, rather than working immediately to alleviate it. But, as Spelman points out, Arendt's tendency to collapse the distance between the sufferer and the viewer "touched in the flesh" by their pain also forecloses any reciprocal relationship to, or communication with, the suffering subject, whose pain can only function as a mute incitement. Spelman attaches a particular importance to the ability of the sufferer to bear witness to his or her own pain. As she writes, "Feeling for others in their suffering can simply be a way of asserting authority over them to the extent that such feeling leaves no room for them to have a view about what their suffering means, or what the most appropriate response to it is." In place of Arendt's purely somatic relationship to suffering, Spelman argues for a cognitive relationship in which compassion is "fine tuned" through a reciprocal exchange between sufferer and witness, based on an awareness of their "shared vulnerability."[24] Here the Other is not simply a passive vehicle for the viewer's own pleasure, enlightenment, or self-congratulation, but is able to exercise his or her own agency: to speak back to the viewer.

Spelman's analysis reveals the complex calibration involved in our relationship to suffering; too close an identification and the viewer subsumes the suffering Other and collapses the very real divisions that exist between them; too distant a relationship and the other is reduced to object and spectacle. Sierra is committed to reinforcing the object-status of his participants, in the hope that an exaggerated objectification and exploitation (even inducing them to openly proclaim their exploited status within his work) will be sufficient to overcome the viewer's practiced capacity for denial (of their own guilt, of the Other's humanity). The only possibility for political change rests, then, with the transformed consciousness of the viewer in the face of the self-evident suffering of the Other, not with the autonomous actions of the poor or working-class populations from which Sierra draws many of his participants. The other option, to allow his participants some independent agency or to engage them as individual subjects with specific needs (outside their function as ciphers of marginality), would simply reproduce the patronizing philanthropy of the bourgeoisie. This accounts for Sierra's odd notion of moral rectitude, in which the decision to provide his participants with minimal compensation is justified by his own honesty in not wanting to pose as a "generous" individual:

> Paying more than what they expect, or in a way that suits my conscience, is useless. . . . That would suggest that I'm a good guy and that I did my bit towards saving these souls. Ridiculous! If I can find someone prepared to hold up a wall for 65 Euros, I'd be showing you a true fact. If I pay double that, I'd be showing my generosity.[25]

Here again we encounter Sierra's striking faith in the metaphysics of presence and the consciousness-shattering power of "true facts," actual bodies, and the literal reenactment of the brutal logic of capitalist exchange. However, the persistence of global poverty can hardly be attributed to the fact that the privileged classes are simply ignorant of its existence and the suffering it entails (and that, once confronted with this reality, they would be shamed into action). The very categories ("privileged" viewers, the "public," the "art scene," the "cultural world") we rely on to talk about this work are hopelessly abstract. There are real class differences in contemporary society, and there are clearly people who benefit quite directly from the global exploitation of labor, and who have no interest whatsoever in seeing this labor as an absolute evil (neoconservative political ideology is devoted in large measure to providing a justification for precisely this sort of unforgiving self-interest). At the same time, there are many people in the "cultural world" and beyond whose knowledge of, and resistance to, social injustice runs quite a bit deeper than that provided by the occasional "flight to Manila or Medellín."

Do we take Sierra and his critics at their word and assume that they really believe a performance in which an illegal worker sits in a cardboard box for four hours in a gallery is going to change anyone's consciousness of racism or class oppression? Or do we assume instead that Sierra's work is intended less for an actual viewer than a hypothetical one, that it functions as a kind of speculative proposition about the relationship between the (autonomous) space of art and the social real? It is this *propositional* nature that links his work most clearly to the Conceptualist tradition (as Medina writes, Sierra "casts the spectator as one of the actors in a philosophical drama").[26] But, along with this philosophical approach comes a tendency to reduce the individual elements in Sierra's projects to one-dimensional postulates: the "cultural world" of the gallery or biennial is a space of heedless denial and ethical indifference, while the Other of bourgeois society is reduced to an interchangeable signifier of marginality or abjection (the prostitute-beggar-illegal worker-migrant). This composition is completed by the arrival of the viewer, who remains blind to oppression until Sierra "drags" it back into the sequestered world of art.[27] This is why some of Sierra's projects threaten to reproduce the appropriation of suffering described by Spelman. The socio-political world of exploitation against which the idealized world of autonomous art is tested remains flattened and specular (like the shantytown-as-scenic backdrop in Francis Alÿs's *Faith*). The "real" which Sierra seeks to transplant into the space of art is never presented in terms of organizational practices or social forms in which the poor possess any agency, but only via images of coercion and confinement, exploitation and victimization. As a result, any reciprocal, cognitive form of compassion, as described by Spelman, is foreclosed.

The seriousness with which Sierra engages the social aesthetics of class difference and economic exploitation is undeniable. Ultimately, however, critical accounts of his work remain unpersuasive. We repeatedly encounter the same formulations centered on notions of shock and revelation, as the "public is exposed in its class character and terror."[28] There is little attempt to address the more complex trajectories of meaning and affect created by the representation of human suffering, or to clearly differentiate Sierra's effort to elicit discomfort, guilt, and obligation in his (implicitly bourgeois) viewers from the obvious parallels provided by the broader history of liberal reform represented by Jacob Riis. This is, perhaps, less a reflection on Sierra's work than on the limitations of contemporary art theory and criticism. Nonetheless, Sierra's commitment to Conceptualist textuality exists in an uneasy relationship with his interest in emergent art practices that involve or incorporate human subjects as active participants. For Sierra the tension between these two registers is inherently critical and productive, but there is a persistent risk in his work that it becomes merely iterative, reproducing the same forms of un-self-conscious projection and pseudo-transcendence that he deplores in his art world audience.

THE INVENTION OF THE PUBLIC — 2

The works of both Sierra and Riis act as a semiotic and affective relay among three subject positions: the artist/reformer, the class Other (whose presence legitimates the reformer's authority), and the public. The artist/reformer mediates between the viewer and the impoverished Other (they share the viewer's privilege, even as they claim a special access to the self-understanding of the poor). In each case, the work constitutes an appeal issued to the public on behalf of the re-presented Other. What is the nature of this appeal? And what more can we learn about the viewer whose "class character" will be "exposed" by the spectacle of poverty and suffering? The viewer or public implied by Sierra's work is defined by two conditions. First, it is assumed that viewers possess an intrinsic, but moribund, capacity for empathy and compassion that can be awakened through the presentation of evidence of suffering and social injustice. Second, within the complex triangulation of his work the viewer's agency is of singular importance. The artist can only present "facts" (amplified or stylized, perhaps, but authenticated ultimately by the sheer physical presence of the Other). The beggar, the prostitute, the laborer, and the drug user, in turn, serve as a kind of passive material—instructed, acted upon, sequestered, and organized in order to produce a particular affect or response in the viewer, to play upon the viewer's conscience. Only the viewer or public retains the power to act decisively (whether this involves a transformation in their own consciousness of violence and class difference, or a more pragmatic intervention into the actual living conditions of the victims of capitalist exploitation).

Sierra's work is also linked with Riis's through its location in urban space (the streets of Birmingham, Mexico City, or Madrid). It is in the city, of course, that the long-established hierarchies of agrarian wealth and poverty are unsettled and new narratives emerge to account for the persistence of class differences in the midst of the plenitude of urban-industrial capitalism. It is also in the city that modern concepts of the public, and a "public sphere," first emerge. The work of Sierra and Riis serves as a fitting introduction to the questions I'll examine in the final chapter of this book. In particular, I'll be focusing on projects that address issues of class, race, and spatial autonomy in two different cities. As Ala Plastica's work in Buenos Aires suggests, the division between the rural and the urban is problematic both geopolitically and discursively. There is, for example, a clear correlation between the discourse of international development and contemporary notions of urban "renewal" or "regeneration" within the larger umbrella of neoliberal economic policy. At the same time, there are significant differences in the way in which social and political forces are modulated at each site. I'll begin this examination by providing a more thorough analysis of the concept of the public. For Sierra, the public is simultaneously the reviled cause of suffering (through its manifest indifference and its self-interested participation in the system of capitalism) and the only possible solution (through its mobilized or transformed conscience). A properly enlightened public functions as the court of appeal within which social conflict can be resolved and reconciled. The concept of the public is two-sided: first the naive or insensible public that enters the gallery space; and second the newly reflective and compassionate public that emerges after exposure to the work of art. The public in Sierra's work is thus a *potential* waiting to be activated.

As I noted in chapter 2, the modern concept of the public is associated with the rise of a mercantile middle-class struggling for political representation against the absolutist rulers of seventeenth- and eighteenth-century Europe. It is first articulated in the work of Enlightenment thinkers such as Thomas Hobbes, John Locke, and Jean-Jacques Rousseau. As early as the 1650s, Hobbes described a "Covenant" in which "men agree amongst themselves, to submit to some Man, or Assembly of men, voluntarily, on confidence to be protected by him against all others."[29] Notoriously, Hobbes insisted that mankind lived in a state of natural aggression, "of every man against every man," that could only be overcome through the consent of individuals to sacrifice their autonomy and be ruled by a monarch who could guarantee a collective peace.[30] What sets Hobbes's ideas apart from earlier doctrines of divine right is his insistence that the leadership of the "soveraigne" must be based on the consent of the governed: the divinely willed authority of the monarch now requires a pragmatic justification. However, Hobbes left intact the legitimacy of political domination itself: once the principle of the covenant is established, the ruler has absolute power over the ruled.

It was only subsequently, in Locke's *Two Treatises of Government* (1690) and Rousseau's *Treatise du Contrat Social* (1762), that Hobbes's covenant was made dependent on an ongoing process of democratic will formation. In his critique of Filmer's *Patriarcha* in the first *Treatise*, Locke argues that political authority must be based on the consent of "free men" and anchored in a justification subject to reasoned consent and debate.[31] At the center of Locke's model of political power was the concept of a social contract in which man (formerly in a "state of nature") agreed to surrender some degree of his autonomy in order to enter into society and form a government. The basis of this government's power was not the will of a monarch, but the will of the people themselves ("a collective body of men"), expressed in the form of a legislature ("call them 'senate,' 'parliament,' or what you please").[32] If the (transcendent) signifier of divine right was a god whose authority was beyond rational debate ("so high . . . that thought can scarce reach it," as Locke writes), the signifier of liberal democracy was the "will of the people" embodied in the institution of Parliament.[33] The public is open, where the monarchy is closed, and it represents the populace as a whole, as opposed to the narrow, familial self-interest of the aristocracy.

The concept of the public challenges the metaphysical certainty of absolutist rule. It is precisely a non-metaphysical mode of authority that depends on the experientially specific interaction of bodies in space and the contingency of human deliberation. This somatic dimension binds the public and the aesthetic in the early modern period. Nowhere is that linkage more evident than in the emergence of the salon, or public art exhibition, in eighteenth-century France. By the early 1700s factions within the nobility, along with rising bourgeois financial elites, were pressuring Louis XV to open the bureaucratic and institutional channels of state power to new actors, and, by implication, to acknowledge the possibility that the identity of the French "people" might be formed independently of monarchical will. The public, as such, was not a stable, singular entity but a space of conflict and contestation, based around competing claims of political representation, self-interest, and inclusion.

With the consolidation of the salon in the 1730s, the commissioning and exhibiting of art became a key site in the struggle to define this nascent French public. Works of art that had previously been sequestered in palaces or churches were presented for the first time in a free and open public forum. The response to this work was no longer assumed to be simple veneration, but rather, the kind of autonomous judgment that had previously been the prerogative of royal and aristocratic authority. The collective space of the salon, as the art historian Thomas Crow has demonstrated, was unique in pre-Revolutionary France, as visitors from across the range of social orders jostled for space in the grand galleries of the Louvre—not as artisan and aristocrat, but as citizen-viewers, each bearing a singular, and equally valid, opinion. "Long before liberalism could be tried out in the larger arena of political life," Crow writes, "the exhibition space provided a kind of temporary model in microcosm."[34]

The freedom of judgment tolerated in the salon was due in part to the distance separating the objects on display (paintings of historical and mythological subjects, portraits, etc.) from the realities of daily political and social life in France. While salon works could be proximate to current social concerns, through allegorical and historical references or genre scenes, for example, they were sufficiently separate (by and large) to insulate the salon from the kind of policing that would have accompanied the free expression of opinions in other, more formally political, contexts.[35] In fact, this very distance is what allowed the salon to function as a training ground for liberalism, facilitating a para-political deliberative exchange that mirrored the process of "real" political discourse without the concrete risks and consequences. This distance reflects a crucial stage in the transition to modern art. As the work of art becomes less directly accountable to a specific patron, it achieves a quasi-autonomy under the protection of the salon, which is obligated to preserve a degree of openness with regard to the specific content of work commensurate with the ideals of a liberal public sphere and an emergent form of civil society.

Civil society (from the Latin *civitas*, which refers to both a political subject—the citizen—and a form of collective settlement—the city) is a complex term that describes the capacity of individual subjects to engage in substantive debate over political issues, as well as the agency whereby this debate, in the form of a consensus or "general will," could be transformed into an instrument of political decision making. This "covenant," or social contract, rests on two key assumptions: the existence of a public sphere within which debate may take place among "equals," and the possibility that this debate can result in the formation of a common social will. The social contract thus necessitates a process of dialogue—prior to and out of which civil society and eventually the state are formed, and from which they derive their authority. But this scenario immediately raises questions of origin: Did the "will" pre-exist civil society, or is it created (or imposed) by civil society? Is civil society the space within which this public will can be produced—an incubator, so to speak, of social consensus? Or, on the other hand, is it the natural and organic outgrowth of an a priori common humanity? And if this common humanity doesn't exist, how can we assume that any amount of dialogue and debate will result in a consensus?

These ontological uncertainties are complicated by a series of epistemological questions. Liberal democracy is based on a mimetic circuit that begins with an original social will that is "represented" by the consensus reached by civil society in the process of public deliberation. This consensus is in turn represented by the state, which engages in political decision making that is the direct expression of the needs and interests of civil society. In each case, the intervening institution (the public sphere, civil society, and the state) is seen as the transparent carrier of a prior will. In conventional liberal political theory, it is presumed that the institutions of representative democracy exercise little or no mediating function: they constitute the self-identical voice of "the people."[36] However, these institutions, far from acting as the unmediated expression of a general public voice, tend, in eighteenth-century Europe, to be biased toward the specific interests of the bourgeoisie (the "public" at this point consisted, of course, of property-owning white men). While the openness and transparency of the early public sphere was a strategic necessity when the bourgeoisie was taking power for itself, it became a significant liability when representatives of the poor and working-class used it to advance their own claims for political power. The primary function of Locke's "commonwealth," for example, was the preservation of property, and the references to this fact in the *Second Treatise* border on the obsessive.[37]

The privileging of property as a precondition for public agency introduces a central tension into liberal discourse. On the one hand, the concept of the public challenges the stasis of social roles prescribed by divine right. The public isn't a fixed entity, but rather a process or mode of interaction that is available to all. But this openness can be sustained only so long as it is never fully tested: so long as the public sphere is limited to like-minded members of the same property-owning class. The "public" thus retains a metaphysical dimension. On the one hand, it refers to a physically proximate, empirically verifiable process of social exchange and deliberation, and on the other, it is an as yet unrealized ideal, limited for now to a select few (propertied men). Property introduces a second point of tension as well. The public actor enters into political exchange with a commitment to acknowledge and respect the differences represented by other actors and with an implicit willingness to revise his or her own beliefs in response to these others and on behalf of a collective good. But the possession of property is premised on an unyielding self-interest and individualism. Within the pedagogy of capital, as described by thinkers such as Adam Smith and Anne-Robert-Jacques Turgot, the sole priority is to enrich and aggrandize oneself, often at the expense of others. The boundaries between the motivations of the "private" self of the market, and the "public" self of civil society are notoriously difficult to maintain.

It is precisely this tension between self-interest and altruism, and between self and Other, that defines the aesthetic as a central category of Enlightenment thought. In the writings of Hume, Kant, Schiller, and Shaftesbury, the aesthetic comes to embody a cosmopolitan openness to difference: a willingness to set aside our normal acquisitive self-interest when confronting objects in the world and to proceed instead from the point of view of an enlightened "disinterest." Rather than subjecting the object to a rigorous conceptual classification, we simply let it work on us in all its uncategorizable alterity. Through our interactions with works of art we learn to approach the world as such from a less instrumentalizing and self-interested perspective. As Schiller suggests, this "aesthetic education" is necessary to prepare us for participation in the public realm of democratic will-formation. It encourages us to see the other's point of view, and to treat our fellow subjects not as "means to an end," but as equal interlocutors. The aesthetic emerges, then, as a necessary counterpoint to the market system; its role is to literally instantiate the kind of "public" that would be able to resist the pressure toward possessive individualism exerted by capitalism.

As we saw in our earlier discussion of Schiller, it was specifically the autonomy of aesthetic experience that gave it this transformative or redemptive power: its absolute segregation from the a priori demands and expectations of both the viewer and the market (the collapsing together of these two is of signal importance). The work of art, free from all external determination, mirrors for the viewer a form of monadic selfhood that requires neither the recognition nor the subordination of an Other. This notion of autonomy expresses both a faith in the emancipatory power of the aesthetic and an underlying pessimism about the possibilities of social interaction *until* this therapeutic regression has been carried out. Of course, autonomy always possessed a dual nature, providing both a critical distance from the overdetermined world of the market and a space in which our complicity with this world might be transcended (and denied). Over time, the continual pressure to devise formal innovations capable of maintaining the level of hermeneutic resistance necessary to defer cognitive possession ran up against the inevitable tendency of these innovations to become conventionalized and normative, necessitating a new, strategic, relationship to the principle of aesthetic autonomy. Thus, while the goal of critical distanciation remained consistent within the avant-garde tradition, its mode of production was gradually inverted, so that the necessary transformation is produced by the strategic *disruption* of aesthetic autonomy (rather than its preservation). It is this inversion that Sierra hopes to achieve by revealing the ostensibly hidden linkages between aesthetic freedom and economic exploitation. Nonetheless, Sierra still depends on the principle of autonomy itself (or rather, he requires that the credulous viewer continue to believe in its existence) in order for the gesture of "dislocating" a beggar from the street to the gallery to retain its cathartic power.

As the preceding discussion suggests, there is a symptomatic transposition within the modernist tradition between the concept of the public (autonomous from the market, and capable of the reciprocal openness necessary for democratic interaction) and the aesthetic, as the process by which this public is produced. For Sierra as well as Schiller, the public is not fixed but is a potential awaiting activation: a form of latent agency currently thwarted by the self-interest inculcated by the market. Autonomy or freedom from external determination, in this tradition, is thus a precondition for a certain kind of action in the world with redemptive implications. The persistence of what we might term an aesthetic model of agency is evident in contemporary critical theory. It achieves its most sophisticated expression in the work of Gilles Deleuze. For Deleuze, any form of being that depends even partially on an external determinant (i.e., a relation to an Other) will inevitably devolve into instrumentalizing violence and an oppositional relationship to difference (the Hegelian "labor of the negative"). Instead of seeking its Other externally, a properly Deleuzean mode of being will recognize its own already *intrinsically* plural nature (Deleuze relies here on a Bergsonian notion of internal differentiation of the self via an *élan vital*). Thus, being must be autonomous and desire wholly immanent (or rather, autonomy is recoded as immanence). A productive, immanent, desire has no external object and therefore will never attempt to possess, negate, or objectify the Other. Instead it will seek to couple with other, similarly transformed, desiring "machines" in various non-instrumentalizing permutations intended only to expand and multiply "joyful passions."

As I noted in chapter 1, for the thinkers of Deleuze's generation the lesson of May '68 was clear. The revolution failed because human subjectivity was not prepared to sustain it: as a result, the transgressive energies unleashed by the "events" were easily enough recuperated and bureaucratized. In the wake of a failed insurrection that sought not simply to "take" power but to redefine it, it was necessary to start over from the beginning, to rethink identity from the ground up, to be present at the "dawn of the world," as Deleuze writes, before the vast, destructive, apparatus of human knowledge, language, and subjectivity came into existence.[38] The desiring body, rather than the (implicitly) Cartesian consciousness, became the privileged locus of being for Deleuze. He turned to Spinoza's concept of conatus to provide a more detailed account of the specific forms of action enabled by this body. In place of the vulgar humanist vocabulary of "feelings," "intentions," or "ideas," Spinoza describes a form of being based on the experience of bodily intensities and affects. Within this radically depersonalized realm, consciousness is reduced to an exercise in physics. Anything that enhances the body's "power of action" is good and joyful, while anything that decreases its power is associated with "sadness" and impotence.[39] The expansion of this power becomes the primary determinant of ethical judgment. Thus, according to Spinoza, "the more every man endeavors and is able to seek his own advantage, that is, to preserve his own being, the more he is endowed with virtue. On the other hand, in so far as he neglects to preserve what is to his advantage, that is, his own being, to that extent he is weak."[40] Deleuze reiterates this view in *Expressionism in Philosophy*. "What is evil?" he writes. "There are no evils save the reduction of our power of action."[41] Here the metaphysics of property shares common ground with the metaphysics of desire. In each case the pragmatic testing of ethical claims through a process of mediated exchange is rendered unnecessary by the a priori ethical value assigned to the expansion of a conative power of action.

While it would be churlish to object to any philosophical system that promises to increase joyful passion, there remain certain tensions in Deleuze's model of being, especially around the ethics of intersubjective exchange. In his essay "The Limits of Individuation" Peter Hallward provides a useful contrast between Michel Foucault's notion of a "specific" subject and Deleuze's "singular" subject. The singular subject is *"aspecific,"* as Hallward writes:

> If a specific individual is one that exists as part of a relationship to a context, to other individuals and to itself, a singular individual is one that like a Creator-god transcends all such relations. A singularity creates the medium of its own existence or "expression" in Spinoza's sense. . . . The singular recognizes no limits. The specific, on the other hand exists only in the medium of relations with others, and turns ultimately on the confrontation of limits.[42]

Here is autonomy writ large, as the very precondition for a redemptive model of human existence. The monadic body resists all forms of predication or interdependence: of subject to object, of signifier to referent, of self to other. Its desire and its capacity for creative transformation are endless and unconstrained. All restrictions on this conative drive, whether the semantic protocols of conventional language or the consciousness of the Other, are intolerable. But what, if anything, regulates this insatiable striving for power? What differentiates Deleuze's notion of desire from a bourgeois conatus that is equally committed to the infinite expansion of self and the endless accumulation of power?[43]

For Spinoza the answer is simple: the conative drive is always oriented by the overarching ethical authority of god. Because we are all equal attributes of god, we are all part of the same univocal self ("God is the immanent, not transient, cause of all things").[44] We need only overcome our "bondage" to "vague experience" and recognize that we are not discrete, potentially antagonistic, subjects, but rather, extensions of a single divine substance. "The mind's utmost advantage or its highest good is knowledge of God," according to Spinoza. "That is an absolutely infinite being, and one without whom nothing can be or be conceived. . . . The absolute virtue of the mind is to understand. But the highest thing the mind can understand is God. Therefore the highest virtue of the mind is to understand or know God."[45] When conflicts do arise among men, they are reconciled through their knowledge of god, which is both proof and precondition of their "common" virtue:

> Someone may ask: "What if the highest good of those who pursue virtue were not common to all? Would it not then follow . . . that men who live by the guidance of reason, that is, men in so far as they agree in nature, would be contrary to one another?" Let him take this reply, that it arises not by accident but from the very nature of reason that men's highest good is common to all, because this is deduced from the very essence of man in so far as that is defined by reason, and because man could neither be nor be conceived if he did not have the ability to enjoy this highest good. For it belongs to the essence of the human mind to have an adequate knowledge of the eternal and infinite essence of God.[46]

For Spinoza the univocity of being depends on the essential unity of an omnipotent god and the individual believer. Deleuze replaces this metaphysical principle with another form of divine creation—the (implicitly redemptive) creativity of desire itself. As Hallward notes, "All actual existent individuals . . . are simply so many *immediate* articulations of one and the same creative force, variously termed desire or desiring production, life, *élan vital*, matter-energy, the virtual or power." As a result, there can be no direct relationship or communication between or among singularities, precisely because the very concept of their discrete individuality is an illusion. "What distinguishes one creature from another is determined by their direct, immediate relations to the Creator," not by their (mediated) relationship with or to each other.[47] In *Deleuze and the Philosophy of Creation*, Hallward describes Deleuze's work in terms of a *"theophanic* conception of things, whereby every individual process or thing is conceived as a manifestation or expression of God or a conceptual equivalent of God (pure creative potential, force, energy, life . . .)." This "affirmation of an expressive or creative immanence," as Hallward writes, "does not so much eliminate the question of transcendence as distribute it throughout creation as a whole."[48]

The Deleuzean subject, withdrawn from all "linked and connected flows," no longer looks outside itself for a determinative moment.[49] The singularity of the corporeal body as a locus of liberatory action and as a mode of being (if not of subjectivity per se) has the effect of foreclosing any form of social experience based on discursive exchange. As a result, Deleuze must locate the preconditions for intersubjectivity or community in devices such as "cosmic memory" that perform a typically aesthetic function in allowing for the unmediated reconciliation of the individual with the social, or the one and the many.[50] This aesthetic function is typified in Deleuze's theory of the univocity of being, as outlined by Hallward. As expressive bodies, we are able to sense or intuit our essential commonalty with other bodies. As Deleuze writes, paraphrasing Spinoza, "God produces things in all attributes at once. Because the attributes are all equal, there is an identity of connection between modes differing in attribute."[51] The natural harmony that exists between and among individual bodies obviates the need for any discursive rationality; as individual beings we are all united as attributes of a greater force (god for Spinoza; cosmic memory for Deleuze), drawn together by the commonalty of a "joyful passion."[52]

Unfortunately, according to Deleuze, most of us live in ignorance or denial of the univocity of being. As Hallward writes, we remain "trapped in the delusions of ontological equivocity or dualism—the belief that we are subjects as distinct from objects, and thus subjects who represent, figure, or otherwise interpret objects."[53] Here Deleuze mirrors Spinoza's bleak assessment of man's capacity for conscious action. "Men are deceived," as Spinoza writes, "because they think themselves free, and the sole reason for thinking so is that they are conscious of their own actions, and ignorant of the causes by which those actions are determined."[54] Until we overcome our naive faith in our own conscious agency and come to recognize the "hidden" laws that structure and predetermine our ostensibly volitional actions, we will remain in "bondage."[55] The only hope for overcoming this bondage lies in the discovery of our true condition as "contingent fragments of a vital or creative energy pulsing through and beyond the whole of actuality." This crucial discovery will be facilitated, not surprisingly, by our exposure to suitably radical forms of art and philosophy that jolt us out of our naive attachment to equivocal, relational subjectivity and the "very notion of traditional self-consciousness, of the self as the mediator of objects, of other selves, and of itself." Hence, the perennial avant-garde campaign to "free" us from the "shackles of mediation" and from the "long error" of representation.[56] We return again to the claims of therapeutic dislocation or de-centering outlined in chapter 1, to Jacques Rancière's notion of a "sensible or perceptual shock caused . . . by that which resists signification," or the "constant shock" produced by Santiago Sierra's work as he "exposes" the class character of his audience.[57]

This discussion returns us as well to the curious circularity I identified above in the modern constitution of the public and the aesthetic around the concept of autonomy. Advanced art must be autonomous from the market and from the debased tastes of the public influenced by it. The public, in turn, will be freed from the self-interest of the market by the experience of advanced art. I would suggest that what we normally describe as the growing autonomy of art in the modern period can be more accurately understood as a property of the audience itself, that freedom and autonomy among the *public* is the precondition for *art's* autonomy. One of the distinctive characteristics of the modern public is its indeterminate and independent nature, its capacity to choose freely, to invent the form of government most appropriate to its needs rather than remaining subordinate to the transcendent authority of God or king. It is, of course, this same autonomy that leads to Schiller's fears of the depraved tastes of the German reading public. Once free to select which cultural forms and practices to venerate, the public may make the "wrong" choice (ghost stories rather than philosophy; romance novels rather than edifying poetry). This accounts for the modern artist's perennial disappointment with the perceived limitations of the philistine viewer (and the intrinsic appeal of the notion that they make their work instead for a selective, quasi-aristocratic, cadre of advanced viewers). With the process of modern desacralization, art loses its millennial association with absolutist power, and the reverence and obeisance of the viewer guaranteed by this association. From this perspective, the persistent attempts by artists working in the avant-garde tradition to assault, shock, dislocate, and otherwise overwhelm the (benumbed) viewer can be seen as a way to reclaim the sovereignty and suasive power over the viewer's consciousness enjoyed by the pre-modern artist.

Shock, disruption, or ontic dislocation are accorded an intrinsically liberatory power in the tradition of avant-garde art, capable of revealing new, critical, insight into the formation of individual and collective identity. However, the actual forms of reception and affect set in motion by the experience of disruption or dislocation are considerably more complex, and potentially ambivalent. As I noted in my earlier discussion of May '68, the "pedagogy" of shock often confuses critique or revelation with punishment. Schiller's desire to chastise middle-class readers for their bad taste, or Sierra's evident frustration with the blinkered ignorance of the "cultural world," exist in an uneasy tension with their claim to either improve or enlighten the public. But why should the projective aggression evident in a range of avant-garde practices *necessarily* induce greater insight or self-transformation on the part of the viewer rather than simple defensiveness?[58] In fact, dislocation or disruption is probably closest to trauma in its psychological effects (the production of a radical break that threatens to destroy or destabilize the individual's sense of psychic or existential security). But trauma, far from generating new insight, is defined precisely by the arrest or reification of certain patterns of thought or bodily response—by the continual reenactment, repetition, or reiteration of the traumatic event in the consciousness of the subject, or through embodied forms of memory (as in the somatic symptoms of post-traumatic stress disorder, intrusive memories, etc.). Arrested in the limbic system of the mind, trauma has no history, no sense of time or transformation, and is always experienced anew. Further, the notion of shock or rupture, as it is deployed in the context of contemporary art theory and criticism, fails to account for the discontinuity between the pre-subjective regression ostensibly effected by avant-garde art and the subjective states of agency and identity necessary to act on the insights achieved by this regression. The "self" that is disrupted, dislocated, or ruptured can't at the same time possess the coherence necessary to comprehend and internalize a new critical perspective.

As we saw in Sierra's work, this approach tends to reduce the public to an abstraction, or rather, to project onto the actual viewers of a given work (in all their potential diversity and differentiation) the characteristics of a stereotypical "bourgeois" viewer (complacent privilege, indifference to the suffering of others, etc.). There is a consequent loss of tactical specificity in the artist's understanding of the public; the same rhetorical strategy is deployed regardless of context, situation, or audience. The universalization of this mode of address and of the implied viewer implies in turn an inattention to the complex forms of displacement, projection, and transference set in motion by a given social composition or network (the relay of gazes in Sierra's *Person Saying a Phrase*, e.g., and their relationship to a much older tradition of class voyeurism). Along with this comes an inability to differentiate among the members of an audience or set of viewers or participants, and a reluctance to understand how these differences might be negotiated through practice (rather than simply conjured away by epiphanic disruption). Individuals remain undifferentiated for Deleuze precisely because they are only ever, at their root, singular manifestations of a universal creative energy or desire. As Hallward notes, for Deleuze any form of direct, relational, exchange involving the negotiation or mediation of differences is foreclosed precisely because these ostensible "differences" are simply an illusion, an artifact of our reliance on a destructive Cartesian subjectivity.[59]

Deleuze's vitalist notion of a creative energy brings us back to the ethical valorization of desire. The discovery of our dislocated (and internally differentiated) nature is endowed with an intrinsically liberatory or redemptive power. But what if the "de-centered" condition of bourgeois subjectivity is not, as I've already suggested, such an explosive secret? And who is to say that a bourgeois conatus is not equally, and in the final analysis, less concerned with the things that one acquires than with the sheer sense of expansive power that acquisition provides? What matters most for the bourgeois subject is not the fact of possessing, objectifying, or incorporating a given property or thing, but rather, the extension of one's power and potential for action (cf. the suum), for which possession is merely a pretext.[60]

How, then, do we determine the ethical valence of a given social inter-action? The revelation of immanent desire (and the sense of shock or dislocation that either precipitates or accompanies this revelation) is assumed to exercise a necessarily positive effect, but an analysis of the impact of this discovery on the individual's subsequent conduct would require "mediated" interaction among subjects, and forms of intersubjective representation (of self to Other) that are proscribed by Deleuze. It would require, in fact, a situationally grounded notion of ethics, which can only be determined through a pragmatic assessment of the modes and effects of social interaction at a given site. This is, for me, a key point of differentiation between the textual, propositional, approach of artists such as Sierra, and the dialogical, collaborative projects under discussion here. For Sierra, the arrangement and deployment of human bodies in particular configurations is assumed a priori to reveal or expose certain contradictions within the discursive system of aesthetic autonomy, regardless of the responses of actual viewers or audience members. The collaborative process, on the other hand, occasions a reciprocal testing of both ethical and aesthetic norms, the outcome of which can only be determined through the subsequent forms of social interaction mobilized by a given work.

Neither approach is necessarily superior, and each has its own limitations and its own potentials. For myself, I am less confident in the redemptive power of ontological regression and cognitive disruption, and somewhat more sanguine about the creative possibilities of "mediated" intersubjective exchange. The goal, in either case, is a transformation of human consciousness in a way that enhances our capacity for the compassionate recognition of difference, both within ourselves and in others. In one case the ability of a certain form of disruption or dislocation to produce this transformation is taken as axiomatic, while in the other this transformation is achieved, or not, through a form of practical or experiential production, the outcome of which is not predetermined. The projects I'll examine next are based on a specific, rather than a generic, understanding of their participants as defined through a complex set of investments and identifications that traverse class and geography, self-interest and conviviality. In this respect they share a great deal with the rural projects I've already examined in chapter 2. However, they take as their primary field of operation urban space and the broader context of urban political economy. I'll examine projects developed in Hamburg, Germany, and Houston,

Texas. If the most relevant set of institutional protocols for the projects discussed in chapter 2 derived from the discourse of global development and the operations of NGOs, in the case of the projects discussed here they can be found in the processes of urban renewal or regeneration.

The discourse of urban renewal implies a system of benign remediation in which a previously vital but now degraded cultural or geopolitical space (a neighborhood, a community) is redeveloped, improved, or otherwise brought back to "life." Of course, it is quite often the case that the renewal process functions in practice to facilitate the relocation of an existing population (typically poor or working class) in order to reclaim a given site for forms of economic development that primarily benefit the middle and upper classes. Here space, as a site of speculative investment, is abstracted from the needs and the identities of the people who have actually inhabited that space over time. Thus, we have the curious process by which development agencies market the cultural associations embedded in a particular neighborhood to potential buyers/investors (as evidence of its charm, its historical singularity, or its resistance to suburban sterility) only after removing the actual population whose lives formed the basis of these associations. As with the projects discussed in chapter 2, questions of agency, solidarity, and sovereignty will play a central role in the analysis of the works examined here. If Riis and Sierra hope to mobilize a sympathetic middle-class audience on behalf of the urban poor or the immiserated victims of globalization, the projects under discussion here ask if it's possible to rethink the category of victimhood itself and for the sufferer, to use Spelman's language, to speak back. It's helpful to begin by situating these projects in the context of historical connections between art, culture, and urban regeneration that are most explicitly revealed in the traditions of "public art."

3 — THE BOULEVARDS OF THE INNER CITY

The term "public art" carries with it an obvious connotation. It refers to the creation of sculpture and murals for parks, plazas, airports, and other nominally public spaces, and funded through municipal, state, federal (and occasionally private) arts patronage. These works, the Picasso in Chicago's Daley Square or Calder's *La Grande Vitesse* in Grand Rapids, Michigan, for example, are often integrated with larger urban planning or "revitalization" schemes. Public art is thus linked to the history of architecture as well as a tradition of commemorative sculpture and mural painting that extends back to antiquity. The term "public art" first emerged in the United States during the late 1960s in conjunction with National Endowment for the Arts and General Services Administration initiatives, such as the "Art in Public Places," "Art in Architecture," and "Percent for Art" programs. It is associated with an expansive, philanthropic view of government characteristic of the Great Society era. In this view the state is obligated not simply to guarantee the basic rights provided by classic liberalism (the protection of property, military defense, and so on), but to actively ameliorate the social costs imposed by the ongoing expansion of industrial, and postindustrial, capitalism. At the risk of overgeneralizing, the mission of early public art programs was to ensure that the cultural good of art was equitably distributed and not solely dependent on the (implicitly elitist) delivery mechanisms of the private art market.

Over the past forty years the field of public art has expanded dramatically to encompass an international network of artists, commissioning agencies, publications, and funding protocols. While the core belief system of public art remains intact (the idea that art should be accessible to people in their daily lives), the movement has lost much of its ideological coherence. There are a number of reasons for this. First, in the United States the ameliorative concept of the state, dominant during the late 1960s and early '70s, has been severely eroded by over three decades of concerted attack by right-wing politicians, foundations, and activists eager to demonize the state and redeem the market system (and evangelical Christianity) as the primary mechanisms of social cohesion. Art funding agencies at the federal, state, and local level have seen their budgets slashed. While innovative projects continue to be produced, public art is increasingly dependent on "partnership" arrangements with private-sector entities (redevelopment agencies, tourism boards, corporations, etc.) whose definition of the public good is often politically ambivalent. Public art has become a standard urban amenity, recognizable in a now routinized landscape of neon-enhanced people-movers, fiber art curtains, and generic sculpture trails. At the same time, the last twenty years have witnessed a proliferation of art projects that address audiences outside galleries and museums, with little or no reference to the institutions and conventions of traditional public art. Today we find artists working in areas as diverse as digital media, performance, and community-based practice claiming some investment in the public sphere. As a result of these two factors, public art today is distinguished less by its commitment to a "public" audience (however that might be defined) than by its relationship to the mechanisms of urban planning and by a commissioning process focused on the creation of permanent or quasi-permanent murals and sculptural projects.

Although it would be left to the Johnson administration to organize a formal program of funding for public art, the philosophical framework was established under JFK. In a lecture at Amherst College in 1963, Kennedy celebrated the artist as "the last champion of the individual mind and sensibility against an intrusive society and an officious state." Rather than the state dictating to the artist, the artist would educate the state, by acting as an independent, willfully individual voice of conscience ("If sometimes our great artists have been the most critical of our society, it is because their sensitivity and their concern for justice . . . makes [the artist] aware that our Nation falls short of its highest potential").[61] For Kennedy, and advocates such as his cultural advisor August Hecksher, the experience of art was understood to have a therapeutic effect on the American body politic. The artist represented the creative and intellectual freedom of the United States against the stale conformity of the Soviet Union. The critical discourse of art demonstrated the inherent superiority of American culture, while also providing a kind of inoculation against the critical, anti-capitalist, appeal of communism at the height of the Cold War. This curious combination of political pragmatism and artistic romanticism led to the paradoxical concept of state-sponsored art that, at the same time, embodied a symbolic resistance to state authority.

This approach was effective in overcoming resistance to federal arts funding among members of Congress who feared, precisely, the artistic meddling of an "officious state." It also provided a useful framework for insulating artists from direct political pressure, and would influence the subsequent reliance of the NEA on "peer review" panels (composed of other artists and arts professionals) for adjudicating grants. These virtues notwithstanding, when it came to actually funding public art under the early GSA and NEA programs, quasi-metaphysical concepts of "artistic spirit" and "personal vision" were of limited value. What, specifically, were the artistic "truths" against which the artist would measure the state? What expertise justified the elevation of the artist to the post of ethical exemplar for the nation? And in what language would the "great artist" tutor American society? The answer to this final question is evident from even a cursory review of projects funded by the Art in Architecture and Art in Public Places programs during the late 1960s and '70s. Guidebooks published at the time present an uninterrupted vista of stone obelisks, biomorphic blobs, jutting metal girders, and angular neon: a veritable boneyard of abstraction drawn from the formal traditions of modernist sculpture. In fact, the public art programs of the 1960s were distinguished from earlier traditions of mural painting or memorial sculpture by their overt commitment to the challenging, formally complex language of avant-garde art. If the artist was the new moral compass of the nation, he would speak to us in a vocabulary of rough-hewn granite, painted steel, and poured concrete.

The predilection for abstraction has much to do with the spirit of the times. By the late 1960s abstraction had become safely canonical (via a formalist version of modern art history codified by Herbert Read, Irving Sandler, Clement Greenberg, and others) while still retaining an aura of radical experimentation. In her book *Spirit Poles and Flying Pigs* Erika Lee Doss associates the rise of abstraction with the outlook of a "well-educated, liberal cadre of arts professionals" that came to dominate early public art policy and funding.[62] This nascent subculture of artists, arts administrators, consultants, and critics reflected the technocratic optimism of the New Frontier, as the "best and the brightest" struggled to solve recalcitrant social problems with the most up-to-date analytic tools. Doss's cadres would take the open-ended justifications for federal arts funding adumbrated by Hecksher and others and mold them into a coherent public art policy centered around the commissioning of large, abstract sculptures in plazas, federal office buildings, airports, and other public spaces. The largesse of the Art in Public Places and Art in Architecture programs soon gave rise to a new professional: the "public artist" who survives through an ongoing series of commissions, or the gallery-based artist who is able to open up a lucrative subspecialty in public projects. The dominant figures during the first decade of the public art movement were, with a few exceptions, uniformly committed to abstraction (e.g., Louise Nevelson, Alexander Calder, Peter Voulkas, George Rickey, Athena Tacha, Mark Di Suvero, Stephen Antonakos, Tony Smith, etc.).

Doss traces the bias toward abstraction to a complex cultural and political dynamic. Public art advocates shared the conventional modernist antipathy to realist or representational art, which was compromised by its association with the artistic traditions of Fascism and Stalinism on the one hand, and vulgar consumer culture on the other.[63] Abstract art, and the very complexity of abstraction as a process, fit quite naturally with the self-image of public art professionals as an intellectual elite in command of a specialized technical language that allowed them to see the world in new ways. It represented a kind of self-contained, "value free" system of meaning with which to improve and civilize viewers unaccustomed to the white cube of the gallery. As Doss writes:

> Modern abstract art was seen as a great unifying force because it was seemingly apolitical and rational. Because it was non-figurative, the postwar argument went, abstract art could not be used to prop up any deviant political ideology. Because it concentrated on itself—on the physical properties of paint, for instance, or steel—abstract art suppressed any romantic or subjective overtones and was thus inherently reasonable. . . . The postwar elite saw abstraction as the ideal form to "cultivate" the masses. They also saw themselves as the voices of cultural authority . . . and rejected public distaste for abstraction as philistinism.[64]

Early public art professionals sought to confront the viewer with mysterious, uncategorizable totems set down in the midst of the banal, commercialized, urban landscape like alien spacecraft. Freed from the deadening cultural force field of the museum, Louise Nevelson's cryptic black pillars or Tony Smith's geometric steel modules would challenge the viewer's preconceptions, producing liberal, self-reflexive citizens rather than mindless drones. We encounter again here the promise of the Enlightenment aesthetic encouraging a cosmopolitan openness to new experience. We encounter as well the belief, outlined in Thomas Crow's analysis of the eighteenth-century salon, that the experience of art could prepare the viewer to be a more effective participant in public, political discourse. Despite these historical parallels, there is a crucial difference between the galleries of the Louvre and the streets of New York, Chicago, or Seattle. The artists of the 1960s and '70s could no longer speak to their public in the lingua franca of biblical narrative, national history, and virtuoso realism. They relied instead on the esoteric formal language of abstraction. But without the ritualized sanctity of the museum to buffer and contextualize the epistemological shock of this unfamiliar tongue, abstract works were often experienced as alienating and unintelligible.

The spatial and epistemological shift from the museum to the street revealed an underlying tension in abstraction as a public discourse during the 1960s and '70s. On the one hand, abstract public art would unite viewers into a civilizing *sensus communis* through its ecumenical formal language. On the other, abstraction was positioned as a destabilizing interruption in the semantic field of urban space, challenging the viewer's preconceptions (Richard Serra's work is emblematic of this approach). The conflict, between public space as a site of coherence and unification and a site at which existing unities and identifications are called into question, is reflected in the genealogy of the public, outlined previously. It was necessary for the nascent bourgeois state to speak on behalf of all of its citizens in order to challenge aristocratic elites who sought to cloak naked self-interest in the guise of national patrimony. At the same time, this global concept of the public implied that it was possible to identify a single set of interests representing all of society, and required the imposition of a false unity on a population that was, in fact, disparate and fractious. The public, as a political construct, is defined by this Janus-faced condition. As a result, abstract public art was not always experienced as an incitement to civic dialogue. The history of the field is replete with stories of well-intentioned projects greeted with indifference, scorn, and outright hostility (Gary Rieveschl and Michael Fotheringham's *Concord Heritage Gateway* [1989]; Stephen Antonakos's *Neons for the Tacoma Dome* [1984]; and, most notoriously, Richard Serra's *Tilted Arc* [1981]).

By the late 1980s these controversies would catalyze a broad interrogation of the methods and imperatives of public art, and art's function in public, especially urban, space. This critique concentrated on two aspects of the established public art tradition. First, artists and critics, such as Rosalyn Deutsch, Patricia Phillips, Arlene Raven, Martha Rosler, and Krzysztof Wodiczko, questioned the ways in which the public itself was defined within this tradition.[65] During the 1970s public art practice coalesced into a set of standardized commissioning protocols and funding bureaucracies. Within this system, projects were often planned by teams of artists, designers, and administrators, and imposed on a given site with little reference to the specific concerns of the people who actually lived and worked there. While the artist was privileged in all of his or her exemplary individuality, the public was treated as an undifferentiated and essentially passive mass on whom a work of art would be benevolently conferred. Consultation, when it did occur, typically involved forums in which completed proposals were presented for "feedback." The only agency left to the public was the simple act of registering its approval or disapproval.[66] Further, there was little recognition that the public itself was a mosaic, not a monolith, composed of numerous constituencies, factions, and interests. The second area of critique concerned the reliance of first-generation public artists on abstraction. It soon became evident that the vaunted "complexity" of abstraction as a formal language did little to prevent abstract works from functioning at the same level of kitschlike simplicity as the most conventional hero-on-a-horse monument. In fact, the process of formal reduction and the lack of a specific referent typical of abstract sculpture made it relatively easy for works to be "détourned" into municipal logos or banal graphic advertisements for a city's commitment to high culture.

The relationship between art and public space in the 1980s was complicated by significant changes in the political economy of urban America, as capital began to flow back into cities for the first time since the 1960s. Vast swathes of land-banked property in Baltimore, Chicago, Cleveland, New York, San Francisco, and other cities became available for investment and redevelopment. The vacuum into which this capital flowed was created thirty years before, as the white middle class began to abandon America's urban centers in a rush precipitated by black migration, subsidized by federal highway construction and mortgage programs, and accelerated by a series of destructive urban rebellions during the 1960s. As a result, property values and tax revenues plummeted and America's inner cities were faced with deteriorating housing stock, a disappearing job base, and a crumbling public-service infrastructure (education, health care, etc.). Moreover, movement out of the inner city for black families was circumscribed in many places by de facto housing segregation well into the 1970s. The results were entirely predictable: rising crime rates, unemployment, drug economies, and violence. Although many black communities managed to thrive despite these challenges, the image of the American inner city, relentlessly portrayed in the news and entertainment media of the 1970s, was uniformly bleak, even apocalyptic. This process of cultural abjection was a necessary precondition for the reinvestment strategies of the 1980s. In a reiteration of nineteenth-century colonialist discourse, the "inner city" had to be seen as uncivilized, dangerous, and ill-used by its current inhabitants to justify the widespread displacement of poor and working-class populations and to clear the ground, both physically and ideologically, for widespread reinvestment.

For a brief period, during the late 1960s, the federal government attempted to reverse the decline of America's urban districts through innovative "community action" programs that delivered funding directly to inner city neighborhoods (under the Office of Economic Opportunity). This approach was motivated by the concern that money passing through the apparatus of city government would, inevitably, be siphoned off by political and economic elites. Community Action Programs sought to give some modest support directly to communities, and even, at its most radical, to allow these communities a say in how the money might be spent (via the principle of "maximum feasible participation").[67] This experiment was, however, short-lived and underfunded, as congressional conservatives soon rallied, attacking the programs as dangerously radical and communistic. It would be left to Richard Nixon to construct a new paradigm for federal urban subsidy that eliminated the unpleasantness of direct interaction with the poor and working class. His solution was developed as part of a broader set of "New Federalism" policies which intended to reverse the perceived excesses of Great Society–era state intervention by returning decision making (and money spending) power to the state and local level.[68] Federal housing and urban infrastructure funds were bundled into "block grants" which required matching support from the local private sector. Inevitably, this meant involving real estate developers, bankers, corporate investors, and large property owners, who soon grasped the potential benefits of block grants in facilitating large-scale gentrification schemes.

Since block grants utilized public monies, it was necessary to maintain at least the pretense that they would assist the urban poor rather than simply provide taxpayer subsidies to already affluent corporate investors and real estate interests. In this view the state represents, and mediates among, the interests of *all* of its citizens, not just the rich and powerful. This returns us to an underlying contradiction in the modern concept of the state, or, more accurately, its bifurcation into two conflicting paradigms. As I suggested above, the generosity of the early public sphere stood in latent conflict with the economic hierarchies of capital (imbedded in concepts of the state through the stipulation of property ownership as a precondition for citizenship). This contradiction placed ongoing pressure on the coherence of liberalism as a political ideology. In order to resolve this contradiction it was necessary to construct a political narrative in which the ownership of property, rather than being a product of contingent social and historical conditions, was instead a reflection of the individual's innate capacities. The ability to accumulate property becomes a test of one's fitness as a subject, based not on the arbitrary legacies of birth or blood, but on one's ability to extract value from nature. If some members of society suffer from poverty or want, it's simply a result of personal failure, not an indication of some more systematic set of forces that require the adjudication of the state.

Are profound discrepancies of wealth solely the product of individual rectitude, or the lack thereof? Or are there structural forces operating within society (e.g., racism, class-based access to capital, education, and business networks, etc.) that predetermine to some extent our ability to succeed, no matter how much we sacrifice? If one accepts the latter position, then the state is susceptible to public demands that it intervene in these forces, through regulation of the market system or by offering ameliorative relief to those damaged by them (e.g., unemployment insurance, social security, health care, public housing, etc.). In the modern era this conflict manifests itself openly during periods of economic and social crisis (the Progressive era, the Great Depression, the 1960s), when the dominant political narrative (i.e., that the market system represents an equitable system for rewarding individual merit) is hardest to maintain. During these periods the state is forced to take up a regulatory and critical relationship to the imperatives of the market. The self-interested depredations of a privileged economic class replace the self-interested depredations of a privileged aristocracy as the target of this regulatory impulse. This ameliorative view of the state was, and is, intolerable to conservatives, who argue that, far from helping to buffer its citizens from the dysfunctional effects of capitalism (cyclical unemployment and depression, downward pressure on wages and benefits, lack of corporate accountability, etc.), the state should seek every possible way to reinforce the discipline of the marketplace and to reward, rather than penalize, the wealthy.

The 1980s was a period of political realignment, as the ameliorative state that came to influence during the 1960s was displaced by a conservative model of the state, embodied in the rise of Reaganism. This transition was, however, gradual and not absolute. Block grant funding made it possible to sustain the still necessary fiction of an ameliorative state (coming to the rescue of "our" deteriorating cities) while effectively turning federal funding decisions over to municipal governments that were far more responsive, and vulnerable, to entrenched economic interests. Once the linkage between the economic process of urban redevelopment and the compensatory benevolence of the liberal state was established, it was possible to jettison even the nominal demand for "consultation" with the poor required by early block grant guidelines. This occurred through a discursive shift in which "the city" (seen as diseased or damaged) was disassociated from its actual residents. The city became an abstraction to be "reborn" aesthetically, in the form of new office towers, pedestrian malls, and shopping arcades, even as its residents were being expelled by the development process. This is why art, with its redemptive, quasi-spiritual associations, played such a crucial role in urban gentrification during the 1980s. It provided a ready-made set of metaphors and images ("urban renaissance," and even the city itself as a "work of art") that transformed the crass, bottom-line calculations of the real estate speculator into the ennobling cultural aspirations of a Florentine prince. The linkage between culture and commercial property investment was pioneered by real estate firms like the Rouse Company, whose "festival marketplace" concept was franchised in New York's Seaport Village, Boston's Faneuil Hall, and, most famously, Baltimore's Harborplace.[69] By the early 1990s, the NEA, under John Frohnmayer, was giving funding for "public" art programs directly to developers such as Rouse through an "Art in the Marketplace" program.[70]

The basic methodology of urban redevelopment was well established by the mid-1980s. Initial experiments in Baltimore, New York, Los Angeles, and elsewhere provided a template that has been applied nationally and internationally since, and which continues to pattern our uses and perceptions of urban space. Public art was, from its inception, linked with real estate development (Calder's *La Grande Vitesse*, e.g., was part of an urban renewal scheme in downtown Grand Rapids), but it was during the 1980s that the public art genre itself was uncoupled from public funding and incorporated into the process of speculative real estate development.

A guide to commercial real estate in Washington, D.C., produced during the late 1980s notes:

> When shopping for space, discerning tenants of course, consider economics, location, parking, and transportation. . . . But the sculptures and paintings on display can be an added enticement. As a result of the increasingly soft rental market, a tenant does not pay substantially more for aesthetically pleasing surroundings. These properties have a competitive edge, however, and their higher occupancy rates reflect it.[71]

It is, of course, not technically accurate to refer to art in this context as "public art," since the spaces in question were privately controlled and policed. However, these works made use of the conventions of the public art genre (and the ameliorative associations of public space itself). The granite-clad corporate atria, shopping arcades, and urban "parks" of America's gentrifying downtowns were filled with large paintings and sculptures, bringing the calming salve of art to people in the midst of their workday routines. Developers could present themselves as munificent corporate citizens while giving their properties a "competitive edge." In fact, they were often able to trade the provision of publicly accessible amenities (such as art) for increases in the commercial footage allowed in a given building. "Art," precisely because it was perceived as a general public good, could be exchanged for permission to violate zoning regulations intended to place some limits on the private monopolization of space.[72] This perception is rooted, however tenuously, in the historical function of art as an open field of cultural inquiry, free from the demands of both the market and the state, and able to provide a critical perspective on the operations of each. In the privatized public art of the 1980s this political function is decanted into a set of aesthetic protocols intended to enhance, rather than question, these operations.[73]

The commercial appropriation of public art was symptomatic of a broader erosion of the institutional and spatial boundaries between the public sphere and the private sector that began during the Reagan era in the United States, and which continues to this day. It was Ronald Reagan who initiated the relentless drive to remove all cultural and political barriers to the imperatives of the market system. The state was to abandon any regulatory relationship to the private sector, reducing corporate oversight, eliminating all forms of public assistance that might offer a nominal alternative to low-wage labor, and privatizing its most basic functions (education, social security and, more recently, defense). Reaganism in the U.S. was mirrored by Thatcherism in the U.K., which was characterized by a similar set of practices, including attacks on organized labor (the miners' strike in the U.K. in 1984–85 and Reagan's breaking of the air traffic controller's union in 1981) and the promulgation of public-private "partnerships" in urban redevelopment, most evident in Thatcher's support for the scheme to gentrify London's Dockland's area and the "urban renaissance" movement in the U.S. during the 1980s.[74]

From the early days of public art, in which certain signature sculptures came to function as monumental logos for the revitalized city (the Daley Plaza Picasso in Chicago, Calder's *Grand Vitesse*), to the role of art galleries and studio spaces as spearheads of the gentrification process in New York's Lower East Side, to the most recent paeans to the "Creative City"—in which hives of energetic designers, software engineers, and advertising executives swaddled in art galleries, cinemas, and coffee shops, provide the new engine of postindustrial capitalism—culture and the arts have played a central role in framing urban renewal as a creative or ameliorative process.[75] In each case, the destructive component of urban redevelopment, the often-coerced displacement of poor and working-class populations, is elided. The essential mechanisms of the renewal process are by now well established, and have migrated around the globe. We find relevant examples in Belfast, Buenos Aires, Sydney, Osaka, and Bilbao, among many other cities. The mythos of the entrepreneurial creative city has even penetrated into those European countries that still retain some semblance of a traditional welfare state apparatus, as is evident in organizations such as Creative Amsterdam, which seeks to "stimulate the creative industries" in the city by linking Amsterdam's venerable history of art production ("Rembrandt's paintings") with such contemporary manifestations of the creative spirit as the television show *Big Brother* and the recent campaigns of the KesselsKramer advertising agency.[76]

The proliferation of urban regeneration schemes during the 1990s was paralleled in the U.K. and continental Europe by the increasing institutionalization of "community art" practices, which initially emerged during the 1960s and '70s in conjunction with broader movements for social and political change.[77] By the late 1990s, community art was largely uncoupled from its roots in local activism, as Tony Blair's New Labor movement celebrated its ability to enhance the "social capital" of the poor and working class. More often than not, the rhetoric of "social inclusion" that began circulating at the time reinforced conventional notions of poverty as a product of personal failure (to be remedied by the "self-esteem" inculcated by exposure to the arts).[78] It coincided with a growing convergence between a de-radicalized Marxism, associated with the retrenchment of the Labor Party of Great Britain in the face of Thatcher's populist appeal, and the centrism of Tony Blair and Anthony Giddens's "Third Way" rhetoric.[79] New Labor policies were promulgated through an influential network of think tanks and institutes, such as Demos and Comedia.

The bellwether expression of New Labor cultural policy was François Matarasso's *Use or Ornament?*, published by Comedia in 1997.[80] While employing the (obligatory) language of "participation" and "self-determination," Matarasso argued for the use of art to facilitate social "stability" rather than political transformation.[81] Exposure to the arts, according to Matarasso, would encourage "personal growth," "enhance confidence," and improve the "social contacts and employability" of participants. We return, once again, to Jacob Riis's blind beggar and the pedagogy of the free market. Rather than selling pencils in the street, the poor are encouraged to ignite their creative, entrepreneurial, spirit through the emulation of artistic subjectivity. Community art, Matarasso continues, "produces social change which can be seen, evaluated and broadly planned," and can function as a "cost effective element of a community development strategy." His notion of social change as something to be "planned" and administered by the state, on behalf of the disenfranchised, is clearly at odds with an understanding of social change as a process set in motion by the constituents of the state, in response to their own demands and in resistance to the various complicities and interdependencies that define the state's relationship to the market. Community art, under the mandate of New Labor, will encourage "social cohesion" but not political solidarity. It will seek to acclimate the working class to the forms of subjectivity demanded by capital, but not to question the demands themselves.[82]

The projects that I'll examine in the final section of this chapter have been created out of the complex economic, political, and cultural forces set in motion by urban development and regeneration. They are part of a broader, informal, body of art practice that engages with the cultural and spatial politics of the city. We find parallel examples in the art and media production associated with the Prestes Maia occupations in São Paulo, the Caracas Urban Think Tank in Venezuela, Torolab in Tijuana, Tranvía Cero in Quito, Mapa Teatro in Bogata, City Arts in Dublin, Temescal Amity Works in Oakland, Transforma in New Orleans, Max Rameau's *Take Back the Land* project in Liberty City, Florida, and Ultra Red in Los Angeles, among many others. The projects developed by these groups range from more-overt activism (demonstrations, occupations), to performance-based works, to experimental urban research, to extended collaborative engagements with specific communities. In the work of Park Fiction in Hamburg, Germany, and Project Row Houses in Houston, Texas, existing communities were faced with the threat of dislocation as a result of rising property values and incipient gentrification in adjacent neighborhoods. In each of these projects, systems of art production intersect with the demands of activist work, producing symptomatic interference patterns in the protocols and orientations of each. These points of tension, differentiation, and replication are of particular importance for my analysis. Processes of displacement and issues of property and spatial sovereignty play a central role in this work. Who can claim space in the city? Who is the audience for actions designed to demand social justice? How is resistance produced through a given site or practice? And what forms of creative agency can be mobilized in this process? As with the projects discussed in chapter 2, this work involves an improvisational understanding of site and situation, and a nuanced, tactical, relationship to existing institutional and discursive systems.

PARK FICTION: DESIRE, RESISTANCE, AND COMPLICITY — 4

It's awful. The men with the fancy suits have always been our enemies, and now suddenly they're supposed to be our friends. I can't deal with that. I'm afraid they tricked us somehow. That's what capitalism is all about.

A LOCAL ACTIVIST FOLLOWING THE AGREEMENT IN 1996 THAT ALLOWED THE HAFENSTRAßE SQUATTERS TO PURCHASE OCCUPIED BUILDINGS FROM THE CITY OF HAMBURG AT A FRACTION OF THEIR MARKET VALUE

The story of Park Fiction begins in the autumn of 1981, long before the park itself was imagined, when squatters occupied several vacant city-owned buildings in Hamburg's harbor-front neighborhood (on St.Pauli-

Hafenstraße and Bernhard-Nocht-Straße). Like cities elsewhere in Europe and the United States, the recession of the 1970s, combined with the forces of suburbanization, left large areas of downtown Hamburg derelict. During the 1980s the Hafenstraße squatters consolidated their control over the occupied buildings, organizing an alternative institutional network that included a daycare, school, cafe, soup kitchen, library, legal aid clinic, and even a radio station. The area became a center for leftist organizing in Hamburg, hosting numerous political demonstrations and fending off regular attacks from fascist gangs. It also became an organizational hub for the larger "Autonomia" movement, which originated in northern Italy during the 1970s and soon spread to France and Germany, as well as Greece. The Hafenstraße squatters formalized their occupation in 1982, receiving a temporary contract from the city council that protected them from eviction. Nonetheless, they faced ongoing police harassment (conservative political leaders claimed they were harboring fugitives from the Red Army Faction), arbitrary arrests, forced inspections, and the interruption of electrical service.

In 1986 the squatter's temporary contract expired and the city attempted to remove them, leading to an extended period of militant conflict (the so-called "barricade days"). While the Hamburg police were able to clear several of the buildings by force, the squatters retained a base of operations in three larger buildings. Historian George Katsiaficas describes the next stage in the conflict:

> In response to these attacks, the movement unleashed its own counteroffensive, marching more than ten thousand strong around a "black block" of at least fifteen hundred militants carrying a banner reading "Build Revolutionary Dual Power!" At the end of the march, the black block beat back the police in heavy fighting. The next day, fires broke out in thirteen department stores in Hamburg, causing damages estimated at over $10 million. Over the next months, while the city government floundered, the movement kept the pressure up. On "Day X," April 23, 1987, small groups of Autonomen again retaliated, attacking houses of city officials, court buildings, city offices and radio Hamburg. In all, more than thirty targets were hit in a fifteen-minute period.[83]

Following several more days of street battles, Hamburg Mayor Klaus von Dohnanyi proposed a compromise that would turn control of the buildings over to a corporation composed of squatters and sympathetic city council members, thus giving the squatters legal status. The corporation would then lease the buildings back to the squatters. This agreement remained in place for six months before conservative politicians, led by Henning Voscherau, refused to honor it, leading to Dohnanyi's resignation and years of protracted negotiations and sporadic police harassment. Throughout this period, the city was never able to fully remove the squatters, in large part due to their own well-organized resistance as well as the broader public sympathy they had gained both in Hamburg and internationally, which made a violent confrontation and removal unacceptable. Finally, in 1996, now-mayor Voscherau agreed to a new compromise which allowed the remaining squatters to purchase an entire block of occupied buildings for one and a half million dollars, or about a third of its market value. The squatters contributed 10 percent of the cost, while the Nuremberg-based Umwelt Bank, which invests in environmental projects, provided the balance in the form of a loan.[84]

While the Hafenstraße has survived, and many of its alternative institutions (schools, etc.) still exist, the community remains one of the poorest in the city, with a high percentage of Turkish *Gastarbeiter*.[85] At the same time, it is under increasing pressure from the development process in surrounding downtown neighborhoods. The very visibility and centrality of the Hafenstraße has increased its vulnerability, as it is located in close proximity to some of the city's most expensive hotels and a large public market. According to Park Fiction member Christoph Schäfer, "Things that might be tolerated in other places as interesting alternative flavors are automatically confronting power and the dominating ideology in this location. Every step you take is symbolic."[86] As early as 1983 mayor Dohnanyi began promoting urban development "enterprise" zones in the city's downtown and waterfront areas. Today even the notorious Reeperbahn red-light district in St. Pauli is becoming fashionable, as the artists and musicians originally attracted by cheap rents are being displaced by luxury apartments, advertising agencies, and nightclubs catering to teenage drinkers.[87] The work of Park Fiction grew out of this complex urban space, poised between a militant and contentious past and a future increasingly ordered by the imperatives of real estate speculation and the cultural proclivities of Hamburg's well-compensated cadres of immaterial labor. Their work can be seen in many ways as a hinge between these two moments.

In my analysis of Dialogue's work in India I focused primarily on what might be termed the micropolitics of collaborative practice: the protocols developed by Dialogue to facilitate intersubjective exchange and the various forms of resistance, distanciation, accommodation, and engagement awakened by their presence in Kopweda. In my discussion of Park Fiction's work I will frame my analysis more broadly in order to address the macropolitical nature of collaborative work at the level of larger institutional and social formations. The point of crisis that initially catalyzed Park Fiction came in 1994 when the city sought to build high-rise office buildings and apartments on a small piece of land in St. Pauli overlooking the Elbe River. The development would have effectively barricaded the Hafenstraße from the waterfront. A diverse group of residents, including activists, musicians, artists, social workers, teachers, and priests (many of them associated with the protests of the 1980s) formed the Hafenrandverein (Harbour Edge Association) to oppose the development process. Hamburg-based artists Christoph Schäfer and Cathy Skene developed the initial Park Fiction proposal, which evolved through ongoing discussions with the Hafenrandverein. The project team, which expanded and contracted over the years, eventually grew to include Simone Borgstede, Margit Czenki, Dirk Mescher, Thomas Ortmann, Klaus Petersen, Ellen Schmeisser, Sabine Stoevesand, Axel Wiest and, a bit later, architect Günther Greis.

Schäfer, Skene, and Czenki, a filmmaker who taught for many years in one of Hafenstraße's experimental schools, had a particular interest in the development of new forms of cultural and artistic practice.[88] As Schäfer has written, "After eighties style militant activism had lost its momentum, after the squat had been legalized, after the former fighters had retreated into their houses, after private had become private again, we had to find different ways, if we wanted to open public space as a field of dispute."[89] This "different way" involved the facilitation of a parallel planning process that undermined the bureaucratic hierarchies of conventional planning while retaining a sufficient level of organizational and political coherence to operate within existing circuits of public policy and decision making. The members of the Park Fiction collective visited hundreds of Hafenstraße residents in their homes to solicit their participation, gave numerous presentations to school and community groups, and staged film screenings, musical performances, exhibitions, raves, and other public events designed to mobilize community involvement and provide venues in which residents could describe and articulate their wishes and proposals for the park site (see plates 13 and 14).[90]

They reinvented the planning process "like a game," according to Schäfer, constructing a "planning container" out of an old shipping container filled with various planning "tools." These included a "clay modeling office," a phone hotline "for people who get inspired late at night," a "wish archive," and a mobile planning "Action Kit" replete with "questionnaires, maps, a dicta-phone, an un-foldable harbor panorama, and an instant camera to capture ideas." In each case, an ironic or whimsical reinstantiation of the methods of conventional planning was used to demystify the authority and technical complexity of the planning process and encourage their collaborators to visualize their own desires for the park.[91] By producing a "little parallel knowledge universe" and creating at least the appearance of a strong community consensus in support of a clearly elaborated alternative use for the site, Park Fiction was able to disrupt and redirect the orderly flow of the official planning process.[92] As Schäfer writes, "For a short moment in time, we had made the rules of the game, had a complex, lively idea of what we were doing, firm ground under our feet—and they [city officials] were in the stupid position, and looking boring and just like what they are: people who just block things."[93]

This sense of playfulness is evident in the proposals generated by the Hafenstraße's residents, which ranged from a strawberry-shaped tree-house to a "Pirate Fountain" featuring images of female pirates Anne Bonny and Mary Read (a sly reference to Hamburg's historical associations with piracy, symbolized by the skull and crossbones, the unofficial symbol of the St. Pauli football team). The Park Fiction collective held a series of community forums to select a final set of projects and organized the design and construction process in further meetings with residents, administrators, an architect, and Park Fiction team members. By 2003 several key features of the park had been completed, including a "Palm Island" (with lifesize metallic palm trees) encircled by a long bench from Barcelona, a field of grass laid over an undulating concrete foundation to create the appearance of a vast, green "flying carpet," a large mosaic, a tulip-patterned synthetic rubber field (which references the "tulip period" in early modern Turkey, when the Ottoman Empire began a rapprochement with the West), and a dog park complete with poodle-shaped hedges and gates (an homage to the Pudel Club, an important experimental music club located nearby), along with a boule field, community gardens, and play areas for children (see plate 15).

The experience of coming upon the park in the midst of Hamburg's gentrifying waterfront is revelatory. After passing through blocks of chic cafes, marble-clad office buildings, and banal street furniture, the park appears like an exuberant mirage, emerging incongruously from the bland, homogenous landscape of urban redevelopment. It is both literally and figuratively an island, but at the same time it remains linked to the urban space of Hamburg, and the broader context of globalization. Its towering metal palm trees echo the looming industrial cranes of Hamburg's nearby docks. The Alhambra-inspired mosaic, the Barcelona bench, and the flying carpet lawn all reference the city's long history as a major port (dating back to the Hanseatic League) and a crossroads of cultural and commercial exchange with the rest of the world. Moving further east from the park, along Bernhard-Nocht-Straße, leads one past the remaining buildings controlled by the Hafenstraße occupation. The park is thus poised between encroaching gentrification and the embattled remains of the "old" St. Pauli of political insurrection and the sex trade. It acts as a spatial equivalent for the practice of Park Fiction itself, serving simultaneously as a domestication of this militant past (violent protest is transposed into play) and a monument to its survival and ongoing reinvention. The park is heavily used by local residents and is often filled with skateboarders, dog walkers, families, musicians, and flirting couples. It has helped to transform street life in the Hafenstraße and provides one of the few joyful public spaces in an area in which space is increasingly privatized and constrained.

Perhaps the most significant effect of the park is the sense of ownership and identification that it provides for Hafenstraße's residents. Political change is produced and sustained in three ways: transformations in institutional protocols (expansion of the franchise, new forms of public policy, legislative or judicial regulation, structural reorientation of the relationship between public authority and the private sector, erosion or outright elimination of conventional market systems, etc.); the inculcation of new belief systems or value systems within a broad social network (the normalization of new notions of racial- or gender-based equity, e.g., or the production of new forms of solidarity); and, finally, through claims of spatial autonomy which result in the literal physical occupation and control of space (through the transfer or redefinition of ownership, the creation of new boundaries or borders, new spatial identities, etc.). All of these forms of change begin, of course, with the transformation of individual consciousness over time, and each overlaps, and intersects, with the other. As with Dialogue's work in Kopaweda, Park Fiction is constituted around a deliberate, collectively realized, claiming of space. The park was created as an island, a physically discrete zone of play, action, and coming together, against the grain of the dominant development paradigm (which would have instead used the space for an office building). It thus stands as a constant reminder of the difference (and survival) of the Hafenstraße, and an informal monument to the creative and improvisational nature of the occupation itself.

The process of creating the park required the ability to shift between an expressive modality, mindful of multiple subjectivities and desires, and a tactical modality which would allow the Park Fiction team to negotiate effectively with the city (the process of "being in bed with bureaucracy," as they describe it). The capacity to shuttle between these two modes was crucial to the project's success. Park Fiction was extremely sensitive to the complex and idiosyncratic conditions necessary to solicit creative participation. They thus sought to multiply the points of access and modes of expression available to residents, using everything from modeling clay to answering machines to cameras to interviews and questionnaires. Rather than reiterating the familiar call-and-response cycle of demonstration and police counterattack, Schäfer, Skene, Czenki, and their collaborators sought to reconfigure resistance through a process of cultural displacement. The "fiction" of a park, in place of the looming reality of a banal office building, was produced by a lateral movement. Instead of proceeding from a moment of negation (demanding that the city simply stop its planned development), Park Fiction began with a gesture that was positive, productive, and indeterminant: imagining something new and unexpected in its place. As Schäfer notes, "We developed a parallel and approachable planning process for a real place, connecting arts and social movements, without falling into the trap of taking the 'legal' path of limited participation suggested by the bureaucratic system."[94]

Their work proceeded neither through a direct, frontal confrontation with the state in the public space of the street, nor through full complicity with existing bureaucratic channels, but rather by working in the space between overt activism and formal state protocols (existing systems of planning and consultation, e.g., that inevitably privilege the development community and political elites). At the same time, the implied threat of direct conflict or violence provided the ground against which Park Fiction's ongoing negotiations with municipal agencies unfolded. As part of its development plan, the city was preparing to demolish the Hafenkrankenhaus, a popular hospital that served the Hafenstraße community and was only a short distance from the park site. Schäfer describes the community's response:

> After the government had cleared the first wing of the hospital, to their surprise, the empty building was squatted by activists. The squatters were strongly supported in the neighborhood, there were weekly demonstrations, and for the first time ever, even a strike in the red light district during those demonstrations. The movement was getting out of hand, '97 was an election year, and suddenly the government was ready to negotiate about the hospital and all the other problems in St.Pauli.[95]

It was in part the proximate danger of renewed militancy and the formation of new solidarities in the Hafenstraße that provided the Park Fiction collective with the political leverage necessary to enact their plans.[96] The city was clearly anxious to defuse the unrest aroused in St. Pauli by the hospital protests. By supporting the park, city officials could demonstrate their generosity and beneficence to the community at relatively little cost. From this perspective the park could be seen as a way to buy off the Hafenstraße, and the Park Fiction team could be accused of acting as middlemen in the process of redirecting the community's potential for resistance into a safely cultural form.

We encounter here an inverted (and equally disabling) variant of the reform/revolution dynamic I outlined in my discussion of May '68 in chapter 2, in which withdrawal into a semi-autonomous zone of cultural production was seen as the only way to preserve the purity of a revolutionary vision tainted by the reformist compromises of party politics. This analysis can easily enough be reversed. The only way to avoid complicity with the existing (and implicitly monolithic) capitalist system is to abjure merely "cultural" interventions and instead to pursue direct, revolutionary action (street demonstrations, attacks on property, etc.). Anything less will only serve to legitimate the system (showing that it can respond to appeals for greater equity or social justice without altering the underlying distribution of political and economic power). This logic can be extended back to the original purchase of the buildings occupied by the Hafenstraße squatters. While this action effectively gave legitimacy and permanence to the occupation, some activists nonetheless viewed it as a "trick" designed to co-opt resistance (transforming militants into property owners rather than challenging the principle of private property itself). Thus, the "authentic" political foundation upon which the cultural action of the park depended (the existence of a network of activists able to live, work, and organize in the occupied houses without the threat of eviction or displacement) was itself initially perceived by some as a reformist compromise (releasing political pressures that might have otherwise led to demands for more substantial change).

What is missing in each of these analytic frameworks is a sense of the necessary interdependence between "cultural" and "political" action, and a more complex understanding of cause and effect in the production of social change. Significant transformations in the distribution of power or resources in a society only come about in response to forms of social or political instability that threaten the legitimacy of the state apparatus or the market system (organized violence or insurrection, massive demonstrations or work stoppages, or the emergence of new forms of solidarity and new emancipatory narratives). But this instability in and of itself is no guarantee that the resulting changes will be progressive or egalitarian rather than authoritarian and conservative. There is a complex interrelationship among the three modes of transformation I outlined above (changes in institutional structures and protocols, changes in values and belief systems, and new claims of spatial sovereignty). Political change occurs across these various registers and is oriented by a diverse, and contentious, group of individual and institutional actors (political representatives, activists and militants, newly mobilized communities, NGOs, etc.). Each of these actors, in turn, can be situated along a continuum of positions, ranging from those who advocate an absolute overturning of existing structures of power, to those who support more gradual or piecemeal change, to those who reject change entirely and seek instead to turn back the clock to some earlier moment of ostensibly greater social stability, hierarchy, or cohesion.

There is a perennial tension among these positions, and a necessary interdependence between the discourses of revolutionary and reformist political action. Moreover, the parameters of change available at any given historical moment are always partially determined by the political narratives and institutional conventions set in place during earlier periods of transformation. Park Fiction's success (its ability to sustain a several-year-long process of negotiation leading to the appropriation of city property and the mobilization of significant public resources for the construction of the park) was not only due to the militancy surrounding the Hafenkrankenhaus demolition; it was also due to the fact that some form of public consultation or participation has become a normalized component of the development process, even if it is now largely symbolic. And the fact that an obligation exists to consult with the communities targeted by planners in the first place is the product of an earlier moment of political resistance and contestation, now enshrined (or reified) in the conventions of urban development. Participatory planning approaches emerged out of the political ferment of the 1960s as activists sought to gain greater control over their own communities and the decision-making processes of metropolitan governments (in opposition to the top-down, hierarchical nature of conventional urban and regional planning in the 1950s).[97] These gestures gained currency against the background of widespread political militance among the urban poor and working class that was especially pronounced in the United States and western Europe. Park Fiction was able to reactualize this participatory tradition through playful and improvisational techniques ranging from beer-fueled *charettes* in the "Planning Container," to raves, to workshops with school children. As a result, they could confront Hamburg's planning authorities with the desires of the Hafenstraße community, formalized in a specific set of counterproposals. As Schäfer notes, "When the politicians entered the scene, they found themselves in a complex field, where they had difficulty moving."[98]

We discover here a temporal parallel to the capillary movement of political change that I outlined earlier (in which calls for more thoroughgoing change, while not fully realized, nonetheless exert pressure on those holding more moderate positions, and who are often more capable of producing actual institutional change). Here, the political conflicts of the past achieve a kind of partial victory when they force the accommodation of new standards (of consultation, participation, political representation, etc.). These are, inevitably, eroded and compromised over time (and they can just as easily be conservative as liberal, or radical), but they retain a latent power that can be remobilized (and even expanded upon) during subsequent moments of crisis. In this context, the avant-garde tendency to define each new mode of practice, each new "movement," as constituting an absolute break with, or supercession of, the compromised or failed conventions of the past is a particular liability. Dialogical practice requires a more nuanced understanding of the temporal, as well as spatial, interdeterminancies that produce political transformation.

While Schäfer describes Park Fiction's approach as a form of parapolitical subversion (bypassing the "'legal' path of limited participation suggested by the bureaucratic system"), the fact remains that the park was brought into existence via formal channels of public arts funding. It was supported by Hamburg's Municipal Culture Department, which invited Schäfer and Cathy Skene to submit a proposal to their Art in Public Space program. They requested funding for the Park Fiction project, which was already generating enthusiastic support among the residents of the Hafenstraße. Once the city decided to finance the project, Park Fiction began an extended process of negotiation. Perhaps the most symptomatic element in this process was a "round table" installed near the park site, which featured seating for neighborhood residents on one side and city authorities on the other. It was at this table that the members of Park Fiction were able to win a key concession from the city, when officials from the Municipal Culture Department agreed to give the collective direct control over the finances allocated by the Art in Public Space program for the construction of the park (a move that had previously been blocked by the conservative Senator for Urban Development).[99]

"Round tables are a dangerous thing," Schäfer writes, "as their name suggests an equal power balance that conceals the unequal status of the participants. Also, speaking with bureaucrats means to half-accept their dominant way of thinking and negotiating."[100] Both literally and figuratively, then, the table represents the movement from indeterminant desire to determinant action. This is the point in a conventional analysis at which the ostensible autonomy of aesthetic creativity (embodied in the singular "wishes" of the Hafenstraße's residents, unconstrained by the propriety of bourgeois taste or technical practicality) is sacrificed on the altar of instrumental action and bureaucratic appropriation. Schäfer himself is not immune to this formulation, insisting that Park Fiction's work was "opposed to the principle of consensus."[101] As we saw in chapter 2, the concept of consensus or agreement has become an almost reflexively pejorative term in contemporary art theory and criticism. The complex processes involved in reaching even a provisional form of consensus have been collapsed into a hypostatized caricature, co-extensive with the most authoritarian forms of coercion and hierarchy. But the "wishes" or "desires" of the Hafenstraße residents, while exuberant, were hardly transgressive or revolutionary per se, and their facilitation certainly required a degree of formal cooperation (among the residents, within the Park Fiction team, and among representatives of the team, the community, and the city). At the same time, this cooperation can't be reduced to the simple denial or conferral of consent, but, rather, depended on a complex technics of collaboration.

Park Fiction's work requires an analysis that is less reliant on a simple opposition between (aesthetic) play and (instrumental) work, between a realm of pure "collective desire" and the impure world of bureaucratic compromise and consensus, or between an absolute revolution or over-turning and mere reform. As with the other dialogical projects I've discussed, there is another mode of labor that unfolds at the intersection of the creative and the practical. This labor is, by necessity, multivalent and contradictory. Just as Park Fiction was obliged to "half accept" the "dominant way of thinking" embodied by city officials, so too the city's Municipal Culture Department was forced to accommodate the demands and modes of expression articulated by the members of Park Fiction and the Hafenstraße community. The result was a subtle but not insignificant re-coding of the political apparatus assigned the task of regulating public space in Hamburg. And, despite the compromises and exclusions implicit in the very notion of the Hafenstraße as a "community," Park Fiction did manage to create a concrete and sustainable space that embodies the collective power and singular imagination of the residents and continues to serve as a stage for ongoing resistance and organizing. During the most recent anti-gentrification protests in St. Pauli, in response to attempts to develop Bernhard-Nocht-Straße, the park functioned as a model of creative dissent. It is necessary here to recall both the tactical and the affective significance of enclosure and spatial sovereignty, whether in the sanctuary of a Pila Gudi in central India, the occupation of an abandoned building, or the incongruous sight of a vast green carpet of grass unfurling toward the cranes and derricks of Hamburg's docks.

From his fifth-floor office, Garnet Coleman can almost see the gleaming new urban lofts lapping at the edge of Houston's Third Ward. . . . Yuppies, empty nesters, childless couples—mainly white and Hispanic people with enough money to drop $250,000—are starting to move in. And Coleman, an intense, chain-smoking power broker who represents the neighborhood in the Texas legislature, isn't happy about it. "You can tell a neighborhood's turning," he says with dismay, "when you see them out at night walking their dogs."
JOHN BUNTIN, "LAND RUSH: GENTRIFICATION IN HOUSTON"

Notwithstanding the success of Park Fiction, the most recent plans for the development of Hamburg's waterfront (under the rather unimaginative theme of "HafenCity") call for over six million square feet of new construction, ranging from condos and apartments to corporate offices and retail. HafenCity's projected cultural amenities will include the Elbphilharmonie concert hall, HafenCity University, and the obligatory specimen of celebrity architecture (a "spectacular" science center designed by Rem Koolhaas and OMA).[102] Against the formidable array of corporate, financial, and governmental resources devoted to this undertaking, the ability of the St. Pauli community to carve out a small zone of autonomy can seem both heroic and quixotic. Despite the colorful anti-gentrification marches and unconventional planning techniques, the flying carpet lawn and the tartan field, is Park Fiction's work simply another "lesson in futility," gesturing vainly toward a never-to-be-realized utopian future? Are we back, again, to Francis Alÿs's college students shoveling vainly in the dunes of Ventanilla?

The goal of *When Faith Moves Mountains* was to present a visual corollary for the odd combination of joyful abandon and Sisyphean resignation that Alÿs associates with Latin America's resistance to modernization. Its temporary nature, the fact that the wind would soon return the dune to its original state and that nothing fundamental in the environment would be altered, is part of its meaning. In the same way, the labor of Latin America is destined to be swallowed up and made invisible by the forces of uneven development. While the park was never meant to perform a purely symbolic function (as its ongoing use as a site of both recreation and resistance suggests), it does serve to represent the agency of the Hafenstraße community in claiming space (while also echoing the original occupations of the early 1980s). However, its symbolic or representational significance is based on the durability of the park; the fact that it is *not* temporary or ephemeral, but rather, marks a permanent or quasi-permanent concession of space (and power) extracted from the state and development community. Its continuity over time, its status as tradition, is key to this meaning, and to the meaning of the performative interactions that have unfolded subsequently within it.

As I've already noted, all modernist art practice makes some claim of political efficacy, even if this claim lies in the refusal or negation of efficacy itself (which is assigned a compensatory or symbolic value). The salient question concerns the nature, scale, and locus of this efficacy. Is the work intended to transform the consciousness of an individual viewer, a group, or a hypothetical viewer-yet-to-be? Does it originate in the imagination of a single artist or out of the intersubjective weave of a larger collective? Is its effect immediate or graduated, ephemeral or sustained? While the park did play an integral role in the ensemble of social forces that successfully opposed gentrification in St. Pauli, it can hardly be expected, on its own, to halt or defer the broader process of capitalist redevelopment in Hamburg. Its significance doesn't lie in a simple calculation of political efficacy—a sudden and absolute revolution, or a single, seismic, shift in political consciousness—but in its contribution to an emerging mosaic of oppositional practices that is both local in effect and international in scope. Although these practices remain largely uncoordinated and situational, they are nevertheless framed by a similar set of concerns. What does political resistance look like when there are no guarantees? When there is no assurance that any given action or event is destined to succeed simply because it follows a single emancipatory telos or revolutionary *grand recit* (whether this narrative ends with the freeing of desire or the freeing of the proletariat)? In the absence of an imminent overturning of the "system," change becomes sustainable and extensive only through a *cumulative* process of reciprocal testing that moves between practical experience and reflective insight.

For many of the artists under discussion here, this process begins with the experiential knowledge generated through collective or collaborative practice and an increased sensitivity to the complex registers of repression and resistance, agency and instrumentalization, which structure any given site or context. It also entails an ongoing commitment to the creation of new relationships and affiliations with other collectives, activist organizations, and NGOs, in order to develop a more formal and coherent understanding of the specific insights generated through practice. Thus, Park Fiction has convened a series of international symposia and meetings related to urban activism, establishing connections with groups from Maclovio Rojas in Mexico to Sarai Media Lab in India. NICA's work in Myanmar was centered around residency and exchange programs, and Amadou Kane Sy of Huit Facettes recently helped establish a new art center in the coastal village of Mbodiene devoted to intercultural exchange. As I noted in the introduction, while these projects are oriented by the forms of creative praxis that unfold in a given situation, their very ubiquity, from the streets of Yangon to the villages of Bastar, from Senegal to Germany, suggests the global emergence of a new paradigm of artistic production.

For Park Fiction and Project Row Houses, the groups under discussion here, this paradigm focuses on questions of spatial sovereignty and the discourse of redevelopment. Project Row Houses (PRH) in Houston, Texas, provides a revealing counterpoint to the work of Park Fiction. In each case, an urban neighborhood was faced with the threat of gentrification and a literal negation or removal of its population. And in each case, instead of responding to this threat with a gesture of refusal, the artists involved began with an action that was creative and indeterminant. They began by visualizing something new and unexpected through an act of appropriation that was both physical (the assertion of control over real property) and discursive. Thus, each group was able to reclaim and reinvent the language of urban regeneration or renewal that is so often used as an alibi for the outright destruction of working-class communities (implicitly defined as broken, pathological, or degenerate). Project Row Houses was produced in Houston's Third Ward, a historically black community just south of the city's downtown area. This once-vital neighborhood has deteriorated over the past thirty years as city and public services have contracted and middle-class African Americans have relocated to the suburbs (an unintended consequence of desegregation). Insurance-based arson became so common that one resident, Benjamin Benson, began bicycling to local fires with his saxophone to play a requiem as the houses went up in flames. At the same time, the neighborhood's proximity to the city center has recently placed it in the path of gentrification. According to a study by the Institute for Regional Forecasting at the University of Houston, assessment values for property in five Third Ward neighborhoods increased at the rate of 10 percent per year between 2000 and 2005.[103]

Project Row Houses was founded in 1993 by Rick Lowe, a young artist who moved to Houston from Alabama in 1985. In the early 1990s Lowe worked with a Third Ward community center named SHAPE (Self Help for African People Through Education), which was conducting a survey of deteriorating or unsafe buildings in the area as part of an urban triage plan intended to arrest blight and improve the neighborhood. They identified twenty-two abandoned homes in one block as among the worst in the area and encouraged the city to tear them all down. The buildings were primarily "shotgun"-style cottages, an architectural form that originated in New Orleans but is common throughout the southeastern United States. Built between the post–Civil War period and the 1930s, shotgun cottages are narrow, with each room lined up after the next on an axis extending back into the lot. They typically have high ceilings to dissipate heat and are built on raised piers to prevent flood damage. Lowe viewed the houses not as symptoms of decline, but as physical links to the past history of the Third Ward, and he argued for their preservation. The shotgun house came to function as both a heuristic and mnemonic device for Lowe, who sought to reactivate it through an unusual rapprochement between the work of African American painter John Biggers and Joseph Beuys, whose concept of art as a form of "social sculpture" Lowe found appealing.

Biggers's canvases and murals commemorate African American life during the 1940s and '50s, with a particular focus on the shotgun house neighborhoods of the American South (he grew up in Gastonia, North Carolina). While Biggers's images are tinged with nostalgia, they also capture something very important about black culture in the Jim Crow era. One of the effects of segregation was the creation of tight-knit, diverse, and self-reliant black communities. As Elmo Johnson, a pastor in Houston's largely black Fourth Ward notes: "This neighborhood had everything it needed. We were our own little self-contained community." This compulsory autonomy, the extended kin networks, the solidarity and diversity of people thrown together by racist exclusion and violence, helped provide the social foundation for the emergence of the Civil Rights movement.[104] For Lowe, Beuys's work sanctioned the imaginative leap from the representational world of Biggers's canvases to "real time."[105] As he recalls:

We passed these little shot-gun houses, and that was the first time I started to think about the houses—you know, the scale of the houses, and how as artists we could utilize those houses as a way of reflecting something to the community. . . . We were talking about tearing them down and we all agreed that this would be the correct course of action. But maybe after looking at John Biggers work and really thinking about it, driving to that corner again one day and looking and all of the sudden I thought, "Ah-ha! Wow! Look at that."[106]

Lowe met with Biggers, who taught for many years at Texas Southern University in Houston. Biggers explained the history of the shotgun house to Lowe and described the way in which its formal structure—a series of interconnected rooms terminating in an enclosed back courtyard—facilitated a division between the public and private spaces of the home, while also creating a deliberate opening from the home into the public space of the sidewalk through the inclusion of a large front porch. For Biggers, the vitality of a shotgun house community depended on a combination of factors. In addition to the architectural program of the house itself, these included a tradition of mutual assistance that created a social safety net within the community, a respect for education, a vibrant culture of music and story telling and a spirit of creative necessity and bricolage, and a level of economic sustainability based in large part on a network of locally owned businesses and service providers.[107]

Lowe sought to transform the shotgun house from a sign of the neighborhood's deterioration into a focal point for its reinvention. Using seed money from the National Endowment for the Arts and private foundations, he was able to purchase the original twenty-two houses slated for demolition. He worked with students at Rice University's School of Architecture to renovate the structures into prototypes of affordable housing, preserving key elements such as the front and rear porches, the pier-and-beam construction, and metal roofs. He set aside seven renovated houses to serve as transitional homes for single mothers in the Third Ward, who were provided with training, education, and assistance for a one-to-two-year period. Another eight houses were used to establish an innovative artist-in-residence program. Artists and writers such as Sam Durant, Julie Mehretu, Quincy Troupe, Alice Walker, Fred Wilson, and Chen Zhen spent up to six months living in the Third Ward. Due to the dearth of pro-

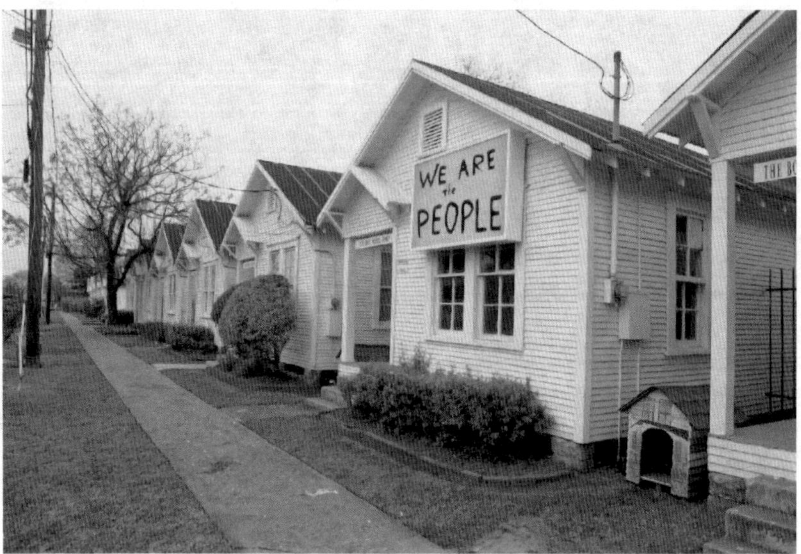

FIGURE 14 *We Are the People*, installation by Sam Durant, Project Row Houses, Houston, Texas (2003). Courtesy of Project Row Houses.

grams for children in the area, the artist-in-residence houses became a magnet for neighborhood kids, leading to the creation of a mentoring program with artists and writers that now serves fifty local children a year.

Project Row Houses eventually grew to involve numerous local churches, schools, community groups, and individual residents. In the process, Lowe's perception of his own function as an artist began to change (his previous work had been primarily painting and installation-based). He came to see his artistic practice as a way to "uncover the meaning of the place and create opportunities for people to give that meaning a place to live."[108] The institutional relationships that Lowe established, both in the Third Ward and within the city of Houston more generally, were paralleled by engagements at the level of individual subjects and subjectivities. Lowe worked with Eugene Howard, who moved back to the neighborhood after twenty years of incarceration, helping him to establish and brand a barbecue catering business. Another resident, named Kenya, functioned as the neighborhood's "one person black power movement," according to Lowe.[109] Dressed in black army fatigues, beret, and gloves, he took on the task of patrolling the neighborhood on his bike, watching over local kids on their way home from school. While many residents viewed

Kenya as an eccentric, to Lowe he represented a contemporary expression of the tradition of mutual assistance associated with the old shotgun house communities. Lowe created a public banner featuring an idealized image of Kenya to acknowledge his importance to the neighborhood and to help shift perceptions of him among Third Ward residents. Lowe cites many similar gestures of initiative and conviviality, such as Cookie Love's Wash n' Fold, a service created by a local woman who uses a grocery cart to pick up laundry from residents in the morning, take it to a laundromat for cleaning, and return it to them at the end of the day. Although each is relatively modest, when taken in the aggregate these actions help to define the community and ensure its resilience and integrity.

Even as Lowe was working to preserve and commemorate the living traditions of the Third Ward, local developers began eyeing the area, having successfully initiated the gentrification of the nearby Fourth Ward (another historically black downtown neighborhood). PRH inadvertently abetted the gentrification process via the publicity that the project generated for the community, which effectively reinforced the traditional role of the arts in making black or working-class neighborhoods seem safe or inviting to middle-class whites. At the same time, as Lowe contends, "the neighborhood would have been earmarked for gentrification because of its central location. . . . Before we came in the Planning Department had already replanned the property as if the houses were gone. So something was going to happen with or without our intervention."[110] If Lowe and his collaborators were going to prevent Project Row Houses from being swallowed up in a sea of loft-style condos and dog-walking yuppies, they would have to effect a scalar shift in their thinking. They established a Community Development Corporation (CDC) and began buying and renovating additional homes to create a larger stock of affordable housing. This marks a key transition in the trajectory of PRH, reflecting a more ambitious and strategic understanding of the forces at work in urban redevelopment.

Lowe was certainly not alone in his concern about gentrification in downtown Houston. A number of political leaders with links to the city's African American community were alarmed after seeing the displacement that occurred as a result of redevelopment in the Fourth Ward. Lowe and PRH found an ally in Texas State Representative Garnet Coleman, who developed his own unorthodox approach to challenging gentrification.[111] Coleman, whose family has lived in the Third Ward for over a century, uses "tax increment financing" (TIF) to buy up property for use as low-income rental housing. TIF zones typically funnel the increased property tax revenues brought about by gentrification in a given neighborhood into infrastructure improvements that will attract additional investment. Coleman, who controls the board of the Midtown TIF district (which includes parts of the Third Ward), has instead directed ten million dollars into the purchase of property over the past five years. He plans to turn control of the land over to local churches and CDCs, with deeds requiring that it be used only for affordable housing. "We can give tax abatements out the wazoo for lofts and condominiums," Coleman argues. "The question is what are our values and whether or not we are willing to spend the same money on people who need a nice, affordable, clean place to live."[112]

Lowe's effort to link the present-day Third Ward to a set of vital cultural traditions was an essential component of this broader process of resistance. In order for the mechanisms of traditional redevelopment to function effectively (the exercise of eminent domain, razing of existing housing, etc.), it is first necessary to define the targeted area as irredeemably blighted or derelict. This is an essentially cultural and discursive process that allows developers to create an implicit linkage between the physical or material decline of a given community (deteriorating housing stock and infrastructure, reduced economic base, etc.) and the character of its inhabitants, whose removal or displacement is thereby rendered less objectionable. Houston developer Larry S. Davis employed precisely this tactic in justifying the removal of poor and working-class residents that occurred as a result of gentrification in the Fourth Ward, which was spearheaded by his own development company. "When you look at what they were being displaced from," Davis argues, "the houses were totally rundown; they should have been torn down. . . . The only culture displaced was a culture of needles and syringes."[113] Davis's ironic notion of "culture" is used here to reinforce the traditional conservative view of the poor and working class as an amoral rabble. Lowe's commitment to reframing the meaning of the Third Ward through the celebration of its cultural and architectural history and its traditions of mutual assistance challenges this perception.

In reacting to the threat of gentrification the PRH team could have engaged in what Lowe defines as a conventional "horizontal" form of resistance, barricading the neighborhood against external threats defined along class and race lines. And, in fact, local residents did launch an informal protest campaign under the slogan "The Third Ward Is Not For Sale." At the same time, Lowe felt it was necessary to supplement this approach. Rather than taking a stand against "any kind of change," he advocated a form of redevelopment that both sustained and enhanced the neighborhood's diversity. "I just felt that seeking diversity was the right thing," Lowe states, "in the sense of trying to instill a community based on desegregation culture."[114] Lowe's notion of a "desegregation culture" is complicated by the diffraction patterns of race and class. Segregation had the effect of confining people on the basis of their race, not their class. In fact, the class diversity of black communities in the Jim Crow era (in particular, the presence of a middle class) was often seen as exercising a positive, stabilizing influence. At the same time, de facto and de jure forms of segregation and redlining insured that property values remained relatively stable despite this class diversity (the black middle class didn't have the option of moving elsewhere). Thus, segregation-era neighborhoods were economically diverse but racially homogeneous.

"Diversity" today, in the context of the Third Ward, must be understood differently. If the gentrification process were allowed to move forward it would entail the gradual displacement of a relatively homogeneous working-class population by an equally homogeneous population of middle- and upper-middle-class homebuyers, many of whom would also be white or Hispanic. Here an initial class diversity (represented by the incursion of new homeowners) is divisive, because their presence would increase property values and housing costs, eventually forcing working-class residents out. The effect of gentrification today is to produce neighborhoods that are economically homogeneous while allowing for some nominal racial diversity. The result is a kind of informal segregation of the poor and working class in conditions of deteriorating housing and limited social services. As in the Third Ward, this class homogeneity is frequently reproduced and reinforced along racial or ethnic lines.

We typically associate the concept of diversity with attempts to challenge hegemonic cultural formations, defined through exclusionary categories of racial or ethnic identity. Here incidental differences of race or ethnicity are assigned fixed and prejudicial value within an artificial hierarchy. Social justice is achieved by attempting to overturn or erode this hierarchy, returning these differences to merely incidental status, with no bearing on the general determination of one's worth, freedom, or opportunity. As I've noted above, to speak of class "diversity" is an altogether more ambivalent matter. Class-based identities carry meaning in a fundamentally different way. Unless one subscribes to the conservative belief that class differences simply reflect the unbiased verdict of the market pronounced on the individual, class differentiation in and of itself is necessarily symptomatic of an underlying inequality, whereas racial or ethnic difference is only contingently so. The "problem" of racism isn't the actual racial identity of the individual (understood as the genetic attributes of skin color, hair type, etc.), but the fact that a given society has chosen to use these attributes as an (arbitrary) marker for discriminatory practices. The "problem" of class difference resides in class identity itself, which reflects and reproduces a systematic form of economic domination that is often, although not always, inflected by racial or ethnic differentiation.

In the absence of a fundamental reorientation of the broader system of neoliberal capitalism, how do we define and articulate political resistance? Is class diversity tolerable if we can mitigate its local effects (rather than the global fact of its existence) via some form of ameliorative or compensatory action by the state or other non-market actors? Or, to be more specific, would gentrification in the Third Ward be less objectionable if it was possible to prevent the displacement of poor and working-class residents? And what kind of "community" would result? This question would appear to be central to Lowe's notion of diversity. Lowe accepts the inevitability of some middle- or upper-income housing in the area, but he also insists on the importance of a large pool of rental housing for low-income residents, as well as programs to assist homebuyers from the neighborhood.[115] However, in trying to cultivate this diversity (and in challenging the "culture of needles" rhetoric of developers like Larry Davis) PRH risks replicating certain problematic patterns we've already identified in the history of urban reform. Here the exemplary Third Ward residents—the convict-turned-caterer, the diligent laundry woman—demonstrate their fidelity to the entrepreneurial spirit demanded by the market rather than engaging in organized resistance directed at the broader system of exploitation that defines the Third Ward as "working class" in the first place.

Is this yet another moment of repetition? Are the participants in Project Row House any better off than Jacob Riis's pencil-selling beggar, reassuring his benefactors of his willingness to abjure charity and "earn" his way in the world? Has the sympathetic passerby on the streets of New York been replaced by the fellowship panel of the NEA or the Ford Foundation, only too happy to fund art programs that promise to transform the impoverished into productive workers? And what are the implications of Lowe's effort to replace the absent black middle class of doctors, lawyers, and accountants with artists and poets? From this perspective, PRH could be viewed as a modern-day settlement house seeking to inculcate properly bourgeois values among its poor and working-class neighbors.[116] But surely this criticism misunderstands both the limitations and the possibilities of dialogical, collaborative practice. The PRH team can only work with the cultural conditions that exist in the Third Ward at this historical moment. They can inflect these conditions, sometimes in a quite profound manner, but they can't transform the Third Ward of today into the Hafenstraße of the mid-1980s. The more pertinent question is whether these practices challenge the imperatives of urban redevelopment in ways that are reflective, sustainable, and generative. By this standard, PRH's capacity to resist both the economic and cultural movement of the gentrification process is significant. As with all of the projects under discussion here, PRH seeks to remain open to the creative potential of practice—its capacity to disclose new possibilities, new modes of political and cultural transformation—while at the same time coming to terms with the existing forces and historical preconditions in place at a given site.

In the absence of the binding force exercised by segregation on the shotgun house neighborhoods of the 1950s, how is community defined in the Third Ward today? What kinds of community, what forms of solidarity, are possible without the threat of an external determinant that functions only to subsume (gentrification) or sequester (segregation)? This is the question that PRH's work raises, and it returns us, finally, to the issues of collectivity and identity with which this book began. In the case of both Park Fiction and PRH we can observe a process of sovereign expression, a claiming of space and collective identity, that is by necessity defensive (each community faces the possibility of removal or displacement) but that nonetheless seeks to preserve internal differentiation and diversity. It is the capacity to shuttle between these two modalities, to define community diachronically, that I find distinctive in so many of these projects. Community here is founded on neither an immanent, quasi-metaphysical substrate nor on the paradoxical revelation of our existential singularity, but on a series of relational encounters that require the ongoing negotiation of difference as well as identity.

The goal of resistance for PRH is not to halt or arrest redevelopment in its entirety, but to insure that the improvements that come with redevelopment (increased jobs, improved infrastructure and services, etc.) benefit everyone and not just the white and Hispanic middle class seeking an "urban" lifestyle in the Third Ward. They mobilized the anodyne discourse of redevelopment ("renewal," "regeneration," etc.), taking advantage of an obligation for participatory involvement that was extracted through past political struggle. We are left, then, with a final question. What is the relationship between the kinds of local or situational action we see in the projects of PRH and Park Fiction, and the pervasive system of neoliberal capitalism that has been a subtheme of the work discussed throughout this book? What possible threat does it pose to global capitalism if a small community in Houston or Hamburg is preserved from the wrecking ball, or a few villagers in central India are able to talk together at a water pump? From one perspective, it could be argued that the work of such groups actually sustains the ongoing existence of a larger system of economic exploitation that would otherwise collapse if only these "contradictions" (poverty, homelessness, unemployment, gentrification, etc.), and the social suffering they entail, were allowed to continue and intensify. Here the goal of political resistance is to publicize and even exacerbate these tensions in order to provoke a heightened critical consciousness among the poor and working class, who are the potential agents of true revolutionary change.

This is a tactical position akin to the view, common during May '68, that by provoking the police through arson, property damage, and open confrontation, it would be possible to "expose" the hidden propensity for violence lurking beneath the benign facade of the liberal state.[117] The street performances of barricades, occupations, police truncheons, and tear gas were intended in part for a hypothetical, yet-to-be-politicized viewer, whose outrage at such an open display of savagery by the forces of order would catalyze their support for a general overthrow of the state.[118] We can see as well in this analysis the significant epistemological and behavioralist overlaps between the discourse of political and artistic vanguards. The political activist is charged with awakening the working class, multitude, or precariat to its revolutionary mission by revealing the hidden contradictions of capitalist power and the systemic roots of what are otherwise perceived as merely individual or epiphenomenal forms of suffering or injustice. The avant-garde artist also seeks to disclose that which was hidden, through the revelatory power of an aesthetic encounter that awakens the viewer to the operation of hegemonic forms of power, identity, or community.

Chantal Mouffe, in her essay "Artistic Activism and Agonistic Spaces," reiterates this view. In a formulation that should by now be familiar to us, Mouffe contrasts a naive, Habermasian notion of public space based on "consensus," with an "agonistic" notion of democracy in which "public space is the battleground where different hegemonic projects are confronted, without any possibility of final reconciliation." "Critical art" practices, according to Mouffe, "foment dissensus," seeking to "unveil all that is repressed by the dominant consensus" (the only possible kind) and thereby making "visible what the dominant consensus tends to obscure and obliterate."[119] What is strangely absent from this veritable orgy of unmasking and exposure is any meaningful account of the actual reception of the initial revelatory gesture. It is as if the "truth" of capitalism were a simple objective fact, like a new species of animal or a recently discovered planet, the existence of which could be proven to a skeptical viewer through the presentation of previously unseen evidence. Here the complex process of representation is reduced to a kind of unmediated, theophanic epiphany. Once having received this truth, the viewer will naturally and spontaneously feel compelled to take up revolutionary struggle. But, as we saw in our earlier discussion of images of poverty and suffering, the ostensible self-evidence of any representational gesture can never be assumed.[120]

This discourse is apparent in the writing of artists as well as theorists. A recent manifesto by the architectural collective BAVO bemoans the "blackmail of constructive critique" ("Either you offer constructive criticism with concrete solutions to go with it or you shut up!"), which they associate with the proliferation of a naive, accommodationist "NGO" art, in which "commitment is understood as the constant production of innovative micro-solutions—so-called 'pocket revolutions'—to the real, everyday problems people encounter in their immediate life world." Such work is antithetical to "deep criticism" and a repudiation of a properly "critical art practice that throws fundamental questions at the ruling order and tirelessly confronts it with its inconvenient truths." A truly *"radical"* critique, according to BAVO, "cannot immediately be made productive within the existing order *since the latter is radically put into question"* (italics in original).[121] Such a critique begins "from the premise that there is something so fundamentally wrong with the existing order that every attempt at making it better, however well intended, will always be perverted by it, and that one should aim for nothing less than the radical subversion of that order."[122] BAVO simply inverts the terms of the blackmail; precisely in trying to improve existing conditions, the artist becomes complicit with the dominant social order.

Here the capacity for a critical epistemological distance (from which one might grasp the interconnected totality of the capitalist system) is collapsed into a literalized notion of political distance or withdrawal (from the "real, everyday problems" of life). "Deep" criticism is, by definition, unproductive, unable to function within the existing institutional and discursive circuits of capitalism because its very depth constitutes a kind of scandal, intolerable to the ruling order, and because the ruling order's capacity to blunt, assimilate, and disarm resistance is absolute. Therefore, BAVO insists on a quasi-hygienic separation between merely reformist institutions and what they term "radical social resistance movements." But here, again, we face a dilemma. Who determines which social resistance movements are sufficiently "radical" and which are not? And what precisely would constitute the "radical subversion" of the "existing order" at this historical moment? How, in fact, do we define the "ruling" or "existing" order in the first place? What are its constituent elements? How do they interrelate and synchronize? Are there moments or locations at which these elements are permeable, discontinuous, or open to intervention, or are they entirely fixed, static, and unchanging?

BAVO returns us, yet again, to the Manichean reform/revolution dynamic I discussed earlier in my analysis of May '68. And am I not, in my own way, simply reaffirming this division with my presentation of projects that are so clearly grounded in the local and the situational? Do these projects offer nothing more than "pocket revolutions," isolated moments of transgression or resistance that will never coalesce into a coherent whole capable of toppling the vast apparatus of neoliberal capitalism? I would suggest that this interpretation is belied by the efforts toward global exchange among practitioners that I outlined above, and by the capacity of groups such as PRH, Ala Plastica, and others to initiate significant scalar shifts in their practice. It is true, however, that I have tended to concentrate on projects that have been generated out of very specific situations and contexts (the condition of water pumps in Kopaweda, the creation of an art center in Yangoon, resistance to gentrification in the Hafenstraße). It's necessary here to differentiate between a rhetorical mode of critique (which seeks to mobilize viewers or readers via the enunciative reiteration of an a priori truth claim, judgment, or accusation) and forms of practice in which critique and critical distance are produced a posteriori, through reciprocal engagement with a specific network of social forces and actors.

Here the orientation and trajectory of critical insight aren't predetermined, but rather, depend on the collaborator's response to the contradictions, possibilities, and points of resistance thrown up by the problem-at-hand (the bureaucratic systems of the Burmese government, the social ecology of water collection, the cultural politics of urban renewal). All of these elements are subject to engagement and transformation. While these projects clearly presuppose an underlying set of ethical and creative values (a commitment to the collaborative process, a resistance to the hierarchies of neoliberalism, etc.), they also generate an important second-order form of knowledge as these abstract criteria are tested against the pragmatic demands of social transformation at a given site (cf. Böhler's "dialogical action," Scott's notion of métis). Certainly this approach can lend itself to a naive faith in technical problem solving, or a tunnel vision that attempts to resolve problems rooted in the broader system of global capitalism with initiatives that suggest that both the cause and solution of these problems are somehow purely local and even individual in nature. I would contend, however, that what makes many of the projects I've examined here distinct is precisely the dual consciousness of both the local and the global implications and interconnections of a given site and situation. In each case, we encounter a clear rejection of a neoliberal discourse that would locate the cause of poverty or suffering in the moral character of the individual, along with an equally clear understanding that resistance to this discourse must begin with individual action.

This doesn't mean that each project openly espouses the immediate overthrow of world capitalism (here, again, we encounter the difference between rhetorical and pragmatic approaches). In fact, one of the most important aspects of this work is its unorthodox and often indirect relationship to conventional forms of political struggle. The members of Dialogue didn't begin their work in Kopaweda by announcing their intention to transform gender relations in the village, and Park Fiction didn't launch their experiment in "desiring production" by blockading access to the contested land in the Hafenstraße. However, the global synchrony of neoliberalism remains a central frame of reference for this work. This is evident in Park Fiction's linkages with urban activist groups in other countries; in Huit Facette's commitment to "south/south" organizing; in Ala Plastica's attempts to challenge the IIRSA at the regional level; and in Dialogue's promotion of Adivasi solidarity in the context of the corporate penetration of central India. While it is certainly necessary to remain cognizant of neoliberalism's remarkable capacity to co-opt political and cultural dissent, BAVO's instinctive distaste for "the problems of daily life" remains problematic. It is symptomatic of certain lacunae in current Left cultural theory, which continues to depend on a teleological orientation to political transformation, defined as the absolute overturning of a monolithic ruling order or undifferentiated capitalist system.

As I've already suggested, the conventional navigational markers for political resistance (and critique) have been transformed over the past thirty years by the vicissitudes of "actually existing Communism," the increasing adaptability of neoliberal capitalism, and the emergence of New Social Movements and new models of class (e.g., the Autonomia movement). Nevertheless, a simplistic and totalizing notion of revolution continues to function as a kind of phantom limb for many artists, theorists, and activists. I would contend that there is much to be learned from the ways in which people respond to, and resolve, the struggles they confront in everyday life. In fact, our most meaningful engagement with the pressures exerted by capitalism occurs precisely through our daily experience at the intersubjective and even haptic level. Unless we can grasp the complex imbrication of the local and the global, of individual consciousness and collective action, which frames this experience, our understanding of political change will remain impoverished and needlessly abstract. The creation of new knowledge regarding political and social transformation, and the specific role that art can play in facilitating this transformation, requires a process of both learning and un-learning via practice. This must,

of course, be combined with an acute consciousness of historical precedent and existing theoretical paradigms, but it is equally necessary to recognize the specific insights generated by practice that might challenge or
contradict both. It is this slow process of learning and un-learning that is
unfolding across a range of collaborative art projects today.

NOTES

Introduction

1. *Complete Edition of the Oxford English Dictionary* (1987), s.v. "collaboration."
2. In the epigraph that begins this chapter, Adorno is referencing Hegel's discussion of "the One and the Many" in *Wissenschaft der Logik* (1812). See G. W. F. Hegel, *Science of Logic*, translated by A. V. Miller, foreword by J. N. Findlay (London: Allen and Unwin, 1969), 163–78.
3. Green, *The Third Hand*.
4. See, e.g., Epstein and Prak, *Guilds, Innovation, and the European Economy*; and Parker, *The Subversive Stitch*.
5. For a useful survey of collaborative and collective practice in the post–Second World War period, see Stimson and Sholette, *Collectivism after Modernism*.
6. See, e.g., Butler and Mark, *WACK! Art and the Feminist Revolution*. I discuss Suzanne Lacy's work in greater detail in my *Conversation Pieces*.
7. Enwezor, "The Production of Social Space as Artwork," 225.
8. For useful overviews, see Harvey, *A Brief History of Neoliberalism*; and Bauman, *Globalization*. It was the neoconservative sociologist Daniel Bell who predicted over thirty years ago, in *The Cultural Contradictions of Capitalism* (1975), that the result of increasing economic and scientific rationalization would be a thirst for transcendence among the population at large—a demand for a new spiritual framework to give order, meaning, and a moral justification to the culture of unrepentant individualism and hedonistic self-interest promulgated

by the market system. Thus, according to Bell, the "real problem" of modernity is "the problem of belief. . . . It is a spiritual crisis, since the new anchorages have proved illusory and the old ones have become submerged." A virulently anti-modern religious fundamentalism may not have been quite what Bell had in mind when he sought to identify a new spiritual ethos for capitalism, but it's what we have ended up with, and it now exists in an uneasy, but disturbingly effective, alliance with the interests of financial and economic elites in the United States (as demonstrated by the success of the revanchist Republican Party during the early 2000s) (see Bell, *The Coming of Post-Industrial Society*, 26).

9. See Ackerman and Duvall, *A Force More Powerful*.

10. See Boal, *Theater of the Oppressed*. For a survey of community arts practice in a national perspective, see Fitzgerald, *An Outburst of Frankness*.

11. Other artists associated with this tendency include Jeremy Deller, Phil Collins, Christine Hill, and Pierre Huyghe. Their works, largely developed in the context of international exhibitions and biennials, have attracted widespread critical, curatorial, and institutional support via commissions, catalogs, museum acquisitions, and exhibitions. After achieving international prominence only about ten years ago, Hirschhorn's work is already in the collections of the Museum of Modern Art in New York, the Kunstsammlung Nordrhein-Westfalen in Dusseldorf, the Philadelphia Museum of Art, the Stedelijk Museum voor Actuele Kunst in Ghent, the Tate Gallery in London, the Renaissance Society at the University of Chicago, and the Walker Art Center in Minneapolis. Tiravanija, to cite another example, has had solo exhibitions at the Museum of Modern Art, the Los Angeles County Museum of Art, the Wexner Center for the Arts in Columbus, and the Philadelphia Museum of Art. He has been awarded a Gordon Matta-Clark Foundation Award, the Louis Comfort Tiffany Foundation Biennial Competition Award, a National Endowment for the Arts Visual Artists Fellowship, the Central Kunstpreis, the Hugo Boss Award, and the Smithsonian American Art Museum's Lucelia Artist Award, as well as being appointed a curator of the 2003 Venice Biennale.

12. This counterpoint is not intended to suggest that projects produced within art institutions are necessarily more compromised or less authentic, or that projects produced outside these institutions (but, inevitably, within others) are somehow more pure or uncorrupt. Clearly, each institutional setting carries its own constraints and its own possibilities. As I will argue, the very language of purity and co-option so often employed in the analysis of collaborative work is symptomatic of certain limitations within the field of contemporary art theory. It's worth noting the symptomatic ambivalence that the mainstream art world continues to display toward certain modes of activist, collaborative practice.

When the curators of *Documenta* decided to include the work of Le Groupe Amos, Huit Facettes, and Park Fiction in *Documenta 11*, they were careful to sequester it in the "lounge-like atmosphere" of the Documenta-Halle, away from official gallery spaces (see Kerr, "Warming to the Global: Documenta XI," 23).

13. I think there are two important distinctions to be made about the treatment of contemporary art by the discipline of art history. First, the artist is generally still alive to dispute or challenge the historian's assessment, and can claim some countervailing authority. This is particularly relevant given the increasing frequency with which artists also function as critics and theorists in their own right. And second, the contemporary viewer, or participant, is also available as a resource for the analysis of reception at a level of proximity and detail that is seldom accessible to historians of earlier periods. Both of these factors implicitly challenge the hermeneutic monopoly that the historian typically enjoys. As a result, contemporary art history poses something of a threat to traditional art historical discourse: the threat of unregulated and multiple claims of interpretational authority. Moreover, both of these factors tend to undermine the perception that the discipline of art history is defined by a capacity for critical detachment or a more objective, less interested, relationship to its object of study. Reception is precisely something we *can* address as historians of the contemporary. Not in order to recover the "real," or originary, meaning of a given work, but because there is a mode of experience that occurs at the site of reception that is significant and worthy of analysis. These concerns are further complicated by contemporary collaborative or participatory art practices. In analyzing this work it's necessary to overcome the tendency to simply project the specific social and institutional determinants of the museum or gallery space onto the widely varying sites, situations, and constituencies that are characteristic of contemporary collaborative practice. More specifically, it's necessary to overcome the long-standing tendency to frame critical analysis around the assumed characteristics of a hypothetical bourgeois subject, regardless of the specific class identity or cultural background of actual viewers and participants.

14. My use of the term "patrimony" is deliberate. One of the most troubling aspects of the homogenizing of art theory over the past fifteen years has been the gradual recession of feminist approaches and the literal disappearance of women theorists. Figures such as Hélène Cixous, Simone de Beauvoir, Teresa de Lauretis, bell hooks, Luce Irigaray, Julia Kristeva, Juliet Mitchell, Eve Sedgwick, Gayatri Spivak, and Michele Wallace, who were widely read and cited in art and media criticism during the 1980s, are rarely encountered in contemporary art writing or scholarly research.

15. Cusset, *French Theory*, xiv.

16. See Bourdieu, *Homo Academicus*; and Bourdieu, *The Field of Cultural Production.*

17. Dosse, *History of Structuralism*, 2:271.

Chapter One: Autonomy, Antagonism, and the Aesthetic

1. Augustine, *Confessions*, bk. II, chap. XIV, sec. 17.

2. Ricoeur, *From Text to Action*, 6.

3. El Lissitzky cited in Craig, "Try Again, Fail Again, Fail Better," 99.

4. It should come as no surprise that Lissitzky was committed to a strategy of defamiliarization or sensory derangement typical of the interwar European avant-garde. Maria Gough offers a revealing analysis of this facet of Lissitzky's work in her discussion of his *Kabinett der Abstrakten*, produced for the Hannover Provincial Museum in 1928. The *Kabinett*, designed to display contemporary painting and sculpture, exemplifies Lissitzky's notion of a *Demonstrationsraüme*, or "demonstration space." Through the use of alternating black and gray wall lathing Lissitzky sought to "activate" the spectator through a conspicuous "optical dynamic" (*optische Dynamik*) set against the very ground on which the works of art were displayed. What was "demonstrated," according to Gough, was precisely the contingency of the exhibition space itself: "The relationship between work and visitor was to be transformed chiefly through the invention of devices that solicit . . . not only the latter's active participation but also, and most especially, his or her sensory disorientation" (Gough, "Constructivism Disoriented," 78). "Lissitzky's theory of activation," Gough reiterates, "is not . . . to be mistaken for a theory of mastery. To be activated . . . is to be disoriented, corporeally undone" (114). Gough's analysis relates directly to issues of participation and viewer "activation" which will be taken up again later in this chapter.

5. Gough, "Constructivism Disoriented," 247, 256–57.

6. The British critic Kate Bush, writing in *Artforum*, provides a typical example, evoking the overwhelming "blizzard of images and words" hurled at the viewer by artist Thomas Hirschhorn, which, she says, are "powered by a sense of urgency and incomprehension in the face of catastrophe that leaves us, under his unforgiving neon, nowhere to hide" (see Bush, "Best of 2001," 94).

7. Lars Bang Larsen, "Questioning the Social: Ethics and Aesthetics in Contemporary Art," presented at the Momentum International Art Conference "Questioning the Social: Ethics and Aesthetics in Contemporary Art," May 26, 2000, in Moss, Norway. Available online at http://kunst.no/questioning/essays/pdf/larsen.pdf.

8. The introductory quote is taken from an unpublished interview with Margit Czenki and Christoph Schäfer by Noel Hefele (August 2005) conducted as part

of *Groundworks: Environmental Collaboration in Contemporary Art*, an exhibition I curated for the Regina Gouger Miller Gallery at Carnegie Mellon University in 2005. See *Groundworks: Environmental Collaboration in Contemporary Art*, edited by Grant Kester (Pittsburgh: Carnegie Mellon University / Regina Gouger Miller Gallery, 2005). The *Groundworks* exhibition was part of a larger project that included a set of site-specific commissions organized by Tim Collins and Reiko Goto through Carnegie Mellon's Studio for Creative Inquiry. Commissioned artists included Helen and Newton Harrison, Walter Hood and Alma Du Solier, Jackie Brookner, Stephanie Flom and Ann Rosenthal, Laurie Palmer, Tom and Connie Merriman, and 3 Rivers 2nd Nature.

9. Park Fiction, "Artist's Statement," *Groundworks* exhibition (2005).

10. Ibid.

11. Ibid.

12. See, e.g., the grassroots campaign in India against Coca Cola's efforts to privatize water at the website of the India Resource Center, http://www.india resource.org/.

13. This and the following quotes are from an unpublished interview with Navjot Altaf by the author (July 2005), conducted as part of the *Groundworks* exhibition.

14. Altaf, "Contemporary Art, Issues of Praxis, and Art-Collaboration," *Towards New Art History: Studies in Indian Art*, 88–98.

15. See Kester, *Conversation Pieces*.

16. Bishop, "The Social Turn," 179. The Bourriaud quote that introduces this chapter is taken from *Relational Aesthetics* (29). Portions of the following discussion were previously published in "Aesthetic Enactment: Loraine Leeson's Reparative Practice," in *Art for Change-Loraine Leeson: Works from 1975–2005*, edited by Katja Jedermann, Birgit Kammerlohr, Nanna Lüth, Carmen Mörsch, Thorsten Streichhardt, and Jole Wilcke (Berlin: Neue Gesellschaft für Bildende Kunst Berlin, 2005), 70–87.

17. Ibid., 9.

18. Ibid., 28, 9.

19. According to Michael Hardt and Antonio Negri in *Empire*, the primary fulcrum of political change is now assigned to "intellectual, immaterial, and communicative labor power," meaning, designers, technicians, media workers, etc. (29). This analysis of the dwindling relevance of industrial labor and the corollary rise of a new technical intelligentsia will be familiar to anyone with a general knowledge of recent sociology as it's been advanced in one form or another for the past several decades (from André Gorz's *Farewell to the Working Class*, to Daniel Bell's *The Coming of Post-industrial Society*, to Robert Reich's discussion of the "symbolic analyst" class in *The Work of Nations*). Moreover, the

interdependence of industrial labor and a technical-managerial cadre has been a feature of capitalism for at least a century (evident in steel and automobile production in the United States by the early 1900s). Hardt and Negri seek to remobilize St. Simon's concept of an emancipatory avant-garde centered in the arts and sciences. While it is no doubt flattering to the average software designer or university professor to find him or herself suddenly placed at the levers of history, there are obvious reasons to remain somewhat skeptical of this analysis, not the least of which is the assumption that graphic designers or advertising copywriters, as a class, are necessarily predisposed to use their technical skills in the service of a revolutionary political project. For another version of this argument, see McKenzie Wark's *Hacker Manifesto*, which postulates a "hacker class" of subversive artists, scientists, and researchers poised to seize control of the global "information commons." Hardt and Negri's dismissal of the agricultural working class notwithstanding, it's worth noting that agricultural labor continues to be the primary form of survival for some 80 percent of the world's population, and a key site for current labor organizing and political struggles over land reform and water access.

20. Bourriaud, *Relational Aesthetics*, 60.

21. Ibid., 91.

22. Ibid., 31, 45.

23. Bishop, "Antagonism and Relational Aesthetics," 65.

24. As I will discuss shortly, it is fitting that Hirschhorn would appropriate this phrase from an icon of the May '68 generation (Jean-Luc Godard, who famously pronounced, "I don't make political films, I make films politically").

25. These include Alix Lambert's *Wedding Piece* (1992), in which she married and divorced four different people "in record time," according to Bourriaud, and Angela Bulloch's café installation in which seated visitors triggered an audio loop consisting of a Kraftwerk song. In many of the works that Bourriaud describes, the positions of artist, collaborator, and viewer, far from being destabilized, remain highly conventional. Aside from offering the viewer some nominal form of social interaction (taking a flyer, eating food, etc.), the artist never relinquishes control. The work is organized or arranged beforehand, and set in place before the viewer, who is "summoned," in Bourriaud's words, to consume the assembled spectacle ("Exchanges are raw matter," as Bourriaud writes) (see Bourriaud, *Relational Aesthetics*, 31).

26. Bourriaud's account of relational practice is characterized by an unresolved tension between conviviality ("the beholder as neighbor") and a prescriptive desire to put the beholder in an "awkward position" or a "disconcerting situation" (Bourriaud, *Relational Aesthetics*, 43, 37, 31).

27. Claire Bishop criticizes Bourriaud's "naïve" and uncritical model of relational practice from the theoretical perspective of Ernesto Laclau and Chan-

tal Mouffe, who have been criticized in turn for naively celebrating the liberatory potential of the market system. See, e.g., Slavoj Žižek's discussion of the "de-politicization of the economy" in Laclau's thought, in Butler, Laclau, and Žižek, *Contingency, Hegemony, and Universality,* 316–23; and see Bertram, "New Reflections on the 'Revolutionary' Politics of Ernesto Laclau and Chantal Mouffe," 81–110.

28. See Bishop, "Antagonism and Relational Aesthetics," 57.

29. Bishop, "The Social Turn," 183.

30. See "Duration, Performativity, and Critique" in Kester, *Conversation Pieces.*

31. Woodmansee, in *The Author, Art, and the Market,* quotes Schiller: "Instead of being used by good writers for more noble purposes [the desire to read] is being misused by mediocre pen pushers and avaricious publishers to peddle their poor merchandise without regard for the cost in public taste and morality. . . . Mindless, tasteless, and pernicious novels, dramatized stories, so-called journals for the ladies and the like . . . are completely destroying the few healthy principles that our playwrights had left intact" (29). An interesting contemporary example of this dynamic, outside the European context, occurs in the widespread consternation among the Japanese literary establishment in response to the emergence of cellphone novels, or *keitai shosetsu* (see Goodyear, "I Love Novels," 62–68).

32. Woodmansee, *The Author, Art, and the Market,* 74.

33. Many German poets greeted the demand for literature created by the new reading public as an opportunity rather than a threat. Gottfried August Bürger, one of the most popular writers of the Sturm und Drang movement, called for a reform of German literature in order to make it more broadly accessible. Shouldn't the poet, Bürger asked, "descend [from Mount Olympus] and walk the earth, as Apollo did . . . and frequent the homes of mortals, both palaces and huts, and write poetry that is equally understandable and entertaining for all humankind?" (quoted in ibid., 61). "Get to know the people," Bürger urged his fellow poets in an essay published in 1776. "Eavesdrop on the ballads and popular songs under the linden in the village, in the bleach-yard, and in the spinning room" (quoted in ibid., 62). Bürger evoked the division between a demanding, and implicitly aristocratic, poetic practice and the cultural forms of the spinning room and the bleach-yard (notably, sites of labor rather than leisure). As Woodmansee shows, far from disparaging the ballads, songs, and stories of German laborers as symptoms of their ignorance or lack of cultivation, Bürger views them as the basis for the renewal and revitalization of poetry: cultural traditions to be engaged with, and learned from. Following his early commercial success, Friedrich Schiller shared Bürger's enthusiasm for populist art. However, after his subsequent plays failed to attract an audience, he struggled to survive as a writer. He was rescued from the vicissitudes of the

market by the timely patronage of the Duke of Augustenburg. It was under the Duke's support that he wrote his famous *Letters on the Aesthetic Education of Man.* By the early 1790s, Schiller's attitude toward the new literary market had changed dramatically, and he published a scathing critique of Bürger (he "does not deserve the name of poet"). Arguing that the "degraded" taste of the "vulgar multitude" threatened to destroy German poetry and literature, he chastised Bürger, who "frequently mingles with the people, to whom he ought merely to condescend, and instead of elevating them to himself jokingly and playfully, he is often pleased to make himself their equal" (quoted in ibid., 72, 78).

34. Ibid., 18.

35. Quoted in ibid., 78.

36. Quoted in Ibid., 21.

37. Quoted in ibid., 29.

38. Ibid., 11. As Moritz writes, the work of art "does not have its purpose outside itself, and does not exist for the sake of the perfection of anything else, but rather for the sake of its own internal perfection" (quoted in ibid., 18).

39. Quoted in ibid., 21. Here is Schiller, in a similar vein: "But how is the artist to protect himself against the corruption of the age which besets him on all sides? By disdaining its opinion. Let him direct his gaze upwards, to the dignity of his calling and the universal Law, not downwards towards Fortune and the needs of daily life" (quoted in ibid., 57).

40. Quoted in ibid., 19, 20. "To love Him selfishly, as a source of private gains, would be to make of Him a mere instrument or means of pleasure. We are enjoined to love God disinterestedly" (quoted in ibid., 19).

41. Ibid., 19, 20. "Beauty in a work of art is not pure and unalloyed for me until I completely eliminate the special relation to myself and contemplate it as something that has been brought forth entirely for its own sake" (quoted in ibid., 20).

42. Schiller, *On the Aesthetic Education of Man*, 7, 25.

43. Ibid., 45.

44. Ibid., 37, 25. "Among the lower and more numerous classes we are confronted with crude, lawless instincts, unleashed with the loosening of the bonds of civil order, and hastening with ungovernable fury to their animal satisfactions" (ibid., 25).

45. Ibid., 7. Schiller reiterates the traditional aristocratic complaint about the avarice of the bourgeoisie: "At the present time material needs reign supreme and bend a degraded humanity beneath their tyrannical yoke," and "Utility is the great idol of our age, to which all powers are in thrall" (ibid., 7).

46. Ibid., 157.

47. Ibid., 141.

48. As Schiller writes: "All improvement in the political sphere is to proceed from the ennobling of character. . . . This instrument is Fine Art: such living springs are opened to its immortal exemplars" (ibid., 55); and "It is only through Beauty that man makes his way to Freedom" (ibid., 9).

49. Beauty, as Schiller writes, "accomplishes no particular purpose, neither intellectual nor moral. . . . But precisely thereby something Infinite is achieved. . . . The aesthetic mode [is] the highest of all bounties . . . the gift of humanity itself" (ibid., 147). This leads to the perennial confusion in modern art theory over the relationship "between" the aesthetic and the political. Art may not be political on the basis of its ostensible content, but it clearly claims a causal relationship to the political (for Schiller the raison d'être of aesthetic experience is to "alter the very nature of sensuous man") (ibid., 163).

50. For a more detailed discussion of Greenberg, see Kester, *Conversation Pieces*, 36–46.

51. Starr, *Logics of Failed Revolt*, 114. The avant-garde patrimony includes Antonin Artaud, Georges Bataille, and Friedrich Nietzsche.

52. Certeau, *The Capture of Speech and Other Political Writings*, 10; Guattari, *Molecular Revolution*, 208.

53. For a detailed account of the events of May '68, and the complex and often contradictory range of positions represented by various actors within the movement, see Seidman, *The Imaginary Revolution*.

54. Starr, *Logics of Failed Revolt*, 114.

55. Ibid., 26.

56. Ibid., 8. As Cornelius Castoriadis observed: "The minority in the May events could perhaps have become a majority if it had gone beyond proclamations and demonstrations. But that implied a different sort of dynamic, into which it clearly neither wanted nor was able to enter" (quoted in ibid, 29). And Régis Debray wrote that the students chose to keep "their hands clean—just enough to get them cut off. Deliberate purity, more suicide than accident" (quoted in ibid, 29).

57. Comité d'Action Etudiants-Ecrivains, May 20, 1968, cited in Ross, *May '68 and Its Afterlives*, 77. Here we can see an important point of contact between the outlook of the May '68 *enragés* and the artistic avant-garde: the imperative to claim a position of radical exteriority and purity, which can only be sustained by exposing the duplicity of all other positions.

58. As Barthes writes: "Both sides of the paradigm are glued together in an ultimately complicitous fashion: there is a structural agreement between the contesting and the contested forms. By *subtle subversion* I mean, on the contrary, what is not directly concerned with destruction, evades the paradigm, and seeks some *other* term . . . an eccentric, extraordinary term. An example? Perhaps Bataille . . ." (quoted in Starr, *Logics of Failed Revolt*, 132; italics in original).

59. The opening of a new, "experimental" campus of the University of Paris (VIII) in the Bois de Vincennes was emblematic of the period. Here the revolutionary spirit could be cultivated, preserved, and then gradually titrated back into French society via intellectual and creative production.

60. Starr, *Logics of Failed Revolt*, 32.

61. Barthes, "Inaugural Lecture. Collège du France (1977)," 457.

62. Dosse, *History of Structuralism*, 2:131.

63. Starr, *Logics of Failed Revolt*, 121.

64. Barthes, "The Death of the Author," in *Image-Music-Text*, 147. As Starr writes, paraphrasing Barthes, literature instantiates "a new textual *economy* outside the commercial logics of exchange and substitution, an economy that would thwart the coercive subjection inherent to language (to nomination, representation and linguistic propriety) through the radical plurality of its constituent elements. . . . What we require, as Barthes has written in *S/Z*, is a disseminative textuality that would disperse all criticism, all meta-language, all centered meaning 'within the field of infinite difference,' a productive, nonrepresentational textuality to open up 'a circularity in which no one (not even the author) has an advantage over anyone else'" (Starr, *Logics of Failed Revolt*, 121; italics in original).

65. The Richard Howard translation in *Aspen* magazine (fall/winter 1967) makes the point more clearly than Stephen Heath's version in *Image–Music–Text*.

66. Barthes, "Inaugural Lecture. Collège du France (1977)," 131.

67. Barthes, "The Death of the Author," in *Image–Music–Text*, 147–48.

68. Barthes, *The Pleasure of the Text*, 39.

69. As Hélène Cixous writes in *The Newly Born Woman*: "Everyone knows that a place exists that is not economically or politically indebted to all the vileness and compromise. That is not obliged to reproduce the system. That place is writing." It is, of course, not merely writing, but *littérature* that Cixous evokes here, the para-institutional "worlds" of art, poetry, and theoretical reflection (see Starr, *Logics of Failed Revolt*, 129).

70. Blanchot, *The Space of Literature*, 199.

71. "What is needed if we are to understand social relations . . . is not only a theory of communication, but a theory of games which accepts agonistics as a founding principle. . . . In the ordinary use of discourse . . . the interlocutors use any available ammunition, changing games from one utterance to the next: questions, requests, assertions, and narratives are launched pell-mell into battle" (Lyotard, *The Postmodern Condition*, 16–17).

72. Badiou, "Fifteen Theses on Contemporary Art."

73. Laclau and Mouffe rightly challenge coercive and universalizing notions of collective identity. However, they have some difficulty in differentiating their concept of an agonistic "consensus" from the relatively banal notion of lib-

eral democracy as a forum for competing viewpoints. This position can only be viewed as radical or innovative against the ground of a naively essentialist version of community. In the art world assimilation of their work, "agonism" is often despecified and treated as an intrinsically emancipatory political force, regardless of context or situation (Laclau and Mouffe, *Hegemony and Socialist Strategy*, 123).

74. Derrida, *Politics of Friendship*.

75. Starr, *Logics of Failed Revolt*, 163. See also Cavanagh, "Pseudo-Revolution in Poetic Language."

76. See, e.g., the writings associated with Spontaneist Maoist or "Mao-Spontex" groups in France during the late 1960s and early 1970s, such as La Gauche Proletarienne and Vive La Révolution (see Schnapp and Vidal-Naquet, *The French Student Uprising*).

77. The parallels here to the Kantian notion of *Zweckmässigkeit ohne Zweck*, or "purposiveness without purpose," are clear.

78. "The archeologist," as Foucault writes, "does not take utterances seriously," while the subject, according to Lévi-Strauss, is little more than an "epistemological obstacle" (Dosse, *History of Structuralism*, 2:240, 1:253).

79. Dosse, *History of Structuralism*, 1:318.

80. *Complete Edition of the Oxford English Dictionary* (1987), s.v. "*conatus*" [Latin for "effort; endeavor; impulse"]. Subsequent attempts to resolve the question of agency introduced by the structuralist paradigm typically involved the delineation of various forms of para-agency articulated through a spatial framework (Pierre Bourdieu's "habitus"; Michel de Certeau's notion of "tactical" action, etc.).

81. This is why we encounter such a striking contrast between the rhetoric of authorial renunciation among the post-structuralist generation and the remarkable proliferation of proper names, signature methodologies, and competing theoretical brands. Dosse's two-volume study, *History of Structuralism* (cited above), provides a useful overview of some of the more colorful turf wars waged by the movement's founding fathers in search of scientific "rigor" and intellectual dominance.

82. Sedgwick, *Touching Feeling*, 140.

83. Ibid., 141.

84. Ibid., 144.

85. Ibid.

86. Michel Foucault's preface to Deleuze and Guattari's *Anti-Oedipus* openly acknowledges the theological fervor of the post-structuralist enterprise: "The Christian moralists sought out the traces of the flesh lodged deep within the soul. Deleuze and Guattari, for their part, pursue the slightest traces of fascism in the body" (xiii).

87. The Johns Hopkins Humanities Center convened an international symposium on "The Languages of Criticism and the Sciences of Man" at Johns Hopkins University in Baltimore in October 1966. The symposium proceedings, including Derrida's contribution, were published as *The Structuralist Controversy*, edited by Richard Macksey and Eugenio Donato (Baltimore: Johns Hopkins University Press, 1970).

88. While the structuralist approach experienced some initial resistance from the French academy in the late 1950s and early 1960s, by 1968 structuralist (and post-structuralist) thinkers were being rapidly assimilated into the academic establishment. The long march through the academy occurred even more quickly in the United States, where post-structuralist approaches have attained a dominant position in the arts and humanities. The works of Deleuze, Guattari, Derrida, Lacan, and Lyotard exerted a particularly strong influence in art and architectural history and theory, literary theory, and film studies.

89. Barthes's *Pleasure of the Text* was translated in 1975, Derrida's *Writing and Difference* in 1978, and Baudrillard's *Simulations* in 1983. See also Kotz, *Words to Be Looked At*.

90. The influence of semiotics and narratology was also evident in the work of figures associated with "new" art history, such as Mieke Bal, Norman Bryson, and John Welchman.

91. Of course, this hasn't prevented many "relational" artists from turning to the private art market. Art works, including documentation of ephemeral projects, by figures such as Hirschhorn, Huyghe, Beecroft, Sierra, and others regularly appear at auction.

92. This image of the artist as a detached, nomadic *flaneur* occurs regularly in discussions of Alÿs's work. The critic Martin Patrick describes Alÿs's *Narcotourism* (1996) as "one installment in Alÿs's ongoing investigation of various altered states: travel, intoxication, (potentially) violent behavior, sleep. He has spoken of using the city as a 'laboratory,' and . . . he becomes a test subject himself. Alÿs walks, but he also prowls" (Patrick, "Snapshots from an Indefinite Vacation," 10). And curator Rosa Martinez, in the catalog for Sierra's show in the Spanish Pavilion of the 2003 Venice Biennale, writes of Sierra "moving in twilight zones which enlightened minds might want to conceal" (Martinez, "Merchandise and Death," 23).

93. Thomas, "Pierre Huyghe," 3.

94. Bishop, "The Social Turn," 182.

95. Steinweg, *WORLDPLAY*, unpaginated. Steinweg continues: "The hyperborean subject is the hyperbolic subject of self-transgression and self-surpassing toward an absolute exterior that is Uninhabitability itself, Chaos, Incommensurability as such. It is the subject of a non-identity-building self-assertion, subject of failed anamnesis, of transcendental non-recognizability, subject

without name, without memory, without teleological inscription, subject of transcendental facelessness—barbaric subject."

96. Miessen and Basar, Introduction to *Did Someone Say Participate? An Atlas of Spatial Practice*, 25.

97. Despite the often reductive manner in which post-structuralism has been taken up in the art world, aspects of French thought during this period can be highly productive for the analysis of collaborative and participatory art practices. The work developed at La Borde clinic as part of the "institutional psychotherapy" movement beginning in the mid-1950s is particularly relevant. Jean Oury, along with figures such as Jacques Schotte and Félix Guattari, developed a set of innovative techniques designed to encourage the critical rearticulation of psychotherapeutic practice. These include the notion of a non-instrumental "empty speech" (the concept is taken from Lacan) in which dialogue is not directed toward the communication of a priori information, but rather, is treated as an end in itself, the principle of "evenly hovering attention" in relationship to the social ecology of a given site (which we might apply to Navjot Altaf's work in the village of Kopaweda), and "indirect action," in which specific problems are approached only tangentially, via a principle of adjacency. All of these strategies seek to open up pathways of knowledge that are efficacious but not instrumentalizing, through a more nuanced understanding of the "inter-subjective weave" existing within a given context (see "Institutional Psychotherapy and the La Borde Psychiatric Clinic," in Julian Bourg, *From Revolution to Ethics*, 125–37); Guattari, *Molecular Revolution*; and Oury and Roulot, *Dialogues à La Borde*.

98. Bourriaud, *Relational Aesthetics*, 95.

99. Ibid., 70.

100. Bishop, "The Social Turn," 180. In this essay, Bishop objects to what she terms the "ethical turn" in art criticism, in which artists are "judged by their working process—the degree to which they supply good or bad models for collaboration—and criticized for any hint of potential exploitation" (180). This criticism assumes that it is possible to distill out a purely "aesthetic" set of criteria for the analysis of art, uncontaminated by ethical considerations. As I've argued above, the model of avant-garde art practice to which Bishop subscribes carries with it an obvious ethical orientation (the privileging of one form of identity over another, the ethical normalization of desire and somatic experience, the artist's custodial relationship to the viewer, etc.). The situation is complicated by the fact that Bishop has yet to provide a substantive account of her own definition of the aesthetic, making it difficult to assess the specific nature of her criticism.

101. See also Rancière, "The Aesthetic Revolution and Its Outcomes," 133.

102. Rancière, "Aesthetics and Politics: Rethinking the Link," lecture given at the

University of California, Berkeley, 2006; transcript posted on 16 Beaver Group website, http://www.16beavergroup.org/.

103. Rancière, "The Aesthetic Revolution and Its Outcomes," 142.

104. As she writes in *Artforum*: "I believe in the continued value of disruption, with all its philosophical anti-humanism, as a form of resistance to instrumental rationality and as a source of transformation. The framework for my essay was Jacques Rancière's articulation of the relationship between politics and aesthetics. In his schema, a political work of art disrupts the relationship among the visible, the sayable and the thinkable without having to use the terms of a message as a vehicle. It transmits meanings in the form of a rupture, rather than simply giving us an 'awareness' of the state of the world. As he writes in *The Politics of Aesthetics*: 'Suitable political art would ensure, at one and the same time, the production of a double effect: the readability of a political significance and a sensible or perceptual shock cause, conversely, by the uncanny, by that which resists signification'" (Bishop, "Another Turn," 24).

105. Bishop, "The Social Turn," 181. This opposition is also evident in the work of Ernesto Laclau and Chantal Mouffe. As Mouffe writes: "To be capable of thinking politics today, and understanding the nature of these new struggles . . . it is indispensable to develop a theory of the subject as a de-centered, de-totalized agent, a subject constructed at the point of intersection of a multiplicity of subject positions between which there exists no a priori or necessary relation. . . . What emerges are entirely new perspectives for political action" (Mouffe, *The Return of the Political*, 12). Slavoj Žižek responds to this claim at length in a series of exchanges with Ernesto Laclau and Judith Butler, published in 2000 as *Contingency, Hegemony, Universality*. As Žižek writes: "I think one should at least *take note* of the fact that the much-praised postmodern 'proliferation of new political subjectivities,' the demise of every 'essentialist' fixation, the assertion of full contingency, occur against the background of a certain silent *renunciation* and *acceptance*: the renunciation of the idea of a global change in the fundamental relations in our society . . . and consequently, the acceptance of the liberal democratic capitalist framework which *remains the same*, the unquestioned background, in all the dynamic proliferation of the multitude of new subjectivities (Žižek, "Holding the Place," 321).

106. Bishop, "Antagonism and Relational Aesthetics," 79.

107. Ibid., 75. The tendency to use other human beings as a compositional device to assault or confound the viewer is evident in the work of a number of contemporary artists. Vanessa Beecroft, an artist who frequently employs young women in her performances, literally describes them as "material . . . a material subject to its own changes. . . . A material in an almost pure state" (Kontova and Gioni, "Vanessa Beecroft," 97).

108. Bishop, "Antagonism and Relational Aesthetics," 73.

109. Martinez, "Merchandise and Death," 43.

110. Ibid., 181.

111. Ibid., 189.

112. Descriptions are at the Guggenheim Collection Online website, http://www
.guggenheim.org/new-york/collections/collection-online. The text reads: "When
Faith Moves Mountains (2002), was completed for the third Bienal Iberoameri-
cana de Lima in a desolate landscape just outside the Peruvian capital. The
work is neither a traditional sculpture nor an Earthwork, and nothing was
added or built in the landscape. That the participants managed to move the
dune only a small distance mattered less than the potential for mythmaking in
their collective act; what was 'made' then was a powerful allegory, a metaphor
for human will, and an occasion for a story to be told and potentially passed on
endlessly in the oral tradition. For Alÿs, the transitory nature of such an action
is the stuff of contemporary myth." Here is Alÿs himself, writing in *Artforum*:
"When *Faith Moves Mountains* is a project of linear geological displacement. It
has been germinating ever since I first visited Lima, with Cuauhtémoc Medina,
the Mexican curator and critic. We were there for the last Lima Bienal, in October 2000, about a year before the Fujimori dictatorship finally collapsed. The
city was in turmoil. There were clashes on the street and the resistance movement strengthened. It was a desperate situation, and I felt that it called for an
epic response, a '*beau geste*' at once futile and heroic, absurd and urgent. Insinuating a social allegory into those circumstances seemed to me more fitting
than engaging in some sculptural exercise: (Alÿs, "A Thousand Words," 147).

Chapter Two: The Genius of the Place

Medina et al., *Francis Alÿs: When Faith Moves Mountains*, 90. My discussion of
Alÿs's work includes material first published in my essay "Lessons in Futility:
Francis Alÿs and the Legacy of May '68." See plate 2.

1. Ferguson, *Francis Alÿs: Politics of Rehearsal* (Los Angeles: Hammer Museum,
2007), 114.

2. Medina, Ferguson, and Fisher, *Francis Alÿs*, 118.

3. The museum installation, as noted above, provides little evidence of the complex process of solicitation, negotiation, and persuasion necessary to enlist a
group of several hundred students in the act of shoveling sand for a day. This
absence can be ascribed to two factors. First, the event, according to Alÿs, is
far too complex to be adequately represented in a museum context. "What was
experienced at the dune," as Alÿs notes, could never "be translated into documentation, since the intensity of the moment cannot be reproduced" (Medina
et al., *Francis Alÿs: When Faith Moves Mountains*, 70). Second, the installa-

tion itself is not obliged to act as a final or definitive account of the event, but rather, exists autonomously from it. Alÿs and his commentators attach a particular importance to the ways in which a given project or performance generates a kind of afterlife, in the form of stories, gossip, and rumors that follow in its wake. The meaning of a project is no more to be found in the original event than in the network of interpretations and references produced through its circulation as "myth," both locally and in the art world. There is no original meaning to be transmitted or reproduced with greater or lesser fidelity, but only subsequent iterations. To treat the installation as in some way bound to the specificity of the event (as documentation, record, or facsimile) would, by this account, entail a naive, "referential" view of its purpose.

Thus, we have the striking assertion that the very fact that Alÿs's work is discussed, gossiped about, or otherwise publicized (by critics, curators, etc.) constitutes a subversive effacement of his authorial power (he "withdraw[s] as the artistic subject of his work," according to the critic Jean Fisher), while also empowering the audience to participate in the construction, or "translation," of an ever-changing story. While I acknowledge the necessary independence of an installation from its catalyzing event, I believe that the questions raised by the *Faith* installation are somewhat more complex. Alÿs has no difficulty presenting material in the museum installation that is clearly intended to document his own experience as the creator and initiator of this project (e-mails with philosophical musings, exchanges with his collaborators, sketches, etc.). Moreover, Alÿs included transcribed statements from some student volunteers from the University of Lima in a book on the *Faith* project published in Madrid (the voices or opinions of the shantytown residents are nowhere in evidence). But his relationship to this material is decidedly ambivalent (these statements are absent from the museum installation of the work, the accompanying catalog, and the Phaidon monograph) (see Fisher, "In the Spirit of Conviviality," 115).

4. Medina, *Francis Alÿs: When Faith Moves Mountains*, 18. The performance is described as "a project by Francis Alÿs in collaboration with Cuauhtémoc Medina and Rafael Ortega."

5. Installation text at Hammer Museum (2007). The text continues: "[*When Faith Moves Mountains*] never intended to promote the idea of passivity, but to concentrate in the same space and time the logic of an economy that, despite having been supplied with all the features of modernity, resists (or never meets) the expectations of modernization and neo-liberalism. It wants to pervert the dogma of 'efficiency'. To evoke and poeticize such economy made us in a certain way accomplices of the evils of underdevelopment. Helio Oiticica's motto, 'Da adversidade vivemos' can be read either as a description of the role of culture in the socially divided context of Latin America, or as an open confession of the way the Latin American artist takes advantage of those circumstances

as raw matter to produce art. Future minds will have to decide if this attitude is more cynical than siding with the evils of development."

6. Alÿs describes *Rehearsal II* as "a metaphor of Mexico's ambiguous affair with Modernity, forever arousing, and yet, always delaying the moment 'it' will happen" (Ferguson, *Francis Alÿs: Politics of Rehearsal*, 88). The video of the *Rehearsal II* performance also includes the following quote: "That image, of a sort of history that is not being carried out, that is not being effective, is something that runs in a very direct relation to the experience of the Latin American modernists, who are always in a state of waiting, of let's see what day history is, in fact, going to visit us. Let's see what day development will actually roll through here. Let's see what day we'll actually get to experience being masters of time."

7. Ferguson, *Francis Alÿs: Politics of Rehearsal*, 79.

8. Installation text at Hammer Museum (2007). The *Lupita* performance, in which a woman repetitively pours water back and forth from one vessel to another, is "a reflection on the struggle against the pressures of being productive" (Ferguson, *Francis Alÿs: Politics of Rehearsal*, 54).

9. "It's what you did at the University of Mexico, for instance, to get people to participate in the 1986 student strike" (Medina et al., *Francis Alÿs: When Faith Moves Mountains*, 104).

10. According to the main essay in the book documenting *When Faith Moves Mountains*, collective action has been rendered irrelevant by the "new technology of appearances" of a "dismantled postmodern society." While no author is identified, it can probably be assumed that the essay represents Alÿs, Medina, and Ortega's collective wisdom regarding the project (Medina et al., *Francis Alÿs: When Faith Moves Mountains*, 120).

11. This claim of futility is all the more striking given the numerous examples of organized resistance to neoliberalism in Mexico and Central and South America over the past fifteen years, ranging from Sem Terra, the Brazilian landless worker's movement, to the Zapatista Army of National Liberation in Mexico, to Argentina's unemployed worker's movement, to PRATEC (the Andean Project of Peasant Technologies) in Peru. See, e.g., Santos, *Another Production is Possible*.

12. Fisher, "In the Spirit of Conviviality," 116. Alÿs relies on a similar contrast, asking how can art "remain politically significant without assuming a doctrinaire standpoint or aspiring to become social activism?" (Ferguson, *Francis Alÿs: Politics of Rehearsal*, 101).

13. Ferguson, *Francis Alÿs: Politics of Rehearsal*, 12.

14. Ibid., 39.

15. Ibid., 40.

16. Installation text at Hammer Museum (2007).

17. Ventanilla is one of several sites on the outskirts of Lima that have become cen-

ters for rural peasants displaced by military clashes between the Peruvian army and the Shining Path guerillas. It is also on the itinerary of several U.S.-based churches seeking to evangelize the poor of Latin America. See, e.g., the schedule for "Fishing for Jesus," a 2007 evangelical mission to Lima sponsored by Travel in Missions and available at their website, http://www.travelinmissions .com/: "This day we will visit the shanty town areas where we can make an outreach to the community (Ventanilla), the poorest people in the nation. This afternoon we will visit the Indian market of Peru. Highly recommended for souvenirs. On time have dinner and transfer to the international airport Jorge Chavez in Lima to take our flight back home."

18. Medina et al., *Francis Alÿs: When Faith Moves Mountains*, 24.

19. Ibid., 143.

20. Ibid.

21. Ibid.

22. Ibid., 96.

23. Ibid., 104.

24. Ibid., 72. There was clearly an esprit de corps among the students at the dune, but it appears to be closer to the conventional solidarity of soldiers or workers (refusing to abandon each other in the face of an enemy or a laborious and demanding task).

25. Alÿs, "A Thousand Words," 147.

26. Ferguson, *Francis Alÿs: Politics of Rehearsal*, 114.

27. As Fisher writes: "The space of freedom opened up by *When Faith Moves Mountains* provides the conditions of possibility for a new thought of the political, here understood . . . as 'conviviality,' or the founding moment of community" (Fisher, "In the Spirit of Conviviality," 112).

28. The Adivasi are a "scheduled tribe," a category recognized by the Indian Constitution for the purposes of antidiscrimination policies, civil rights protection, and preferential treatment in higher education admissions. Along with the "scheduled castes" they make up the population previously labeled "untouchables" (approximately 25 percent of India's total population). For a recent study of contemporary Adivasi life, see Munshi, *Adivasi Life Stories*.

29. Cited in Narendra, "Bastar in the Shadow of Globalization," in *Indigenous Survival in the Modern World*, an online publication of the Finnish group Global Platform (www.globalplatform.fi/). Organized opposition to these forces began in the mid-1970s, when the Bengal worker Shankar Guha Niyogi formed the Chhattisgarh Mines Shramik Sangh (CMSS). More recent activist and Adivasi rights groups active in Bastar include Adivasi Samata Manch.

30. This terminology effects a significant displacement: no longer the "first" or original inhabitants, but rather the uncivilized or primitive inhabitants (those who "dwell in the forests").

31. Dip Kapoor, "Normative Implications of Social Movement Theories for Adivasi (original dweller) Social Movements, Popular Education/Praxis and Social Change in India," paper presented at the 22nd Annual National Conference of the Canadian Association for the Study of Adult Education at Dalhousie University/University of King's College, Halifax, Nova Scotia, May 29–31, 2003 (available online at the University of Toronto, Ontario Institute for Studies in Education website, http://www.oise.utoronto.ca/oise/).

32. The Naxalites are an informal network of Maoist groups that emerged initially in Naxalbari in West Bengal during the late 1960s. Their actions are directed primarily at large landowners and the Indian state, and they engage in ongoing skirmishes with the Indian military in several states. Chhattisgarh is also the home of the Chhattisgarh Mukti Morcha (Chhattisgarh Liberation Front), which was formed in 1983 to protect tribal and peasant mine workers in the region. The CMM motto is "Virodh Nahi Vikalp" (Not Resistance, but Alternative). The CMM today works for social justice for Adivisi and peasant communities and has been especially active in challenging development projects that seek to isolate and disempower the rural poor. The CMM also participates in electoral politics and has seated members in the State Assembly.

33. Kapoor concludes: "The assimilation of Adivasi struggles into the anti-development/environmentalist agenda, the modern-reformist agenda or the socialist project neglects history, i.e., that Adivasi people have always fought against outside oppression on their own terms. Their history of resistance long precedes the advent of developmentalism, environmentalism or socialism. Whether or not the Kondhs go 'environmentalist' or become 'rights/justice oriented' and recognize the 'failed promise of development' by the state, is dependent on a process of popular education that seeks to widen the scope and purpose of such movements to include state-centered-developmentalist critique, resistance, articulation of new visions of the good life and/or make demands on the state to fulfill its commitments to the Adivasis. In these instances, a process of popular education would also seek to have Adivasis consider the possibility of joining in solidarity with other groups that profess such agendas, thereby essentially inviting them to participate in a wider process of resistance and redefinition of social structures and values. Ideally, this would be an Adivasi decision and not the result of some populist mobilization engineered to co-opt them into a struggle that is not of their design or choosing" (Dip Kapoor, "Normative Implications of Social Movement Theories for Adivasi (original dweller) Social Movements, Popular Education/Praxis and Social Change in India," 6).

34. Other members of the collaborative team in Kondagaon have included Anita Baghel, Lata Baghel, Shakila Baghel, Gangadevi, Punivati, Shabnam, and Shanti Nag. Altaf first came to Bastar in 1996 to study Adivasi memorial pillars and the

representation of the female body in Adviasi art. She met Shantibai, Gessuram, and Rajkumar while working at Shilpi Gram in Kondagaon, where she came to learn Adivasi craft techniques (bell metal work, casting, wood carving, etc.). Shilpi Gram was established by the Adivasi artist Jaidev Baighel during the 1980s to encourage collaborative interactions among Adivasi and non-Adivasi artists from India and beyond. Altaf and her colleagues eventually sought to develop their own projects independently of Jaidev, which led to the creation of Dialogue. The full name of the center is "DIALOGUE—Interactive Artists Association Practice" (DIAAP). Only Maria tribal members can own property in Kondagaon, so the land for Dialogue was purchased by Shantibai and Geesuram (who are both Maria) and turned into a trust. Navjot is also a member of Sahmat, a group formed in Delhi in 1989 by artists, activists, and journalists following the murder of a street theater activist. Sahmat (http://www.sahmat .org/) organizes political interventions through media and public actions that challenge Hindu fundamentalist and right-wing parties in India.

35. "They say that when it was a smaller pump and it was open, only one person could sit or fill up water or wash clothes, and only men could have a bath, because only men could do this sort of thing in the open. But with our structure the women feel quite protected and can bathe. Because it's cooling they like to spend more time there. The larger pump sites allow one person to wash their clothes and another person to get water for drinking in the same space. In the regular pumps you have to wait and use the pump site one person at a time" (interview with Navjot Altaf by author, April 2, 2007, Kondagaon District, Bastar, Chhattisgarh, India).

36. Bishop, "Antagonism and Relational Aesthetics," 79.

37. There are potential connections here to John Dewey's analysis of the relationship between ethics and aesthetics (see Hickman, *Pragmatism and Post-Postmodernism*).

38. "So for them, it was, 'OK, that person is dead and we can remember them,' but for us, it was, 'What was made on *that* pillar? What forms? Why that image of a woman in a car? Why this narrative?' All that they started seeing from a different perspective. This is a work of art, it's not just for ritualistic purposes, somebody has *made* it, with this purpose, with the history of this woman. We found out that that woman who had died was the head of a Panchayat [an assembly of village elders] and that she had once traveled in a car, so people wanted to remember her as a significant person in her village. We would discuss the representation, the way it was made as an artist would, and this affected them; this they found very interesting" (interview with Navjot Altaf by author, April 4, 2007, Kondagaon District, Bastar, Chhattisgarh, India).

39. Baghel is under continual pressure from buyers and collectors to enlarge or

otherwise modify his work within a relatively narrow formal framework. Collectors will often request that he reproduce an existing motif at a larger scale in order to fill a specific space, or that he combine elements from two or more existing pieces to create a more dramatic effect, regardless of the relationship of the new image to Adivasi symbolism. In an interview between Altaf and Baghel, Altaf comments: "My Adivasi colleague, Jaidev Baghel, . . . invited me to Bastar where he had a huge studio and a tradition of working in wood. . . . I met a number of artists there trained at Shilpi Gram, sponsored either by the government or by handicrafts boards. They were producing art *en masse*. It became clear during conversations with them that they got neither time nor opportunity to experiment. Perhaps they did want to experiment because they were inspired by the contemporary situation. But Jaidev showed me a piece of sculpture that he had done as an experimental piece when he was inspired to see contemporary art at the Bharat Bhavan. It got rejected when he sent it for selection. They said, 'It can't be Jaidev Baghel's!'" (interview available at VASL Artists' Collective website, http://www.vaslart.org/).

40. The ability to take time away from work and to have a separate space to make her own art was decisive ("The time in my studio is my *own* time," as she notes in an interview). The workshop, like the Nalpar site, encouraged a process of self-cultivation (interview with Shantibai by author, April 4, 2007, Kondagaon District, Bastar, Chhattisgarh, India).

41. Kapur, *When Was Modernism*; Subramanyan, *The Living Tradition*.

42. The translation occurred across Hindi, English, and Halbi (the Adivasi dialect spoken in Kondagaon). Key words or terms included "criticism" (*Alochana*), "dialogue" (*Samvadh*), "work" or "labor" (*Kaam*), "interaction" (*Lenden*), "exchange of thoughts or ideas" (*Akal Banta Banti*), and "working cooperatively or collaboratively" (*Kalasahyog* or *Baithiya*), among many others.

43. Irigaray, *To Speak Is Never Neutral*.

44. Interview with Navjot Altaf by author, April 4, 2007, Kondagaon District, Bastar, Chhattisgarh, India.

45. The group also included an administrative assistant (Mor Lissa Ba). In 2006, Kane Sy and his wife and collaborator Muhsana Ali formed a collective called Portes et Passages du Retour, along with several other artists, architects, and sociologists. They are currently developing a Holistic Art Center devoted to intercultural exchanges and residencies in the village of Mbodiene on the coast of Senegal.

46. Kane-Sy and Huit Facettes, "Beyond Post-ism," 25.

47. Patrick Deegan, unpublished interview with Amadou Kane-Sy, spring 2005; conducted as part of the *Groundworks* exhibition.

48. See, e.g., Dennis Galvan's research on democracy and identity in Senegal: Gal-

van, *The State Must Be Our Master of Fire*; Galvan and Sil, *Reconfiguring Institutions across Time and Space*; and Galvan, "Political Turnover and Social Change in Senegal."

49. Patrick Deegan, unpublished interview with Amadou Kane-Sy, Spring 2005.

50. Enwezor, "The Production of Social Space as Artwork," 244.

51. Ibid., 245.

52. In his essay "Reflections on Art, Contemporaneity, and Urban Existence in Dakar," Kane-Sy writes: "It's in Dakar that the major decisions involving the country are taken. It's also in Dakar that the private or state corporations and companies make the urban framework the overall domain of the expression, blossoming and popularization of the arts. . . . It is also in the urban zone that almost all the places of popularization, expression and commercialization of artistic and cultural creations are concentrated. For that reason it is habitual to think that art may, and must, rhyme with urban existence alone. Well, this isn't the case, since many artistic and cultural projects in the contemporary arts have witnessed the context of their realization shift increasingly towards semi-urban areas, or even rural ones" (37).

53. Collins and Goto's innovative *3 Rivers 2nd Nature* project explores the complex cultural and environmental interrelationship between rural and urban space in the Monongahela River Valley around Pittsburgh, Pennsylvania. See: http://3r2n.collinsandgoto.com/. Ian Hunter and Celia Larner of Littoral have developed a range of innovative projects at the intersection of art, agriculture, and rural life over the past twenty years; see the Littoral website, http://www.littoral.org.uk/.

54. Moens, "The Hamdallaye Studios." Moens works as an animator at Atelier Graphoui (a group of Belgian animators who worked with Huit Facettes in Hamdallaye).

55. See Starr, *Logics of Failed Revolt*, 134, 144, 141. See also Bataille, *The Accursed Share*. According to Bataille, poetry evokes "the order to come," while for Bernard Sichére, of the *Tel Quel* group, revolutionary practices address a proletariat "that does not yet exist, but remains to be constituted" (quoted in Starr, *Logics of Failed Revolt*, 158–59).

56. Rancière, "The Aesthetic Revolution and Its Outcomes," 150–51.

57. Rancière, "The Emancipated Spectator," 278.

58. Ibid., 280.

59. Barthes, *S/Z*, 4.

60. Rancière, "The Emancipated Spectator," 279. Rancière proposes a similar dynamic in *The Ignorant Schoolmaster*, where he contrasts traditional educational methods (in which the instructor seeks to replicate a pre-existing knowledge in the mind of the passive student), with "emancipation," in which students create their own knowledge in response to their own needs. Drawing on the work of

the nineteenth-century educational theorist Joseph Jacotot, Rancière evokes a form of emancipatory teaching that awakens self-esteem among those "stagnating in the swamp of self-contempt." If Rancière is eager to do away with the hierarchical distinction between teacher and student he is less prepared to sacrifice a spatialized concept of authority. Whether in the form of catalyst or content, agency must always be located somewhere else. Thus, the teacher is displaced by the book. The book allows each student the freedom to produce his or her own autonomous meaning via a process of creative "translation." Rather than conveying a pre-existing and fixed meaning, like the teacher, the meaning of the book is intrinsically fluid and available. Oral instruction, via the embodied teacher is only ever authoritarian and logocentric. The text, on the other hand, is more dialogical and reciprocal than another human being. *The Ignorant Schoolmaster: Five Lessons in Intellectual Emancipation*, translated by Kristin Ross (Stanford: Stanford University Press, 1991), 6–7.

61. As David Wellbery notes in his study of early modern aesthetics, "The style of the poem must not reveal any intentional working or cultivation, but rather must appear as an improvisation, a natural outgrowth of the subject matter" (Wellbery, *Lessing's "Laocoön*," 82). As Wellbery argues, the process of secularization had the effect of gradually taking language out of the realm of ritual. Language becomes more functional (allowing for the assembly and exchange of complex ideas, new forms of linguistic and written communication, etc.). But, as a result, language also begins to lose its intuitive immediacy—its capacity to transmit divine meaning through a process that transcends the constraints of linguistic signification or deliberative exchange. The aesthetic seeks to recover the naturalness and immediacy of metaphysical experience and to provide a form of knowledge that is given to the viewer all at once, without the labor of interpretation or translation.

62. Nancy, *The Inoperative Community*, 35.

63. See, e.g., Derrida, "Structure, Sign, and Play in the Discourse of the Human Sciences." Here is Derrida on the "free play" of the signifier: "There are thus two interpretations of interpretation, of structure, of sign, of free play. The one seeks to decipher, dreams of deciphering, a truth or an origin that is free from free play and from the order of the sign, and lives like an exile from the necessity of interpretation. The other, which is no longer turned toward the origin, affirms free play and tries to pass beyond man and humanism, the name man being the name of that being who, throughout the history of metaphysics or of onto-theology—in other words, through the history of all of his history—has dreamed of full presence, the reassuring foundation, the origin and the end of the game" (294). This level of analysis has been stunted in the early traditions of art history and theory as well. In attempting to build a new theoretical framework for the history of art in the late nineteenth and early twentieth centuries,

both Alois Riegl and Heinrich Wölfflin choose to limit their research to visual and optical experience. Significantly, they associate the haptic and the tactile with backwards "oriental" cultures, still reliant on the reassurance of physical touch and direct contact with the world, as opposed to (implicitly) advanced Europeans, who've learned to master their world through optical distancing and abstraction.

64. As the economic historian Robert Heilbroner famously observed: "As late as the fourteenth or fifteenth century there was no such thing as land in the sense of freely salable, rent-producing property. . . . A medieval nobleman in good standing would no more have thought of selling his land than the governor of Connecticut would think of selling a few counties to the governor of Rhode Island" (Heilbroner, *The Worldly Philosophers*, 28). This section includes material first published in the catalog I edited for *Groundworks: Environmental Collaboration in Contemporary Art*.

65. Polanyi, *The Great Transformation*.

66. Grotius, *De jure belli ac pacis libri tres*, 186.

67. Grotius cited in Olivecrona, "Locke's Theory of Appropriation," 330.

68. Olivecrona, "Locke's Theory of Appropriation," 330–31.

69. In *On the Law of Nature and of Nations* (1672), Pufendorf notes that "ownership" doesn't function by "physically and intrinsically affect[ing] things themselves." Rather, it produces what he describes as a "moral effect in relation to other men" (see *The Political Writings of Samuel Pufendorf*, 175). John Locke also establishes his defense of property through recourse to the "extension of personality" model. He describes a process by which the labor of the subject's body (supervised by the mind) "mixes" the subject's personality with nature (via extraction or cultivation). Through this mixing, one infuses objects with one's personality and is thereby entitled to remove them from the commons and claim them as one's sole property (see Locke, *Two Treatises of Government*, 134).

70. As C. B. Macpherson notes, property should be understood not as a "thing" to be possessed, but as a "right" to be exercised or performed (MacPherson, "The Meaning of Property," 3).

71. This is clear in Locke's discussion of property, in which his will is co-extensive with the labor or property of his horse or servant—all are simply vehicles for his own achievement of subject status: "Thus the Grass my horse has bit; the Turfs my Servant has cut; and the Ore I have digg'd in any place where I have a right to them in common with others, become my Property, without the assignation or consent of any body. The labor that was mine, removing them out of that common state they were in, hath fixed my Property in them (Locke, "Of Property," 18).

72. While Locke is a staunch advocate of the idea that "every man has a property in

his own person," this principle comes into conflict with the "extension of personality," which allows one person to possess the labor of another as his or her property. In a society in which the bulk of the common land has already been engrossed, one segment of the population will, inevitably, be forced to sell their labor to the other. Thus, the juridically free worker is granted property-right in his own labor in a situation in which his only possible option is to then surrender that "property" in exchange for wages. That is, the act of granting the worker property in his own labor is only allowed in order for it to then be made available to others.

73. Resistance to early notions of bourgeois individualism and privatism took many forms. The most pertinent, in the case of England, include groups such as the Diggers, the Levellers, and the Ranters, whose commitment to communal notions of property in the mid-1600s was attacked as blasphemy. The classic study of this period is Hill, *The World Turned Upside Down*.

74. See Kester, "The Faculty of Possession."

75. While bourgeois ideology attempts to cover over this contingency, to "retranscendentalize," it remains central to the history of liberal thought. The cyclical process by which this contingency is denied, then revealed, then concealed again, extends back at least as far as the 1848 revolution in France. After a century and a half during which the ostensible universality of bourgeois identity has been repeatedly challenged, exposed, and questioned, it seems clear that the revelatory gesture itself has become an integral part of the apparatus of bourgeois power. This doesn't mean that it's futile to challenge any form of power that claims transcendent status, only that the process of challenging that power is considerably more complex than the simple act of "exposing" its contingent nature.

76. Wilberforce, *A Practical View of the Prevailing Religious System of Professed Christians in the Higher and Middle Classes in This Country Contrasted with Real Christianity*, 150.

77. The laws of creative labor can only be discovered after the fact of creation. For a useful comparative analysis of "creative" and "reiterative" labor in a Marxist context, see Sánchez Vásquez, *The Philosophy of Praxis*.

78. In his essay "That Obscure Object of Desire: The Art of Art History," Donald Preziosi remarks on the relatively undeveloped nature of reception theory in the discipline of art history. As he writes: "The viewer has been seen largely as a passive reader or consumer of images: the end of the line, so to speak, the targeted audience or inadvertent interceptor of a transmission. . . . This logocentric paradigm is given a characteristic slant or trajectory so as to privilege the maker or artist as an essentially active, originary force, in complementary contrast to the essentially passive consumer or reader of works. It involves no great leap of the imagination to see that the paradigm simultaneously serves

as a validating apparatus to privilege the role or function of the historian or critic as a legitimate and unvested diviner of intentionality on behalf of lay beholders" (24–25).

79. Hans Joas has written on the importance of "role taking" in intersubjective exchange, as participants "anticipate the way partners in action would potentially behave in response and create an inner representation of that response." Drawing on the work of George Herbert Mead, he describes the "anticipation of the situation-specific behavior of a partner in action": "If an actor can objectify his own behavior in the same manner as his partner, then what develops is an evaluative scale for spontaneous instinctive impulses, as these come to be seen in connection with anticipated reactions to the expression of these impulses. . . . The task for the actor is to create by himself a synthesis of the representations of the expectations, which may very well diverge from one another. The 'self' that thereby emerges is then a point of reference for unitary self-appraisal and for action orientation" (Joas, *The Creativity of Action*, 187–88). See also Maurice Merleau-Ponty's work on bodily schema in *Phenomenology of Perception*.

80. Joas, *The Creativity of Action*, 169–70.

81. "This notion of squandered energies refers in the first place to the way in which southern countries' economies are the constant expression of failed modernization. It is no accident that they seem to be under the curse of an eternal return: to start a process of development over again every five or ten years and leave it incomplete after coming across new obstacles" (Medina, "Maximum Effort, Minimum Result," 178).

82. The International Bank for Reconstruction and Development (now part of the World Bank Group) and the International Monetary Fund (IMF) were both established in 1944.

83. As the Swiss development scholar Gilbert Rist has observed: "*From 1949 onwards, often without realizing it, more than two billion inhabitants of the planet found themselves changing their name, being 'officially' regarded as they appeared in the eyes of others, called upon to deepen their Westernization, by repudiating their own values.* No longer African, Latin American, or Asian . . . they were now simply 'underdeveloped'" (Rist, *The History of Development*, 79; italics in original).

84. Rist, *The History of Development*, 109–14.

85. Neoliberal economic theory, which originated in the work of Chicago School economists under the influence of Friedrich von Hayek, provided an effective ideological template for expanding capital in the post–Second World War period. It was mobilized in conjunction with certain strategic shifts in the projection of corporate power: the increasing centralization of control by transnational financial and managerial elites; the spatial segregation of production,

which works to disempower and disaggregate labor; and the ongoing erosion of the state's capacity to impose any significant regulatory limits on corporate interests. These processes have been germinating for decades—with offshore sourcing, beginning in the late 1950s, and the contraction of the state's regulatory and ameliorative role in the United States, beginning with the backlash against community action programs in the late 1960s and continuing through Richard Nixon's New Federalism initiatives in the early 1970s and on to Clinton's "welfare reforms" in the 1990s.

86. Due in part to the negative publicity that the Structural Adjustment Program received, it was renamed the Poverty Reduction Strategy Initiative in 2000. The fundamental structure of the program remained unchanged, however.

87. Interview with Margaret Thatcher by Douglas Keay, *Women's Own*, October 31, 1987, 8–10.

88. Rist, *The History of Development*, 173. For Rist, the only possible motivation for humanitarian relief programs is to deflect criticisms of World Bank economic policies ("making people believe" that structural adjustment is harmless). But one can certainly acknowledge some degree of ideological calculation at the World Bank without dismissing the entire system of humanitarian assistance as a cynical ploy.

89. Agamben, *Homo Sacer*, 133; Hardt and Negri, *Empire*, 36.

90. Guattari and Negri, *Communists like Us*, 139.

91. This view complements Peter Starr's analysis of the "logics of failed revolt" in May 1968. As Starr observes: "The logics of failed revolt meticulously occult the incremental advance, that specifically historical remainder that makes a difference. That is to say, they are grounded in an essentialist tautology whereby failure is presumed to equal failure (and nothing else), whereby the social system that returns on the far side of a revolutionary episode is deemed the same as that against which revolution was brought" (Starr, *Logics of Failed Revolt*, 21).

92. Hardt and Negri, *Empire*, 43.

93. This either implies too much (effectively ignoring the ongoing economic and political domination of a handful of countries and central banks and the increasing consolidation of major corporations, not to mention the unilateral military policies of post–9/11 America) or too little (who would deny that there is a complex reciprocity among key state players, banks, and corporate boards at the global level?). For a contrasting perspective, consider the comments of Vladislav Sukov, former deputy chief of staff of the president of the Russian Federation in 2006: "For all globalization's benefits, all the talk of friendship, the Americans count their dividends at home, the British count theirs—and we count ours. The majority count their losses. So when they tell us that sovereignty is outdated, as is the nation-state, we should ask ourselves what they are up to" (quoted in Specter, "Kremlin, Inc.," 59). It should be noted that Hardt

and Negri would subsequently embrace the decidedly centralizing (and conventionally liberal) concept of an international "Magna Carta," in which "global aristocracies" (multinational corporations and nation-states) would compel the global "monarch" (presumably the United States) to act more responsibly (Hardt and Negri, "Why We Need a Multilateral Magna Carta" (2004), available at the InterActivist Network website, http://info.interactivist.net/).

94. Hardt and Negri's analysis of political change owes a great deal to the influence of Gilles Deleuze. As this material has been taken up in contemporary art theory, the result, as with the Marcus Steinweg passage cited above, can border on self-parody. Akseli Virtanen and Jussi Vähämäki, writing in *Framework: The Finnish Art Review*, describe a Deleuzean utopia in which "people are set in motion, flow and spread without the limitations of direction, origin and meaning. Only such setting in motion, flowing and spreading unleashes movement and desire. Or, thinking can advance, move and touch only when it takes meaning to the point of collapse, far beyond society and its requirements" (31). Any possible external predication of the singular individual is forbidden. All that is left, then, is a kind of social physics of "attraction" and "rejection" in which "good relations" are those "that add power, extend and combine," and "bad relations" are those that "take apart, isolate and suffocate. . . . When we come across something that is right for us, we link to it, combine with it and devour it" (33).

95. Deleuze, "On Human Rights."

96. See Eribon, *Michel Foucault*, 258–62.

97. Foucault quoted in Keenan, "The 'Paradox' of Knowledge and Power," 20–21. Foucault's statement concludes: "We must reject the division of tasks that is all too often offered: individuals can get indignant and speak out, while it is governments that reflect and act. It is true that good governments like the hallowed indignation of the governed, provided it remains lyrical. I believe that we must realize how often, though, it is the rulers who speak, who can only and want only to speak. Experience shows that we can and must reject the theatrical role of pure and simple indignation that we are offered. Amnesty International, Terre des Hommes, [and] Médecins du Monde are initiatives which have created a new right: the right of private individuals actually to intervene in the order of politics and international strategies. The will of individuals must inscribe itself in a reality over which governments have wanted to reserve a monopoly for themselves—a monopoly that we must uproot little by little every day."

98. Some oppositional movements have engaged in armed conflict with state authorities (the Maoist Naxalites in central India, the Tamil Tigers in Sri Lanka, until their defeat in 2009), but they are primarily concerned with achieving political or territorial autonomy, not in leading a global communist revolu-

tion. And in some cases their commitment to social justice for minority and indigenous communities is linked with a pattern of human rights abuses (the killing of civilians or the use of child soldiers and suicide bombers by the Tamil Tigers, e.g.). The Zapatista Army of National Liberation, or EZLN, in Mexico is a notable exception. While they ceased formal armed resistance in 1994, they continue to suffer from ongoing military harassment in Chiapas.

99. It should also be noted that Chavez has instituted significant restrictions on the freedom of the press in Venezuela and ignored criticisms of human rights abuses within his government. In 2008, he expelled members of Human Rights Watch who released a report detailing his growing, punitive, control over the media and the judiciary in Venezuela (see Human Rights Watch, *A Decade under Chavez*; see also Vivanco and Wilkinson, "Hugo Chávez versus Human Rights," 68).

100. There have been a series of important gatherings over the past decade bringing together representatives from activist groups, NGOs, and other formal and informal organizations working against neoliberalism. Among the most well organized were the "Encuentros for Humanity and against Neoliberalism" during the 1990s (held in Chiapas in 1996, Barcelona in 1997, and Belem in 1999) and the (ongoing) annual World Social Forum.

101. See Lavaca Collective, *Sin Patrón*; and Santos, *Another Production Is Possible*. Santos's work is of particular importance. His "Reinventing Social Emancipation" project has involved the collaborative efforts of dozens of scholars, researchers, and activists in developing case studies of alternatives to neoliberalism in the global south (focusing specifically on Brazil, Colombia, India, Mozambique, and South Africa). The first three volumes of a projected five-volume series have already been published. These include the aforementioned *Another Production Is Possible*, as well as *Democratizing Democracy: Beyond the Liberal Democratic Canon* (2005), and *Another Knowledge Is Possible: Beyond Northern Epistemologies* (2007).

102. Hardt and Negri, *Empire*, 36. See also Bamford, *The Shadow Factory*.

103. Of course, even those movements that are often presented as exemplary models of organized resistance to neoliberalism are not free of contradiction. See, e.g., the extensive critical analysis of the Landless Peasant Worker's Movement in Brazil (Movimento dos Trabalhadores Rurais Sem-Terra, or MST), in Santos, *Another Production Is Possible*, 146–240.

104. For a critical, but balanced, assessment of the politics of non-governmental organizations, see Incite! Women of Color against Violence, *The Revolution Will Not Be Funded*.

105. Venues have included Redcat Gallery at the Disney/Cal Arts Theater in Los Angeles, the Venice Biennale, the Herning Kunstmuseum, and the Arken Museum of Modern Art in Denmark.

106. "Their African clothing, e.g., was based on the idea of combining the look of an engineer, a practical social worker, and the kind of uniforms preferred by imperialist armies" (Steiner, "Radical Democracy," 52).

107. Larsen, "Superflex."

108. Nacking, "An Exchange between Åsa Nacking and Superflex."

109. Steiner, "Radical Democracy."

110. The English author Richard North offers the following "propositions" on ethical capitalism, from a talk at London's Institute of Contemporary Art in 2002:

> 1. Good is done by firms involved in cigarettes, animal research facilities, oil, chemicals, landfills, drink, pornography, 'sweatshops,' and flowers grown in the tropics. Much less good is done by organics, windmills, 'fair' trade suppliers, 'development' NGOs.
>
> 2. It is a matter of debate what production systems and goods and services produce good, so it pays us to remember that describing CSR [Corporate Social Responsibility] or ethical business is contested territory. Firms going for 'corporate social responsibility' can much more easily achieve political correctness than real good.
>
> 3. NGOs do not have a monopoly on understanding virtue. NGOs are romantic, idealist and propagandist. The public, media and corporations have been unwise to sub-contract so much ethical thinking to them.
>
> 4. Firms, instead of claiming to be 'ethical,' should say they are catering to a particular fashion, taste or market sector. The owners, managers and staff may share that taste, but they should remember that there will be others who, perhaps rightly, think them fools.
>
> 5. Ethics is like politics. I believe in the market as a force for good in rather the way a Conservative might think that self-reliance is good for the poor; I believe 'leftist' reform often does damage. Similar cases can be made for capitalism 'red in tooth and claw' vs. 'Third Way' capitalism incorporating an NGO agenda. (see the archive for North's website, at http://richarddnorth.com/archive). North, whose most recent book is *Let's Scrap the BBC: Ten Years to Set Broadcasters Free*, is affiliated with the Social Affairs Unit, a London-based conservative think tank (see North's bio at his website, http://richarddnorth.com/rdn-bio).

111. Here is Superflex, from an interview with Åsa Nacking: "Yes, the [Biogas] project may be seen as a utopia for a specific group of users, namely the African family. We do not wish to impose a prevailing ideology on people—the families are perfectly free to choose. Nor is the Biogas project a gift. We might compare it to a western family buying a car, they will usually only do so if they need one and if their finances allow. We are interested in the opportunity that the Biogas system presents for the individual families. They now have more

time to do something else but gather firewood. Inherent in it is an opportunity for productivity, even if we have no definite proof that this will follow" (Nacking, "An Exchange between Åsa Nacking and Superflex," 28).

112. Unpublished interview with Rasmus Nielsen of Superflex by Sarah Lookofsky, August 2004, translated from Danish by Sarah Lookofsky. *Realizing the Potential of Africa's Youth,* a 2009 report from Denmark's Commission on Africa, in which Danida played a leading role, advocates a developmental process capable of "unleashing African entrepreneurship" and encouraging "microfinancing," in language almost identical to that employed by Superflex. As the report notes: "The Africa Commission proposes private sector–led growth as the most effective way to create more and better jobs. . . . Focus must be on increasing competitiveness of private enterprises, including agro-business. This will require strong partnerships between the public and the private sector to eliminate barriers to growth. Growth driven by private investments also leads to higher revenues for governments to finance vital social services and infrastructure. It will contribute to reducing aid dependency of developing countries" (Africa Commission, *Realizing the Potential of Africa's Youth,* 6).

113. The cartoons are reproduced at the Superflex website, http://www.superflex .net/tools/supergas/comic.shtml/.

114. See Chege, "The Return of Multiparty Politics," 47–74.

115. Nacking, "An Exchange between Åsa Nacking and Superflex," 29.

116. See Laxmi Murthy, "Banking on Poor Women: Grameen Bank," *Infochange India News,* http://www.infochangeindia.org. See also Feiner and Barker, "Microcredit and Women's Poverty," 7–8.

117. "Micro-Credit Improves Cash Flow but Doesn't Create Wealth" (interview with Dr. Sudhirendar Sharma), *Infochange India News,* http://www.infochange india.org. A recent essay by Jaya Sharma of Nirantar, a Delhi-based women's resource center, describes some of the drawbacks of the micro-credit system. It's worth quoting at length: "Banks enjoy higher rates of return than they could ever dream of getting from individual men or corporations due to extremely low transaction costs, since poor women undertake the role of pressurizing each other to repay. Corporations gain easy access to vast rural markets with micro-credit-based women's collectives serving both as consumers and sellers of their products. Donors find a route to ensuring self-sustainability of NGOs they support since a share of the often higher-than-market rate of interest being charged to the women goes to the NGOs managing micro-credit interventions. Several studies draw attention to the rise in women's indebtedness as a result of back-to-back lending, higher incidence of violence in the event of women being unable to bring into the family the credit that is expected of them, and the tremendous pressure on women to repay which can compel them to migrate. There have even been reported instances of default-

ing women being imprisoned. The most popular model of micro credit in India is that of self-help groups (SHGS). A qualitative study of SHG interventions in Andhra Pradesh and Gujarat undertaken by Nirantar . . . offers insights into the micro-credit phenomenon through voices of women who are part of SHGS. A district-level official linked to a national level SHG program sponsored by the ministry of rural development explained why the program focused on women: 'Women cannot go anywhere, they can be located easily; they cannot run away leaving their homes; they can be easily persuaded to repay as they feel shame more quickly and consider non-repayment as a betrayal of family honor'" (Jaya Sharma, "Grameen Myth," *The Times of India* [Bombay], November 6, 2006, 18). Sharma also points to the political implication of the shift from subsidy as a right (evident in the reduction or elimination of agricultural subsidies) and its replacement by the financial burden of credit.

118. An instructive comparison could be made here with Simon Grennan and Christopher Sperandio's "worker-designed" candy bar in *We Got It!*, which was part of Mary Jane Jacobs's *Culture in Action* exhibition in Chicago in 1993.

119. Junior Achievement is a school-based program designed to "inspire" young people to "dream big" by learning the basic tenets of "work readiness, entrepreneurship and financial literacy" (see the Junior Achievement website at http://www.ja.org/).

120. O'Connor, *The Fiscal Crisis of the State*; Offe, *Contradictions of the Welfare State*; Piven and Cloward, *Regulating the Poor*.

121. See Scharpf and Schmidt, *Welfare and Work in the Open Economy*.

122. Kuzma and Osborne, "Art of Welfare," 124.

123. Kwon, *One Place after Another*, 46.

124. Huit Facettes-Interaction, "Glocal Challenge," 101.

125. See Chambers, "Participatory Rural Appraisal (PRA)," 1266.

126. See, e.g., Cooke and Kothari, *Participation: The New Tyranny?*; Hickey and Mohan, *Participation: From Tyranny to Transformation?*; Williams, "Evaluating Participatory Development"; Gellar, "The Ratched-McMurphy Model Revisited"; and Green, "Participatory Development and the Appropriation of Agency in Southern Tanzania."

127. All quotes from Joas, *The Creativity of Action*, 160. In Joas's description, site or situation can catalyze a movement between modes of intentionality and receptivity. In conventional artistic expression (and specifically in textual modes of production), cognition precedes and orients action (an idea or image is visualized and then brought into existence) and the relationship to site is primarily teleological and possessive (site is a resource from which an object or image will be extracted). In the work of Dialogue, Ala Plastica, and others, cognition occurs in and through action, not prior to it. Practice itself enables a process of reflection that further modifies the direction and nature of subsequent action.

128. Interview with Silvina Babich and Alejandro Meitin of Ala Plastica by author, November 8, 2007, San Diego, California; translation by Annie Mendoza.

129. The passage below, from an essay by Marc Legér, is typical. Legér seeks to expose "the obscene underside of so-called dialogical collaboration," contrasting a reviled (but undefined) "community art" practice with the "critical," "agitational" work of Vitaly Komar and Alexander Melamid. As Legér writes: "In two of its most recent manifestations, Nicolas Bourriaud's 'relational aesthetics' and Grant Kester's 'dialogical aesthetics,' political claims and social protest are to be renounced in favor of dialogical interaction (a word entirely denuded of its basis in the class analysis of the Russian formalists) where the artist is expected to renounce all claims to authority and authorship" (Legér, "For the De-Incapacitation of Community Art Practice," 293).

130. Christens and Speer, "Tyranny/Transformation," par. 20.

131. Ala Plastica's name carries two meanings, either "plastic wing" (they began working in conjunction with a theater group, so they initially identified themselves as the "plastic," or sculptural, "wing" of a larger collective) or "in the manner of" plasticity or art (e-mail exchange with Ala Plastica, November 25, 2008).

132. In its effort to facilitate the extraction of raw materials from the Rio de la Plata, the Integration of Regional Infrastructure in South America (IIRSA) is working in a tradition that extends back five centuries. The river's name ("River of Silver") is based on its role as a transportation route for Peruvian silver being moved to the coast by the Spanish for shipment home.

133. The IIRSA was established in 1970 in Caracas, Venezuela. It has country offices in Buenos Aires, La Paz, Brasilia, Bogota, Quito, Madrid, and Lima. Its shareholders include Argentina, Brazil, Bolivia, Chile, Colombia, Costa Rica, Dominican Republic, Ecuador, Jamaica, México, Panama, Paraguay, Peru, Spain, Trinidad and Tobago, Uruguay, Venezuela, and fifteen private banks in the region. The IIRSA website is http://www.iirsa.org/.

134. This work was initially developed in collaboration with Ian Hunter and Celia Larner of Projects Environment (which later became Littoral). For parallel examples, see Mel Chin's *Revival Field* (1990–present) and Helen and Newton Harrison's *Breathing Space for the Sava River* (1988–89).

135. Interview with Silvina Babich and Alejandro Meitin of Ala Plastica, by author, November 8, 2007, San Diego, California; translation by Annie Mendoza.

136. The project grew out of dialogues with the Austrian-based group Abseits vom Netz, founded by Erwin Posarnig. The term "AA" referred to the Argentina/Austria connection (e-mail from Ala Plastica, December 9, 2008).

137. See Scott, *Seeing Like a State*, 311.

138. The quote is taken from Ala Plastica's unpublished description of the *Camino de la Sal* project. This work shares certain common features with Pablo Sanaguano's work with Kichwa-speaking indigenous communities in Ecuador.

139. Scott, *Seeing Like a State*, 311–16. Michel de Certeau invokes métis as a corollary to "tactics" in *The Practice of Everyday Life*: "Many everyday practices are tactical in character . . . clever tricks, knowing how to get away with things, 'hunters cunning,' maneuvers, polymorphic simulations, joyful discoveries, poetic as well as warlike. The Greeks called these 'ways of operating' métis. But they go much further back. . . . They also show the extent to which intelligence is inseparable from the everyday struggles and pleasures that it articulates" (xix–xx).

140. Here, Ala Plastica cites the influence of John Holloway, a sociology professor at the University of Puebla in Mexico and the author of *Change the World without Taking Power: The Meaning of Revolution Today*: "We get close to local agents with whom we speak regarding the aspects that are related to the historical reality, climate or topographical changes, water power, production, etc. of the areas they reside in. From there, diverse conversations and approaches regarding the utopia of the residents and the potential of the distinct areas happen over a specified period of time. From there, what begins to emerge is something that we call a local calling (*vocación del lugar*). We then usually begin to develop some workshops that awaken an interest because they value the local resources that reconnect people to their own sense of agency (*su poder hacer* or power to do)." From the author's interview with Silvina Babich and Alejandro Meitin of Ala Plastica, November 8, 2007, San Diego, California (translation by Annie Mendoza); unless otherwise noted, all other Ala Plastica quotes are from this interview.

141. Kwon, *One Place after Another*.

142. Jennifer Flores Sternad, "Interview with Ala Plastica in La Plata, Argentina" (July 1, 2007), available on the LatinArt.com website, http://www.latinart.com/.

143. Interview with Jay Koh and Chu Chu Yuan by the author, conducted between December 2008 and January 2009.

144. E.g.: "To educate and organize the Myanmar women to uphold the tradition, culture, and to safeguard one's own lineage and religion with a view to combat the infiltration and influences of foreign culture which could lead to social problems" ("Reply from the Union of Myanmar to the Questionnaire on Implementation of the Beijing Platform for Action," undated, but released following the Fourth World Conference on Women held in Beijing in 1995; available online at www.un.org/womenwatch/daw/followup/responses/Myanmar.pdf).

145. Provided by Jay Koh.

146. The Alliance Française, British Council, and American Center were also told to close their cultural centers, but instead incorporated them into their embassies, thus providing them with diplomatic protection. As Chu Yuan notes: "The

only social space in Burma where you could get people from various ethnicities to interact would be in the arts, among writers, musicians, and visual artists. So we tried to emphasize cross-group and interethnic exchanges in our events and in our training programs and discussions. We would foreground ideas of interculturalism, plurality, diversity, and equality, but only using examples from outside. We'd never make direct reference to the situation in Burma. It's very unusual for anyone from the majority ethnic group, the Burmans, to admit that there is inequality among the various ethnic nationalities in Burma. Even the Burman artists would insist that there is no problem and that all people in Burma are equal. But we also worked with Kachin, Shan, Indian, and Chin young people, as well as with a Kachin Baptist organization, and they would sometimes say things about their lives that would acknowledge this problem indirectly, even if they wouldn't discuss it openly" (interview with Jay Koh and Chu Chu Yuan by the author, conducted between December 2008 and January 2009; unless otherwise noted, all subsequent quotes from Koh and Chu Yuan are from this interview).

147. Koh and Chu Yuan were told that there was no precedent for their request and that the scope of their activities was so broad that it would require approval from several different ministries. Moreover, the approval process could not be concurrent but would require working through each separate ministerial bureaucracy in turn (interview with Jay Koh and Chu Chu Yuan by the author, conducted between December 2008 and January 2009).

148. NICA has received support from Arts Network Asia, Singapore International Foundation, Singapore Lee Foundation, Asian Arts Council New York, Heinrich Boel Foundation Asia Center, Japan Foundation, and the Prince Claus Fund in the Netherlands.

149. Following the putsch of Prime Minister Khin Nyunt in 2004, the Myanmar government began cracking down on all international NGOs operating in the country. The regime required the International Committee of the Red Cross to use the regime's own approved translators when interviewing detainees (making it impossible to conduct open interviews) and otherwise attempted to frustrate their assistance work (restricting their movement through the country, etc.). The ongoing harassment led to a voluntary closure of the ICRC field offices.

150. Koh has written about his experience with varying modes of verbal and nonverbal communication. As he describes it: "Working across communities, for me, involves the ability to switch between mindsets in order to gain a deep understanding of local contexts and histories that uphold local cultural practices, especially in identifying embedded divisions. . . . While ways of speaking in the West are mostly low-context and direct and can be confrontational, dia-

logue in the East and South tends to be more circular and reserved, and meanings conveyed can be highly dependent on context" (Koh, "Mediating Across Divides and In Between Layers," unpublished lecture, 2007).

151. As Koh elaborates: "We are different than NGOs in that we work only for concepts or visions we believe in and do not need to report to or be accountable to managerial structures that aren't organic and central to that vision. We don't follow rules that have been set up locally to control and feed on foreign groups. We don't rent spaces in our names, to avoid the higher rates charged to foreigners or go[ing] through banking rules established by the state, which can use up what little funding we have. We don't need to engage in publicity like the NGOs in order to sustain ourselves and 'sell' our work to an international donor audience" (interview with Jay Koh and Chu Chu Yuan by the author, conducted between December 2008 and January 2009).

152. Interview with Jay Koh and Chu Chu Yuan by the author, conducted between December 2008 and January 2009.

153. Koh's most recent project involves the creation of what he describes as "Sites of Rights and Expression" throughout Myanmar using cheap, Internet-ready laptops purchased on eBay. As he notes, "We just need to be a step ahead of state surveillance and control, and exercise creativity" (ibid.).

154. According to Chu Yuan: "Even though we faced hostility from certain groups who spread malicious rumors about us (which was very distressing for me), I knew that everyone, whether they liked us or not, was watching and learning from what we were doing, how we were doing it, and we also freely gave out information on how to access funding and opportunities outside, and various artist-run initiatives that they could study. We wanted to increase people's awareness and capacity to help themselves, especially in Myanmar, where the situation seems extremely bleak, on a daily basis. Many of the foreign artists and educators we invited and hosted sustained their relations as well as collaborated with the local artists and youth well after they left Burma" (interview with Jay Koh and Chu Chu Yuan by the author, conducted between December 2008 and January 2009). George Packer, in an essay on present-day Myanmar published in *The New Yorker*, cites the experience of the Burmese activist Thar Gyi, who has developed collaborative theatrical productions of *Romeo and Juliet*, *Rent*, and Sartre's *No Exit*, to "encourage young Burmese to develop their talents and transcend inertia and helplessness." According to Gyi: "American people say that political changes will change the condition in our country. That's true. But I think we need to develop our own capacities. We are not ready for democracy. We don't have any good platform, good foundation, to get those changes" (Packer, "Letter from Rangoon," 47). Chu Yuan elaborates on this point in my interview with her, noting that NGOs operating in Myanmar for many years have told her that "there are absolutely no foundations set,

no practices, protocols, and processes established, for mutual consultation, debate and discussion, and working out disagreements, for working together, between various peoples and groups in Myanmar. One of their staff told me many believe that civil war will break out once military rule ends in Myanmar. . . . Of course, this cannot in any way make an excuse for the military's oppressive and abusive rule, but many believe that an immediate introduction of Western-style democracy will be disastrous for Burma."

Chapter Three: Eminent Domain: Art and Urban Space

1. Riis's "Blind Man" is identified as the father of the "notorious Blanche Douglass." Blanche Douglass was implicated in the murder of Jennie Cramer in West Haven, Connecticut, in 1882. See "Jennie Cramer's Death; Blanche Douglass's Admissions and Confessions," *New York Times*, May 20, 1882, 1.

2. Riis, *How the Other Half Lives*, 186.

3. The contents of the book were originally published as a series of articles in the London *Morning Chronicle* in the late 1840s.

4. Riis himself writes about the blind beggar in *How the Other Half Lives*, noting: "The blind beggar alone is winked at in New York's streets, because the authorities do not know what else to do with him. There is no provision for him anywhere after he is old enough to strike out for himself. The annual pittance of thirty or forty dollars which he receives from the city serves to keep his landlord in good humor; for the rest his misfortune and his thin disguise of selling pencils on the street corners must provide" (189).

5. Mayhew, *London Labour and the London Poor*, 1:395.

6. Riis, *How the Other Half Lives*, 189.

7. Ibid.; Mayhew, *London Labour and the London Poor*, 1:395.

8. Stange, "Jacob Riis and Urban Visual Culture," 274–303.

9. "A man stood at the corner of Fifth Avenue and Fourteenth Street the other day, looking gloomily at the carriages that rolled by, carrying the wealth and fashion of the avenues to and from the big stores down town. He was poor, and hungry, and ragged. This thought was in his mind: 'They behind their well-fed teams have no thought for the morrow; they know hunger only by name, and ride down to spend in an hours shopping what would keep me and my little ones from want a whole year.' There rose up before him the picture of those little ones crying for bread around the cold and cheerless hearth—then he sprang into the throng and slashed about him with a knife, blindly seeking to kill, to revenge" (Riis, *How the Other Half Lives*, 199–200).

10. Riis, *How the Other Half Lives*, 226.

11. Cited in Trachtenburg, Introduction to *Paul Strand: Essays on His Life and Work*, 16.

12. In an interview from the 1970s, Strand notes: "I felt they [the subjects of his early photographs on the streets of New York] were all people whom life had battered into some sort of extraordinary interest and, in a way, nobility. The woman in *Blind Woman* had an absolutely unforgettable and noble face" (cited in Homer, *Alfred Steiglitz and the American Avant-Garde*, 251).

13. Jim Drobnick, "Sonic Intimidation," 72.

14. Medina, "Aduana/Customs," 233, 17.

15. Ibid, 19.

16. Rosa Martínez, "Merchandise and Death," 21.

17. Rosa Martínez, "Interview with Santiago Sierra," 189.

18. Ibid., 189, 197.

19. Ibid., 201.

20. Ibid., 175. This approach parallels the symbolic displacement of aggression onto the viewer or reader that I examined in my discussion of post-structuralist poetics in the wake of May '68. Claire Bishop, while lamenting what she calls an "ethical turn" in recent art criticism, nonetheless identifies the primary locus of aesthetic experience in the strategic production of shame or guilt in the viewer (in order to awaken a presumably dormant ethical sensibility). In an interview from 2009, she praises Santiago Sierra projects such as *Workers Facing a Wall* (2002) and *Workers Facing a Corner* (2002) as "very tough pieces." "Being invited to scrutinize these people while they stood in silence," she continues, "produced a difficult knot of affect. If it was guilt, it was a superegoic, liberal guilt produced in relation to being complicit with a position of power that I didn't want to assume. It was akin to the self-awareness felt in relationship to minimalist sculpture, but now charged with identification and disgust and awkwardness." Whether consciously or not, Bishop here echoes Schiller's insistence two centuries before that the task of art is to humanize the "cold heart" and "proud self-sufficiency" of a rational, calculating aristocratic class. However, the simple assertion that momentary squeamishness before a tableau vivant of exploitation will lead inevitably to a heightened capacity for empathy overlooks both the pleasures of masochism and the complex psychic economy, outlined above, that operates in our relationship to the suffering of the Other (see Austin, "Trauma, Antagonism, and the Bodies of Others").

21. We find a typical example of this interpretation in an essay by the critic Jean-Ernest Joos for the journal *Parachute*. After praising the "formal dimension—the beauty even—of Sierra's work," Joos goes on to insist that "the value of Sierra's project lies . . . in the simple fact that it reproduces the true circumstances of an encounter with another." He elaborates on these "true" circumstances in a discussion of Pierre Huyghe's *The Third Memory* (1999), which centered on the film *Dog Day Afternoon* and the relationship between Al Pacino and the actual figure he portrays in the film (John Wojtowicz). Huyghe,

according to Joss, "recreates a triangular structure, wherein the viewer is placed in such a way as to see the otherwise impossible spectacle of the material contemporaneity of Pacino and Wojtowicz. What this means is that suddenly the position of the viewer is de-centered in relation to the position he occupies in the 'society of the spectacle'" (Joos, "Being One among Others," 77–78, 86–87).

22. Spelman, *Fruits of Sorrow*, 120, 114.

23. Ibid., 67.

24. Ibid., 70, 87, 120.

25. Rosa Martínez, "Interview with Santiago Sierra," 207, 211.

26. Cuauhtémoc Medina, "Aduana/Customs," 243.

27. Ibid.

28. Ibid. This is Medina again.

29. Hobbes, *Leviathan*, 90.

30. Ibid., 64, 89.

31. Locke, *Two Treatises of Government*, 10.

32. Ibid., 168.

33. Ibid., 10.

34. Crow, *Painters and Public Life in Eighteenth-Century Paris*, 18.

35. Despite their centrality during the early to mid–nineteenth century, the salon and academy were clearly intermediary institutions, marking the gradual transition from direct religious and courtly patronage to the rise of the modern art market. By the late nineteenth century, the salon would become synonymous with mediocrity, and a range of new movements emerged that viewed the "public" demands and standards of the academy as an intolerable constraint on individual creativity and innovation. Impressionism, with its strong links to a nascent international network of dealers and collectors, was symptomatic of this shift. The academic system, which preserved at least a notional commitment to art as a form of public culture entitled to state patronage and subject to public adjudication, is replaced by a system of private dealers and collectors which bears a more complex, and ambiguous, relationship to the public. On one hand, the market provides artists with an unprecedented level of freedom; they are no longer forced to reproduce the hidebound conventions of past artistic practice or submit themselves to the conformist demands of academic elders jealous of their talents. On the other, it involves a process of "re-privatization," as the work of art is channeled through a closed network of spaces and personalities: the artist's studio, the dealer's gallery, and the collector's living room. This hardly means that Paul Durand-Ruel or Duncan Philips were latter day Medicis, dictating color and composition to Picasso and Matisse. The modern collector was no longer buying slavish veneration, but rather, the radical individuality of the artistic personality itself. The liberal cosmopolitanism of the aesthetic is projected onto the artist, who emerges as a

paradigm of modern subjectivity: a creative, entrepreneurial spirit, unbounded by social or artistic convention.

36. Rousseau argues that these institutions are literally un-representable: "Soverignty [*sic*] cannot be represented, for the same reason that it cannot be alienated. It consists essentially of the general will, and will cannot be represented. Either it is itself or it is different. There is no middle term" (Barker, Introduction to *Social Contract: Essays by Locke, Hume, and Rousseau*, 372).

37. See Locke, *Two Treatises of Government*, 168, 184, 190.

38. Deleuze and Guattari, *A Thousand Plateaus*, 309.

39. Deleuze, *Expressionism in Philosophy*, 262.

40. Spinoza, *"Ethics," preceded by "On the Improvement of the Understanding,"* 166. "By virtue and power I mean the same thing; that is virtue in so far as it is related to man, is man's very essence, or nature, in so far as he has power to bring about that which can be understood solely through the laws of his own nature" (156).

41. Deleuze, *Expressionism in Philosophy: Spinoza*, 246.

42. Hallward, "The Limits of Individuation, or How to Distinguish Deleuze and Foucault," 93.

43. As Julian Bourg notes: "Is all action good simply because it is action? The problem of immanent vitalism is that one simply knocks to another level the evaluative criteria by which discriminations are made. Changing the name of evaluative criteria does not necessarily change the constitutive and formal fact that evaluation is taking place. In this case the evaluative criterion becomes, rather than law, duty or other recognizable standards, life in search of its extension" (Bourg, *From Revolution to Ethics*, 155).

44. Spinoza, *"Ethics," preceded by "On the Improvement of the Understanding,"* 59.

45. Ibid., 112, 169.

46. Ibid., 174.

47. Hallward, "The Limits of Individuation, or How to Distinguish Deleuze and Foucault," 95.

48. Hallward, *Out of This World*, 4, 6.

49. Deleuze and Guattari, *Anti-Oedipus*, 9.

50. Deleuze, *Bergsonism*, 111.

51. Deleuze, *Expressionism in Philosophy*, 110.

52. Ibid., 240.

53. Hallward, "The Limits of Individuation, or How to Distinguish Deleuze and Foucault," 96.

54. Spinoza, *"Ethics," preceded by "On the Improvement of the Understanding,"* 108 (cf. Eve Kosofsky Sedgwick's analysis of "paranoid" knowledge in *Touching Feeling: Affect, Pedagogy, and Performativity*).

55. The corollaries with elements of both Marxism (and Louis Althusser's notion

of ideology) and structuralism are evident. It's worth noting that Althusser was one of the first thinkers to bring Spinoza into dialogue with the traditions of Western Marxism and Continental Theory. In fact, Althusser relies heavily on Spinoza in his work. As Perry Anderson notes: "'Structuring causality' as a mode of production in [Althusser's] *Reading Capital* was a secularized version of Spinoza's conception of God as a *causa immanens*. . . . Althusser's passionate attack on the ideological illusions of immediate experience as opposed to the scientific knowledge proper to theory alone, and on all notions of men or classes as conscious subjects of history, instead of as involuntary 'supports' of social relations, was an exact reproduction of Spinoza's denunciation of *experientia vaga* as the source of all error, and his remorseless insistence that the archetypical delusion was men's belief that they were in any way free in their volition, when in fact they were permanently governed by laws of which they were unconscious" (Anderson, *Considerations on Western Marxism*, 65).

56. Hallward, "The Limits of Individuation, or How to Distinguish Deleuze and Foucault," 96, 97.

57. "An aesthetic politics always defines itself by a certain recasting of the distribution of the sensible, a reconfiguration of the given perceptual forms. . . . The dream of a suitable political work of art is in fact the dream of disrupting the relationship between the visible, the sayable, and the thinkable without having to use the terms of a message as a vehicle. It is the dream of an art that would transmit meanings in the form of a rupture with the very logic of meaningful situations. As a matter of fact, political art cannot work in the simple form of a meaningful spectacle that would lead to an 'awareness' of the state of the world. Suitable political art would ensure, at one and the same time, the production of a double effect: the readability of a political signification and a sensible or perceptual shock caused, conversely, by the uncanny, by that which resists signification" (Rancière, *The Politics of Aesthetics*, 63).

58. Guy Debord writes of "passive spectators who . . . *should be forced into action*" by Situationist détournement (see Raunig, *Art and Revolution*, 176 [italics are Debord's]).

59. We encounter a corollary here to Elizabeth Spelman's analysis of Hannah Arendt's notion of suffering, which collapses the distance between the sufferer and the viewer "touched in the flesh" by their pain. As a result, there is no possibility of any reciprocal relationship to, or communication with, the suffering subject, whose pain can only function as a mute incitement.

60. For Kant, possession is not simply a question of physical (or "empirical") possession; rather, it must be morally justifiable and legally protected even when the individual does not actually possess, inhabit, or make use of a given object or piece of property. *The Metaphysics of Morals* (1797), 83.

61. Wetenhall, "Camelot's Legacy to Public Art," 152.

62. Doss, *Spirit Poles and Flying Pigs*, 43.

63. The NEA avoided the funding of representational or commemorative public art projects well into the 1980s (see Doss, *Spirit Poles and Flying Pigs*, 51–52).

64. Ibid., 46.

65. See, e.g., Phillips, "Out of Order"; and Deutsch, *Evictions*.

66. *Going Public: A Field Guide to Developments in Art in Public Places*, edited by Jeffrey L. Cruikshank and Pam Korza and published in 1988, is emblematic of this tendency. While it includes lengthy and detailed discussions of the logistics of the commissioning process, it devotes almost no space to a consideration of how the public might be involved in this process.

67. See Rubin, "Maximum Feasible Participation," 14–29.

68. See Conlan, *From New Federalism to Devolution*.

69. James Rouse's vision for gentrification first emerged during the mid-1950s, when he was a young mortgage banker in the Washington, D.C. area. In "No Slums in Ten Years: A Workable Program for Urban Renewal" (1955) Rouse outlined his plan for the elimination of the "vast stretches of filth, congestion, and disorder" of Washington, D.C.'s slums. The report contains, in embryonic form, one of Rouse's favorite urban renewal mechanisms, the "public-private partnership," in which city agencies use powers of eminent domain to relocate poor, inner-city residents and provide low cost land to private developers. At the center of this process is a "Redevelopment Land Agency": a "pace-setting, trail blazing, profit venture with broad business support and a community gleam in its eye" ("No Slums in Ten Years: A Workable Program for Urban Renewal," A Report to The Commissioners of the District of Columbia by James W. Rouse and Nathaniel S. Keith, January 1955 [unpublished]).

70. Doss, Spirit *Poles and Flying Pigs*, 89.

71. Kester, "The Ruins that Profit Wrought," 21.

72. The perception is evident in *The New Urban Landscape* exhibition at Battery Park City in 1988, which featured commissioned works by "socially-engaged artists," such as Nam June Paik, Vito Acconci, Dan Graham, and others, scattered around the towering "World Financial Center," a banal upscale development anxious to market itself as a vibrant urban space. The exhibition was staged in part as a compensatory gesture for the failure of the project developers to provide low- or moderate-income housing (see Deutsch, *Evictions*, 91).

73. See Miles, *Art, Space, and the City*.

74. The work of Peter Dunn and Loraine Leeson, including the Docklands Community Poster Project (1981–91), the East London Health Project (1978–81), and the Bethnal Green Hospital Campaign (1977–78), provide an important example of cultural resistance during this period (see Kester, "Aesthetic Enactment"). See also the history of The Art of Change website, at http://www.arte-ofchange.com/content/history-arte-art-change; and the bio for

Loraine Leeson at the University of East London, London East Research Institute website, http://www.uel.ac.uk/londoneast/gallery/loraine_leeson/index .htm.

75. See, e.g., Vancouver's "Creative City" website, http://vancouver.ca/creativecity/.

76. "The television concept, *Big Brother*, Marcel Wanders' *Knotted Chair*, the Rietveld Academy, Dick Bruna's *Miffy* books, Paul Verhoeven's film *Basic Instinct*, advertising campaigns by KesselsKramer, Rembrandt's paintings, fashion by Viktor & Rolf . . . These are only a few of the creative calling cards of the Amsterdam Metropolitan Area. Creative Amsterdam was set up to further strengthen the creative industries in the region" (from the "Creative Amsterdam" website, http://www.creativeamsterdam.nl/). For a critical overview of "Creative City" rhetoric in Europe, see *Variant* 34 (Spring 2009), available at http://www.variant.org.uk/.

77. Here's a formal definition of community art from the Greater London Arts Association: "The term *community arts* does not refer to any specific activity or group of activities; rather it defines an approach to creative activity, embracing many kinds of events and in a wide range of media. . . . The approach used in community arts enjoins both artists and local people within their various communities to use appropriate art forms as a means of communication and expression, in a way that critically uses and develops traditional art forms, adapting them to present day needs and developing new forms. Frequently the approach involves people on a collective basis, encourages the use of a collective statement but does not neglect individual development or the need for individual expression. . . . Community arts proposes the use of art to effect social change and affect social policies, and encompasses the expression of political action, effecting environmental change and developing the understanding and use of established systems of communication and change. It also uses art forms to enjoy and develop people's particular cultural heritages. . . . Community arts activists operate in areas of deprivation, using the term 'deprivation' to include financial, cultural, environmental or educational deprivation" (quoted in Kelly, *Community, Art, and the State*, 1–2).

78. According to the U.K. Cabinet Office, "social exclusion" is a "shorthand term for what can happen when people or areas suffer from a combination of linked problems such as unemployment, poor skills, low incomes, poor housing, a high crime environment and family breakdown" (quoted in Jermyn, *The Arts and Social Exclusion*, 2).

79. Under the influence of figures such as Martin Jacques and Stuart Hall, *Marxism Today*, the theoretical journal of Great Britain's Communist Party, played a central role in attempts to renew Marxist political analysis in the face of Thatcherism during the 1980s (through the concept of "New Times"). The journal ceased publication in 1991.

80. Matarasso was appointed to the Arts Council of England as East Midland Chair in 2005.

81. This transformation is not unique to the U.K. As I discuss at some length in my *Conversation Pieces*, concepts of "participation" and "empowerment" that first emerged in more deliberately egalitarian contexts during the 1960s and '70s have also been appropriated in the United States by conservative political movements to justify the withdrawal of social services and state obligations and to reinstate a traditional, Victorian, notion of poverty as a sign of individual weakness or moral failure.

82. This bureaucratized model of "community art," particularly prevalent in Ireland and the U.K., has been deservedly criticized by writers such as Rebecca Gordon Nesbitt, Stewart Martin, and others (see Martin, "Critique of Relational Aesthetics"; and Nesbitt, "The New Bohemia"). *Variant* magazine in Scotland has provided some of the most consistently thoughtful coverage of this issue; see http://www.variant.org.uk.

83. Katsiaficas, *The Subversion of Politics*, 125–26. Katsiaficas continues: "The city then declared the occupied houses 'Public Enemy Number 1,' and the squatters braced themselves for fresh attacks. Steel doors were installed, bars were mounted in the windows, and barbed wire was hung on the sides and roofs of buildings. In early November, the city promised to clear out and tear down the houses within fourteen days. The squatters painted a new slogan on the side of one of the houses—Don't count our days, count yours!—and barricaded the houses. . . . Netting was hung on the second stories of the houses to ward off the use of ladders, and patrols on the roofs guarded against helicopter landings. Four thousand police arrived from all over Germany."

84. Stephen Kinzer, "Hamburg Journal: Squatters Victorious! (A Checkbook Did It)," *New York Times*, January 5, 1996, A-4.

85. According to Schäfer, the influx of East Germans following reunification led to an increase in anti-immigration rhetoric and in the deportation of Turkish immigrants. Hamburg emerged as a center for organizing by the German Nationalist Party (NDP). Neo-Nazi skinheads traditionally exercised a strong influence in the brothels of the Repperbahn red-light district in the St. Pauli area.

86. Schäfer, "The City is Unwritten," 41.

87. Travel writer William Cook describes the conventional trajectory of gentrification in the Reeperbahn: "What has happened [in the Reeperbahn] is what has occurred in lots of Red Light districts worldwide. The sex trade drives prices down, drawing in artists, writers and musicians, who do not mind living somewhere seedy and cannot afford to live elsewhere. These outsiders make the area chic, attracting mainstream creative industries, such as advertising and film-making, and more prestigious leisure outlets, such as upscale restaurants

and hotels. Like London's Soho, the Reeperbahn is still a Red Light district, but nowadays it is also the most fashionable part of town" (Cook, "Turn Off the Red Light," 27).

88. Czenki's film, *Park Fiction: Desires Will Leave the House and Take to the Streets* (1999), provides detailed documentation of the creative process involved in bringing the park into existence. For more information, see the Park Fiction website, http://www.parkfiction.org.

89. Park Fiction's work was also influenced by Hamburg's underground music scene, reflecting the permeability between art and adjacent zones of cultural production characteristic of contemporary collaborative art practice. As Schäfer continues: "The same year, silently, a new mode of operating appeared, a shift towards a different way of moving. Probably it was to be felt and practiced first in cultural fields not recognized as political at all. What started then feels like a turning point, a change of paradigm, and we are in the midst of it now. For me, it started with music, and that came from Chicago and Detroit. Acid House . . . More than probably any music style before, House, for a decisive moment in time, was more about mixing (so basically: playing records) than about bands. When punks questioned the band-audience relation by storming the stage, house was more about people dancing, and not about people being the audience in the first place. Consumers became producers, irreversibly. What also started with Acid was the conscious idea and ability to create situations—Ambient carries that quality in its name, chill out zones sprung up everywhere, and with Rave, the temporary and unauthorized use of empty buildings, factories, hangars, farmland, banks—became a mass activity. Maybe it was the use of m.d.m.a., that gave everybody the sudden ability to trust each other, and to see oneself as a person or part of a collective, that has the power to construct situations, now, and in a smooth way." (Schäfer, "The City is Unwritten," 40).

90. Schäfer describes a typical example of the interactions involved in this process, in an unpublished interview from 2005: "With the 'Action Kit' I visited a meeting of Turkish women in the Community Center. It has an un-foldable harbor panorama, and all kinds of materials and examples in it. It's a bit like a parody of a salesman's suitcase. Before it was my turn, an Avon lady was presenting her make-up stuff. So we both had our presentation kits with us, a very funny situation. It was so funny, that talking about the park became of course much easier." (Noel Hefele, unpublished interview with Christoph Schäfer, August 2005, conducted in conjunction with the exhibition *Groundworks: Environmental Collaboration in Contemporary Art.*)

91. The preceding descriptions are taken from the Noel Hefele interview. Schäfer provides another example of Park Fiction's working process in the Hefele interview: "A young woman, Nesrin, came to a colleague with a sociological back-

ground with a drawing of a 'sky mirror.' A device that would allow the sky to be mirrored into the park—I was told. I asked the colleague: 'That sounds like an interesting idea—can you show it to me?' But the drawing never showed up. We noted down the idea anyway. Later I went to see Nesrin myself and tried to find out what her idea was. We had a long and complicated talk. After a while it came out, she wanted a kind of screen under which there was always sunshine. Nice idea! We talked and wondered how this might be possible (at least it's possible once a year on the Red Square in Moscow), but came to no conclusion. Later Nesrin designed the tulip-patterned-tartan-field. For a long time I thought this was only a cheap substitute for the original, very poetic idea. But now, on a warm evening, everybody is sitting around the tulip-patterned field, with all the kids playing on it—and somehow it is exactly the original thing: a piece of heaven mirrored into the park."

92. Park Fiction work can be related to what Oskar Negt and Alexander Kluge describe as a "counter-public sphere," or *Gegenöffentlichkeit* (see Negt and Kluge, *The Public Sphere and Experience*).

93. Schäfer, "The City is Unwritten," 44.

94. Ibid.

95. Ibid.

96. In November of 2002, St. Pauli was the scene of demonstrations and blockades protesting the city's destruction of an unauthorized trailer park (the "Bauwagenplatz Bambule") used by an alternative community that lived out of car trailers and modified buses. The Bauwagenplatz protest attracted widespread support from St. Pauli's activist networks, and was eventually quashed following a violent police eviction.

97. See, for example, e.g., John Friedmann, *Planning in the Public Domain: From Knowledge to Action* (Princeton, NJ: Princeton University Press, 1987).

98. Schäfer, "The City is Unwritten," 44.

99. Ibid, 45. Schäfer further elaborates: "As a sign of trust, we demanded that the budget for the project, blocked by the Senator for urban development, would be transferred to our bank account before the elections. So it happened and we could start."

100. Ibid. Schäfer elaborated on the significance of the round table in a recent e-mail exchange:

> "Round table" is an idiom, and a tricky one as well. 'Round tables' became highly popular during the [German] "unification" process to bring citizens and administrators and party members together. They are usually a device to calm down conflict. They have been criticized a lot, because the "round" is often a camouflage for real existing hierarchies; especially if the state or the administration picks the people who are allowed to sit at such a "round

table" (for instance: people from administration, citizens, shop owners, the local police, teachers from the school). A "round table" can be a tool to break the power of neighborhood self-organization.

In our case, we demanded a round table to bring all sectors of administration responsible for a possible park/solution to the table. On our side it was basically the initiative, the neighborhood. It was quite open, but at the same time, the people sent to the round table had to have the power to make decisions. With a lively social movement behind you, you can achieve something with a round table. As an institution I find it rather dangerous. We needed the round table from 1997 to 2002. It was then cancelled by the right wing government. But the park was nearly finished by then. The round table had a clear goal—find a solution everybody accepts for the park—and was more or less steering itself. The chair was a guy from an urban planning department. Following rule number one from Saul Alinsky's book for activists (or Ibn Khaldoun's book on "nomadic warfare") it was vital to have the table in our territory (that is in the school, the local community center etc.). In the beginning we would make special arrangements (decorate the hall with paintings, etc) to create an atmosphere that would not allow administrators to hide behind their files. This worked wonders at the beginning and all the "hard decisions" (that cost the city money) were made in the first four to six meetings, within three or four months. (E-mail to author, June 28, 2009).

101. "Our idea of the 'urban' is opposed to the principle of consensus—although you share a space, you do not have to agree. Now a very private idea (maybe of happiness) becomes a very public work, open for many layers of interpretation and use" (Noel Hefele, unpublished interview with Christoph Schäfer, August 2005).

102. "HafenCity Hamburg is one of the most important inner-city development projects in Europe, which will enlarge Hamburg's downtown area by forty percent within twenty years. This generates not only ten kilometers of a new public water line but additionally, due to the lift of the area caused by flood protection measures, a new topography, and consequently a new definition of public and private spaces. . . . Forty thousand people will work in HafenCity, about 12,000 people will live here and far more will be visitors on a daily basis. Major cultural institutions are under development, e.g. the Elbphilharmonie, a concert hall with 2,200 seats, a newly designed building by Herzog & de Meuron on top of an existing storage building, an international maritime museum to be opened in Summer 2008, and a spectacular science center by Rem Koolhaas (OMA) to be finished in 2012" (from the "HafenCity Hamburg" website, http://www.hafencity.com).

103. "From 2000 to 2005, property values have appreciated at an unprecedented rate. Five Third Ward area neighborhoods—Broadmoor, Belfort Park, Southcrest, Overbrook and South Park—have had annual average assessment increases of 10 percent or more during the five-year period, according to a study by Evert Crawford of Crawford Realty Advisors in conjunction with the University of Houston's Institute for Regional Forecasting. Andover Place, Kennedy Heights, Denver, Brentwood and Washington Place neighborhoods also show impressive property value increases. All have had nine percent or better annual growth since 2000" (M. Madere, "Neighborhood Home Sales: Third Ward Property Values Are Soaring, Joint Study Says," *Houston Chronicle*, May 17, 2006, B-3).

104. Elmo Johnson is quoted in Buntin, "Land Rush." There is much for contemporary artists and critics concerned with collaborative practice to learn from the organizational protocols of the civil rights movement. For an excellent study of the complex forms of collective decision making and action in the movement, see Polletta, *Freedom Is an Endless Meeting.*

105. As Lowe notes: "It was during that time when I started to really see my role as an artist as trying to uncover the meaning of the place and creating opportunities for people to give that meaning a place to live within the project in reality—in real time. And so it went from children in the neighborhood to church groups, museum groups, corporate groups, and a wide range of other professionals with technical expertise, from architects, historians, to attorneys, to people who conceptualized programs. For sure, all the programs of Project Row Houses didn't come from me. They came from inviting people who are really good at developing programs—giving them the space to be involved and letting them see what the possibilities were in terms of program development (from an unpublished discussion between Tom Finkelpearl, Rick Lowe, and Mark Stern, November 2004 and July 2005, to be published in a forthcoming book on art and social cooperation by Tom Finkelpearl).

106. Ibid.

107. Lowe elaborates: "Art was among the things John Biggers pointed out that were vital for good communities. He was speaking of art in broader terms. More like creativity out of necessity than 'art.' He talked about how people used creativity to take the old worn rags that they got from some place and turned them into a wedding dress, or the tools they made, instead of buying them, to carry out their work, or the quilts that were made from scraps, or the gumbo that was made from scraps of food that could feed many. He never really talked about it in terms of paintings, sculpture, etc. however, he would reference the music and story telling and things like that" (e-mail from Rick Lowe to the author, August 4, 2009).

108. From an unpublished discussion between Tom Finkelpearl, Rick Lowe, and

Mark Stern, November 2004 and July 2005, to be published in a forthcoming book on art and social cooperation by Tom Finkelpearl.

109. Lecture by Rick Lowe in the Visual Arts Department at the University of California, San Diego, March 4, 2009.

110. From an unpublished discussion between Tom Finkelpearl, Rick Lowe, and Mark Stern, November 2004 and July 2005, to be published in a forthcoming book on art and social cooperation by Tom Finkelpearl.

111. According to Coleman, "We learned a lot from the debacle in the Fourth Ward. So it would be stupid not to respond to the negative byproducts of rapid development. We want to find people who will make this community better by becoming part of its fabric, not by changing its fabric" (Kris Axtman, "After Years in the Suburbs, Many Blacks Return to City Life," *Christian Science Monitor*, April 29, 2004, 1).

112. Ibid.

113. Larry S. Davis is quoted in Buntin, "Land Rush," 24.

114. From an unpublished discussion between Tom Finkelpearl, Rick Lowe, and Mark Stern, November 2004 and July 2005, to be published in a forthcoming book on art and social cooperation by Tom Finkelpearl.

115. As Lowe elaborates: "I've been trying to work on this idea of what role artists, and arts and cultural organizations, should play in terms of community development. . . . Market developers' interest in community development is profit-driven. They don't care who gets served; they don't care who's paying. And then you have Community Development Corporations who are interested in who gets served by the development. Now Project Row Houses has a community development corporation also, but what role does it play? As an arts and cultural institution the role is to try to look into what values come out of these developments from a human standpoint. What does the development project mean? The CDC says it needs to serve low-income populations, but what does it mean if a development serves low-income populations in relation to market development of high-end real estate? I want to explore what those things mean and create opportunities to have dialogue in a meaningful way" (from an unpublished discussion between Tom Finkelpearl, Rick Lowe, and Mark Stern, November 2004 and July 2005, to be published in a forthcoming book on art and social cooperation by Tom Finkelpearl). With the successful creation of a PRH CDC, as Lowe notes, "the challenge . . . is getting the houses on the land. It's becoming easier now with the downturn in the economy. During the boom, builders were not interested in taking on small, less profitable projects. The row house community development corporation is doing thirty units with the 30% money [provided by the Tax Increment Financing Zone]. Maybe we'll do more. I'm not sure" (e-mail from Rick Lowe to the author, August 4, 2009).

116. See Davis, *Spearheads for Reform*.

117. The alternate interpretation was that open attack on the forces of order by a disorganized and undisciplined movement changed nothing and simply gave the state permission to unleash its far greater capacity for violence, while also providing the French right wing with a point of unification. As Jacques Lacan suggested during the upheavals of May '68, the enragés *needed* the state to respond violently to legitimate their own perceived radicality ("What you, as revolutionaries, aspire to is a Master. You will have one") (quoted in Starr, *Logics of Failed Revolt*, 20). See also Debray, "A Modest Contribution to the Rites and Ceremonies of the Tenth Anniversary."

118. The existence of widespread public support for the May '68 protests during the initial phases of the movement was due in part to shock over the fact that police violence was being visited upon the sons and daughters of the bourgeoisie, rather than workers and immigrants (see Seidman, *The Imaginary Revolution*).

119. Mouffe, "Artistic Activism and Agonistic Spaces," 4. Mouffe's use of "agonism" as a model for political discourse can be read against Renato Poggioli's thoughtful analysis of "agonistic sacrifice" (on behalf of "the people," posterity, etc.) as a key component of the modern artistic avant-garde (see Poggioli, *The Theory of the Avant-Garde*, 61–77).

120. Riis, Sierra, and the Yes Men each in their own way assume the existence of a receptive viewer who can be provoked into some recognition of human suffering (Riis) or the injustices of bourgeois liberalism (Sierra and the Yes Men). But this transformative recognition (of complicity, responsibility, or guilt) depends on a concept of civil society (in which appeals to quasi-universal notions of justice or equity can be transmitted through the mechanisms of the public sphere) that is equally part of the traditions of bourgeois liberalism. Even as Michel Foucault objected to the role of the "mediating third" in the modern judicial system (the judge who oversees and adjudicates), his work with various French NGOs and his "investigations" into the French prison system nevertheless positioned the French public in a similar role (see Bourg, *From Revolution to Ethics*, 91).

121. "Always Choose the Worst Option: Artistic Resistance and the Strategy of Over-Identification," BAVO Collective, June 26, 2008, pp. 24, 20, available at the BAVO Project website, http://www.bavo.biz/. BAVO consists of Gideon Boie and Matthias Pauwels, working out of Rotterdam and Brussels, respectively. BAVO continues: "To break out of this impasse, we argue that art should enter into alliances with radical social resistance movements (and therefore not with government authorities, developers, etc.), with social movements that demand a radical transformation of the existing order. Art must take care not to be a cosmetic operation that merely assuages structural injustices temporarily for a specific group. This hot-wiring of radical artistic activism and radi-

cal political activism is still a relatively unexplored area today. We therefore want to issue the following call to socially engaged artists: 'Artists . . . one more effort to be really political!'"

122. "Always Choose the Worst Option: Artistic Resistance and the Strategy of Over-Identification," BAVO Collective, June 26, 2008, 28. It is noteworthy that both Chantal Mouffe and BAVO cite the Yes Men as a paradigmatic example of a "really political" or "critical" art practice. The Yes Men are known for posing as representatives of various private corporations and governmental agencies (Dow Chemical, the World Trade Organization, etc.) and insinuating them-selves into conferences or press appearances, during which they present out-rageously exaggerated or uncharacteristically honest versions of neoliberal ide-ology (Dow Chemical accepting full responsibility for the Bhopal disaster and offering restitution; a WTO representative advocating slavery as a solution to world poverty, etc.). BAVO praises the Yes Men for catalyzing a subversive pro-cess of "over identification." "The critical effectiveness of the Yes Men consists in being *too* honest and sympathetic towards the WTO [World Trade Organiza-tion], thereby they succeed in bringing into the open the 'neo-liberal utopia of unlimited exploitation,' as Bourdieu phrased it" (ibid., 30). The appeal of the Yes Men for both BAVO and Mouffe would seem to lie less in their integration with a given "radical social resistance movement" (BAVO provides no explanation of what constitutes a "radical social resistance movement" or how the Yes Men are related to such movements), than it does with their rhetorical position, which confirms their own image of the subversive artist or intellectual "bring-ing into the open" the repressed truth of neoliberal exploitation. The artist thus becomes the embodied agent of Mouffe's notion of "agonistic" resistance, simultaneously sustaining and critiquing democracy. The Yes Men amplify the effects of global capitalism through parodic reenactment, "ruthlessly dishing up the system in its most extreme form" and thereby "pushing people who might otherwise have a more nuanced or relativist attitude towards the cur-rent state of affairs to the point where they cannot bare [*sic*] it any longer and feel compelled to take a radical stance" (ibid., 32). We might describe this as the *Borat* strategy, in which a given set of attitudes (anti-Semitism, misogyny, homophobia, etc.) are taken to an extreme, on the assumption that the viewer possesses a latent capacity for ethical discrimination that can be reawakened by the shock of overidentification. However, as with Sacha Baron-Cohen's fa-mous namesake, the capacity of some viewers to identify with even the most outrageous beliefs should never be underestimated, and *Borat* can just as easily encourage and indulge these beliefs as he can challenge them. BAVO cites a Yes Men performance in which they posed as WTO representatives offering a pro-posal to recycle the feces of McDonald's customers as a food source to solve world hunger, leading several audience members to walk out. At the same time,

they acknowledge that in other Yes Men performances, audiences, far from being shocked into a more "radical stance," sit quietly, greeting equally outrageous proposals with either indifference or polite applause. In fact, it seems likely that those who walked out in "disbelief" and "anger" did so not because they suddenly recognized the repressed truth of capitalism but because they realized that they were the butt (no pun intended) of a deliberately vulgar joke. This is not intended as a critique of the Yes Men's work, but rather as a demonstration of the unreflective reiteration of certain tropes associated with the awakening of the viewer's conscious (BAVO speaks of mobilizing the viewer's capacity for "disgust" and "shame" [31] in contemporary art theory), and the need for more nuanced models of reception.

REFERENCES

Articles and Essays

Altaf, Navjot. "Contemporary Art, Issues of Praxis, and Art-Collaboration: My Bastar Interventions and Interrogations." In *Towards New Art History: Studies in Indian Art*, edited by Shivaji Panikkar, Parul Dave Mukherji, and Deeptha Achara. New Delhi: D. K. Printworld, 2003.

Alÿs, Francis. "A Thousand Words: Francis Alÿs Talks about *When Faith Moves Mountains*." *Artforum* 40, no. 10 (summer 2002): 147.

Austin, Julia. "Trauma, Antagonism, and the Bodies of Others: A Dialogue on Delegated Performance." *Performance Paradigm* 5, no. 1 (May 2009).

Badiou, Alain. "Fifteen Theses on Contemporary Art." *Lacanian Ink*, no. 23 (2004): 100–19.

Barthes, Roland. "The Death of the Author." *Aspen* (fall/winter 1967): n.p.

———. "The Death of the Author." In *Image–Music–Text*, translated by Stephen Heath, 142–48. New York: Hill and Wang, 1977.

———. "Inaugural Lecture. Collège du France (1977)." In *A Roland Barthes Reader*, edited by Susan Sontag, 457–78. London: Vintage, 1993.

Bertram, Benjamin. "New Reflections on the 'Revolutionary' Politics of Ernesto Laclau and Chantal Mouffe." *boundary 2* 22, no. 3 (autumn 1995): 81–110.

Bishop, Claire. "Another Turn." *Artforum* 44, no. 9 (May 2006): 3.

———. "Antagonism and Relational Aesthetics." *October* 110 (fall 2004): 51–80.

———. "The Social Turn: Collaboration and Its Discontents." *Artforum* 44, no. 6 (February 2006): 179–85.

Buntin, John. "Land Rush: Gentrification in Houston." *Governing Magazine*, March 2006.

Bush, Kate. "Best of 2001." *Artforum* 39, no. 4 (December 2001): 94.

Cavanagh, Clare. "Pseudo-Revolution in Poetic Language: Julia Kristeva and the Russian Avant-Garde." *Slavic Review* 52, no. 2 (summer 1993): 283–97.

Chambers, Robert. "Participatory Rural Appraisal (PRA): Analysis of Experience." *World Development* 22, no. 9 (September 1994): 1253–68.

Chege, Michael. "The Return of Multiparty Politics." In *Beyond Capitalism vs. Socialism in Tanzania and Kenya*, edited by Joel D. Barkan. London: Lynne Rienner Publishers, 1994.

Christens, Brian, and Paul W. Speer. "Tyranny/Transformation: Power and Paradox in Participatory Development." Review of Bill Cooke and Uma Kothari, eds., *Participation: The New Tyranny?* (2001) and Samuel Hickey and Giles Mohan, eds., *Participation: From Tyranny to Transformation?* (2004). *Forum Qualitative Sozialforschung / Forum: Qualitative Social Research* 7, no. 2, http://nbn-resolving.de/urn:nbn:de:0114-fqs0602223.

Cook, William. "Turn Off the Red Light." *CNN Traveller*, March/April 2008, 27.

Craig, Stephen. "Try Again, Fail Again, Fail Better." In *Public Art: A Reader*, edited by Florian Matzner. 2nd rev. ed. Ostfildern, Ger.: Hatje Cantz, 2004.

Debray, Régis. "A Modest Contribution to the Rites and Ceremonies of the Tenth Anniversary." Translated by John Howe. *New Left Review* 115 (May–June 1979): 45–65.

Deleuze, Gilles. "On Human Rights." In *L'Abecedaire de Gilles Deleuze*, with Claire Parnet, directed by Pierre-André Boutang. Paris: Video Editions Montparnasse, 1996.

Derrida, Jacques. "Structure, Sign, and Play in the Discourse of the Human Sciences." In *Writing and Difference*, translated by Alan Bass. London: Routledge, 1978.

Drobnick, Jim. "Sonic Intimidation: Santiago Sierra." *One Hour Empire* 1 (fall 2008): 72–77.

Enwezor, Okwui. "The Production of Social Space as Artwork: Protocols of Community in the Work of Le Groupe Amos and Huit Facettes." In *Collectivism after Modernism: The Art of Social Imagination after 1945*, edited by Blake Stimson and Gregory Sholette. Minneapolis: University of Minnesota Press, 2007.

Feiner, Susan F., and Drucilla K. Barker. "Microcredit and Women's Poverty: Granting This Year's Nobel Peace Prize to Microcredit Guru Muhammad Yunus Affirms Neoliberalism." *Dollars and Sense: The Magazine of Economic Justice* 268 (November/December 2006): 2189–210.

Fisher, Jean. "In the Spirit of Conviviality: When Faith Moves Mountains." In

Francis Alÿs, edited by Cuauhtémoc Medina, Russell Ferguson, and Jean Fisher. London: Phaidon, 2007.

Foucault, Michel. Preface to *Anti-Oedipus: Capitalism and Schizophrenia*, by Gilles Deleuze and Félix Guattari; translated by Robert Hurley, Mark Seem, and Helen R. Lane; introduction by Mark Seem. Minneapolis: University of Minnesota Press, 1983.

Galvan, Dennis. "Political Turnover and Social Change in Senegal." *Journal of Democracy* 12, no. 3 (July 2001): 51–62.

Gellar, Sheldon. "The Ratched-McMurphy Model Revisited: A Critique of Participatory Development Models, Strategies, and Projects." *Issue: A Journal of Africanist Opinion* 14 (1985): 25–28.

Goodyear, Dana. "I Love Novels: Young Women Develop a Genre for the Cellular Age." *The New Yorker*, December 22, 2008.

Gough, Maria. "Constructivism Disoriented: El Lissitzky's Dresden and Hannover *Demonstrationsraüme*." In *Situating El Lissitzky: Vitebsk, Berlin, Moscow*, edited by Nancy Perloff and Brian Reed. Los Angeles: Getty Research Institute, 2003.

Green, Maia. "Participatory Development and the Appropriation of Agency in Southern Tanzania." *Critique of Anthropology* 20, no. 1 (March 2000): 67–89.

Hallward, Peter. "The Limits of Individuation, or How to Distinguish Deleuze and Foucault." *Angelaki: Journal of the Theoretical Humanities* 5, no. 2 (August 2000): 93–111.

Huit Facettes-Interaction. "Glocal Challenge." In *Ground Works: Environmental Collaboration in Contemporary Art*, edited by Grant Kester. Pittsburgh: Carnegie Mellon University/Regina Gouger Miller Gallery, 2005.

Jermyn, Helen. *The Arts and Social Exclusion: A Report*. London: Arts Council of England, 2001.

Joos, Jean-Ernest. "Being One among Others: The Uniqueness of the Artist in the Face of Anonymity." *Parachute: Contemporary Art Magazine*, January 1, 2003.

Kane-Sy, Amadou. "Reflections on Art, Contemporaneity, and Urban Existence in Dakar." In *Africas: The Artist and the City*, edited by Josep Subirós. Barcelona: Centre de Cultura Contemporania de Barcelona, 2001.

Kane-Sy, Amadou, and Huit Facettes. "Beyond Post-ism." Translated by Jennifer Taylor-Gaida. *Springerin*, January 2003.

Keay, Douglas. "Interview with Margaret Thatcher." *Women's Own*, October 31, 1987.

Keenan, Tom. "The 'Paradox' of Knowledge and Power: Reading Foucault on a Bias." *Political Theory* 15, no. 1 (February 1987): 5–37.

Kelly, Owen. *Community, Art, and the State: Storming the Citadels*. London: Comedia, 1984.

Kerr, Merrily. "Warming to the Global: Documenta XI." *NY Arts Magazine*, September 2002.

Kester, Grant. "Aesthetic Enactment: Loraine Leeson's Reparative Practice." In *Art for Change: Loraine Leeson, 1975–2005*, edited by Katja Jedermann, Birgit Kammerlohr, Nanna Lüth, Carmen Mörsch, Thorsten Streichhardt, and Jole Wilcke. Berlin: Neue Gesellschaft für Bildende Kunst Berlin, 2005.

———. "Lessons in Futility: Francis Alÿs and the Legacy of May '68." *Third Text* 99, no. 23 (July 2009): 407–20.

———. "The Ruins that Profit Wrought: DC's Devastating Developments." *New Art Examiner*, June 1989.

Kontova, Helena, and Massimiliano Gioni. "Vanessa Beecroft: Skin Trade." *Flash Art* 36, no. 228 (January–February 2003): 94–97.

Kuzma, Marta, and Peter Osborne, eds. "Art of Welfare." Special issue, *Verksted* 7 (2006).

Larsen, Lars Bang. "Superflex: Art and Biogas." *Siski: The Nordic Art Review* 12, no. 3 (fall 1997): 7–11.

Léger, Marc. "For the De-Incapacitation of Community Art Practice." *Journal of Aesthetics and Protest*, no. 6 (2008): 290–96.

Locke, John. "Of Property." In *Property: Mainstream and Critical Positions*, edited by C. B. MacPherson. Toronto: University of Toronto Press, 1978.

MacPherson, C. B. "The Meaning of Property." Introductory essay in *Property: Mainstream and Critical Positions*, edited by C. B. MacPherson. Toronto: University of Toronto Press, 1978.

Martin, Stewart. "Critique of Relational Aesthetics." *Third Text* 21, no. 4 (July 2007): 369–86.

Martinez, Rosa. "Entrevista a Santiago Sierra/Interview with Santiago Sierra." In *Santiago Sierra*, catalog of the Spanish Pavilion, Venice Biennial 2003, curated by Rosa Martinez. Madrid: Ministerio de Asuntos Exteriores, Dirección General de Relaciones Culturales y Científicas/Turner, 2003.

———. "Merchandise and Death." In *Santiago Sierra*, catalog of the Spanish Pavilion, Venice Biennial 2003, curated by Rosa Martinez. Madrid: Ministerio de Asuntos Exteriores, Dirección General de Relaciones Culturales y Científicas/Turner, 2003.

Medina, Cuauhtémoc. "Aduana/Customs." In *Santiago Sierra*, catalog of the Spanish Pavilion, Venice Biennial 2003, curated by Rosa Martinez. Madrid: Ministerio de Asuntos Exteriores, Dirección General de Relaciones Culturales y Científicas/Turner, 2003.

———. "Maximum Effort, Minimum Result." In *Francis Alÿs: When Faith Moves Mountains*, by Cuauhtémoc Medina et al. Madrid: Turner Publications, 2005.

Miessen, Markus, and Shumon Basar. Introduction to *Did Someone Say Partici-*

pate? An Atlas of Spatial Practice, edited by Markus Miessen and Shumon Basar. Cambridge, Mass.: MIT Press, 2006.

Moens, Aline. "The Hamdallaye Studios: Animated Films by Villagers." *Animation World Magazine*, April 1, 1998.

Mouffe, Chantal. "Artistic Activism and Agonistic Spaces." *Art and Research: A Journal of Ideas, Contexts, and Methods* 1, no. 2 (summer 2007): 1–5.

Nacking, Åsa. "An Exchange between Åsa Nacking and Superflex." Translated by Kjersti Board. *Afterall* (spring/summer 1999): 27–30.

Nesbitt, Rebecca Gordon. "The New Bohemia." *Variant* 32 (summer 2008): 5–8.

Olivecrona, Karl. "Locke's Theory of Appropriation." In *John Locke: Critical Assessments*, edited by Richard Ashcraft. London: Routledge, 1991.

Packer, George. "Letter from Rangoon: Can the Burmese People Rescue Themselves?" *The New Yorker*, August 25, 2008.

Patrick, Martin. "Snapshots from an Indefinite Vacation: Francis Alÿs and Photography." *Afterimage* 34, no. 6 (May–June 2007): 8–11.

Phillips, Patricia C. "Out of Order: The Public Art Machine." *Artforum* 27, no. 4 (December 1988): 92–96.

Preziosi, Donald. "That Obscure Object of Desire: The Art of Art History." *boundary 2* 13, no. 2/3 (winter/spring 1985): 1–41.

Rancière, Jacques. "The Aesthetic Revolution and Its Outcomes." *New Left Review* 14 (March–April 2002): 133–51.

———. "The Emancipated Spectator." *Artforum* 45, no. 7 (March 2007): 271–80.

Rubin, Lillian B. "Maximum Feasible Participation: The Origins, Implications, and Present Status." In *Evaluating the War on Poverty*, edited by Louis A. Ferman. *Annals of the American Academy of Political and Social Science* 385, no. 1. Philadelphia: American Academy of Political and Social Science, 1969.

Schäfer, Christoph. "The City is Unwritten: Urban Experiences and Thoughts Seen Through Park Fiction." In *Making Their Own Plans: City Repair, Resource Center, Park Fiction, Can Masdeu*, edited by Brett Bloom and Ava Bromberg. Chicago: White Walls, 2004.

Sharma, Jaya. "Grameen Myth." *The Times of India* (Bombay), November 6, 2006.

Specter, Michael. "Kremlin, Inc." *The New Yorker*, January 29, 2007.

Stange, Maren. "Jacob Riis and Urban Visual Culture: The Lantern Slide Exhibition as Entertainment and Ideology." *Journal of Urban History* 15, no. 3 (May 1989): 274–303.

Steiner, Barbara. "Radical Democracy: Acknowledging the Complexities and Contingencies." *NU: The Nordic Art Review* 2 (August 1999): 50–55.

Steinweg, Marcus. *WORLDPLAY*. In *Thomas Hirschhorn: "Utopia, Utopia = One World, One War, One Army, One Dress."* Boston: Institute of Contemporary Art, 2005.

Thomas, Rachel. "Pierre Huyghe: Streamside Day" (curatorial statement). Dublin: Irish Museum of Modern Art, 2005.

Trachtenburg, Allan. Introduction to *Paul Strand: Essays on His Life and Work*, edited by Maren Stange. New York: Aperture, 1990.

Virtanen, Akseli, and Jussi Vähämäki. "The Structure of Change: An Introduction." *Framework: The Finnish Art Review* 4 (December 2005): 30–33.

Vivanco, Jose Miguel, and Daniel Wilkinson. "Hugo Chávez versus Human Rights." *New York Review of Books*, November 6, 2008.

Wetenhall, John. "Camelot's Legacy to Public Art: Aesthetic Ideology in the New Frontier." In *Critical Issues in Public Art: Content, Context, and Controversy*, edited by Harriet F. Senie and Sally Webster. Washington, D.C.: Smithsonian Institution Press, 1992.

Williams, Glyn. "Evaluating Participatory Development: Tyranny, Power and (re)Politicization." *Third World Quarterly* 25, no. 3 (2004): 557–78.

Žižek, Slavoj. "Holding the Place." In *Contingency, Hegemony, Universality: Contemporary Dialogues on the Left*, by Judith Butler, Ernesto Laclau, and Slavoj Žižek. London: Verso, 2000.

Books and Catalogs

Ackerman, Peter, and Jack Duvall. *A Force More Powerful: A Century of Non-Violent Conflict*. New York: Palgrave, 2000.

Adorno, T. W. *Aesthetic Theory*. Edited by Gretel Adorno and Rolf Tiedemann, translated by C. Lenhardt. London: Routledge, 1984.

Africa Commission. *Realizing the Potential of Africa's Youth: Report of the African Commission*. 2nd ed. Copenhagen: Secretariat of the Africa Commission, Ministry of Foreign Affairs of Denmark, 2009.

Agamben, Giorgio. *Homo Sacer: Sovereign Power and Bare Life*. Translated by Daniel Heller-Roazen. Stanford, Calif.: Stanford University Press, 1998.

Anderson, Perry. *Considerations on Western Marxism*. London: Verso, 1979.

Augustine. *Confessions*. Translated and edited by Albert C. Outler. Dallas: Southern Methodist University, 1955.

Bamford, James. *The Shadow Factory: The Ultra-Secret NSA from 9/11 to the Eavesdropping on America*. New York: Doubleday, 2008.

Barkan, Joel D., ed. *Beyond Capitalism vs. Socialism in Tanzania and Kenya*. London: Lynne Rienner Publishers, 1994.

Barker, Sir Ernest. Introduction to *Social Contract: Essays by Locke, Hume, and Rousseau*. London: Oxford University Press, 1948.

Barthes, Roland. *A Roland Barthes Reader*. Edited by Susan Sontag. London: Vintage, 1993.

———. *Image–Music–Text*. Translated by Stephen Heath. New York: Hill and Wang, 1977.

———. *The Pleasure of the Text*. Translated by Richard Miller. New York: Farrar, Straus and Giroux, 1975.

———. *S/Z: An Essay*. Translated by Richard Miller, preface by Richard Howard. New York: Hill and Wang, 1975.

Bataille, Georges. *The Accursed Share*. Translated by Robert Hurley. 3 vols. in 2. New York: Zone Books, 1991.

Baudrillard, Jean. *Simulations*. Translated by Phil Beitchman, Paul Foss, and Paul Patton. New York: Semiotext, 1983.

Bauman, Zygmunt. *Globalization: The Human Consequences*. New York: Columbia University Press, 1998.

Bell, Daniel. *The Coming of Post-Industrial Society: A Venture in Social Forecasting*. New York: Basic Books, 1973.

Blanchot, Maurice. *The Space of Literature*. Translated with an introduction by Ann Smock Lincoln. Nebraska: University of Nebraska Press, 1982.

Bloom, Brett, and Ava Bromberg, eds. *Making Their Own Plans: City Repair, Resource Center, Park Fiction, Can Masdeu*. Chicago: White Walls, 2004.

Boal, Augusto. *Theater of the Oppressed*. London: Pluto Press, 1979.

Bourdieu, Pierre. *The Field of Cultural Production*. Edited by Randal Johnson. New York: Columbia University Press, 1993.

———. *Homo Academicus*. Stanford, Calif.: Stanford University Press, 1990.

Bourg, Julian. *From Revolution to Ethics: May 1968 and Contemporary French Thought*. Montreal: McGill–Queen's University Press, 2007.

Bourriaud, Nicolas. *Relational Aesthetics*. Translated by Simon Pleasance and Fronza Woods with the participation of Mathieu Copeland. Dijon: Les Presses du Réel, 2002.

Butler, Cornelia, and Lisa Gabrielle Mark, eds. *WACK! Art and the Feminist Revolution*. Cambridge, Mass.: MIT Press/Los Angeles Museum of Contemporary Art, 2007.

Butler, Judith, Ernesto Laclau, and Slavoj Žižek. *Contingency, Hegemony, and Universality: Contemporary Dialogues on the Left*. London: Verso, 2000.

Certeau, Michel de. *The Capture of Speech and Other Political Writings*. Edited with an introduction by Luce Girard, translated with an afterword by Tom Conley. Minneapolis: University of Minnesota Press, 1997.

———. *The Practice of Everyday Life*. Translated by Steven Rendall. Berkeley: University of California Press, 1984.

Conlan, Timothy. *From New Federalism to Devolution: Twenty-Five Years of Intergovernmental Reform*. Washington, D.C.: Brookings Institution, 1998.

Cooke, Bill, and Uma Kothari, eds. *Participation: The New Tyranny?* New York: Zed Books, 2001.

Crow, Thomas E. *Painters and Public Life in Eighteenth-Century Paris*. New Haven, Conn.: Yale University Press, 1985.

Cruikshank, Jeffrey L., and Pam Korza. *Going Public: A Field Guide to Developments in Art in Public Places*. Amherst: Arts Extension Service/National Endowment for the Arts, University of Massachusetts, 1988.

Cusset, François. *French Theory: How Foucault, Derrida, Deleuze and Company Transformed the Intellectual Life of the United States*. Translated by Jeff Fort with Josephine Berganza and Marlon Jones. Minneapolis: University of Minnesota Press, 2008.

Davis, Allen F. *Spearheads for Reform: The Social Settlements and the Progressive Movement, 1890–1914*. New Brunswick, N.J.: Rutgers University Press, 1985.

Deleuze, Gilles. *Bergsonism*. Translated by Hugh Tomlinson and Barbara Habberjam. New York: Zone Books, 1991.

———. *Difference and Repetition*. Translated by Paul Patton. New York: Columbia University Press, 1994.

———. *Expressionism in Philosophy: Spinoza*. Translated by Martin Joughin. New York: Zone Books, 1992.

Deleuze, Gilles, and Félix Guattari. *Anti-Oedipus: Capitalism and Schizophrenia*. Translated by Robert Hurley, Mark Seem, and Helen R. Lane; introduction by Mark Seem. Minneapolis: University of Minnesota Press, 1983.

———. *A Thousand Plateaus: Capitalism and Schizophrenia*. Translated by Brian Massumi. New York: Continuum, 2004.

Derrida, Jacques. *Politics of Friendship*. Translated by George Collins. London: Verso, 1997.

———. *Writing and Difference*. Translated by Alan Bass. London: Routledge, 1978.

Deutsch, Rosalyn. *Evictions: Art and Spatial Politics*. Cambridge, Mass.: MIT Press, 1996.

Doss, Erika Lee. *Spirit Poles and Flying Pigs: Public Art and Cultural Democracy in American Communities*. Washington, D.C.: Smithsonian Institution Press, 1995.

Dosse, Françoise. *History of Structuralism*. Translated by Deborah Glassman. 2 vols. Minneapolis: University of Minnesota Press, 1997.

Epstein, S. R., and Maarten Prak, eds. *Guilds, Innovation, and the European Economy, 1400–1800*. Cambridge: Cambridge University Press, 2008.

Eribon, Didier. *Michel Foucault*. Translated by Betty Wing. Cambridge, Mass.: Harvard University Press, 1991.

Ferguson, Russell. *Francis Alÿs: Politics of Rehearsal*. Los Angeles: Hammer Museum, 2007.

Fitzgerald, Sandy, ed. *An Outburst of Frankness: Community Arts in Ireland—A Reader*. Dublin: New Island/Tasc, 2004.

Florida, Richard. *The Rise of the Creative Class: And How It's Transforming Work, Leisure, Community, and Everyday Life*. New York: Basic Books, 2003.

Friedmann, John. *Planning in the Public Domain: From Knowledge to Action.* Princeton, N.J.: Princeton University Press, 1987.

Galvan, Dennis. *The State Must Be Our Master of Fire: How Peasants Craft Culturally Sustainable Development in Senegal.* Berkeley: University of California Press, 2004.

Galvan, Dennis, and Rudra Sil, eds. *Reconfiguring Institutions across Time and Space: Syncretic Responses to Challenges of Political and Economic Transformation.* Hampshire: Palgrave Macmillan, 2007.

Gorz, André. *Farewell to the Working Class.* London: Pluto Press, 2001.

Green, Charles. *The Third Hand: Collaboration in Art from Conceptualism to Postmodernism.* Minneapolis: University of Minnesota Press, 2001.

Grotius, Hugo. *De jure belli ac pacis libri tres.* Vol. 2, bk. 1. Translated by Francis W. Kelsey with collaboration of Arthur E. R. Boak, Henry A. Sanders, Jesses S. Reeves, and Herbert W. Wright. Introduction by James Brown Scott. Oxford: Clarendon Press, 1925.

Guattari, Félix. *Molecular Revolution: Psychiatry and Politics.* Translated by Rosemary Sheed. Introduction by David Cooper. London: Penguin Books, 1984.

Guattari, Félix, and Toni Negri. *Communists like Us: New Spaces of Liberty, New Lines of Alliance.* Translated by Michael Ryan. New York: Semiotext, 1990.

Hallward, Peter. *Out of This World: Deleuze and the Philosophy of Creation.* London: Verso, 2006.

Hardt, Michael, and Antonio Negri. *Empire.* Cambridge, Mass.: Harvard University Press, 2000.

Harvey, David. *A Brief History of Neoliberalism.* New York: Oxford University Press, 2005.

Heilbroner, Robert. *The Worldly Philosophers: The Lives, Times, and Ideas of the Great Economic Thinkers.* New York: Touchstone, 1999.

Hickey, Samuel, and Giles Mohan. *Participation: From Tyranny to Transformation?* New York: Zed Books, 2004.

Hickman, Larry. *Pragmatism and Post-Postmodernism: Lessons from John Dewey.* New York: Fordham University Press, 2007.

Hill, Christopher. *The World Turned Upside Down: Radical Ideas during the English Revolution.* London: Penguin, 1975.

Hobbes, Thomas. *Leviathan.* Introduction by A. D. Lindsay. London: J. M. Dent and Sons, 1934.

Holloway, John. *Change the World without Taking Power: The Meaning of Revolution Today.* London: Pluto Press, 2005.

Homer, William Innes. *Alfred Steiglitz and the American Avant-Garde.* Boston: New York Graphic Society, 1977.

Human Rights Watch. *A Decade under Chavez: Political Intolerance and Lost*

Opportunities for Advancing Human Rights in Venezuela. New York: Human Rights Watch, 2008.

Incite! Women of Color against Violence, eds. *The Revolution Will Not Be Funded: Beyond the Non-Profit Industrial Complex*. Boston: South End Press, 2007.

Irigaray, Luce. *Between East and West: From Singularity to Community*. Translated by Stephen Pluhacek. New York: Columbia University Press, 2002.

———. *To Speak Is Never Neutral*. New York: Routledge, 2002.

Joas, Hans. *The Creativity of Action*. Translated by Jeremy Gaines and Paul Keast. Chicago: University of Chicago Press, 1996.

Kant, Immanuel. *The Metaphysics of Morals*. Introduction, translation, and notes by Mary Gregor. Cambridge: Cambridge University Press, 1991.

Kapur, Geeta. *When Was Modernism: Essays on Contemporary Cultural Practices in India*. Delhi: Tulika Books, 2000.

Katsiaficas, George. *The Subversion of Politics: European Autonomous Social Movements and the Decolonization of Everyday Life*. Atlantic Highlands, N.J.: Humanities Press, 1997.

Kelly, Owen. *Community, Art, and the State: Storming the Citadels*. London: Comedia, 1984.

Kester, Grant. *Conversation Pieces: Community and Communication in Modern Art*. Berkeley: University of California Press, 2004.

———. "The Faculty of Possession: Property and the Aesthetic in English Culture, 1730–1850." Ph.D. diss., University of Rochester, 1996.

———, ed. *Groundworks: Environmental Collaboration in Contemporary Art*. Pittsburgh: Carnegie Mellon University/Regina Gouger Miller Gallery, 2005.

Kotz, Liz. *Words to Be Looked At: Language in 1960s Art*. Cambridge, Mass.: MIT Press, 2007.

Kwon, Miwon. *One Place after Another: Site Specific Art and Locational Identity*. Cambridge, Mass.: MIT Press, 2004.

Laclau, Ernesto, and Chantal Mouffe. *Hegemony and Socialist Strategy: Towards a Radical Democratic Politics*. London: Verso, 1985.

Lavaca Collective. *Sin Patrón: Stories from Argentina's Worker-Run Factories*. Foreword by Naomi Klein and Avi Lewis. Chicago: Haymarket Books, 2007.

Light, Andrew, John O'Neill, and Alan Howard. *Environmental Values*. London: Routledge Press, 2008.

Locke, John. *Two Treatises of Government*. With a supplement, *Patriarcha*, by Robert Filmer. Edited with an introduction by Thomas I. Cook. New York: Hafner Publishing, 1969.

Lyotard, Jean-François. *The Postmodern Condition: A Report on Knowledge*. Translated by Geoff Bennington and Brian Massumi. Foreword by Fredric Jameson. Minneapolis: University of Minnesota Press, 1984.

Macksey, Richard, and Eugenio Donato, eds. *The Structuralist Controversy*. Baltimore: Johns Hopkins University Press, 1970.

Matzner, Florian, ed. *Public Art: A Reader*. 2nd rev. ed. Ostfildern, Ger.: Hatje Cantz, 2004.

Mayhew, Henry. *London Labour and the London Poor*. 4 vols. With a new introduction by John D. Rosenberg. New York: Dover Publications, 1968.

Medina, Cuauhtémoc, Susan Buck-Morss, Gustavo Buntinx, Gerardo Mosquera, Lucy Lippard, and Corinne Diserens (contributor). *Francis Alÿs: When Faith Moves Mountains*. Madrid: Turner Publications, 2005.

Medina, Cuauhtémoc, Russell Ferguson, and Jean Fisher. *Francis Alÿs*. London: Phaidon, 2007.

Merleau-Ponty, Maurice. *Phenomenology of Perception*. Translated by Colin Smith. London: Routledge, 2002.

Miessen, Markus, and Shumono Basar, eds. *Did Someone Say Participate? An Atlas of Spatial Practice*. Cambridge, Mass.: MIT Press, 2006.

Miles, Malcolm. *Art, Space, and the City*. London: Routledge, 1997.

Mouffe, Chantal. *The Return of the Political*. London: Verso, 1993.

Munshi, Indra. *Adivasi Life Stories: Context, Constraints, and Choices*. Jaipur: Rawat Publications, 2007.

Nancy, Jean-Luc. *The Inoperative Community*. Edited by Peter Connor, translated by Peter Connor, Lisa Garbus, Michael Holland, and Simona Sawhney. Minneapolis: University of Minnesota Press, 1991.

Negt, Oskar, and Alexander Kluge. *The Public Sphere and Experience: Towards an Analysis of the Bourgeois and Proletarian Public Sphere*. Translated by Peter Labanyi, Jamie Owen Daniel, and Assenka Oksiloff. Minneapolis: University of Minnesota Press, 1993.

O'Connor, James. *The Fiscal Crisis of the State*. New York: St. Martins Press, 1971.

Offe, Claus. *Contradictions of the Welfare State*. Edited by John Keane. Cambridge, Mass.: MIT Press, 1984.

Oury, Jean, and Danielle Roulot. *Dialogues à La Borde: Psychopathologie et structure institutionnelle*. Paris: Hermann, 2008.

Parker, Rozsika. *The Subversive Stitch: Embroidery and the Making of the Feminine*. New York: Routledge, 1989.

Piven, Francis Fox, and Richard Cloward. *Regulating the Poor: The Functions of Public Welfare*. New York: Vintage, 1971.

Poggioli, Renato. *The Theory of the Avant-Garde*. Translated by Gerald Fitzgerald. Cambridge, Mass.: Belknap/Harvard University Press, 1968.

Polanyi, Karl. *The Great Transformation*. Boston: Beacon Press, 1944.

Polletta, Francesca. *Freedom Is an Endless Meeting: Democracy in American Social Movements*. Chicago: University of Chicago Press, 2002.

Pufendorf, Samuel. *The Political Writings of Samuel Pufendorf*. Edited by Craig L. Carr, translated by Michale J. Seidler. New York: Oxford University Press, 1994.

Quattrocchi, Angelo, and Tom Nairn. *The Beginning of the End: France, May 1968*. London: Verso, 1998.

Rancière, Jacques. *The Politics of Aesthetics*. Translated by Gabriel Rockhill. London: Continuum, 2004.

Raunig, Gerald. *Art and Revolution: Transversal Activism in the Long Twentieth Century*. Los Angeles: Semiotext, 2007.

Reich, Robert B. *The Work of Nations: Preparing Ourselves for 21st Century Capitalism*. New York: Vintage, 1992.

Ricoeur, Paul. *From Text to Action*. Translated by Kathleen Blamey and John B. Thompson. Essays in Hermeneutics, no. 2. Evanston, Ill.: Northwestern University Press, 1991.

Riis, Jacob. *How the Other Half Lives: Studies among the Tenements of New York*. Introduction by Donald N. Bigelow. New York: Hill and Wang, 1957.

Rist, Gilbert. *The History of Development: From Western Origins to Global Faith*. Translated by Patrick Camiller. London: Zed Books, 1997.

Ross, Kristin. *May '68 and Its Afterlives*. Chicago: University of Chicago Press, 2002.

Sánchez Vásquez, Adolfo. *The Philosophy of Praxis*. London: Merlin Press, 1977.

Santos, Boaventura de Sousa, ed. *Another Knowledge Is Possible: Beyond Northern Epistemologies*. Reinventing Social Emancipation, no. 3. London: Verso, 2007.

———. *Another Production Is Possible: Beyond the Capitalist Canon*. Reinventing Social Emancipation, no. 2. London: Verso, 2006.

———. *Democratizing Democracy: Beyond the Liberal Democratic Canon*. Reinventing Social Emancipation, no. 1. London: Verso, 2005.

Scharpf, Fritz Wilhelm, and Vivien A. Schmidt, eds. *Welfare and Work in the Open Economy*. 2 vols. Oxford: Oxford University Press, 2001.

Schiller, Friedrich. *On the Aesthetic Education of Man*. Edited and translated by Elizabeth M. Wilkinson and L. A. Willoughby. Oxford: Oxford University Press/Clarendon Press, 1987.

Schnapp, Alain, and Pierre Vidal-Naquet, eds. *The French Student Uprising, November 1967–June 1968: An Analytical Record*. Boston: Beacon Press, 1971.

Scott, James C. *Seeing Like a State: How Certain Schemes to Improve the Human Condition Have Failed*. New Haven, Conn.: Yale University Press, 1998.

Sedgwick, Eve Kosofsky. *Touching Feeling: Affect, Pedagogy, and Performativity*. Durham, N.C.: Duke University Press, 2003.

Seidman, Michael. *The Imaginary Revolution: Parisian Students and Workers in 1968*. New York: Berghahn Books, 2004.

Senie, Harriet F., and Sally Webster, eds. *Critical Issues in Public Art: Content,*

Context and Controversy. Washington, D.C.: Smithsonian Institution Press, 1992.

Spelman, Elizabeth V. *Fruits of Sorrow: Framing Our Attention to Suffering*. Boston: Beacon Press, 1997.

Spinoza, Benedictus de. *"Ethics," preceded by "On the Improvement of the Understanding."* Edited with an introduction by James Gutmann. New York: Hafner Press, 1949.

Stange, Maren, ed. *Paul Strand: Essays on His Life and Work*. New York: Aperture, 1990.

Starr, Paul. *Logics of Failed Revolt: French Theory after May '68*. Stanford, Calif.: Stanford University Press, 1995.

Stimson, Blake, and Gregory Sholette, eds. *Collectivism after Modernism: The Art of Social Imagination after 1945*. Minneapolis: University of Minnesota Press, 2007.

Subramanyan, K. G. *The Living Tradition: Perspectives on Modern Indian Art*. Calcutta: Seagull Books, 1987.

Wark, McKenzie. *Hacker Manifesto*. Cambridge, Mass.: Harvard University Press, 2004.

Wellbery, David E. *Lessing's "Laocoön": Semiotics and Aesthetics in the Age of Reason*. Cambridge: Cambridge University Press, 1984.

Wilberforce, William. *A Practical View of the Prevailing Religious System of Professed Christians in the Higher and Middle Classes in This Country Contrasted with Real Christianity*. London: T. Cadell, 1797.

Woodmansee, Martha. *The Author, Art, and the Market: Rereading the History of Aesthetics*. New York: Columbia University Press, 1994.

INDEX

Page numbers in *italics* and those followed by "n" indicate figures or tables and endnotes, respectively. "Plate" refers to color plates.

Danish welfare state, 133–35

David, Jacques-Louis, 160

Davis, Larry S., 218, 220

Debray, Régis, 237n56

debt entrapment in microcredit systems, 130

de-centering: evangelical Christianity and, 110; of international exchange, 98; Spinoza and, 182; of subject, 31, 51–52, 61, 242n105

deconstruction, 23, 56, 62

"deep criticism," 223–24

Deleuze, Gilles, 121–22, 155, 178–82, 256n94

dependence theorists, 117

Derrida, Jacques: on "free play" of the signifier, 251n63; on friendship, 49; at Johns Hopkins Humanities Center, 53, 240n87; Renaut on, 13–14; on speech vs. text, 105

desire: Alÿs's *When Faith Moves Mountains* and, 75; Chu's *Offering of the Mind* and, 150; Deleuze on creativity of, 180–81, 184; post-structuralism on, 50

detachment. *See* autonomy, aesthetic

development: Ala Plastica vs. IIRSA, 140–45; Alÿs's *When Faith Moves Mountains* and, 69–72; humanitarian relief programs, 119–20, 255n88; mechanisms of, 116–17; neoliberal structural adjustment policies, 117–19, 255n86; "participatory" model, 136–37; *Realizing the Potential of Africa's Youth* (Denmark's Commission on Africa), 259n112; Superflex's critique of, 127–33. *See also* urban renewal and gentrification

development organizations. *See* nongovernmental organizations (NGOs) and aid agencies

dialogical practice: co-presence of bodies in real time and, 114; materiality and, 138–39; meaningful loss of intentionality, 115; openness to site and, 139; "projects" vs. "initiatives" and, 138; quasi-dialogical action, 137; temporal and spatial indeterminacies, 209. *See also* collaboration and collective experience; *specific projects*

Dialogue (India): overview, 27–28, 78; agency and, 138; Ateliers d'Hamdallaye compared to, 99; collective experience and co-laboring, 88–90; culture, ritual, and the modern vs. pre-modern, 86–88; hierarchies and ethics, 93–95; Nalpar water pump sites, 76–83, *79*, 248n34, plates 3–6; name of, 248n34; Pilla Gudi ("children's temples"), 27–28, 84–86, plates 7–9; Shilpi Gram workshops and gender, 90–95; Superflex compared to, 136

difference: Barthes on, 238n64; bourgeois subjectivity and, 111–12; the class Other, 155–72, *158*, 220, 265n4, 266n12; Deleuze on, 178; Dialogue and, 28, 64; disruption and, 185; *Documenta* and, 62; openness to, 176; post-structuralism and, 49–50; "working through," 95

Dim, Moustapha, 96

"disruption" (Bishop), 61–63, 242n104. *See also* rupture

distance and distanciation: Alÿs's *When Faith Moves Mountains* and, 72–73; epistemological and political, collapse of, 224; exclusion vs. necessary distance, 38, 40; immersion and, movement between, 139; salon works and, 174; stasis vs. interaction, 89–90; Superflex and, 128

diversity, Project Row Houses and, 219–20

divine right concept, 106

Doctors Without Borders, 124

Documenta and *Documenta II*, 62, 231n12

Dog Day Afternoon (film), 266n21

Dohnanyi, Klaus von, 200–201

Dondagaon, Chhattisgarh, India, 77. *See also* Dialogue (India)

the instantaneous, labor and, 104–5
institutional psychotherapy movement,
    241n97
intellectual baroque, 14
intentionality, 114–15, 260n127
interloper role, 144
intrinsic value in art, 39–40
Irigaray, Luce, 94, 100

Jacob, Mary Jane, 260n118
Jacotot, Joseph, 251n60
Joas, Hans, 114–15, 137, 254n79, 260n127
Johnson, Elmo, 214
Joos, Jean-Ernest, 266n21
jouissance, textual, 48–49

Kabinett der Abstrakten (Lissitzky), 232n4
Kane Sy, Amadou, 96–99, 212, 249n45,
    250n52
Kant, Immanuel, 112, 269n60
Kapoor, Dip, 78, 247n33
Kapur, Geeta, 91–93
Katsiaficas, George, 200, 272n83
Kennedy, John F., 188
Kenya (Third Ward resident, Houston),
    216–17
knowledge and epistemology: collabo-
    rative art practices and, 10; collective
    projects and experiential knowledge,
    112; local, 142–44; métis, 143; Sedg-
    wick's "paranoid knowing," 52–53
Koh, Jay, 145–52, 263n147, 263n150,
    264n153
Kolla aboriginal groups, 142
Kopaweda, Chhattisgarh, India, 76–83,
    79, 84, 86, plates 3–6. *See also* Dialogue
    (India)
Korza, Pam, 270n66
Kristeva, Julia, 49, 57, 102
Kwon, Miwon, 144

labor: agricultural, 234n19; Alÿs's *When
    Faith Moves Mountains* and, 67, 69–71,

74–75, 100, 211; of artist vs. viewer,
    100–101; Bourriaud on relational prac-
    tice and, 30; Dialogue and co-laboring,
    90; failed or futile, 69–70, 100; global,
    121; the instantaneous and, 104–5;
    intellectual eclipsing industrial, 233n19;
    moral economy of, 157–59; Nalpar
    water pump sites and, 79–81; Park Fic-
    tion and, 210; praxis, representation,
    and, 100–106; property, liberal human-
    ism, and the bourgeois subject, 106–12;
    semantic, 71; voluntary, 74–75
Lacan, Jacques, 278n117
Laclau, Ernesto, 49, 234n27, 238n73,
    242n105
Lambert, Alix, 234n25
landless workers, 73
language: as battleground, 48; Derrida
    on text vs. speech, 105; empty speech,
    241n97; fascism of, 46; in Myanmar,
    149, 263n150; semiotic model of expres-
    sion, 113–14; verbal and haptic experi-
    ence vs., 105–6; Wellbery on immediacy
    and, 251n61. *See also* textual production
    and politics
Larsen, Lars Bang, 22–24
Leeson, Loraine, 270n74
Lefort, Claude, 44–45
Legér, Marc, 261n129
Letters on the Aesthetic Education of Man
    (Schiller), 36, 41–42, 43
Lévi-Strauss, Claude, 239n78
liberalism: bourgeois subject and liberal
    humanism, 106–12, 117; and public,
    concept of, 174–76. *See also* bourgeois
    subjectivity; neoliberalism
Lima Biennial (2002), 67. See also *When
    Faith Moves Mountains* (Alÿs)
Lissitzky, El, 19–21, 232n4
local knowledge, 142–44
Locke, John, 173, 176, 252n69, 252nn71–72
London Labour and the London Poor
    (Mayhew), 154–59

water pump sites and, 82–83; as quasi-
hegemonic, 12–13; rapprochement
with contemporary art, 54–58, 240n88;
rupture and desire, 49–52; Sedgwick's
"paranoid knowing," 52–53; social cohesion, impossibility of, 49; synchronic
identity bias, 82; as synonymous with
critical theory, 54; tension within, 13–14
poverty: blind beggar theme, 155–63, *158*,
265n1, 266n12; community art and, 198;
deserving vs. undeserving poor, 157–59;
ignorance of privileged classes and,
160; Sierra and, 162–71
pre-modern vs. modern art, 87–88, *88*
Preziosi, Donald, 253n78
PRH. *See* Project Row Houses
private dealers and collectors, 267n35
production and productive practices:
Continental philosophy, assimilation
of, 11–12; ex nihilo creativity, 112–13;
mass production, 249n39; paradigm
shift in, 10–11. *See also* textual production
productivity, Alÿs's *When Faith Moves
Mountains* and, 70
project-based vs. site-specific art, 135–40
Project Row Houses (PRH), Houston: diversity and resistance to gentrification,
217–22; institutional relationships, 216;
Park Fiction compared to, 213; shotgun
houses and renovation, 214–16, *216*
property, 106–8, 176, 194, 252nn69–72
protest and resistance: anti-globalization,
124; to bourgeois individualism,
253n73; Ghandi's spinning wheel as
symbol of, 91–93; Hafenstraße squatters, Hamburg, 200–201; "horizontal,"
218–19; May '68 *enragés*, 43–48, 178,
237nn56–57, 255n91; Park Fiction and,
205; Project Row Houses and, 217–22;
solidarity and violence, interrelationship of, with, 83; St. Pauli, Hamburg,
200–201, 206, 274n96
provocation: assumptions about viewer,

278n120; Bishop on Hirschhorn and,
61–62; in nineteenth century, 34; orthopedic aesthetic and, 35–36; Project Row
Houses and, 222; Sierra and, 62, 165.
See also revolution; rupture; shock
the public: autonomy, shock, and, 182–85;
Deleuze and Spinoza on, 178–82; development of concept, 172–77; German
aesthetic philosophy and, 38–39; private dealers and collectors and, 267n35;
public art and, 191–92; Sierra's stance
on, 177–78
public art: abstraction and, 189–92; commercial appropriation of, 195–97; definition of, 186–87; European community
art practices, 197–98; history of, 187–89;
the "public" and, 191–92; urban renewal
and, 192–95, 197. *See also* Park Fiction;
Project Row Houses
Pufendorf, Samuel Frieherr von, 107,
252n69
purity and contamination, hygienic discourse of, 35

quasi-dialogical action, 137
Quattrocchi, Angelo, 53

race diversity, 219–20
Raituram, 91
Rajkumar, 78, 80, 84–86, 248n34
Rancière, Jacques, 59–61, 102–4, 182,
242n104, 250n60, 269n57
Rashtriya Swayamsevak Sangh (RSS), 77
Ratneshwar, Nath, 77
Reagan, Ronald, 195–97
real estate development, speculative,
195–96
Realizing the Potential of Africa's Youth
(Denmark's Commission on Africa),
259n112
reception theory, Preziosi on, 231n13,
253n78. *See also* viewer and audience
receptivity and intentionality, movement
between, 260n127

Nalpar water pump sites and, 79–81, plate 3. *See also* gender

Woodmansee, Martha, 38–40

"WORDPLAY" (Steinweg), 57

workshop as method of production, 95–96

Yes Men, 278n120, 279n122

Žižek, Slavoj, 242n105

Zmijewski, Artur, 100

Grant H. Kester is a professor of Art History and chair
of the Visual Arts department at the University of
California, San Diego. He is the author of *Conversation
Pieces: Community and Communication in Modern Art*
(2004), and the editor of *Art, Activism, Oppositionality:
Essays From* Afterimage (1998).

Library of Congress Cataloging-in-Publication Data
Kester, Grant H.
The one and the many : contemporary collaborative art
in a global context / Grant H. Kester.
p. cm.
Includes bibliographical references and index.
ISBN 978-0-8223-4972-3 (cloth : alk. paper)
ISBN 978-0-8223-4987-7 (pbk. : alk. paper)
1. Artistic collaboration. 2. Creation (Literary, artistic,
etc.) 3. Art—Philosophy. I. Title.
BH301.C84K478 2011
709.05′1—dc22   2011006447